THE GEORGE GUND FOUNDATION
IMPRINT IN AFRICAN AMERICAN STUDIES

The George Gund Foundation has endowed
this imprint to advance understanding of
the history, culture, and current issues
of African Americans.

The publisher gratefully acknowledges the generous contribution to this book provided by the African American Studies Endowment Fund of the University of California Press Associates, which is supported by a major gift from the George Gund Foundation.

Ties That Bind

AMERICAN CROSSROADS

*Edited by Earl Lewis, George Lipsitz, George Sánchez,
Dana Takagi, Laura Briggs, and Nikhil Pal Singh*

Ties That Bind

THE STORY OF AN AFRO-CHEROKEE FAMILY IN SLAVERY AND FREEDOM

Second Edition

Tiya Miles

UNIVERSITY OF CALIFORNIA PRESS

University of California Press, one of the most distinguished university presses in the United States, enriches
lives around the world by advancing scholarship in the
humanities, social sciences, and natural sciences. Its
activities are supported by the UC Press Foundation and
by philanthropic contributions from individuals and
institutions. For more information, visit
www.ucpress.edu.

University of California Press
Oakland, California

Library of Congress Cataloging-in-Publication Data

Miles, Tiya, 1970– author.
    Ties that bind: the story of an Afro-Cherokee family in
slavery and freedom / Tiya Miles. — Second edition.
        p.   cm. — (American crossroads; 14)
    Originally published: 2005.
    Includes bibliographical references and index.
    ISBN 978-0-520-28563-7 (pbk.: alk. paper)
    ISBN 978-0-520-96102-9 (ebook: alk. paper)
    1. Cherokee Indians—History—19th century.
2. Cherokee Indians—Mixed descent.   3. Cherokee
Indians—Kinship.   4. Indian slaves—Georgia—
History—19th century.   5. African Americans—
Georgia.   6. African Americans—Kinship—
Georgia.   7. Blacks—Georgia—Relations with
Indians.   I. Title.   II. Title: Story of an Afro-Cherokee
family in slavery and freedom.   III. Series: American
crossroads; 14.
    E99.C5M553   2015
    975.004'97557—dc23   2015002838

24   23   22   21   20   19   18   17   16   15
10   9   8   7   6   5   4   3   2   1

For my dear grandmother, Alice Banks,
and
in memory of my grandfather, Ardell Banks

CONTENTS

ILLUSTRATIONS

MAPS

PLATES

FIGURES

SHOEBOOTS FAMILY TREE

The spelling of Cherokee names is variable in the records, and names are often difficult
to read. The names given here are taken from the legal statement of William Shoeboots, made in 1888.
William did not give a Cherokee name for himself. Adapted from a tree by Joy Greenwood.

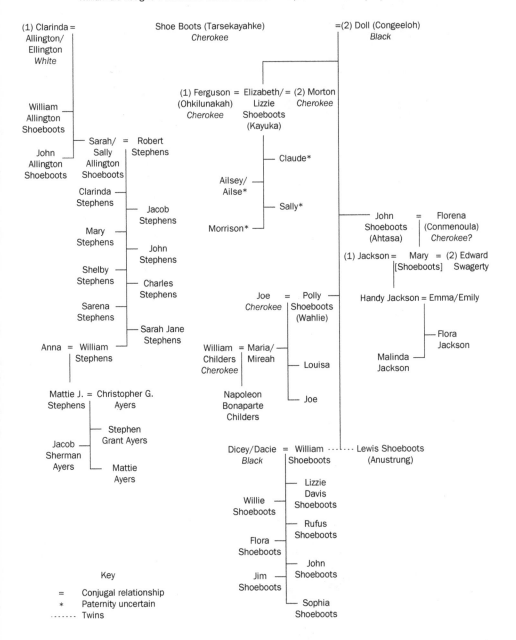

Key

=	Conjugal relationship
*	Paternity uncertain
······	Twins

PREFACE TO THE SECOND EDITION

In September 2005, two months before *Ties That Bind* was released, Diné historian Jennifer Denetdale invited me to give the keynote address at a conference on Native American and African American relations hosted by the University of New Mexico. The title of the conference was "Crossing Breath," a lovely evocation of spirit and interconnection. However, as I knew from researching *Ties That Bind* and from my own experience as a member of an Afro-Native family, the conference planners' focus on black-red interchange was in many ways aspirational. The reality of black and Native relationships, particularly within nations that had once owned black slaves, was rough, tumultuous, and in many ways characterized by conflict. The timing of Professor Denetdale's invitation and my awareness of tensions between black people, Native people, and self-identified Black Indians over issues of personal identity, cultural identification, indigenous authenticity, and political belonging led me to think about a different case of troubled waters and what is necessary to bridge the breach after a devastating storm.

The University of New Mexico conference took place just months after the natural and political disaster of Hurricane Katrina, which devastated the Gulf coast in the summer of 2005 and is now brilliantly captured in the National Book Award–winning novel *Salvage the Bones,* by Jesmyn Ward.[1] I was among the millions of people who saw that horror scene unfold at a distance on my television screen, as the poorest, brownest people in the city of New Orleans and countless coastal parishes succumbed to the ravages of nature. I watched with mounting disbelief as the storm surged, as squalid floodwaters swallowed homes and public buildings, stranding people, taking lives. Women, men, and children directed to designated safe zones found themselves corralled without the basic necessities of life: food, water, or the governmental safeguards that are supposed to support all of this country's citizenry. The tragedy of thousands felled by nature and failed by civic leaders elicited the empathy of many others. It brought those of us who still had our family members near, who still had homes and dry land to stand on, to a point of epiphany: we are, all of us, human beings and therefore deserve compassion, good lives, and the respect of others.

The breach that characterized Hurricane Katrina was both natural and human-made. While the storm overwhelmed the structural defenses of settlements and cities, a slow and inadequate government response made matters worse. If people felt betrayed by nature in August 2005, they also felt abandoned by their political leaders who failed to stem the tide of human suffering. After the storm, there was, and still is, the need for repair on multiple levels: structural repair, political repair, economic repair, and emotional repair. Because it was raw and recent at the time of the New Mexico "Crossing Breath" conference, Katrina became more than the event itself in my mind; it became a metaphor for the storm of slavery in Native American history, for the betrayal of relationships, the devastation of lives, the complicity of tribal governments, and the necessity of repair in slavery's aftermath.

Six years later, I wrote in a *New York Times* Room for Debate forum on Cherokee citizenship conflicts that the history of slavery and racial prejudice in the Cherokee Nation calls for reparations, by which I meant a collaborative project of repair, reconnection, and healing. In closing that piece, I said, "The Cherokee people and the progeny of those once enslaved in their territory share a story. It is a story of colonialism, slavery, removal, Civil War, injustice, survival and resilience, yet and still, one that their ancestors shaped together."[2] My view, reflected in *Ties That Bind* and a second history of Cherokee slavery, *The House on Diamond Hill*,[3] is that historical understanding can contribute to bridging the breach caused by slavery—a social, cultural, economic, and political occurrence of natural disaster–like proportions for its victims as well as its perpetrators.

Ties That Bind is at heart the story of a family formed at the crossroads of colonialism, slavery, and gender domination in the nineteenth-century American Indian South. It is the story of a domestic unit created through what was likely a coercive sexual relationship between a Native slaveholding man, Shoe Boots, and a black enslaved woman, Doll. This was a family whose members occupied vastly different power positions, a family shaped in the context of tremendous change, whose children tested the means and measure of belonging in the Cherokee Nation. In the book, I argue, in the dialogic form of questions, three main ideas: that slavery and anti-black prejudice existed in Cherokee society since at least the late 1700s, that slavery developed in tandem with a growing Cherokee nationalism and suppression of women's direct political influence, and that kinship mitigated the worst effects of slavery for Afro-Cherokee people, who were often accepted by community members. I stress that community acceptance of some Afro-Cherokee individuals occurred alongside the alienation and mistreatment of blacks who were not defined as Cherokee by descent or adoption. I also demonstrate through the pieced-together biography of Doll that the families of enslaved black women were doubly disadvantaged in this matrilineal society because they lacked crucial clan membership in a system in which the children inherited the mother's status.

My sense of the significance of the Shoeboots family story as a means of interpreting the workings of slavery in the Native South and Indian Territory was greatly influenced by the work of several scholars, mainly ethnohistorians, who studied slavery in the Five Tribes and published classic monographs from the late 1970s through the early 1990s. These include historians Theda Perdue, William McLoughlin, Rudi Halliburton, Daniel Littlefield, and James Merrell.[4] Anthropologist Jack Forbes's broad and detailed study of Africans and Native Americans in the colonial period was also highly influential. Anthropologist Circe Sturm's revealing book *Blood Politics* was crucial to my developing work, as she was the first scholar I had read who took up directly, through the use of interviews, the issue of anti-black prejudice among Cherokees.[5] Rather than go on at length about scholarly precursors here, I point your attention to historiographical essays and a database about Afro-Native histories at the New York Public Library's Schomburg Center for Research in Black Culture.[6]

I published *Ties That Bind* with a feeling of trepidation about how it would be received. Given that a Tuscarora academic had vehemently informed me of her disagreement with my argument that Cherokees in the 1800s had marginalized blacks, and a black woman at a public talk had heatedly told me she rejected the possibility that the black "wife" of Shoe Boots could have been a slave, I had reason for concern. In the end, I was grateful for such challenging comments.[7] This critical feedback pushed me to work harder to understand the role of race in Cherokee legislation and to imagine the ways in which an unequal sexual union might at the same time involve intimacy and emotional connection. I was deeply relieved and grateful when the book garnered an overwhelmingly positive response. I also found that after hearing the story of the Shoeboots family, people often wanted to share their own family stories with me. One reader sent census information that by all indications traces the family of Lewis Shoeboots, one of Shoe Boots and Doll's twin sons who was lost to slavery in the South-east.[8] I was moved to receive gifts of beaded jewelry, music, and books, as well as letters and emails, from other readers.[9] They seemed relieved to discover a complex, interracial family story discussed openly and with sensitivity to both African American and Native American experience.

Readers who had criticisms of the work voiced them respectfully and pointed out ways in which it could have spoken more powerfully to them. One Native high school student who read the book with eighty other Native and Latino teenagers in a program sponsored by Pomona College thought my chapter on Cherokee removal was far too short. A Seneca elder said he felt that the book was prescribing what the Cherokee Nation should have done in a way that diminished tribal authority. Most people who had critiques quibbled good-naturedly about genealogical details and the spelling of names. This is not to say that *Ties that Bind* is a perfect book. That is far from the case, and this new edition includes a few minor corrections. Rather, this is to say that the book seems to have met a desire held by many people at the start of a new century to read a documented story that reflects the racial travails of their own mixed-race black, Native, and white families. Because I had managed (after much labor, trial, and error) to relate the material in a narrative interpretive vein, *Ties That Bind* avoids the objectifying distance of a traditional social historical treatment and conveys the story of a Cherokee family, a black family, an American family, with empathy and directness. The book's subject matter, together with an increased public interest in mixed-race identities spurred by the multiracial movement and a new option on the 2000 U.S. census to check more than one box for racial identity, attracted an open-minded readership of scholars, students, and genealogists.

When the book was published in 2005, it was accompanied by a work on the Afro-Creek Grayson family, written by the award-winning historian Claudio Saunt.[10] Since the nearly in tandem publication of my book and Saunt's *Black, White and Indian*, a number of works have been published, symposia organized, and conference panels planned on subjects in the subfield that is often referred to as Afro-Native studies, Black Indian studies, or indigenous slavery studies. These works span historical, anthropological, and literary fields but are situated for the most part in Native American history, ethnohistory, and, increasingly, African American history. Some of the most inspiring work published over the past decade includes Celia Naylor's unflinching look at Cherokee slaves and freedpeople in Indian Territory, Fay Yarbrough's detailed monograph on the racialized legislation of marriage in the Cherokee Nation, Barbara Krauthamer's bold book on slavery and the struggle for citizenship in the Choctaw and Chickasaw nations, David Chang's innovative study of multiracial land use in the Creek Nation, Malinda Maynor Lowery's astute reconstruction of Lumbee history in the Jim Crow era, and Christina Snyder's comprehensive examination of Native slavery in the Southeast.[11] As a result of the visibility of strong work at this intersection of historical streams, numerous books on Native American history, African American history, and trans-Atlantic slavery outside this subfield now attend to interrelated black and Native issues. For instance, Ariela Gross's illuminating treatment of race trials and freedom suits demonstrates the degree to which claims of Native maternal ancestry were critical for blacks. And Rose Stremlau's engaging book on the impact of allotment on Cherokee families delves into the issues of family structure, differential gender ideals, and federal assimilation policy by following a selection of families, some of which were descended from slaveholders.[12]

A plethora of new scholarly work has helped us better understand the causes and effects of colonialism and slavery on Native communities and on the black communities within them. The more layered of these studies also include analyses of women's and gender history or issues of place and land. None of these books upholds the celebratory narrative about natural black and Indian alliance that has sometimes appeared in popular treatments and certainly maintains a place in the popular imagination. As historian James Hugo Johnston documented in the *Journal of Negro History* in the 1920s, relationships between people of African descent and indigenous people in what would become the United States were extensive, longstanding, and multifaceted, consisting of alliances and skirmishes, friendships and feuds.[13] Native Americans and African Americans were people, and they did what people do—made love and war, aided one another and injured one another, joined together and moved apart through the course of lives and generations.

At our present moment, in the second decade of the twenty-first century, the mood writ large of black and Native relations is sobering. Despite the plentiful academic work just described and the pathbreaking *IndiVisible* exhibition coproduced by the Smithsonian Institution's National Museum of the American Indian and National Museum of African American History and Culture, stories still circulate about Afro-Native people who find themselves questioned, criticized, and even ostracized by members of their families and communities.[14] This negative tone is exemplified in the public arena by the recent series of court cases and tribal elections in the Cherokee Nation of Oklahoma that turn on the political status of descendants of slaves within the nation. Historians Celia Naylor and Daniel Littlefield have documented the early struggles of former slaves of Cherokees to attain and maintain citizenship rights in the Cherokee Nation in the late nineteenth and early twentieth centuries.[15] The continuing conflict is over whether descendants of Cherokee-held slaves who cannot adequately demonstrate blood ties via the Dawes Rolls should receive standing and benefits in the nation equal to those of "Cherokees by blood."

Similarly, these descendants argue that the post–Civil War Treaty of 1866, the ties of kin relationships, a shared cultural past, and a moral code that recognizes the human rights abuse of slavery should guarantee their place in the nation. Some Cherokee citizens support this cause; others see the issue through a racial lens and feel that these descendants are "black" rather than "Indian" and therefore not entitled to hard-won resources distributed by tribal governments; some also feel that the descendants' appeal to the United States government for a remedy undermines tribal sovereignty and the right of the Cherokee Nation to determine who is Cherokee.

There were legal challenges to these freedmen and freedwomen descendants' citizenship status in 1997 and 2004, with membership appeals brought in the Cherokee courts by Bernice Rogers Riggs and Lucy Allen. Although Riggs lost her petition, Lucy Allen won in a 2–1 decision by the Cherokee Supreme Court.[16] Principal Chief Chad Smith was among numerous enrolled Cherokees who disagreed with this judgment. Matters came to a head in 2007 when a Cherokee Nation special election resulted in a constitutional amendment that barred approximately 2,800 freedmen and freedwomen descendants from citizenship. Representatives of the U.S. government responded swiftly. The Bureau of Indian Affairs of the Department of the Interior sent a letter to the Cherokee Nation stating that the descendants' citizenship could not be withdrawn. Representative Diane Watson, a Democrat from California, introduced legislation to block $300 million in federal funds earmarked for the Cherokees, and Representative Melvin Watts, a Democrat from North Carolina, submitted an amendment to the federal housing bill to withhold funding from the Cherokee Nation. The Department of Housing and Urban Development suspended more than $37 million that would have been distributed to the nation.[17]

A media firestorm followed. Descendants of freedpeople—such as Marilyn Vann, president of Descendants of Freedmen of the Five Civilized Tribes—protested. Supporters inside and outside the Cherokee Nation argued the case for inclusion. Ojibwe literary scholar and *Indian Country Today* columnist Scott Lyons challenged the merits of the requirement in the new constitutional amendment that citizens be "Cherokee by blood" in a lineage traceable to the Dawes Rolls. He argued that "for well over a century the Cherokee Nation has been a multiracial nation, one whose sovereignty rests largely upon treaty-based relationships with others," and he urged the nation to protect "its hard-won national identity" by upholding its agreement in the Treaty of 1866. Osage literary scholar Robert Warrior wrote an opinion piece asserting that "the moral case against the Cherokees is straightforward" and asked "Native American writers, scholars, and artists, not to mention elected leaders, presidents, and chiefs, to stand up and be counted on the right moral side of this question."[18] A temporary agreement reached in federal court in September 2011 permitted freedpeople's descendants to vote for principal chief. Their participation likely contributed to the election of new principal chief Bill John Baker.[19] Currently, the Department of the Interior is pursuing a clear resolution to the Cherokee freedperson citizenship question through the federal courts.

In her article "Tribes and Tribulations: Beyond Sovereign Immunity and toward Reparation and Reconciliation for the Estelusti" (a term used to refer to Afro-Native people, especially in the Seminole Nation), legal scholar Carla Pratt outlines the histories of slavery in the Cherokee, Creek, Choctaw, Chickasaw, and Seminole tribes, arguing that slavery benefited these nations and individuals within them.[20] She calls for "micro-reparations" for descendants of these slaves from both the U.S. government and the tribal governments. I find her take on the cultural transformation and subjectivity of American Indian slaveowners too monolithic, and she feels that my representation of Cherokee slavery does not go far enough in condemning those who perpetuated it. I hold out hope for a multitribal or United Nations–arbitrated forum for hearing these disputes that is fair, ethical, and outside the bounds of U.S. courts, while Pratt focuses on strategies within the U.S. courts and the waiving of sovereign immunity by Native nations. Nevertheless, I was struck by her article—by her bold recognition that there is a deep wound in black and Native relations. We agree on the need for a rebuilt relationship, for a repair, between former slaveholding nations and the progeny of their former slaves, lest the damage to the spirit of black and red communities continue.

The Cherokee court cases and the vitriol surrounding them are both signs and symptoms of a distance between peoples who at times have been close geographically, culturally, and relationally. This distance has been created and cemented, in large part, by policies of the United States government (such as civilization, slavery, racial color coding, and removal) imposed on these groups, rather than by long-standing cultural values and behaviors rooted in the groups themselves. The sensibility of separation that characterizes the citizenship cases stems from a time when intense racialization, the expansion of slavery, Indian Removal, Jim Crowism, and race-based vigilante terrorism were the norm and when people of color were propelled and sometimes compelled to participate in oppressive systems that left indelible marks on ways of thinking and being. We must not allow our hearts and thoughts to be mired there—to be stuck in a late nineteenth-century logic of race-based exclusion and hierarchy that did not originate in indigenous American or African diasporic communities. It is, I believe, to our detriment and to the detriment of healthy and whole communities to define ourselves and one another within such a frame.

The weight of race in U.S. history is bearing down on us, so much so that we have not escaped its mark. But instead of allowing ill-conceived ideologies and policies of the past to confine us in the present, we can turn to a people's history to aid us in struggles for justice: to provide models of inspiration, to document relational ties that may have been forgotten, and to map places in the landscape with communal significance. In order to move forward from here, we need a full view of the past: long, intricate, and joined to an ethos of healing. To quote Cherokee Nation Principal Chief Baker, who made this comment during the tumult of 2011, "It's time for the healing to begin."[21]

I am grateful for and surprised by the opportunity to issue a new edition of *Ties That Bind* a decade after its initial publication.[22] I hope the book will be viewed not only as a scholarly study but also as a work that furthers a project of relational reunion by telling the story of a shared past. I hope too that readers find within these pages an account that reveals an inspiring, though difficult, history, illustrates the storm of slavery in the Native South, shows causes for the breach in black-Native relations today, and fosters a spirit of reconciliation.

1. Jesmyn Ward, *Salvage the Bones* (New York: Bloomsbury, 2010). For a study of Native people's experience with Hurricane Katrina, see Brian Klopotek, Brenda Lintinger, and John Barbry, "Ordinary and Extraordinary Trauma: Race, Indigeneity, and Hurricane Katrina in Tunica-Biloxi History," *American Indian Culture and Research Journal* 34, no. 2 (2008): 55–77.

2. Tiya Miles, "Why the Freedmen Fight," Room for Debate, *New York Times*, September 15, 2011, www.nytimes.com/roomfordebate/2011/09/15/tribal-sovereignty-vs-racial-justice/wjy-the-freedmen-fight [*sic*].

3. Tiya Miles, *The House on Diamond Hill: A Cherokee Plantation Story* (Chapel Hill: University of North Carolina Press, 2010).

4. Theda Perdue, *Slavery and the Evolution of Cherokee Society, 1540–1866* (Knoxville: University of Tennessee Press, 1979); William McLoughlin, *Cherokee Renascence in the New Republic* (Princeton: Princeton University Press, 1986); Rudi Halliburton, *Red over Black: Black Slavery among the Cherokees* (Westport, Conn.: Greenwood, 1977); Daniel F. Littlefield, *The Cherokee Freedmen: From Emancipation to American Citizenship* (Westport, Conn.: Greenwood, 1979); James Merrell, *The Indians' New World: Catawbas and Their Neighbors from European Contact through the Era of Removal* (New York: Norton, 1991).

5. Jack D. Forbes, *Africans and Native Americans: The Language of Race and the Evolution of Red-Black Peoples* (Urbana: University of Illinois Press, 1993); Circe Sturm, *Blood Politics: Race, Culture, and Identity in the Cherokee Nation of Oklahoma* (Berkeley: University of California Press, 2002).

6. Tiya Miles and Barbara Krauthamer, "Africans and Native Americans," in *A Companion to African American History*, ed. Alton Hornsby Jr. (Oxford: Blackwell, 2005), 121–39; Tiya Miles and Celia E. Naylor-Ojurongbe, "African-Americans in Indian Societies," in *Handbook of North American Indians*, vol. 14, *Southeast*, ed. Raymond Fogelson (Washington, D.C.: Smithsonian, 2004), 753–59; Barbara Krauthamer, "African Americans and Native Americans," in *Origins*, Schomburg Studies on the Black Experience, ed. Howard Dodson and Colin Palmer (East Lansing: Michigan State University Press, 2008), 91–135, and online at *African Americans and Native Americans in North America*, ed. Krauthamer (Ann Arbor: ProQuest Information and Learning, 2005), The Black Experience in the Western Hemisphere, http://bsc.chadwyck.com/search/displayEssayItem ById.do?ItemID=10KRAU&ItemNumber=8&QueryName=essay&fromPage=es sayList; Tiya Miles, "Native Americans and African Americans," in *The New Encyclopedia of Southern Culture*, ed. Charles Reagan Wilson, vol. 24, *Race*, ed. Thomas C. Holt and Laurie B. Green (Chapel Hill: University of North Carolina Press, 2013), 114–20; Sharon P. Holland and Tiya Miles, "Afro-Native Realities," in *The World of Indigenous North America*, ed. Robert Warrior (New York: Routledge, 2014), 224–48.

7. I expect that the Native scholar mentioned here would want it known that she later read the book and expressed appreciation for the finished work. The chapter on Cherokee nationhood would not have been nearly so strong if not for her verbal pushback against my ideas.

8. The following censuses list a Lewis Shoeboots and his family members: 1870 U.S. Census, Colbert County, Alabama, population schedule, Townships Four Range Ten, Leighton Post Office, page 6, citing National Archives (NA) microfilm publication M593, roll 10; 1880 U.S. Census, Colbert County, Alabama, population schedule, Townships Four Range Ten, page 19, citing NA microfilm publication T9, roll 8; 1900 U.S. Census, Colbert County, Alabama, population schedule, Leighton Beat, page 26, citing NA microfilm publication T623, roll 26; 1900 U.S. Census, Concordia County, Louisiana, population schedule, Seventh Ward, page 8, citing NA microfilm publication T623, roll 562; all available as digital images at Heritage Quest Online (http://heritagequestonline.com), accessed May 23, 2014. Notably, this Lewis had a daughter named Elizabeth, as did Shoe Boots and Doll. I am grateful to Rodney Dillon for sharing this information with me.

9. It was through reader feedback that I learned about the existence of a novel that chronicles the experience of Shoe Boots's first wife, Clarinda Allington. See Ilene Shepard Smiddy, *Daughter of Shiloh* (Bloomington, Ind.: 1st Books Library, 2000).

10. Claudio Saunt, *Black, White and Indian: Race and the Unmaking of an American Family* (New York: Oxford University Press, 2005).

11. Celia E. Naylor, *African Cherokees in Indian Territory: From Chattel to Citizens* (Chapel Hill: University of North Carolina Press, 2008); Fay A. Yarbrough, *Race and the Cherokee Nation: Sovereignty in the Nineteenth Century* (Philadelphia: University of Pennsylvania Press, 2008); Barbara Krauthamer, *Black Slaves, Indian Masters: Slavery, Emancipation, and Citizenship in the Native American South* (Chapel Hill: University of North Carolina Press, 2013); David Chang, *The Color of the Land: Race, Nation, and the Politics of Landownership in Oklahoma, 1832–1929* (Chapel Hill: University of North Carolina Press, 2010); Malinda Maynor Lowery, *Lumbee Indians in the Jim Crow South: Race, Identity, and the Making of a Nation* (Chapel Hill: University of North Carolina Press, 2010); Christina Snyder, *Slavery in Indian Country: The Changing Face of Captivity in Early America* (Cambridge, Mass.: Harvard University Press, 2012).

12. Ariela Gross, *What Blood Won't Tell: A History of Race on Trial in America* (Cambridge, Mass.: Harvard University Press, 2008); Rose Stremlau, *Sustaining the Cherokee Family: Kinship and the Allotment of an Indigenous Nation* (Chapel Hill: University of North Carolina Press, 2011).

13. James Hugo Johnston, "Documentary Evidence of the Relations of Negroes and Indians," *Journal of Negro History* 14 (January 1929): 21–43.

14. In July 2014, yet another development occurred in Washington, D.C., with

the formation of the National Congress of Black American Indians, an organization that aims to foster Black Indian cultural, spiritual, and historical affirmation.

15. Naylor, *African Cherokees in Indian Territory;* Littlefield, *Cherokee Freedmen.*

16. See Miles and Naylor-Ojurongbe, "African-Americans in Indian Societies," 758–59; Adam Geller, "Past and Future Collide in Fight over Cherokee Identity," *USA Today,* February 10, 2007.

17. Evelyn Nieves, "Putting to a Vote the Question 'Who Is Cherokee?,' " *New York Times,* March 3, 2007; Murray Evans, "Cherokees Pull Memberships of Freed Slaves," Associated Press, March 4, 2007; Jeninne Lee-St. John, "The Cherokee Nation's New Battle," *Time,* June 21, 2007; Jerry Reynolds, "Housing Amendment Would Punish Cherokee over Freedmen," *Indian Country Today,* July 27, 2007, http://indiancountrytodaymedianetwork.com/2007/07/27/housing-amendment-would-punish-cherokee-over-freedmen-91190; Frank Morris, "Cherokee Tribe Faces Decision on Freedmen," NPR, February 21, 2007, www.npr.org/templates/story/story.php?storyId=7513849; Alex Kellogg, "Cherokee Nation Faces Scrutiny for Expelling Blacks," NPR, September 19, 2011, www.npr.org/2011/09/19/140594124/u-s-government-opposes-cherokee-nations-decision.

18. Scott Richard Lyons, "Cherokee by Text," *Indian Country Today,* October 18, 2007, http://indiancountrytodaymedianetwork.com/2007/10/18/lyons-cherokee-text-91628; Robert Warrior, "Cherokees Flee the Moral High Ground over Freedmen," *News from Indian Country,* August 7, 2007, http://indiancountrynews.net/index.php/news/119-editorialletters/1106-cherokees-flee-the-moral-high-ground-over-freedmen.

19. Lenzy Krehbiel-Burton, "Cherokee Court's Ruling May Affect Baker's Apparent Election Win," *Tulsa World,* October 12, 2011; Brian Daffron, "Bill John Baker, Policy-Maker: An Interview with the New Cherokee Principal Chief," *Indian Country Today,* March 7, 2012, http://indiancountrytodaymedianetwork.com/2012/03/05/bill-john-baker-policy-maker-interview-new-cherokee-principal-chief-101239.

20. Carla D. Pratt, "Tribes and Tribulations: Beyond Sovereign Immunity and toward Reparation and Reconciliation for the Estelusti," *Washington and Lee Race and Ethnic Ancestry Law Journal* 11, no. 1 (Winter 2005): 61–132.

21. Krehbiel-Burton, "Cherokee Court's Ruling."

22. This new edition would not have been possible without the astounding research assistance of graduate students Emily MacGillivray and Michelle Cassidy. I thank them for their excellent work and support.

When I began work on this book several years ago, I wanted to tell a story. I imagined it would be about the intersecting lives of blacks and Indians in nineteenth-century America, about interracial and intercultural alliance, about shared meanings and joint resistance to slavery and colonialism. In the intervening years, however, I found, as veteran storytellers have known for longer than I have been alive, that the "story" is rarely what it seems on the surface and often encompasses many more stories. As I read secondary-source materials on Native American and African American histories in preparation for writing this book, the story that most arrested me was one about a slave woman: a black slave woman, owned by a Cherokee man who would later father her five children. Her name was Doll, his was Shoe Boots, and the tale of their life together was both complicated and painful.

The Shoeboots family[1] story opened up an entire history that I, growing up in an African American family, majoring in Afro-American Studies in college, and studying Native American history in graduate school, had never heard. And yet this story seemed vital to gaining a full understanding of the American past, since it moved through and encompassed key moments, issues, and struggles both in African American and American Indian histories. The more details I uncovered about Doll and Shoe Boots's life and family, the more committed I became to writing into the historical silence that often surrounds interactions between black and Native people.

While conducting research and speaking about this project in public and in academic venues, however, I found that the story of Doll's life in the Cherokee Nation was, in the view of many, an unspeakable thing. The specter of slaveowning Indians stirred up emotional, intellectual, and political trouble for contemporary African Americans and Native Americans alike who remember and imagine this past in differing ways. Some black people, I found, were reluctant to hear about American Indians who engaged in trading and owning slaves because they imagined Indians as the historical protectors of black runaways; still other African Americans were disinterested in hearing about American Indians, thinking that such a focus would siphon attention from black justice struggles. Some Native people felt regretful and even ashamed of this history; others denied it outright. And ironically, like their black counterparts, some Native people saw any engagement with African American history as detracting attention and stealing energy from American Indian justice struggles. It seemed that black slavery within Native American nations was an aspect of history that both black and Native people had willed themselves to forget. Their reactions seemed to echo an assessment made by cultural critic Sharon Holland, that there exists an ever-present attempt in America to "disremember a shared past."[2] For black and Indian peoples in the United States, this imperative to "disremember" is even more pressing, because memory contains not only the suffering we have endured in the vise of colonial expansion, genocide, and slavery but also the suffering we have endured at the hands of one another in this context of brutal oppression.

The desire to disremember, the desperate need to blot out the horrors of the past, is a central theme in Toni Morrison's epic novel of slavery in the United States, *Beloved*. This novel is now considered a classic by many scholars of American literature. In my view, the work still stands alone in its intuitive sense and articulation of the power of the unspoken. The resonant quality of *Beloved*, its enduring ability to mediate between our present selves and shrouded pasts, has echoed in my thoughts throughout the process of writing this book and thus has left an imprint on the story that I tell. In the world of *Beloved*, the memory of the ravages of slavery, of its distortions of human relations, refuses to be suppressed despite desperate attempts by the main characters to suppress it. The memory of slavery continually returns to haunt the protagonist and her family, first as a ghost and later as a flesh-and-blood woman with the power to poison relationships in the present. At the end of the novel, the narrator repeats these words like a mantra: "It was not a story to pass on . . . it was not a story to pass on . . . this was not a story to pass on."[3] And yet, in her remarkable portrayal of the impossibility of remembering, the impossibility of speaking the stories of the slave past, Toni Morrison does pass it on. Even as she denies the possibility of telling her tale, she unveils it layer by layer. She gives us the story in one hand and with the other takes it away. This, I believe, is a necessary feint. For the very stories that pain us so are the maps to our inner worlds, and to the better worlds that we envision for our children. In the words of Laguna Pueblo writer Leslie Marmon Silko, "through the stories we hear who we are."[4]

Recently when I was speaking in a public forum about black and American Indian relations in colonial and early America, a respected Indian elder from a Great Plains tribe impressed on me her strong desire that I cease speaking about this topic. Her fear, as she expressed it, was that documenting the intermarriage of black and Indian people would give the U.S. government just one more reason to declare Native people inauthentic and soluble and then to seize their remaining lands and any vestiges of political autonomy. At the end of a private conversation following the session, the woman said, "Don't write your book; it will destroy us." I was pained by her words, just as she had been pained by mine. I couldn't help but question the efficacy, and even the ethics, of denying the existence of the relationships forged by our forebears. I wondered, too, about the impact of such denial on descendants of black and Indian couples who are too often marginalized in Native and sometimes black communities, as well as on the communal well-being of the many Native nations with mixed-race citizens. I also saw in her formulation of the risk involved in acknowledging black and Indian kinship, a reiteration, indeed a reformation, of the triangulated relationship between Indian, African, and European American people. This relationship has existed ever since African and Native people came into contact in massive numbers during European colonial expansion and the trans-Atlantic slave trade, and it continues to prohibit blacks and Indians from speaking directly with one another, forcing them instead to speak through and against the material and discursive structures of American colonialism. During this conversation, I was reminded of an observation made by black feminist theorist bell hooks more than a decade ago: "For Native Americans, especially those who are black, and for African Americans, it is a gesture of resistance to the dominant culture's ways of thinking about history, identity, and community for us to decolonize our minds, reclaim the word that is our history as it was told to us by our ancestors, not as it has been interpreted by the colonizer."[5] In this elder's plea that I not write, I saw even more reason for doing so. For the void that remains when we refuse to speak of the past is in fact a presence, a presence both haunting and destructive.

It is my hope that black and Native people can bear the weight of this, my telling, and also the weight of the complex history that we share in America. As the court cases pending in the Cherokee Nation and the Seminole Nation about the place and citizenship rights of descendants of black slaves within those tribes demonstrate, this history continues to shape our lives, both separately and together. The following account is a Cherokee story, an African American story, an American story. In the words of historian Nell Irvin Painter, it is a "fully loaded cost accounting" of who we have been and who we can become, as peoples whose lives have been intertwined on this land for centuries.[6] It is a heartfelt and imperfect offering.

ACKNOWLEDGMENTS

Conceiving, researching, writing, and rewriting this book has been an arduous yet fulfilling process that, thankfully, I have not had to undertake alone. The input, advice, words of encouragement, words of caution, research skills, artistry, and empathy of many people made this manuscript possible. I discovered partway through writing it, to my relief and delight, that there existed a community of people willing to nurture this project. I am thankful for the lifelong love and support of my family: my grandmother Alice Banks, who first told me stories and remains my inspiration; my mother, Patricia Miles King, who is my foundation; my husband, Joseph Gone, whose commitment to me and to social justice revived my flagging courage; my father, Benny Miles, and stepmother, Montroue Miles, for continuous encouragement; my stepfather, James King, who understood my intentions from the start; my always-there-when-I-needed-them siblings, Erin and Erik Miles; my sister-in-law, Stephanie Iron Shooter, who asked me why I was writing about Cherokees often enough that I was finally able to articulate an answer; my mother-in-law, Sharon Juelfs, who helped care for my newborn twins while I edited; and my dear friend, Sunita Dhurandhar, who read and edited the manuscript in dissertation form.

I am forever grateful to and in awe of my primary advisors at the University of Minnesota. David Roediger noticed me in a class where I barely said a word, encouraged the seedling of my idea to grow, and convinced me that I could become a writer in historian's clothing. Carol Miller never let me forget that the heart of this project lay in its story. Jean O'Brien rescued me from emotional and archival despair and convinced me that if the Shoeboots lived, I would find records. My additional dissertation committee members, Brenda Child and Angela Dillard, offered constructive criticism that helped to reform my outlook on the work.

Along the journey, I was fortunate enough to meet many more good souls who advised me and shaped the book in significant ways. I am deeply grateful to Raymond Fogelson, Nancy Shoemaker, Peggy Pascoe, Rowena Mc-Clinton, Celia Naylor-Ojurongbe, Deborah King, and Angela Walton-Raji. I am also grateful to my fellow co-organizers of the Dartmouth College conference on African American and Native American relations, Stephanie Morgan and Celia Naylor-Ojurongbe, and to our advisors, Deborah King, Colin Calloway, Vera Palmer, and Judith Byfield. Our collaborative effort on this project and the gathering of people from many walks of life that resulted illuminated both the trauma and the power inherent in this subject.

I owe a great debt of gratitude to genealogist Tressie Nealy, who ferreted out documents at the Oklahoma Historical Society that became essential to this book. I am thankful also to Jack Baker, to Phyllis Adams, and to all the incredibly helpful people at the Oklahoma Historical Society, as well as to Kristina Southwell and John Lovett at the University of Oklahoma Western History Collections. I am grateful to Clara Sue Kidwell at the University of Oklahoma and to Phyllis Murray of the Montford Inn in Norman for making Oklahoma a welcoming place. I greatly appreciate the indispensable research advice and aid of John Aubrey at the Newberry Library, of Dale Couch and Joanne Smalley at the Georgia State Archives, of Todd Butler at the National Archives, and of Julia Autry and Jeff Stancil at the Chief Vann House Historic Site. For invaluable and at times miraculous research assistance, I would like to thank Nerissa Balce, Joy Greenwood, Lingling Zhao, Denene DeQuintal, Paulina Alberto, and Nanette Reepe. For inspiration through the language of visual art, I would like to thank Jean Rorex Bridges, creator of the *Sister Series* representing Cherokee women's history.

I am appreciative of all those, named and unnamed, whose input and faith influenced this project. Thanks especially to Monica McCormick, Randy Heyman, Mimi Kusch, Chalon Emmons, Ms. A. W. Jo Shoeboot, Mr. André Haskell Shoeboot, Josie Fowler, Philip Deloria, Ariela Gross, Greg Dowd, June Howard, Patricia Penn Hilden, Theda Perdue, Daniel F.

Littlefield, Circe Sturm, Claudio Saunt, Réquel Lopes, Mary Young, Wendy St. Jean, Alex Bontemps, Sharon Holland, Theresa O'Nell, Joseph Jordan, Barbara Krauthamer, Robert Warrior, Donald Pease, Jennifer Brody, Brian Ragsdale, Susan Kent, Frances Smith Foster, Beverly Guy-Sheftall, Werner Sollors, Catherine Clinton, Dian Million, Elizabeth Castle, Ray and Sue McClinton, the Wednesday Night Group at Dartmouth College, my dissertation work group—Catherine Griffin, Adrian Gaskins, Marjorie Bryer, Alex Lubin—and participants in the Newberry Library Lannan Summer Institute 2001.

For the funding that allowed me to eat as well as believe that my project might be worthwhile, I am grateful to the Ford Foundation, Dartmouth College, the University of Minnesota Department of American Studies, the University of California, Berkeley, Department of Ethnic Studies, and the Newberry Library in Chicago.

For allowing me to tell this wondrous story, I would like to thank Dolly Shoeboots.

Introduction

FAMILY MATTERS:
THE SHOEBOOTS LEGACY IN THE AMERICAN PAST AND PRESENT

When Ralph Ellison wrote about the history of blacks in Indian Territory in 1979, expressing his sense of wonder at "the sheer unexpectedness of life in these United States," he might well have included the life and times of an uncommon family known as the Shoeboots.[1] The Shoeboots descended from a famed Cherokee warrior named Tarsekayahke, or "Shoe Boots," who, in mid-autumn 1824, appealed to the members of the Cherokee Nation's governing body on behalf of his mixed-race black-Cherokee children. Addressing the council members as "My Friends and Brothers," Shoe Boots said,

> Being in possession of a few Black People and being crost in my affections, I debased myself and took one of my black women by the name of Doll, by her I have had these children named as follows, the oldest Elizabeth about the age of Seventeen, the next the name of John about the age of Eleven, the next the name of Polly about the age of Seven years.
>
> My desire is to have them as free citizens of this nation. Knowing what property I may have, is to be divided amongst the Best of my friends, how can I think of them having bone of my bone and flesh of my flesh to be called their property.[2]

Shoe Boots's rare petition to the Cherokee statesmen requesting freedom and citizenship for his black children points to the Cherokee adoption of African slavery, the historical development of intimate relations between Cherokees and blacks, the creation of new mixed-race Afro-Cherokee families, and the role of the Cherokee nation-state in defining and regulating race as a category of social, political, and economic life.

A famous war veteran and moderately wealthy farmer, Shoe Boots acquired Doll, his first African slave, in the late 1790s. During the next thirty years, Shoe Boots and Doll would live together as master and slave and as intimate lifelong partners. The couple had five children together: Elizabeth, John, Polly, William, and Lewis Shoeboots, all of whom came of age in the Cherokee Nation in the troubled times of slaveholding and Indian Removal. The intimate connection between Shoe Boots and Doll has been recognized by chroniclers of Cherokee history as the first black-Cherokee marriage.[3] In truth, this liaison was unlikely to have been the earliest long-term sexual relationship between a Cherokee and an African, but it *was* the first such relationship to be regulated and recorded by the Cherokee national government. Because of Shoe Boots's fame, the official intervention of Cherokee lawmakers into his sexual affairs, and the sheer duration of this coupling, the story of Shoe Boots and his African "wife" has taken on symbolic meaning in Cherokee history. Today scholars refer to their family dramas as a way to preserve and explain the conceptualization of race and the nature and management of black and Indian relations in the Cherokee past. One Cherokee man explained to anthropologist Circe Sturm, who was seeking to understand the historical treatment of blacks living in the Cherokee Nation: "You know, that's not an easy question to answer because it really depends on the situation. Who, when, what, where: you have to take all that into consideration. Yeah, there was racism. I mean, we were southerners; we had slaves. But we also had a lot of tolerance and openness, and you can see that if you look back at the history, look at the stories themselves . . . look at the story of Shoe Boots. . . . His story will tell you what you need to know."[4] To borrow the language of anthropologist Raymond Fogelson, the Shoeboots family drama is an "epitomizing event" with "compelling qualities and explanatory power" for Cherokees as well as for students of African American, American Indian, and American histories.[5]

Shoe Boots, Doll, their children, and their grandchildren lived through key historical moments: the U.S. colonization of the indigenous Southeast, the formation of the first Native American constitutional government, the systemization of slavery in America and the adoption of slaveholding among

American Indians, the cementing of race as a social category and of blacks as a subjugated racial caste, the removal of southern Indians west of the Mississippi, and the American Civil War. The composite and intersecting stories of the Shoeboots family members' lives thus crystallize and illuminate not only each of these historical moments but also crucial issues in the fields of American studies, American history, and ethnohistory. The existence of diverse African diasporic experiences in the Americas, the processes and impact of colonialism on Native societies, the myriad cycles of enslavement and resistance in the United States, the competing currents of cultural transformation and retention among American Indian groups, and the relationship between nationalism and racial formation all emerge in the Shoeboots family drama. The saga of this family, when understood within the broader contexts of local and national events and ideologies, is therefore rich in possibilities for historical and cultural analysis.

Black feminist theorist Patricia Hill Collins has demonstrated the efficacy of studying the family in order to understand the interrelated nature of race, gender, class, and nation. In her essay "It's All in the Family" she argues that the American family has long been constructed by national policy and associated with the national interest. She demonstrates that through antimiscegenation, inheritance, and similar laws, the U.S. government has legislated into existence an ideal family unit that serves a "dual function as an ideological construction and as a fundamental principle of social organization."[6] The model family, then, defined historically as heterosexual and white, reflects American national ideals concerning Christian mores, the proper role of women, the supremacy of whiteness, the goodness of accumulated wealth, and the moral rectitude of heterosexuality. In addition, Collins explains, the model family serves the function of maintaining the national ideals that it symbolizes, since the white family, and the white woman in particular, is charged with preserving white racial purity through controlled sexual behavior. Bloodlines, as well as the wealth that is passed down from generation to generation through those bloodlines, must be kept pristine and within the family so that peoples defined as undesirable can be readily identified and relegated to the margins of the national body.

As Collins's work suggests, the processes of family making and the state regulation of family units can illuminate the values and dictates of the communities and nations in which families live. The family can thus be read as a barometer for the society, tracing and reflecting the atmospherics of social life and social change. In the case of the Shoeboots clan, a family story encapsulates and reveals social and cultural meanings in dual national contexts: the United States and the Cherokee Nation. In both these locations, the ideal family unit came to be defined and regulated in accordance with concepts of racial difference and black inferiority. After one hundred and fifty years of interaction with British and Euro-American slaveholders, the Cherokee government delegitimized Cherokee families that included black members and outlawed marriage between Cherokees and black slaves, even as it legalized Cherokee-white intermarriage. Thus the existence of the mixed-race, Afro-Cherokee Shoeboots family, as well as its public bid for citizenship rights, disrupted state definitions of the ideal family unit both in the Cherokee Nation and in the United States. Their saga reflects the complexities of colonialism, slavery, racialization, nationalism, and the family as a site of subjugation and resistance.

The story that unfolds here follows episodes in the Shoeboots's lives that foreshadow, overlap, and result from major historical events. In the course of the narrative, two central questions emerge. First, What was the relationship between black slavery and Cherokee kinship norms? This story shows that British and American colonization of the Southeast led to the introduction of African slavery and racial prejudice among Cherokees and other Indian nations. However, in the social context of Cherokee communities, people of African descent were not always defined as "black" and "enslaved"; sometimes they were defined as relatives. Did this alternative definition give rise to a competing status that was disruptive to emergent racial categories? Did kinship ties among Cherokees mediate the ravages of racial slavery, leading to the tribal recognition of Afro-Cherokees and enabling new forms of black resistance?[7] Or did the challenges to recognizing black kin posed by a racially conscious nation-state successfully foreclose these radical possibilities?

And second, What was the relationship between black emancipation and Cherokee sovereignty?[8] The story of the Shoeboots family indicates that liberation for African slaves and self-determination for Cherokee people were often framed in opposition to one another. Cherokees adopted black slavery in part to demonstrate their level of "civilization" in the hopes of forestalling further encroachment by white America. Thereafter the Cherokee Nation legalized slavery and black exclusion to maintain economic growth and independence and to demonstrate a social distance from the subjugated African race. In its qualified support of the Confederacy during the American Civil War the Cherokee Nation again opposed black liberation and Cherokee independence, since many Cherokee leaders had come to view slavery as a core feature of their national character and a key sign of their sovereign rights. Does this integral yet conflicting connection between emancipation and sovereignty mirror historian Edmund Morgan's astute finding regarding liberty and slavery in early America? Morgan concluded: "That two such seemingly contradictory developments were taking place simultaneously over a long period of time . . . is the central paradox of American history."[9] Is it a central paradox as well that in the context of nineteenth-century life in the Cherokee Nation, liberation and self-determination for two oppressed and intimate peoples were positioned as mutually exclusive? Or is it more fitting to emphasize the transitory moments in southeastern Native history in which black and Indian freedom fighters joined forces, recognizing the interdependent relationship between colonialism and slavery and envisioning a conjoined liberation? The emblematic experience of the Shoeboots family urges us to grapple with these questions, even if it sometimes seems that conclusive answers are not forthcoming.

TELLING IT SLANT: NARRATIVE AND HISTORY

While shaping this book I discovered for myself the by now rather obvious truth that historical scholarship is not simply the objective collection and presentation of facts. Rather, writing history consists of selecting elements from an array of evidence and of arranging and rearranging those elements into story lines. As Fogelson once observed in a presidential address to the American Society for Ethnohistory, "the historian makes histories. Histories do not exist as performed narratives awaiting discovery."[10] In a process whereby historical narratives are shaped, not found, constructing a story line for the history of an Afro-Cherokee family in the contexts of colonialism, slavery, and nation-building was a special challenge. While putting bits of evidence into coherent order, I found myself in a quandary. How could I tell the story of a black slave woman *and* the story of her Cherokee master and husband? How could I articulate the Cherokee enslavement of black people *and* the colonization of Cherokees by white people? And as an African American woman and a descendant of slaves, what biases would I bring to the story? It seemed that to capture the multiplicity and contradictory nature of this past, I would have to tell at least two stories—sketch two histories, enter two worlds, enlist two purposes, and sound two calls for justice—at once.

As a result of this conviction, one story line rendered here is the arc of Cherokee history: federal and local challenges to Cherokee nationalism, forced removal, and the rebuilding of the Cherokee Nation in the West. A second story line is the history of black slaves in Native America, a significant location in the African diaspora that many slavery studies overlook. Each of these story lines contains its own pretext and context, its own central themes and events, and its own historiography. And this bifurcation of narratives is exacerbated by a discordant recognition by members of different communities of the relative importance of historical events.[11] Indeed, African Americans and Cherokees, as well as "Black Indians" and "Indian Indians" presently living in Oklahoma, would prioritize the events chronicled in this book in vastly different ways. While many Cherokees view slavery as a marginal chapter in their history, descendants of former slaves owned by Cherokees view it as central to their historical experience and crucial to their rights as citizens in the Cherokee Nation. In the Cherokee Nation of Oklahoma and the Seminole Nation of Oklahoma the conflicts created by these divergent viewpoints are apparent in contemporary struggles over the place and legal rights of blacks in those tribes.

In my endeavor to tell a free story for blacks *and* for Cherokees, I am talking out of both sides of my mouth, sometimes emphasizing Cherokee life, sometimes the lives of blacks among Cherokees, and often attempting to mark the places where "Cherokeeness" and blackness overlap. In the early stages of writing this book, I had hoped to capture the full depth and scope of Cherokee and African American historical experience, but as Toni Morrison has cautioned, to do so is impossible: "Language can never 'pin down' slavery, genocide, war. Nor should it yearn for the arrogance to be able to do so. Its force, its felicity is in its reach toward the ineffable."[12] In writing this ineffable tale I have cast my net wide, hoping to provide a glimpse of untold lives with honesty, complexity, and compassion.

CHAPTER OVERVIEW

This book is organized geographically and chronologically into two parts: the first describes what took place in the Southeast before the forced removal of the Cherokees, and the second portrays events after removal in present-day Oklahoma. Part 1, titled "Bone of My Bone: Slavery, Race, and Nation—East" begins with "Captivity," an introduction to Shoe Boots in his early years as a warrior, in which he kidnapped and married a white adolescent girl from Kentucky. This chapter explores the historical and symbolic meaning of intermarriage between Cherokee men and white women and suggests that the evaluation of these relationships by white onlookers often included a hidden third element—the presence of black slaves. Chapter 2, "Slavery," offers an overview of the development of African slavery among the Cherokees, reprises the debate over the comparison of white and Indian slaveholding, and speculates about Doll's arrival in Cherokee country. Chapter 3, "Motherhood," addresses Doll's experience as Shoe Boots's slave and lover, focusing on her outsider status in Cherokee social and ceremonial life, the birth of her first child, and the convergence of American slave law and Cherokee clan organization in which the child follows the condition of the mother.

Chapter 4, "Property," analyzes the Cherokee historical relationship to property, the development of new forms of property valuation and accumulation, and the Creek War of 1813–1814 in which elite members of the Cherokee and Creek nations, including Shoe Boots, fought to protect this new way of life. Chapter 5, "Christianity," describes the founding of abolitionist Protestant missions in the Cherokee Nation and addresses the impact this new presence had on Cherokee communities, black slaves within those communities, and the Shoeboots family in particular. Chapter 6, "Nationhood," traces the development of the new Cherokee national government in the 1820s, a major turning point in Cherokee history that not only articulated Cherokee sovereignty in a language that U.S. officials could recognize but also legalized Cherokee slaveholding and formalized black exclusion from Cherokee citizenship. Chapter 7, "Gold Rush," discusses the Cherokee gold rush of 1829, the resulting usurpation of the Cherokee government by the state of Georgia, and the ensuing turmoil that resulted for Cherokees and African American slaves.

Part 2, "Of Blood and Bone: Freedom, Kinship, and Citizenship—West" follows the Shoeboots family across the Cherokee Trail of Tears and into Indian Territory of present-day eastern Oklahoma. Chapter 8, "Removal," delineates the history of Indian Removal under the leadership of Andrew Jackson, explores the spiritual and psychological impact of dislocation among Cherokees and their black slaves, and offers an interpretation of why relations between Cherokees and blacks worsened in the aftermath of forced relocation. Chapter 9, "Capture," analyzes the experience of blacks and Afro-Cherokees on the Cherokee lands of Indian Territory by comparing two events: the mass escape known as the Cherokee slave revolt of 1842 and the kidnapping of Doll and Shoe Boots's free granddaughters by slave-catcher-bandits in 1847. Chapter 10, "Freedom," traces the rebuilding of communities by the Shoeboots and other Cherokee families in the West and the eventual disruption of the American Civil War that decimated Cherokee towns even while emancipating black slaves among Cherokees.

The epilogue picks up the Shoeboots family story in the Dawes Allotment era of the 1890s and analyzes Doll and Shoe Boots's youngest son's failed application for Cherokee citizenship. The coda touches on the complicated legacy of this remarkable past for Shoeboots descendants today. It is my hope that, along with other recent contributions to the study of African American and Native American conjoined histories, this book crosses traditional boundaries of subject matter and perspective to contribute fresh and useful findings to our national conversation about race.

PART ONE

Bone of My Bone

Slavery, Race, and Nation——East

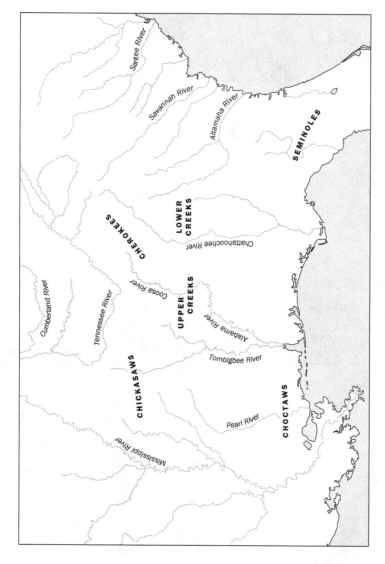

Map 1. Location of the Cherokees relative to other major southern tribes, 1780s–1830s, from Thurman Wilkins, *Cherokee Tragedy* (Norman: University of Oklahoma Press, 1986). Used by permission of the University of Oklahoma Press.

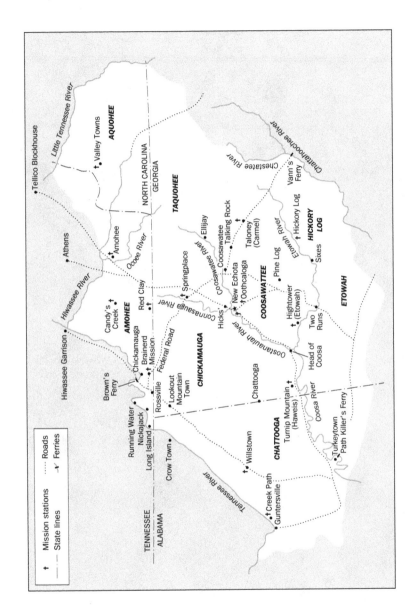

Map 2. The Cherokee Nation, 1817–1823, from Henry Thompson Malone, *Cherokees of the Old South* (Athens: University of Georgia Press, 1956) and Joyce B. Phillips and Paul Gary Phillips, eds., *The Brainerd Journal* (Lincoln: University of Nebraska Press, 1998). Used by permission of the University of Georgia Press.

ONE

Captivity

O, come with me, my white girl fair,
O, come where Mobile's sources flow;
With me my Indian blanket share,
and share with me my bark canoe;
We'll build our cabin in the wild,
Beneath the forest's lofty shade,
With logs on logs traversely piled,
And Barks on barks obliquely laid . . .

Then come with me, my white girl fair,
And thou a hunter's bride shall be;
For thee I'll chase the roebuck there,
And thou shalt dress the feast for me:
O, wild and sweet our feast shall be,
The feast of love and joy is ours;
Then come, my white girl fair, with me,
O, come and bless my sylvan bowers.

SILAS McALPINE
"Ode to John Ridge and Sarah Northrup" (circa 1824)

AT THE TURN OF THE EIGHTEENTH CENTURY, the Cherokee man known as Shoe Boots was a warrior in exile. According to a report of John Howard Payne, a white American journalist, lay historian, and visitor to the Cherokee Nation, Shoe Boots fled his home after accidentally killing a man who refused to sing for him. An ardent music lover, Shoe Boots seems to have become enraged when a bystander would not sing to accompany Shoe Boots's dancing. He then assaulted the man, pummeling him to death.[1] Judging by this account and several others, Shoe Boots was an arresting figure, distinguished in his mode of dress, daring on the battlefield, quixotic and even dangerous in character. Tall, dark, and self-possessed, Shoe Boots was described by one Cherokee contemporary as "about 6 feet 2 or 3 inches high, of slender build, erect, of very dark complexion, straight black hair, and . . . about 180 or 200 pounds."[2] The same acquaintance also said that "Shoe-boots was a very peculiar looking man, from the fact that he was a very tall man—his garb was that of a military officer's style. He wore boots, the legs of which reached above his knees. His hat was that of a British military hat, with a red plume in front. . . . His coat was a British military uniform coat, which was kipped with red scarlet cloth . . . he wore a strap across his shoulders, and on that strap swung a long sword."[3]

After fleeing his home in Cherokee country for fear of retribution, Shoe Boots traveled north to Shawnee territory and joined a band of young men who were incensed at the encroachment of white Kentucky settlers.[4] It was here, in the rolling bluegrass hills, that the story of Shoe Boots's successive "marriages," first to a white woman, and next to a black woman, begins to unfold. The inception of Shoe Boots's relationship with a young Kentuckian named Clarinda was later described by the couple's grandson, William Stephens, as "somewhat romantic."[5] Stephens continued: "At an early day, about the year 1780 . . . the Cherokees made an assault on the village where my grandmother lived at that time, she being then only sixteen years of age, and among others they took my grandmother into captivity, and subsequently one of the raiding band took her to be his wife according to the customs, usages and laws of the Cherokees." Other sources give Clarinda Allington's age as eleven or thirteen at the time of her abduction.[6] The tenor of this episode, misinterpreted as romantic by Stephens, is better captured by Kentucky historian Harry Enoch, who reports that Clarinda's story was an "unhappy" one that was nevertheless "told and retold for many years as part of the country's lore."[7]

When Shoe Boots took up with the Shawnee men who would make their famous raid on Kentucky's Morgan's Station, he would not have been focused on the imminent capture of a young girl. Rather, Shoe Boots and his fellows were motivated by righteous indignation at the gall of white intruders who were pouring into Shawnee territory. By 1792 Kentucky had become a fast-growing state. Settlers were crowding in with their slaves, elevating the population of Lexington to nearly one thousand, clearing forests, depleting wild game, and engaging with Wyandots, Shawnees, Mingos, and Cherokees in armed skirmishes over territory, game, horses and livestock.[8] Three years before the coming of statehood, a wealthy Virginian named Ralph Morgan had founded a settlement and fort on the western "frontier" of the region. The settlement, called Morgan's Station, overlooked Slate Creek and was home to six families, many of which also had emigrated from Virginia in search of land and prosperity.[9] Because of its location as an outpost of Kentucky settlements, Morgan's Station was particularly vulnerable to Indian attacks, especially from Shawnees to the north and Cherokees from the south. Residents were constantly fearful of Indian raids in their first years of settlement, but by the time Kentucky achieved statehood, citizens of Morgan's Station had relaxed their vigilance. They became so comfortable in their new environment that they allowed defenses at the station to deteriorate. An entry gate that formerly had guarded the station was neglected, and fencing that had connected each of the buildings in a protective palisade had been removed for use as firewood.[10]

The settlers now viewed their Indian neighbors as a contained threat, even as they adopted Indian ways to help them survive in the Kentucky wilderness. Like their countryman, the famed Daniel Boone, Kentucky settlers "not only understood [the Indians], they virtually adopted their lifestyle. . . . Early Kentuckians wore buckskin shirts, breechcloths, leggings and moccasins; assumed the nomadic existence of hunter-gatherers; could endure incredible hardship and were capable of extreme brutality to their enemies."[11] Thus, the frontiersmen described by Enoch above became part of a process of Americanization analyzed by scholars Richard Slotkin and Rayna Green, in which white men adopted a unique identity and means of subsistence that depended on the employment of Native ways and the simultaneous extermination of Indians.[12] In the spring of 1793, a group of thirty to forty Shawnee and Cherokee warriors stunned the residents of Kentucky by launching what would later be described as "the last Indian raid in Kentucky."[13] Much of what we know of that raid is based on the eyewitness accounts of early residents of Morgan's Station who were interviewed by a lay oral historian, Reverend John Shane, in the 1840s and 1850s.[14]

Thirty-six-year-old Shoe Boots was among the warriors who camped along the banks of Little Slate Creek on Easter Sunday, 1793.[15] The Indian men are said to have entered Morgan's Station from the south and then to have divided their ranks, with one group entering an isolated cabin to take prisoners and another continuing on to attack the heart of the station. Inside the targeted cabin the woman of the house, Rachel Becraft, and several of her children were visiting with two neighbor girls, Polly Baker and Clarinda Allington. All were taken captive and carried away, while most of the station's residents tried in vain to fend off the second group of raiders. The party of warriors inside the station attacked men, women, and children with muskets and tomahawks. In the words of one eyewitness, James Wade, a small girl was shot by a warrior aiming for her father, and "the women and children were flying in all directions."[16] Only one family, the Martins, was able to flee. Clarinda Allington's grandmother narrowly escaped by running with the Martins as far as she could and hiding inside a hollow fallen tree. By the end of the raid, two settlers would be killed inside the settlement and eleven out of nineteen prisoners would be killed outside the station.[17] The warriors burned the station to the ground, killed livestock, and are said to have captured a few black slaves before taking their leave of the place.

Meanwhile, the small party of bedraggled prisoners was making its way along the Little Sandy River at the command of its captors. As a posse to pursue the Indians formed back at the station, the raiders began killing captives who were slowing the pace of their retreat. At times the raiders even left their captives alone on the long trek toward the territory of present-day Michigan. Clarinda Allington, an adolescent girl who has been described as a "plucky" child, thought that she could find her way back to the Ohio River and urged the other captives to escape with her.[18] They refused to follow Clarinda, however, and also refused to let her go alone. With her bid for escape thwarted, Clarinda, along with her neighbor Polly Baker, was taken south into Cherokee country, while most of the remaining captives were taken north to Detroit.[19] After the raid, President George Washington appointed General "Mad Anthony" Wayne to raise a militia to suppress the midwestern tribes. Wayne's army prevailed in the Battle of Fallen Timbers, and in 1795, a treaty signed by several tribes, including the Shawnee, secured the release of many of the captives from Morgan's Station.[20] Clarinda Allington, then confined in the home of Shoe Boots, was "the last of the captives still being held."[21]

Snatched from her neighbor's home and witness to the killing of friends, Clarinda must have been terrified when she first reached Cherokee country. But she was known as a girl of fortitude and was able to adapt to her new conditions. For a time Clarinda seems to have lived platonically with Shoe Boots, who may have had a Cherokee wife.[22] Within a few years, however, she became Shoe Boots's sexual partner. Sometime between 1794 and 1803, the couple had three children: William, Sarah (or Sally), and John.[23] They also had at least two African slaves—including a teenaged girl named Doll who was not much younger than Clarinda.[24]

It is not clear how Clarinda came to feel about her predicament, since written accounts of her experience were kept by and between white men.

Did she accept Shoe Boots as her husband, or would she always view him as her captor? Did she enjoy living at what must have been a greater level of material comfort in Cherokee country, with a slave of her own? Or did material circumstances have no impact on her experience of forced exile? Though many white people captured by Indians in the eighteenth century later told tales of their difficult adjustment to Native culture, many also came to prefer life among the Indians and chose to remain in Native communities, even when presented with the opportunity to return to their families of origin.[25] According to Indian Agent Silas Dinsmoor, Clarinda was content to live with Shoe Boots; according to his successor, Return Jonathan Meigs, she wanted to return home but could not for fear that she would be compelled to leave her children behind.[26]

Clarinda's Kentucky family was devastated by her capture and tried for years to bring about her return. Payne notes that they even hired local hero William Whitley to track her down and rescue her.[27] Whitley, who had been appointed a major in the Kentucky militia by Governor Isaac Shelby, had gained renown for his zest in fighting Indians. A history of Kentucky published in 1882 recorded how Whitley had acquired his fame, reporting that in 1794, "aggravated by continued Indian raids, [he] led two hundred men against Chickamauga [a Cherokee] village in Tennessee. After resoundingly defeating the Indians, Whitley gave a barbeque at his newly completed home, Sportsman Hill."[28] Now a lieutenant colonel, Whitley traveled to Cherokee country to meet with federal Indian Agent Dinsmoor to discuss Clarinda Allington's return. As Dinsmoor noted in the Cherokee Agency records, "relative to the business of Col. Whitely I am of opinion that the woman who lives with Tuskiaoo [Shoe Boots] will not be willing to leave him . . . she has three fine children by the man and I believe is well satisfied with her situation."[29] Dinsmoor's successor, Agent Return Meigs, inherited the problem. In October 1803, when Clarinda's relatives appeared at the agency, Meigs called in Shoe Boots to ascertain the details of the case. Meigs reported:

This Cherokee man named Tuskingo or Shoeboots being brought before the agent with the said three children and questions being first put to the woman. Do you wish to return to your friends in Kentucky?—Answered Yes if I can carry my children—and the following questions being put to the Cherokee man—Are you willing to let Clarinda Ellington the woman you call your wife go with her children to see her friends in Kentucky? Answered No. If my children are taken away I shall look on it the same as if they were dead. And the said Clarinda therefore declines going to see her friends as she cannot leave her children. The said Tuskingo says that he saved her life at the time she was taken, and therefore thinks he has a right to keep her as his wife. It appears that Tuskingo is a man of very considerable property.[30]

Clarinda Allington, discussed in this report as if she were property, had remained in Cherokee territory for the sake of her children in the view of Agent Meigs. Because Clarinda left no account of her own, we cannot know whether she actively chose to stay with Shoe Boots or whether she was content, as Agent Dinsmoor believed. Perhaps Clarinda was relieved and even elated when a year after this meeting her relatives made an arrangement with Agent Meigs for her and the children to visit Kentucky.[31] According to Payne, Shoe Boots agreed to the trip only on the condition that his family would return to Cherokee country. Payne noted that after an agreement was reached, Clarinda and her children departed from Shoe Boots's home in high style: "Captain Shoe Boots fitted out his wife and children as became his dignity and his wealth. He gave them several fine horses, and abundance of clothes and silver money, and a negro slave, besides a hired servant, to attend them."[32]

This leave-taking is an essential part of the Shoeboots family story not only because of what it would mean for Clarinda's servant, Doll, who was left behind, but also because of what it suggests about the symbolic meaning of idealized (white) womanhood in Cherokee country and how this meaning gets bound up with the practice of owning black slaves. In the lavish description quoted above, Payne highlights Shoe Boots's gentlemanly behavior toward his beloved wife, who had transformed him from a marauding warrior into a man of gentility. However, Clarinda's relationship with Shoe Boots would be represented quite differently in the public forums of her home community, revealing ambivalence about intermarriage between white women and Native men among white Americans, an ambivalence sometimes influenced by the presence of black slaves in these multiracial households.[33]

When Shoe Boots first brought Clarinda to his home in the 1790s, few white women lived with Cherokee families. The majority of interracial marriages took place between white men—often traders—and Cherokee women. For a white man seeking to do business with Indians, marrying an Indian woman was a wise investment, since it allowed him to become more familiar with Cherokee language and culture and offered the added advantage of family and community ties. In 1819 the Cherokee National Council mediated these relationships, passing a resolution meant to protect Cherokee women, requiring that white men legally marry the Cherokee women they called their wives and making it illegal for a white man to have more than one Cherokee wife. The law also dictated that intermarried white men would not have the right to control their Cherokee wives' property, in keeping with Cherokee understanding that women, not men, owned the homes in which they lived.[34] In an 1825 law the Cherokee Council referred to the 1819 act, broadening its provision on polygamy by making it illegal for anyone in the Cherokee Nation to have more than one wife. In addition, the 1825 law was the first to acknowledge the presence of intermarried white *women* in the Nation. Because the Cherokees were a matrilineal tribe in which clan membership, and thus Cherokee belonging, had customarily passed from Cherokee mother to child, the government had to address whether and by what means the children of white women would be considered citizens. The Council thus enacted a special provision for these children, granting them automatic Cherokee citizenship.[35] In essence, the Cherokee government sanctioned marriages between white women and Cherokee men by promising their children an equal place in the nation.

By the time this law legitimating the children of white women and Cherokee men was passed, dominant American definitions of proper feminine virtues, embodied in the idealized type of the white, middle-class "true woman," had begun to influence the thinking of some Cherokees.[36] Members of the Cherokee elite urged their daughters to model themselves after the gentle, chaste, pious women represented in American mass culture.[37] The newspaper *Cherokee Phoenix* reprinted a series of articles on the feminine ideal that defined the goal of female education as "the formation of moral principles and sound affections," raised the query, "Who is a Beautiful Woman," and answered it: "Wherever there is most bosom tranquility, most domestic happiness, there beauty reigns in all its strength." Another article listed the "Qualifications for a Wife" as "Piety, Person, Parts, Patience, Prudence, Providence, Privilege, Parentage, and Portion."[38] The presence of white female missionaries who modeled as well as taught these values further reinforced this notion of womanhood.[39] And a marriage announcement printed in the *Cherokee Phoenix* in 1828 illustrates the ways in which elite Cherokee women were assessed in accordance with a popularized white gender ideal: "The Bride is a quarter white, possesses a fine figure, somewhat tall, beautiful complexion, with dark hair and eyes: her features bear the evidence of amiability and good nature; and on the whole she is an interesting woman. She is a member of the Methodist Church." This wedding story also notes the class standing of the bride, indicated by her parents' property holdings, which "consist[ed] of four log cabins, with a farm."[40]

In a period when the Cherokee Nation was trying to remake itself in the image of the United States to prove its level of civilization, entertaining the complex set of ideas and social practices known today as the ideology of "true womanhood" or "domesticity" represented a pathway to civilized society.[41] For this nascent connection between female virtue and Cherokee civilization echoed a similar relationship between female virtue and American civilization. Properly enacted femininity represented the nobility of the American republic in the nineteenth century, and white women were charged with strengthening the nation's moral fiber through their possession and performance of a series of qualities: piety, purity, deference, and domesticity.[42] White women's spiritual faith and decorum in the home were believed to temper white men's necessary engagement in the defiling world of commerce and politics.[43] White women's tutelage of young children was thought to shape the morality of future statesmen, thus affecting the course of national events.[44] It follows that as these notions filtered into Cherokee communities, some Cherokees would come to believe that Cherokee women exhibiting these characteristics of "true womanhood" could do as much for Cherokee men and the Cherokee Nation. And if Cherokee women could have such an impact, how might the growing number of actual white women marrying Cherokee men help elevate Cherokee society?

Certainly Cherokees living in the 1800s would have answered this query in various and contradicting ways. But Payne seems to have thought that the presence of white women could have uplifting effects, as evidenced by his descriptions of Clarinda Allington, "whose charms, it may be conjectured, had already made a captive of her captor." Shoe Boots, the once-wild Indian, had become a proper gentleman in her presence, evidencing gentleness and commitment, and "ingratiat[ing] himself, by his devotedness and delicacy and decorum still more and more with his captive."[45] Clarinda, in Payne's view, had made her savage husband into a noble man. In his history of the Cherokee Nation, Cherokee historian Emmet Starr clearly espouses the benefits of intermarriage with whites, male or female. In a section titled "Character of the Cherokees" Starr reports that "the Cherokees married more freely with the whites than did the other tribes, and with exceptional results."[46] Daniel Butrick, a Protestant missionary stationed in Cherokee country, not only supported these marriages but also indicated that the federal government did so as well. Butrick made reference to former president Thomas Jefferson, an advocate of white-Indian couplings: "If I am not mistaken the President, or Secretary of War, but a few years since, recommended intermarriages with the Indians as a means of promoting their improvement, but if they had not, I can see no evil in it."[47]

At the same time that white intermarriage represented transformation and civilization for Indians, the means of that transformation proved inherently compromising for white women. By becoming the wives of Indian men and having sexual relations with them, white women forfeited their purity and honor in the eyes of white society. For the salvation of Indian men by intimate association with white women was at the same time a desecration of virtuous white womanhood. Clarinda Allington's reception in Kentucky after her return from Cherokee territory demonstrates this irony. Clarinda's family members, who worked mainly as subsistence farmers and tanners, were unable to bear the cost of care for Clarinda and her three children. The family therefore submitted a petition to the Kentucky assembly, seeking aid for Clarinda:

> When the Treaty of Greenville came on, she was detained by a Cherokee chief . . . and was conducted by a secret route to the Cherokee nation. That her situation there has been extremely distressing owing to the cruelty of her tyrant. For four years after her captivity she was constantly in danger of her life by refusing to become his wife. Self-preservation, however, at length induced her to yield to the embraces of the savage, by whom she has had three children, all now very young. That she has, within a few days since, found means to escape with her children and throwing herself upon the bosom of an aged mother and other relations, who are unfortunately too poor to afford any support to her and her children, and is unable from her long captivity—which induces an ignorance of the manners and employments of white people—to produce any kind of sustenance for herself and her children. Therefore praying that an Act may pass for her relief.[48]

The legislature accepted this narrative of Clarinda's circumstances and awarded her a pension.[49]

The representation here of Clarinda's eventual submission to the sexual appetites of a savage, and her own descent into savagery by virtue of her loss of white ways and adoption of Indian ways, shows the danger of intermarriage for white women. Once sullied by her sexual relations with a Native man, Clarinda's character continued to worsen in the eyes of her community members. James Wade, who had been present at the raid on Morgan's Station, recalled that Clarinda "again married . . . a great deal worse husband than the Indian had made." Wade notes further that Clarinda married a third time, to a "trifling fellow" who was promised on a bet, presumably made with male friends, that he would receive "a cow and calf, perhaps other things, if he wod go and marry her."[50] While Payne, writing in the 1830s as a visitor to the Cherokees, sees Clarinda as Shoe Boots's moral salvation, the white people of Clarinda's hometown see Shoe Boots as the vehicle of her degradation and moral decline. Because she is already tainted by her sexual relationship with an Indian, each successive marriage reveals the depth of Clarinda's ruin, until finally, she can only find a husband if he is paid to take her. Clarinda's dire circumstances in Kentucky were relieved only slightly by the sixteen-year-old slave Mingo, whom Shoe Boots had sent along with her. Too poor to maintain Mingo as her servant, Clarinda bartered him for childcare and "left her children with her brother and gave him the little Negro boy to pay for raising them."[51] If Clarinda was unable to redeem herself in life, perhaps she did so in death. Her grandson recalled that she passed away in 1840, "surrounded by white relatives."[52]

Two highly publicized marriages of Cherokee men to white Christian women in the 1820s also illustrate the contradictory dynamic of white women's symbolic presence in Cherokee communities, as viewed both by Cherokees and whites. Cousins John Ridge and Elias Boudinot (formerly called Buck Watie) of the prominent Ridge family were sent as children to the Moravian Mission School that had been established in Cherokee territory. The boys' acquisition of English literacy and biblical knowledge so exceeded expectations that they were chosen to continue their education in New England. They traveled to the Foreign Mission School in Cornwall, Connecticut, where they lived for almost five years. During their stay in Cornwall, both men, now in their late teens, met the young women they wished to marry. Sarah Northrup (age fourteen) and Harriet Gold (age nineteen) returned their suitors' affections, Harriet's reason being that "she was determined to become a missionary to the Cherokees and knew no better way than as the wife of a leading man of the nation."[53] The parents of both women were undone upon hearing their daughters' intentions and attempted to dissuade them. However, Sarah and Harriet fell ill at the thought of losing their beloveds, and both sets of parents relented in order to restore their daughters' fragile health. The families of Ridge and Boudinot, who preferred that the cousins marry Cherokee women, were also convinced by the entreaties of the young men.[54]

The vitriolic response of white New Englanders to the news of the impending weddings came as a shock and an affront to Ridge and Boudinot, who had been educated to believe in the generosity of Christian values and the particularly liberal nature of white northerners. Local newspapers printed editorials expressing the sentiment that Ridge's fiancée, Sarah, "was to be a squaw with a grubby papoose on her back."[55] Boudinot and his fiancée, Harriet, faced a more graphic, violent protest. Cornwall citizens, led by Harriet's brother, burned images of Elias, Harriet, and Harriet's mother on the town green and threatened to lynch the dark-skinned Elias should he go through with the ceremony. In a letter to her sister and brother-in-law, Harriet recounted the macabre scene that she witnessed from a friend's window: "A painting had before been prepared representing a beautiful young Lady and an Indian. . . . The church bell began to toll . . . Brother Stephen set fire to the barrel of tar, or rather, the funeral pile, the flames rose high and the smoke ascended. . . . My heart truly sung with anguish at the dreadful scene."[56] The scandal was so extreme that the Foreign Mission School closed its doors after the Boudinot-Gold wedding, explaining that "it was best to train youths in their own lands."[57]

In the aftermath of the protests, however, the people of Cornwall, who saw Sarah Northrup in a new light, had a change of heart. Cornwall citizens came to realize that Sarah had married into a prominent Cherokee family with wealth, slaves, and even a famous Indian chief. John Ridge's father, Major Ridge (sometimes called "The Ridge"), was a Cherokee war hero and political leader, making John Ridge something of a prince and thus redeeming Sarah for white womanhood. Historian Marion Starkey writes about the town's changing impression: "The Ridge had come to visit John dressed in broadcloth and driving a coach-and-four. . . . His state was kingly. Cornwall decided to make an Indian princess of Sarah after all."[58] Biographer Thurman Wilkins further explains that "the townspeople even came to think of Sarah Northrup Ridge as a kind of princess who dressed in silk every day and had fifty servants to wait on her." Wilkins quotes from a history of Cornwall in which Sarah was remembered: "She simply said to this [slave], go, and he goeth, and to another one Come, and he did so."[59]

Sarah Northrup Ridge's transformation from squaw to princess depended on a triangular relationship among white women, Cherokee men, and black slaves. Possessing a bevy of slaves to wait on her made Sarah's life with an Indian husband acceptable and even enviable, just as wealth derived from slave labor made Major Ridge worthy of respect. In his description of Clarinda Allington's departure from Shoe Boots's home, Payne successfully reproduces this formula, representing Clarinda as a white-Indian princess by his reference to her finery and slaves.

The early marriage of Shoe Boots to a young white woman serves as a precursor to the saga that unfolds here, and the portrayal of this marriage by Payne can be read as a metaphor for the role of blacks in the Cherokee Nation. Though much of nineteenth-century Cherokee history has been written as a story about Cherokees and whites, it was an invisible third element, the presence of black people, on which the story often turned.

TWO

Slavery

Know all men by these presents that I Mary Steamon of the district of Chickamon GA and Cherokee Nation have this day sold to Joseph Vann of the district of Coosa water and Nation aforesaid the following property: one negro woman slave by the name of Jinney about fifty years old, also her husband named Harry about the same age and her children: Sally thirty-four years old, Charlat twenty-eight years old, George twenty-six, Roseanna twenty-one, Isaac eighteen, Bob sixteen, Harry fourteen, Caty eleven, and Ellack eight years old, and her the said Jinney's grandchildren: Ruben nine, Washington six, Sally three, and Eveline one year old, also ten head of cattle, one sown mare and two colts, one bay horse and poney and one wagon.

Cherokee Supreme Court docket

I want to add my testimony to that of abler pens to convince the people of the Free States what slavery really is. Only by experience can any one realize how deep, and dark, and foul is that pit of abominations.

HARRIET JACOBS
Incidents in the Life of a Slave Girl Written by Herself

WHAT DID IT MEAN to be described in the possessive, categorized in a collective, listed among things? What were the psychic and physical costs of becoming someone owned, of having one's humanity diminished by custom and law, of being fully subject to the authority of another? Sometimes we, as twenty-first-century students of history, think we know the answers to these questions. But Harriet Jacobs, who wrote the exemplary slave narrative *Incidents in the Life of a Slave Girl Written by Herself,* after she had escaped from her master in North Carolina, tells us that we are mistaken. "O virtuous reader!" Jacobs writes, "You never knew what it was to be a slave."[1] Even as we learn more about the conditions and cycles of female enslavement from an ever-growing and important body of scholarship, we seem to perceive less about the raw and utter evil that was chattel slavery in America. The passage of time, the passing away of our great-grandparents who knew the "peculiar institution" firsthand, and, ironically, the wide availability of brutal slavery accounts, have distanced us from this history, anesthetized us to its horrors, and muted our ability to understand its assault on humanity. Literary scholar Saidiya Hartman has unveiled this disassociation in her discussion of representations of violence against slaves, writing that she wants to "call attention to the ease with which such scenes are usually reiterated, the casualness with which they are circulated, and the consequences of this routine display of the slave's ravaged body. Rather than inciting indignation, too often they immure us to pain by virtue of their familiarity." Instead of reproducing such scenes in her book, Hartman directs our attention to what she calls "the sheer unrepresentability of terror."[2] Here Hartman agrees with Jacobs, who impresses on us the unknowability of her experience.

This place of the unrepresentable, the unknowable, and, in the language of Toni Morrison, the "unspeakable," is where the slave lives.[3] It is where a slave woman named Doll Shoeboots lived until her old age. Unlike Harriet Jacobs, though, who told her unknowable story in her own words, Doll did not write. A record of Doll's interior life, her ruminations and fleeting thoughts, might reveal something of her world to us. But like millions of other slave women, Doll left nothing behind that attests to her character, her strategies and ideologies, the quality of her days and years. The available sources on Doll's life are a reflection of that life itself—limited, ambiguous, and fragmented.

To write about Doll, then, is to pay tribute to her life, a life that would otherwise be lost to history. But do not be lulled. To write about Doll is also a wholly inadequate exercise. For every scrap about her past that I have scavenged and reconstructed here might just as well have been captured by a chapter of blank, white pages. "O virtuous reader! You never knew what it was to be a slave."

She was known by the name Doll. It is an evocative name, one that conjures the image of a plaything with vacant eyes; or perhaps it brings to mind a sweet-faced young woman, kind and gentle of spirit. But even the simple fact of Doll's moniker points to absences in what we know about this woman's life. Was Doll the name given her by her mother or grandmother? Or was it attached to her by a former slaveowner as a way to undermine her parents' authority or to simplify the task of addressing his slaves? Would this name resonate with Doll, or was it a label that, when uttered, did violence to her by erasing another name that we will never know? Many historians who mention Doll in passing as part of their accounts of Shoe Boots's life did further violence by misnaming her, calling her anything from Lucy and Lilcy (the apparent name of one of Shoe Boots's sisters) to "the dark faced one" and "the servant woman."[4] By the end of what we know of Doll's life, she is referred to in legal documents as Dolly Shoeboots, a name that could be read as signaling her final and full inclusion in her master/husband's community or as a double erasure of her self, a final remarking of her as the belonging of another.

In South Carolina, where Shoe Boots first acquired her, Doll was a fairly common name for female slaves.[5] However, it was not a common name in the Cherokee tribe in the late 1700s and 1800s, which suggests that this young woman was already known as Doll before she was transported West from the Atlantic coast to the inland region of central Cherokee country. Doll's family, her mother and father, grandparents and siblings, are never mentioned in the Cherokee records. It is as though she sprang up, fully formed, as the slave of Shoe Boots. Where was her first home? Who were her people? What trees did she know? What waters? Was she born in Africa, the Caribbean, America? Did she recall her home as did the young poet Phillis Wheatley, who came to Boston on a slave ship in 1761? Or did she carry with her the story of a father or grandfather who remembered an African past?

It is quite possible that Doll was African born, since Cherokee slaveowners purchased slaves recently arrived from Africa who were said to have spoken their mother tongues.[6] If Doll had undergone a journey in the middle passage, or if her parents had, it is possible that she was Gambian (from the present-day Ivory Coast or Liberia, a favored location among South Carolina planters), or Angolan (from Central Africa, the home of many newly arrived slaves in eighteenth-century South Carolina).[7] Born around 1784, one year after the Paris Peace Treaty concluded the American Revolutionary War, Doll may have lived in a predominantly African environment in the outlying areas or in the sea islands of South Carolina, or she may have lived in close quarters with her master in the city. It is probable that Doll lived near Charleston as a girl or at least passed through that metropolis, since Charleston was a major market for the buying and selling of slaves, and one that the prominent Cherokee slaveowner James Vann frequented on his slave-buying expeditions. Doll may have spoken an African language, and she may also have spoken Gullah, a New World fusion of African languages and English. She may even have known some Cherokee, since in coastal South Carolina many Indian slaves, including Cherokee slaves, were kept on English plantations with African slaves until the mid 1700s.[8]

Doll had another life somewhere before she came into Shoe Boots's hands, before she was passed from man to man, like a gun or a blanket. It is likely that she was Shoe Boots's first slave and that he purchased her to be the helpmate and servant of his Kentucky-born wife, Clarinda Allington. Doll arrived in Cherokee country as a young woman of nearly sixteen, with a strength and subtle beauty that would sustain her in the years to come. A fellow slave once said of her, "Dolly . . . was a tall, strong made woman . . . she was called a fair woman at that time." A Cherokee man and acquaintance of Shoe Boots also remembered Doll as a woman with an imposing presence, saying she was "rather tall and heavy made."[9] These fragmented descriptions of Doll's likeness, frustrating in their lack of detail, suggest nevertheless that her strength of body, and possibly of character, blur the immediate associations inspired by her name. This contradictory image of her, of a barely-out-of-girlhood "doll" who was at the same time tall and strong, holds in tension Doll's objectification and vulnerability as a woman owned and her fortitude as a woman *on her own* in an unforgiving land.

When Doll was captured or purchased by Shoe Boots in the late 1700s, black slavery in Cherokee territory was newly germinating. Cherokees had been aware of Africans at least since the sixteenth century when Spanish explorer Hernando de Soto beached in the Americas, carrying in tow West Indian and African slaves.[10] The slaves from De Soto's expedition (1540) and explorer Juan Pardo's travels (1657), and possibly runaway slaves from the Spanish Colony on Peedee River (1526), were likely the first Africans that Cherokees encountered.[11] The earliest forms of Cherokee and African relations were identification and interdependence. As British settlers planted their first colonies in Virginia and South Carolina, they enslaved Indians as well as Africans to increase their labor pool and to weaken those neighboring Indian groups that they viewed as political and military adversaries. The practice of enslaving Indians (mainly women) alongside Africans (mainly men) brought members of both groups into intimate proximity. A joining of families through intermarriage and a fusion of cultural ways resulted. African folktales featuring a trickster rabbit combined with southeastern Native tales about the same hero; African medicinal practices became enmeshed with Native knowledge about the uses of indigenous plants; African women's basketry patterns were woven into Native women's crafts; and corn, the staple of the southeastern Indian diet, became a signature ingredient of what we now call "soul food."[12] African people and Indian people, including many Cherokees, shared the same lot for nearly a century. The bonds they developed persisted throughout the early 1700s, a period when black slaves escaped to Indian communities in significant numbers, and, paradoxically, when Indian slaves were traded to the West Indies to prevent the likelihood of their escape.[13]

Evidence that black slaves sometimes found protection in Native communities exists mainly in the oral histories of African American and Native American people as well as in the records of British colonists who were frustrated by the deepening of black and Indian relations. One of the best sources for mapping the history of slave escapes to Indian communities are British colonial and early American newspapers. Public historian William Loren Katz and historian Jack Forbes both have noted the ways in which newspaper advertisements for runaway slaves indicate not only the routes that slaves took to find their freedom but also the reality of intermarriage between blacks and Indians in the colonial and early national periods. Katz observed: "Reward notices in colonial newspapers now told of African slaves who 'ran off with his Indian wife' or 'had kin among the Indians' or is 'part-Indian and speaks their language good.'"[14] Many of these advertisements do not specify a particular Indian nation to which slaves were said to be running, and of those that do, a fair number note the Creek Nation, which, along with the related Seminoles, was more open to accepting African slaves than the Cherokees were. Still, some advertisements directly named the Cherokee Nation or indirectly indicated Cherokee territory, such as in the following examples:

Taken up in September last, by the subscriber who commands Fort Prince-George in the Lower Settlements of the Cherokee Nation, a Negro Fellow, named Jack; speaks pretty good English, says he belongs to the estate of John Stobo of Virginia, and that he has been away about Four years (1769).[15]

Run away from my plantation [near Charles Town, South Carolina] . . . two country-born Negro men, named July and Cupid. . . . As they are particu-

larly known at the Indian land, it is supposed they are concealed or har-
boured there (1774).[16]

Came to my plantation, up on Ouslow Island, a Negro wench called Nancy,
otherwise Penny, who says she belonged to a Mr. ___, who died about 18
months ago, and that she went to the Cherokee Nation with her husband
(1793).[17]

Ran-away on Monday last, from the subscriber, living on Peedee . . . three
Negro Fellows, supposed to be making for the Indians, through the state of
Georgia (1801).[18]

These newspaper advertisements from the late 1700s and early 1800s also
indicate a shift in the enslaved population. Here we see African slaves (and
Afro-Indian slaves in many cases) escaping to Indian communities, but we
do not see slaves described as "Indian" running away. This is owing not just
to the planters' tendency to lump African and Native bondspeople together
under the category "Negro" but also to a dramatic decrease in the number
of American Indians held as slaves. Relative to the enslavement of Africans,
the enslavement of Cherokees and other Native peoples in British North
America was short-lived, declining by the 1720s as the British depended less
on intertribal warfare for their own security and realized the inefficiency of
enslaving people in their own homeland.[19] Free Cherokees, perhaps in re-
membrance of their shared experience with African slaves, continued to accept black runaways into their communities in the mid-eighteenth century,
but the knotty circumstances of early Cherokee and African encounters
would soon complicate future interactions.[20] As Indian slavery fell out of
favor in the British colonies, and as more and more African slaves were
dumped onto Native lands, Cherokees and Africans could not help but view
one another through the divisive and refracted lenses of European colonialism and racism.

As British settlers and their slaves swallowed up Cherokee hunting
grounds, Cherokees probably came to view blacks as co-intruders with the
Europeans they accompanied.[21] And as Cherokees took note of the fixed
and inferior position of the Africans, a position increasingly connected to
race or "blackness" in the minds and laws of the British, they may have begun to associate dark skin with low status. These early assessments among
Cherokees led to a gradual, and later, strategic, self-segregation from black
people. Thus, even as Cherokees and Africans developed alliances and de-
pendencies in the early decades of their encounters, they also betrayed and

battled one another, vying for liberty and authority in the expanding morass of European colonial rule. Their relationship came to be characterized by an ever-present theme of contradiction, resulting in simultaneous yet different social, economic, and political experiences at the intersection of African and Cherokee lives.[22]

One central contradiction at this fraught intersection was the gradual Cherokee involvement in the business of the day: the trade in African slaves. This practice seems to have developed, in part, out of the Cherokee tradition of taking Indian captives during wars with other tribes.[23] In intertribal battles, often waged for the purpose of avenging the deaths of loved ones, captives were ransomed, adopted into a family, or killed. War captives were embraced by tribal members when "Beloved Women" or "War Women," the highly respected elders who had the authority to decide the captives' fate, deemed them worthy of standing in the places of deceased clan members.[24] Intertribal battles increased in number and ferocity in the 1700s as tribes sided with particular European colonial powers to protect their people from opposing colonial powers. As British colonists in South Carolina sought cheap agricultural labor in the form of Native captives-turned-slaves, they further interrupted and influenced the balance of intertribal relations. Soon southeastern tribes sought war captives not only to avenge personal losses but also as commodities to be traded for European goods.[25] When colonists abandoned the Indian slave trade and demanded black slaves instead, the existing system of Indian captives-for-goods was easily adjusted. Cherokees and other tribes, whose appetite for European goods was swelling, became hunters and traders of Africans.[26]

In 1730 the Cherokee role as slave traders was written into law with the passage of the Treaty of Dover, enacted in England between King George II and a makeshift "delegation" of seven Cherokees who had no official power within the Cherokee Nation.[27] The treaty stipulated the following about Cherokees and African slaves: "That in the case any Negro slave runs away from his English master into the woods, the Indians of the Cherokee shall see what they can to apprehend him, and bring him back to the plantation from whence he fled, or to the governor's house; and for every Negro which the Indians shall thus retake, they shall have a musket, and a sentinel's unit of clothes. Whereupon we give you a full box of vermillion, with 10,000 flints, and six dozen hatchets." Concurrent with the passage of this treaty, "Slave Catcher" became a common title for some Cherokees.[28]

Though Cherokee complicity in the colonial slave system seems apparent from the language of the Treaty of Dover, it was a complicity that was not fully transparent, officially sanctioned, or unilateral. In the early 1700s British colonial rulers in the southeastern colonies and their superiors in England were distressed by the steady flow of runaway slaves from the British colonies into Indian communities and the Spanish colony of Florida. In an attempt to stem the tide, British officials included slavecatching clauses in many of the treaties they entered into with Native peoples of the Southeast.[29] It was difficult, if not impossible, for Indians to avoid formally agreeing to such clauses if they wanted to gain some measure of legal protection from the spread of European settlements. But even as Cherokees were hunting and trading African slaves, they continued to harbor runaways in their mountain communities, so much so that in 1767, John Stuart, the British superintendent of Southern Indian Affairs, warned that "to prevent the Indian Country [from] becoming an Asylum for Negroes is a Matter of the Utmost consequence to the prosperity of the provinces."[30] Superintendent Stuart had cause for concern, since Cherokees did not strictly enforce the slavecatching provision of the Treaty of Dover.[31] In fact, the Cherokee delegation to London may have intentionally included a loophole in their acceptance of the treaty, which reads: "This small Rope we shew you, is all we have to bind our Slaves with, and may be broken, but you have Iron Chains for yours; however, if we catch your Slaves, we shall bind them as well as we can, and deliver them to our Friends again, and have no Pay for it."[32] While the Cherokee delegation did agree to the provision, they left room for error by explaining in advance that their ropes were not strong enough to hold slaves even if they happened to catch them. The Cherokees strategically inserted these qualifications so that they would have recourse should they fail to capture slaves to the satisfaction of the British Crown. And in fact they did disappoint British expectations at various times by aiding runaways, by keeping black slaves for themselves, and by adopting Africans into their own families. All this amounted to what historian Peter H. Wood has called a "wilderness diplomacy," in which relations between Indians, Africans *and* Europeans were always in a "state of considerable doubt."[33] Interaction between Africans and Cherokees was like the proverbial box of chocolates: you never knew what you were going to get.

This was not a reassuring realization for the British, whose aim was to develop stable and economically productive American colonies. Aware that Cherokees were stealing and sheltering slaves and frightened by the possibility of a black-Indian insurrection, British colonists began purposefully to divide the two groups. In 1775 Stuart again warned that "nothing [could] be more alarming to Carolinians than the idea of an attack from Indians and Negroes."[34] British policy included the goal to "Discourage any Trade or Traffick being carryed on between Indians and Negroes and likewise prevent any Negroe from takeing a wife among the Free Indians, or Free Indians from takeing a Slave a Wife."[35] For the Cherokees, the British desire to sever ties between blacks and Indians crystallized in the form of colonial laws prohibiting white traders from transporting slaves into the Cherokee territory.[36] Colonists also paid Cherokees and other tribes to hunt blacks, at the same time arming blacks to fight Indians.[37] In addition to mandating physical distance and inciting violence between blacks and Indians, colonists attempted to introduce conflict by informing Cherokees that black slaves were to blame for the Cherokee smallpox epidemic of 1739 and for souring trade relations between Cherokees and whites.[38] These divisive activities would continue into the early national period of U.S. history; in 1758 James Glen, governor of South Carolina, informed his successor that "it has been allways the policy of this govert to creat an aversion in them [Indians] to Negroes."[39]

While colonists worked to foment antipathy between Cherokees and Africans, Cherokees were slowly adopting the practice of keeping black slaves for themselves in a manner that simultaneously reproduced and resisted the Euro-American system of slavery.[40] Cherokees and their slaves, who maintained a noteworthy degree of autonomy and mobility, worked side by side on communal town farms. Yet Cherokees valued slaves not just for their physical labor but also for intellectual skills such as knowledge of English and of Euro-American mores. A few Cherokees even married slaves or free blacks and enfolded them into their kinship circles. Examples of these intermarriages derive mainly from oral histories of black and Afro-Cherokee people whose forebears were slaves of Cherokees. One Afro-Cherokee man who was interviewed as part of the Federal Writers' Project during Franklin Roosevelt's Works Progress Administration of the 1930s explained that his grandfather, a slave, had married his Cherokee mistress: "My father was half Cherokee Indian. His father was bought by an Indian woman and she took him for her husband. She died and my grandfather, father and Auntie were bought by John Ross."[41] Another black-Cherokee man who was a former slave said in a WPA interview that his father, born in 1827 in Georgia, was "part Indian on account of his mamma was a Cherokee Indian girl name Downing."[42] A third free black man named Jack Civills is the rare African person described in some detail in the records of the Cherokee Agency. He lived in Cherokee country from the 1780s to 1805, married a Cherokee woman, and operated a tavern and trading post. According to Assistant Indian Agent William Lovely, Civills was "like all people of his colour, too forward . . . the fellow has obtained property by dint of his Industry, this with his equality with these people, appear too much for him to bear [humbly], his Indian connection creates an Idea of Indian Independence."[43]

As the above examples illustrate, Cherokee slaveholding was a loose and flexible practice in comparison to slavery in the American South in the late 1700s, where controlling, punitive, and brutal measures were deeply ingrained. At the turn of the nineteenth century, however, the ideology and enactment of antiblack prejudice would make slow but steady inroads in Cherokee country, affecting African slaves, free blacks in Cherokee territory, and the children who were the products of African-Cherokee marriages. In contrast to previous times, the early 1800s saw a firmer separation between Cherokees and blacks as well as limited intermarriage, a change influenced by a growing acceptance of European racial hierarchies among some Cherokees.[44] As German artisans and British sympathizers in the Revolutionary War brought their African slaves into Cherokee territory, as they began to intermarry with Cherokees, and as they founded individual farms, slaveholding among the Cherokees became more entrenched and systematized.[45] The combination of increasing white-Cherokee intermarriage, a growing slave population, and white racism against blacks negatively influenced Cherokee attitudes toward African people. According to historian Theda Perdue, it was in 1793 that the first expression of Cherokee color prejudice appeared in writing: "In that year Little Turkey sent a letter to Governor William Blount of Tennessee in which he described the Spaniards in the most derogatory terms he could as 'a lying, deceitful, treacherous people, and . . . not real white people, and the few I have seen of them looked like mulattoes, and I would never have anything to say to them.'"[46] Little Turkey's disparagement of "mulattoes" here in comparison with "real white people" reveals a growing racialization of peoples and an attachment of hierarchical value to different racial groups. Interestingly, this quotation also reveals one Cherokee man's attempt to marshal racial prejudice for the strategic purpose of manipulating colonial governments in the interest of himself and his tribe. Little Turkey demonstrates his allegiance to the Americans by distancing himself from the Spanish, whom he defines as mulatto or nearly black.

Cherokee understandings of racial difference and racial hierarchy, as exemplified by Little Turkey's exclamation, were exacerbated by an American program to "civilize" the Cherokees launched in the 1790s. In the wake of the American Revolution, President George Washington and Secretary of War Henry Knox were faced with the dilemma of what to do with the Native peoples whose homelands were now enclosed within the United States. Knox believed it a nobler goal to elevate and assimilate rather than to annihilate the Indians and so proposed that they be incorporated into American life. He felt that if only the Indians could be civilized through the adoption of private property, they could co-exist with white people.[47]

Knox's vision became reality for the Cherokees in 1791, when the tribe signed the Treaty of Holston with the United States in the aftermath of a crushing defeat at the hands of the Americans during the American Revolutionary War, in which the Cherokees had sided with the British. The Treaty of Holston included a program that called for the Cherokees to "be led to a greater degree of civilization, and to become herdsmen and cultivators, instead of remaining in a state of hunters."[48] To encourage Cherokee efforts toward these ends, the United States promised to supply the necessary tools, or "implements of husbandry."[49] The Cherokees were destitute after the ravages of the American Revolution and, as Perdue surmises, must have welcomed the material assistance.[50] But "aid" from the U.S. government came at a cost. The Cherokees would be pushed to re-envision their relationship to the natural world, to reinvent work patterns, and to reshape gender roles. As a letter from George Washington to the Cherokees in 1796 demonstrates, the federal government expected drastic change: "Each of you should get as large a flock of sheep, hogs, and cattle as possible; that you should raise cotton, or flax, and have your wives and daughters taught to spin it up into thread, and weave it into cloth; and that you should plant more corn, and learn to grow wheat."[51] Washington further suggested that some element of surveillance would be included in this plan for Cherokee improvement: "But further, that you may go on right and always keep right, I shall order my beloved man Mr. Dinsmoor, to visit every town in the nation from time to time; to give instructions and advice to those who do not like to be idlers; to see how the flocks and grain fields look; to examine the plows and implements of husbandry; to mark the advances which the women make in spinning and weaving; and to report thereof to the President of the United States."[52]

The president's instructions represented a major disruption of Cherokee customs, especially their subsistence patterns. Before this period and historically in Cherokee society, men and women played prescribed and arguably balanced roles. Men hunted, entered political negotiations with other tribes, and went to war. Women raised corn, gathered and prepared foods, managed the home, and maintained community ties. Cherokee women were considered the owners of their dwellings as well as of the farming tools they used and the household utensils, such as pottery, baskets, and tanned hides that they manufactured. Men had charge of fewer possessions, such as weapons and religious objects, and were dependent on their mothers and wives for shelter when they were not spending time with other men in the shared "town house." No one in Cherokee communities owned the land itself. In the view of federal officials, this lifestyle was backward and wasteful. They felt that Cherokee men were embarrassingly feminized, that Cherokee women were improperly masculinized, and that the vast, uncultivated Cherokee hunting grounds were underutilized. Instead of hunting, the men must farm. Instead of farming, the women must weave. And land must be privately owned and put to efficient use. Inherent in this new American way of life was the practice of owning black slaves, an enterprise that federal officials felt could bring industry and profit to Cherokee towns. So along with plows and looms, Cherokees were implicitly urged to acquire slaves. Benjamin Hawkins, the federal agent assigned to the southeastern tribes in this period, advised the tribes under his purview to take up slaveholding. In 1796 he traveled through Creek and Cherokee territories to assess Indian progress on the road to civilization. Hawkins found the Indians disappointing, since many of them failed to work their slaves hard enough, demonstrating "no economy or management."[53] In all his travels Hawkins found just one "industrious" Indian and described this man as "owning 61 slaves, over 200 horses, 400 cattle, and 300 hogs."[54] Progress and slavery were linked in Hawkins's view, so much so that he developed his own model plantation along the Flint River as an example for the Indians to follow.[55]

Perhaps persuaded by the Hawkins model or by the urging of his white wife, Shoe Boots took up slaveholding sometime around the year 1800, collecting a young African woman from South Carolina and bringing her home to his farm in Cherokee territory.

Snug in the valley of multiple riverbeds, the region where Shoe Boots farmed was choice land where many Cherokees with significant property holdings resided. The towns they built unfolded alongside the rivers and enfolded public squares and town houses, used for meetings and ceremonies. The towns then stretched into individual homes and farm sites, sometimes widely spaced one from another. John Norton, a Mohawk-Cherokee man raised in England who traveled through this area in 1809, described one portion as "the beautiful Valley of Chicamauga" and continued: "This Valley is watered by a stream of the same name, of about twenty yards wide, and is bounded by a ridge of Mountains on each side: it contains many small Villages and is in some places more than twelve miles broad. The soil is generally fertile."[56] Shoe Boots lived just east of the Chickamauga Valley, in a second valley nestled between the Coosa, Etowah, and Oostanaula Rivers, which Norton described as "a fine valley, a continuation of the Chicamauga," where there were "extensive corn fields, with droves of cattle, horses and dogs."[57] Cherokee towns, which once had been across the mountains from one another as far apart as central South Carolina and central Tennessee, had been pushed south toward the Georgia-Tennessee border after the American Revolution.[58] The families occupying this broad swath of fertile ground in the middle of the now-compressed Cherokee country were the most likely members of the tribe to own slaves; therefore, the practice of slaveholding among the Cherokees tended to fall within specific geographical boundaries. In what is now northern Georgia and the southern edge of Tennessee, "on the rich bottom lands along the headwaters of the Coosa and the Savannah," where land was fertile and water plentiful, Cherokees with financial resources built impressive farms and plantations, then constructed wharves near their homes to export their crops conveniently.[59] "Here," Marion Starkey writes, "real Southern plantations, cultivated in part by negro slaves, began to appear by the end of the [eighteenth] century."[60]

Shoe Boots's farm on the Etowah (or Hightower) River, where he lived with his mother, sister, nephew, wife, and children, was seventy acres in size, with an abundance of peach and apple trees.[61] Corn, probably potatoes, and possibly cotton were the major crops produced, which Shoe Boots would have traded to other Cherokees or to nearby white settlers for goods such as light fabrics, linens, hardware, needles, gunpowder, or, more rarely, money.[62] Shoe Boots's neighbor, Sally Hughes, operated a successful ferry that made it possible for farmers in the area to transport their wares.[63] Shoe Boots's simple but respectable property holdings, which would have comprised the farm house, outbuildings, and especially the harvest, increased dramatically with the acquisition of the new slave girl. Doll most likely lived with Shoe Boots and his wife, Clarinda, in their one-and-a-half-story log cabin, which was twenty feet wide by eighteen feet long.[64] Log cabins had become a common form of housing for Cherokees since the Revolution-ary War, replacing homes made of wood and daub (a mud mixture resem-bling plaster).[65] On Shoe Boots's farm, a separate kitchen, fourteen feet square, abutted the cabin. Though there may have been separate slave quar-ters on the land that Shoe Boots and his family occupied, there is no evi-dence of them in the records.[66] Shoe Boots's female relatives probably lived in a separate cabin on the farm, but this building too is not indicated in the records.[67] A freestanding stable and corncrib completed the outbuild-ings. Shoe Boots's compound seems to have been an early and smaller ver-sion of the typical Cherokee slaveowner's home described in a missionary essay:

> The establishment was probably a squarish, two-story house, small by mod-ern standards and quite plain, often unpainted. The farm, for it was a farm, not a plantation, was completed by a few utility shacks, the slave huts, sta-bles and fields. The slaves probably numbered about half a dozen. The men worked the fields with the Indian owner, the women did the domestic work under the direction of the squaw, the children ran free. . . . These Indians were the rich and important men of their tribes, they were men of affairs, and in most cases they were the allies of the missionaries and church members.[68]

Though Shoe Boots was by no means a rich planter, as the owner of slaves, valuable crops, and several "improvements," he was a solid member of a small group of property-owning Cherokees who were beginning to earn profits and stockpile things far beyond what was needed to sustain daily life. The men and women comprising this group might properly be called the Cherokee "middle class," measured not by exact formulations of wealth or position between the Cherokee elite and poor but by their geographi-cal location in this middle region of Cherokee country where a particular kind of property-owning, slaveholding microculture was developing. The boundaries of this middle-class group were elastic and included men and women who owned dozens of slaves as well as men who, like Shoe Boots, owned only a handful. Though distinctions can be made within this slave-holding group, and have been made by historians, those with both mod-est and plentiful means shared qualities that set them apart from most Cherokee people. In the early 1800s the majority of Cherokee families did not own slaves or keep sizable private farms. These subsistence-based fam-ilies who made up the bulk of the Cherokee population tended to live in outlying areas, closer to the Blue Ridge and Appalachian Mountains that span Georgia, South Carolina, and North Carolina.[69] Of the population who lived in the productive middle zone and who began to purchase slaves, a handful amassed enough wealth to comprise a class of elite families by the middle 1800s.

Because most Cherokees did not own slaves, the overall number of slaves in Cherokee territory was small. In 1809 approximately 583 black slaves lived among 12,395 Cherokees, about 5 percent. The number of whites living in Cherokee territory, 341, was even smaller.[70] The scant number of slaves owned by Cherokees in the early 1800s contrasts markedly with the slave population in the neighboring state of Georgia, which was 105,218 by 1810.[71] Despite these small numbers, slaves in the Cherokee tribe were extremely valuable to the propertied families who had begun to accumulate wealth in the late 1700s, since slaves were valued at approximately $200 to $300 each in a period when a log cabin was worth around the same amount.[72] Furthermore, as historian Rowena McClinton has pointed out, the Cherokee tribe's rejection of the concept of individual land ownership made slaves all the more valuable. Whereas vast land holdings contributed greatly to the wealth of southern whites, black slaves were one of the most valuable kinds of property a Cherokee person could own.[73]

Though Shoe Boots was a visible member of the Cherokee middle class, he was not the offspring of a white trader, as were many of his slaveholding compatriots; he spoke little English, had only recently settled into farming, and was slow to acquire human property.[74] Doll was likely his lone slave for her first years on the farm, and African neighbors were few and far between. This situation must have made for a lonely, isolated life for Doll. Even if Shoe Boots's female relatives and wife were considerate to her, Doll must have longed for her own family and for the presence of others who were like her—also African, also enslaved. The rhythms of Doll's daily life on Shoe Boots's farm have not been recorded, but we do know that she arrived at a time when Cherokees were just beginning to incorporate aspects of the U.S. civilization program that pushed for individual property ownership, male farming rather than hunting, and a strictly domestic role for women. Most Cherokee-owned slaves in this period, especially on small farms, were put to work in the fields. Displaced from their customary role, Cherokee women would then devote the majority of their energies to domestic duties, especially spinning and weaving, childcare, and gardening. Thus, Doll may have worked in Shoe Boots's fields alongside Frank, a male slave whom Shoe Boots acquired some time before 1809. At the same time, the likelihood that Doll was purchased for Clarinda suggests that she would have worked in the cabin alongside her mistress. More likely still, on a small farm with few slaves, Doll may have done double duty, dividing her time between the house and fields, hoeing, plowing, cooking, and if Shoe Boots owned cattle as did some of his neighbors, milking as well.

Did it matter to Doll that she cooked and plowed for an Indian master? Did the fact that Shoe Boots was Cherokee make him kind rather than harsh, lax rather than controlling? Or did race and culture have no bearing on the relationship between the enslaver and enslaved? Historians, anthropologists, and demographers of slavery in Indian nations disagree on this point and continue to debate the relative permissiveness of Native American slaveholders. Perdue has suggested in her early work that slavery among Cherokees was, for a time at least, uniquely organized and executed.[75] In contrast, historian Rudi Halliburton has argued that it is a "myth" that "the lives of black slaves owned by Cherokees were considerably easier than those owned by white masters."[76] Monroe Billington has seconded this opinion by measuring slave well-being along yardsticks such as available food and shelter and finding regular similarities between white- and Native-owned slaves.[77] Historian Celia Naylor-Ojurongbe has argued recently that slave women's testimonies of physical abuse by Cherokee masters and mistresses should cause us to question the notion that Native slave systems were more benign.[78] Geographer Michael Doran's analysis situates him between these positions, since he has insisted that though some "full blood" slaveholders treated blacks with relative lenience, the majority of Cherokee slaveholders, who were "mixed bloods," adopted the system as it was practiced in the white South.[79] And anthropologist Raymond Fogelson has suggested that the key variable in the treatment of slaves by Indians *and* whites was likely the number of slaves owned, with larger plantations supporting fewer interactions between masters and slaves and creating a greater fear of insurrection on the part of masters. This assessment is in keeping with the findings of historian Ira Berlin, who argues that treatment of slaves varied drastically even among white slaveholders, depending on factors such as time period, generation, region, type and size of residential arrangements, and crops produced.[80]

In the early 1800s, the period of Doll's first years in Cherokee country, the general conduct of Cherokee slaveowners and the general experience of black slaves were often contradictory, offering yet another example of simultaneous yet different realities. From the oral histories of intermarriage between Cherokees and Africans to the accounts of federal Indian agents assessing Cherokee "progress," the evidence suggests that Cherokee slave-owners were measurably more liberal and less punishing than white ones. On the whole, then, Cherokees who owned slaves were more merciful than white slaveholders. At the same time, though, this picture is complicated by the fact that most black slaves in Cherokee territory were owned by just a few masters with large plantations. On his travels through Cherokee lands in 1809, John Norton noted passing by "the house of a wealthy Cherokee who by trade and agriculture ha[d] acquired a considerable property. He ha[d] many negroes and white servants to attend to the labours of the field, and a capacious building." Later Norton visited "the plantations of the late James Vann, a half Cherokee, the son of a Trader," noting that "he had himself been very successful in trade, and had thereby acquired an immense property; he possessed at his death a hundred negroes employed on different plantations."[81] Just two Cherokee men, then, owned somewhere between one and two hundred (approximately one third) of the nearly six hundred slaves in the Cherokee Nation. Though Norton does not name the first major slaveowner, he does name James Vann, a well-known figure in Cherokee history. Vann amassed property holdings that made him, and later, his son, the richest man in the Cherokee Nation. He kept the majority of his slaves at his plantation manor in the town of Spring Place near the Oostanaula River, where "the house [was] surrounded by a cluster of negro buildings, which [gave] the place the appearance of a village."[82] Vann hired white overseers to run his plantations, and he, along with his hired men, were cruel to the slaves they worked. Vann was described by his missionary neighbors as a frequent drinker and abuser who terrorized his slaves—burning their cabins, whipping them, and "execut[ing]" them "in such a horrible way."[83] Additional evidence supports the German-American missionaries' claim of Vann's violent behavior. He killed his brother-in law in a duel and was later murdered by an unknown assailant. Norton reported that "it is said, that the deceased [Vann], altho' of considerable natural talents and capable of serving his country; on account of his violent disposition was not generally beloved."[84] Though Vann is an exception among Cherokee slaveowners of the early 1800s, many black slaves in Cherokee territory would have suffered his brand of slavery. When most slaves were held by just a handful of men, the practices of one master like Vann would have shaped a common slave experience that mirrored the brutalities of the white South.

There may be no conclusive or satisfying answer to the question of how slavery among Indian tribes compared to slavery in the southern states. Still, it is significant that when slaves speak of their experience in personal narratives and interviews, they overwhelmingly represent Indian masters as preferable to white ones. A primary example comes from escaped slave Henry Bibb, who suffered slavery in Kentucky, Louisiana, and the Cherokee Nation and who wrote the following in his personal account:

> The Indians allow their slaves enough to eat and wear. They have no overseers to whip nor drive them. If a slave offends his master, he sometimes, in a heat of passion, undertakes to chastise him; but it is as often the case as otherwise, that the slave gets the better of the fight, and even flogs his master; for which there is no law to punish him. . . . So far as religious instruction is concerned, they have it on terms of equality. . . . Neither do they separate husbands and wives, nor parents and children. All things considered, if I must be a slave, I had by far, rather be a slave to an Indian, than to a white man.[85]

Though the behaviors that Bibb described as anathema to Indian slaveholding could be found on some Native plantations, his testimony of diminished mistreatment in Indian country is telling. Bibb demarcated crucial differences between various types of masters and found Indian masters to be the lesser evil. Still, he felt that to be a slave was intolerable under any circumstances and revealed that he was committed to escaping slavery at every turn, saying: "Among other good trades I learned the art of running away to perfection. I made a regular business of it, and never gave it up, until I had broken the bands of slavery."[86] Bibb ran away from his Cherokee master just like the others but declined to reveal the man's name in his narrative, seeking instead to protect the reputation of the master who in relative terms was "the most reasonable, and humane slaveholder that [he] ever belonged to."[87]

Likewise, in interviews conducted with former slaves of Indians as part of the Federal Writers' Project, most respondents described their experience of enslavement by Indians as better than enslavement by whites. In the memories of these freedmen and women, Indian masters were consistently more lenient. One former slave of Choctaws proclaimed, "I think dat Indian masters was just naturally kinder any way, leastways mine was."[88] A Creek freedwoman reported: "I have had people who were slaves of white folks back in the old states tell me that they had to work awfully hard and their masters were cruel to them sometimes, but all the Negroes I knew who belonged to Creeks always had plenty of clothes and lots to eat and we all lived in good log cabins we built."[89] Another former slave who married a Cherokee freedman implied that the difference between her and her husband's slave experience was the racial identity of their owners. She asserted: "Lots of people lak me say dat dey was happy in slavery, and dat dey had de worst tribulations after freedom, but I knows dey didn't have no white master and overseer lak we all had on our place."[90] And one Afro-Cherokee man who was the former slave of Cherokees insisted that he was never even told he was a slave and was therefore unqualified to describe the experience of slavery: "But, like I said, my folks never told me about slavery; they never whipped me, always treated [me] like I was one of the family, because I was, so I can't tell anything about them days."[91]

Did Doll also feel like one of the family? Did she prefer Shoe Boots to her South Carolina master? Did she prefer him to crewmen she may have encountered in the middle passage if she was African born? Comparing degrees of enslavement seems a hollow and even barbaric exercise, but it is one that former slaves themselves found it necessary to engage in. The recorded words of freedmen and women who testified to the relative kindness of Native American slaveowners are significant and should give us pause. Their words suggest that slaves recognized a real difference between white and Indian slaveholding practices. Their words also suggest that in 1849, when Henry Bibb published his account, and in the 1920s and 1930s, a period of strident antiblack violence during which former slaves were interviewed, black people saw a political efficacy and even perhaps a personal dignity in elevating their experience among Indians for mainly white interviewers and readers. And finally, their words suggest that those who survived slavery, battered in body and spirit, wanted to recall a space apart from the very worst ravages of that beast and sometimes evoked Indian homes as a rhetorical refuge.

What Doll's experience was in her first few years in Cherokee country, we can only imagine. We can only imagine the crushing loneliness, the fear of being censured, the monotony of hard labor. We can only imagine the sense of encasement and the simultaneous surge of relief at being someplace better than the last place. In the space between history and memory, between the rigid bones of historical documents and the tender flesh of human experience, we can only imagine Doll, a girl of sixteen, a slave for life.

THREE

Motherhood

Children got by an Englishman upon a Negro woman shall be bond or free according to the condition of the mother.

English colony of Virginia statute

Indian males were always told to marry an Indian girl—this was to insure that the children would always have a family. When children were born—they always took the Mother's clan.

HASTINGS SHADE

Deputy Principal Chief of the Cherokee Nation, Oklahoma

SHOE BOOTS'S EURO-AMERICAN "WIFE," Clarinda, had lived in Cherokee country for approximately seven years when Doll was delivered to her doorstep. After witnessing the Shawnee raid on Morgan's Station and being forcibly carried to Cherokee territory by a warrior she did not know, Clarinda's own arrival to that farm must have been traumatic. The two young women, captives of a different color, may have comforted one another. They may have felt something akin to affection at a time when the daily labors of life were backbreaking and when the security and duration of life itself were uncertain. Clarinda and Doll must have worked closely together in and around Shoe Boots's farmhouse, hauling water, gathering wood, tending the vegetable garden, cooking meals, spinning thread, sewing garments, and sharing in the care of Clarinda's three children. Nevertheless, Clarinda was Doll's mistress, and she had been raised in a community where slavery was practiced and corporal punishment of slaves employed. The balance of power between the women was markedly uneven, even if at times their close age and shared experience of captivity colored and recalibrated that balance of power. Like many slave women who have written about their relations with a mistress, Doll may have felt fond of

Clarinda as a young girl but harbored feelings of betrayal and rage as she grew older.

Sexual tension and threat within the household may also have tempered the women's relationship. Like Harriet Jacobs, who devotes a chapter of her narrative, titled "The Jealous Mistress," to the dynamic of white women's anxiety about carnal contact between masters and slaves, Doll may have experienced unwelcome advances at the hands of Shoe Boots and in the presence of Clarinda.[1] If so, those advances would have been differently inflected in a context in which polygamy was practiced. Whereas engagement in multiple sexual relationships was stigmatized in Anglo-American culture, having more than one wife was acceptable among Cherokees. In many cases, these co-wives were close friends who enjoyed the companionship of living in a shared household. Within a cultural framework that allowed the practice of polygyny, Doll may have been more exposed to sexual overtures from her master. At the same time, her master may have been more open to viewing her as a second wife rather than as a temporary sex partner. Either contingency would surely have been an affront to Clarinda, and in 1804 she departed from Shoe Boots's homestead with her three young children in tow.

At the time of Clarinda's leave-taking, Doll had lived and worked on Shoe Boots's farm for approximately five years. She was now experienced in the day-to-day patterns of that place and had likely developed relationships with the people around her, forging a new community for herself. In Clarinda's absence, Doll would have assumed major responsibility for the duties formerly overseen by her mistress. She probably abandoned fieldwork, leaving that to the male slave, Frank, and took charge of the household management—the manufacture of cloth and clothing, food preparation, and cleaning. Keeping the cabin in order would have become Doll's charge; the spinning wheel, woven baskets, pottery, and wood furniture were hers to use and care for.[2] Aggy, a slave girl around eight years old, whom Shoe Boots acquired before 1809, probably aided Doll now just as Doll had once aided Clarinda.

Sometime between 1802 and 1805, Doll's position in the household shifted even more dramatically.[3] She became Shoe Boots's intimate partner—mistress of his bed as well as his home. The course and character of Doll's movement from domestic worker to concubine has not been preserved for history, though it is possible that Doll's initiation into a sexual relationship involved pressure or force. In a dictated letter to the Cherokee Council twenty years after the fact, Shoe Boots described his affair with Doll matter-of-factly: "Being in possession of a few Black People and being crost in my affections, I debased myself and took one of my black women by the name of Doll."[4] The phrase "crost in my affection" here refers to Shoe Boots's anguish at Clarinda's abandonment. Nearly a year after Clarinda's departure, in the early stages of his sexual relationship with Doll, Shoe Boots appealed to Indian Agent Return Jonathan Meigs, lamenting the loss of his children and wife. In a letter to the agent Shoe Boots said: "All people lukes up to God when ther children dies and goes up to God we don't expect to see them anymore on Earth but when ther ar on the Earth we hope to see them and expect to see them. When a man has his children clos to him he can tel wheather ther ar sik or well and would be desires to see them as far as opperunitys will admit, and when we parted we won't to mind any lies that we hard but was to prove tru to each other and when a man takes a wif thar outen to part til God parts them."[5] Shoe Boots's appeals to be reunited with his wife and children were unsuccessful, leaving Doll more exposed to Shoe Boots's desires than she would have been before Clarinda's departure. The void in Shoe Boots's life, created by the loss of his nuclear family, would be filled by "one of [his] black women."

Like the physical brutality visited on enslaved Africans in America, the sexual abuse of black women in slavery has become a familiar topic to students of American history. Historians of black women's experience have documented sexual abuse, rape, and forced breeding in ways that no longer allow for the kind of denial with which the subject was treated in traditional slavery studies. But like the desensitization that can come with repeated exposure to violence in slavery, repeated exposure to stories of rape in slavery can render the topic almost banal. Contemporary women who have suffered a rape in their own lifetimes can perhaps understand some measure of what enslaved women experienced. Female Muslim survivors of the recent Bosnian War who have suffered multiple sexual assaults of the cruelest kind, who have experienced the phallus deployed as a weapon to dehumanize and disempower an entire population, can understand even more. To be an enslaved woman in America was to be utterly exposed to sustained and systematic personal violation, which was also a sustained and systematic assault on the humanity and self-determination of one's community. Against this violence the law offered no protection; American society offered no protection; and members of the slave community attempted to protect themselves and each other at the risk of their lives. To be an enslaved woman was to be subject, always, to the sexual will of another, a sexual will, that when exercised, could serve to increase the master's property through the reproduction of more slaves.

The threat or enactment of sexual assault and exploitation was a facet of everyday life for slave women in antebellum America. A significant number of slave women, nearly 40 percent, according to historian Thelma Jennings's study of the WPA interviews, reported experiencing or witnessing sexual abuse in the slave system.[6] Memories of these experiences permeate the slave narratives, early fiction, and political commentary written by African American women. Harriet Jacobs offers the most thorough account of systematic sexual abuse, describing the sexual awakening of a slave girl in her narrative:

> The slave girl is reared in an atmosphere of licentiousness and fear. The lash and the foul talk of her master and his sons are her teachers. When she is fourteen or fifteen, her owner, his sons, or the overseer, or perhaps all of them, begin to bribe her with presents. If these fail to accomplish their purpose, she is whipped or starved into submission to their will. She may have had religious principles inculcated by some pious mother or grandmother, or some good mistress; she may have a lover, whose good opinion and peace of mind are dear to her heart; or the profligate men who have power over her may be exceedingly odious to her. But resistance is hopeless.[7]

Of her own experience of being harassed by her master, Jacobs wrote: "He told me I was his property; that I must be subject to his will in all things. My soul revolted against the mean tyranny. But where could I turn for protection? No matter whether the slave girl be as black as ebony or as fair as her mistress. In either case, there is no shadow of law to protect her from insult, from violence, or even from death; all these are inflicted by fiends who bear the shape of men."[8] Jacobs's testimony, representative of the testimony of many black women, illustrates both the frequency and the trauma of coerced sexual relations with white men in positions of authority. Often enslaved women who were trapped in these relationships found themselves mistreated or sold by their master and mistress or saw their children—the offspring of these illicit liaisons—sold away.[9]

Some slave women involved in sexual relations with the master, however, occupied a liminal position that afforded them temporary respite from the harsh labor and material deprivation of slavery. Jacobs recalls that as her master pressured her for sex, he threatened to have her sent to the fields if she did not comply, and conversely, promised to build her a cabin of her own where she would not have to work if she agreed to become his concubine. Though Jacobs refused this arrangement, Jennings found that many slave women interviewed preferred concubinage to a white man over forced breeding with another slave: "Concubinage might offer such compensations as better housing and food and a certain status. Undoubtedly, some women did not oppose a liaison with a white man, given their circumstances, whereas all female slaves abhorred breeding."[10] Jennings's observation implies that some enslaved women became concubines because of the benefits associated with that role, an argument that has been complicated by other scholars. Indeed, in discussions of sexual relationships between enslaved women and white men, especially relationships that were long-term and held the promise of material benefits to the slaves, the question of consent on the part of the slave women is often a point of contention. In her literary study of slavery and emancipation in the United States, Saidiya Hartman addresses this question, arguing that according to law, a slave was incapable of giving consent. The state of being enslaved, in fact, denotes a complete lack of free will, which "implies the power to control and determine our actions and identifies the expressive capacity of the self-possessed and intending subject." Therefore, Hartman contends that invoking the idea of slave women's will in matters of sexual relations with their masters misconstrues those relationships and "unmoors the notion of 'force'" implicit in them.[11] To attribute consent or desire to a slave woman engaged in such intimacies, then, masks the exercise of raw power and exploitation at work in these liaisons.

Though some slave women may have "acquiesced" to long-term sexual relations with their masters, their acceptance cannot be viewed or assessed outside the limited options and coercive practices of slavery. A number of these affairs lasted for decades and may have developed into affectionate attachments, but the inherent, vastly differential power relations between a master and his female slave always colored and constrained these relationships. Henry Bibb, whose first wife, Malinda, became the concubine of her master after Bibb escaped, comes close to capturing the complexity of this type of relationship:

> My wife was living in a state of adultery with her master, and had been for the last three years. . . . Whitfield had sold her to this man for the above purposes at a high price, and she was better used than ordinary slaves. . . .

Poor unfortunate woman, I bring no charge of guilt against her. . . . It is consistent with slavery, however, to suppose that she became reconciled to it, from the fact of her sending word to friends and relatives that she was much better treated than she had ever been before. . . . It is also reasonable to suppose that there might have been some kind of attachment formed by living together in this way for years.[12]

Although Bibb's understanding of his wife's relationship with her master is inflected both by the privilege afforded by his gender and by his sense of rejection, his analysis holds in tension the misfortune and fortune, powerlessness and protection, repugnance and attachment that Malinda likely experienced.

In her study of free women of color in Georgia, historian Adele Logan Alexander encounters the complexity of long-term relationships between masters and slaves as well as between white men and free women of color. She situates these relationships within the "inherently coercive environment" of a system in which "the law did not acknowledge the rape of a Black woman by a white man as a crime under any circumstances."[13] The women in Alexander's history engaged in sexual relationships with their masters at best because of unjustly limited options and at worst because of physical force and the lack of legal or social protection. Even when these women benefited materially from their status as concubines, they paid dearly—in the loss of control over their bodies, in the inability to choose the person they wished to love, and in the risk of hurting loved ones in the slave community. As historian Melton McLaurin found in his study of a Missouri murder trial, some slave women were so aggrieved and enraged at their forced concubinage that they resisted violently. McLaurin describes the life of Celia, a slave who was purchased as a teenager to be the sexual partner of her master. When Celia fell in love with another slave and asked her master to leave her be, her master attempted to continue the sexual affair by force. Celia retaliated by murdering her master and paying his unknowing grandson to dispose of the ashes. In 1855 the state of Missouri hanged her for the offense.[14] Celia's grievous case exemplifies a central tension in American slave law that Hartman elucidates: though a slave woman did not have the legal right to decline sex with her master, she could be held legally accountable for acts defined as criminal by the court, such as the forceful refusal to be violated.

As the work of Hartman, Alexander, and McLaurin shows, analysis of the law and its contradictions with regard to enslaved women provides a way of understanding the structures of power in sexual encounters between master and slave. Although their conclusions, derived from American law and culture, can be generalized to slaveholding states and territories in the United States, the applicability of these conclusions to slaveholding American Indian nations is not so straightforward. Despite the fact that notions of governance, race, and gender were changing in the Cherokee Nation, in the early 1800s Cherokees did not share the Anglo-American view that racial difference rendered African people subhuman, nor did Cherokees share in the Anglo-American practice of controlling behavior through an extensive body of laws in this early period.

Instead, Cherokees maintained harmony in their towns by upholding an ethos that called for respecting individual autonomy and therefore abhorring coercion.[15] People were bound to one another not by a controlling authority but by kinship ties and obligations. Cherokees conducted social relationships in accordance to the central understanding that every Cherokee person belonged to a clan and was therefore subject to behavioral expectations and proscriptions. Cherokees believed that women possessed clan and passed it on to their children through bloodlines.[16] Clan membership could thus be obtained in only two ways—through matrilineal descent from Cherokee mother to child or, more rarely, through formal adoption into a clan. Clan membership was at this time the essence of Cherokeeness, the adhesive that bound dispersed Cherokee people into one tribe. According to historian Sarah Hill, the Cherokee words for clan, *hstahlv-i* and *anata-yun-wi,* can be translated as "you and I originate" and "relationship."[17] And as the meanings of these words suggest, belonging to one of the seven Cherokee clans (*Aniwahiya* [Wolf], *Anikawi* [Deer], *Anidjiskwa* [Bird], *Aniwodi* [Red Paint], *Anisahoni* [Blue or Panther], *Anigotigewi* [Wild Potatoes or Blind Savannah], or *Anigilohi* [Twisters or Long Hair]) defined a person as a Cherokee as well as her or his place within the larger group.[18] Hill explains: "Clans embraced the entire population, weaving patterns of relationships and responsibilities into the fabric of kinship. Every individual belonged to a family that extended beyond households, through settlements, and across the nation."[19]

In addition to binding Cherokees together, clan membership shaped and determined interpersonal relations and obligations as well as social and ceremonial practices.[20] The rules of clan dictated that people from the same clan should not intermarry; that a person should not marry into her or his father's clan; that people from the mother's clan, even strangers, were to be treated as close family; and that people from the father's clan were to be treated with respect and protected from harm.[21] Clan served a critical function in organizing ceremonies and in arranging the seating and activities in ceremonial settings. No town was a true town without representatives from each of the seven clans. Finally, and quite importantly, clan served as a control against intratribal violence and as a cloak of protection from injury. An assault inflicted on a clan member would be redressed by someone from the victim's clan, often in the form of an act of justice directed at the perpetrator or a member of the perpetrator's clan. For hundreds of years kinship had been the web that bound Cherokees as a people, and individual Cherokees viewed the world through the intricate netting of this web.

The unwritten code that constituted clan membership as the mechanism of social protection disadvantaged African slaves, because to harm a slave who had no clan would not incur punishment from clan members except when the clan was attempting to protect or recoup its common slave property. In the Cherokee context, then, enslaved women and men would have been particularly vulnerable to abuse—not because the law sanctioned their abuse as it did in white society, but because the protection of Cherokee kinship structure did not extend to them. The vulnerability of black slaves resulted from their importation into Cherokee territory as clanless people, people who were not expected to be integrated into the kinship structure; it did not stem from exclusionary laws and practices developed around the notion of racial difference and black inferiority. If, in the Anglo world, whiteness was equated with freedom, the corollary of freedom in the Cherokee world was clan membership. Africans could become members of Cherokee clans through adoption, and people of African and Cherokee descent could become members of clans if their mothers were Cherokee, but being an African slave and a Cherokee clan member simultaneously was unheard of.

Doll's status as Shoe Boots's slave, then, dovetailed with her clanless position, highlighting and exacerbating her vulnerability. Doll would thus have been susceptible to physical harm in a Cherokee context because she had no relatives to protect and avenge her. Though the root causes were different, enslavement in the Cherokee tribe amounted to a kind of social death for Africans, just as it did in the United States. Sociologist Orlando Patterson has argued that separation from relatives—including ancestors and progeny—was a central aspect of the condition of enslavement: "Not only was the slave denied all claims on, and obligations to, his parents and living blood relatives but, by extension, all such claims and obligations on his more remote ancestors and on his descendants. He was truly a genealogical isolate. Formally isolated in his social relations with those who lived, he was also culturally isolated from the social heritage of his ancestors."[22] This disembodiment from the kinship system was exaggerated in Doll's situation in Cherokee society, where having clan membership entitled one to a life worth preserving and protecting.

Cherokee concepts of clan membership and obligations, and Doll's exclusion from that system, would have affected the inauguration of Shoe Boots and Doll's sexual relationship. At the same time, their affair must have been influenced by Cherokee understandings of women's authority and sexuality, which departed from dominant Euro-American ideas. The notion of patriarchy (rule of the father), in tandem with familial and social pressures that prescribed women's sexual propriety, permeated white southern culture in the nineteenth century. These interrelated ideologies often cooperated to enact white women's deference to men and to position white men as protectors and controllers of their sexuality.[23] In this environment, concepts of white womanhood and black womanhood were intersecting and oppositional. White women, particularly those of the middle and upper classes, were constructed as vessels of purity whose role it was to uphold and instill the values of the community; black women, in contrast, were viewed as embodiments of deviant sexuality, conduits of base instincts and desires.[24] The imposed asexuality of white women and perceived hypersexuality of black women meant that white women's sexual purity would be strictly guarded, while black women's bodies would be subject to rhetorical and physical violation.[25] Though Cherokees would become conversant in these Euro-American notions of womanhood later in the nineteenth century, in 1805 their understandings of women's sexuality would not have supported this dialectic.

Instead, Cherokee conceptions of personal autonomy, relational harmony, and matrilineal family organization shaped women's position in social life. As Theda Perdue has argued, Cherokee women "had their own arena of power over which they retained firm control" and in which domination by men was untenable.[26] Cherokee women were the owners and administrators of their homes. They also had an intimate knowledge of the world outside their cabins, since they traveled over mountainous terrain to gather wood, plants, nuts, and berries; to visit relatives in far-flung towns; and sometimes to assist men in preparing meat and hides in the hunt. In addition, women's primary role in agricultural work, especially corn production, placed them in important economic as well as social and cultural roles.

Furthermore, Cherokee marriage and divorce customs suggest that Cherokee women were understood to be the keepers of their own sexuality. Early records of Cherokee women's sexual experience derive from the findings of white male travelers and traders whose interpretations were culturally biased, making it difficult but necessary to distinguish between observation and interpretation in these documents. Though we cannot be assured of a full or even wholly accurate picture of Cherokee women's sexual lives from these records, they do offer a glimpse of sexual behaviors from which scholars of Native women's history have made consistent inferences. In a comparative review of these accounts, Raymond Fogelson has concluded: "It seems clear that Cherokee women enjoyed notable freedom from, and with, men. They possessed considerable power, which they exercised within the household and in other selected domains."[27] Indeed, it seems that seventeenth- and early-eighteenth-century Cherokees did not forbid or sanction women's premarital sexual relations, though at times older women advised the younger women of their clan about sexual behavior and marriage partners.[28] Cherokee women seem to have chosen their own sexual partners, and once married, could change partners without community censure. If a Cherokee woman desired a divorce, she simply placed her husband's belongings outside the door of her home, an act that compelled him to leave.

Cherokee women's control over their sexual lives shocked European men who visited the Cherokees. In 1775 the Scotch-Irish trader James Adair reported that "the Cheerake are an exception to all civilized or savage nations in having no laws against adultery; they have been a considerable while under a petti-coat government, and allow their women full liberty to plant their brows with horns as oft as they please, without fear of punishment."[29] Louis Philippe, who visited the Cherokees in the 1790s and later became king of France, recorded in his diary: "Marriage is unknown among them. . . . [The Cherokees] are exceedingly casual. If a Cherokee's woman sleeps with another man, all he does is send her away. . . . And all Cherokee women are public women in the full meaning of the phrase: dollars never fail to melt their hearts." In the view of Adair and Louis Philippe, the sexual autonomy of Cherokee women was appalling and detrimental to relations between the sexes. Louis Philippe commented further that since women "can free themselves from dependence due to their weakness only by the nobler feelings they arouse in men," to engage in sexual relations with multiple men erases "the magic of the emotion" and plunges women "into degradation."[30] This may often have been the case in European societies, where women were economically disfavored and therefore needed, for their survival, to secure the commitment of men, but in Cherokee society, where women controlled the production of food, the organization of families, and the administration of households, sexual autonomy did not jeopardize a woman's security.

As an enslaved African woman among Cherokees, Doll stood at the intersection of two significant Cherokee ideologies. Slave women were vulnerable in Cherokee communities owing to their position outside the clan system. At the same time, this vulnerability may have been curbed by an understanding of Cherokee womanhood that respected sexual autonomy. It is likely that Cherokee sexual norms offered some protection to African American women, as suggested by a written legal code adopted by the Cherokees in the 1820s. In 1825 the Cherokee Nation passed the first statute outlawing rape, a law that did not explicitly exclude slave women, as did rape laws in the United States. The legislation reads: "Any persons, whatsoever, who shall lay violent hands *on any female,* by forcibly attempting to ravish her chastity contrary to her consent, abusing her person and committing a rape upon such female, he or they, so offending, upon conviction before any of the district or circuit Judges, for the first offence, shall be punished with fifty lashes upon the bare back, and the left ear cropped off close to the head; for the second offence, one hundred lashes and the other ear cut off; for the third offence, death."[31] Other Cherokee laws passed in the 1820s *did* differentiate between "Negro slaves," Cherokees, and whites; they also differentiated between "Negro women slaves" and Indian and white women. The fact that Cherokee rape law did not spell out a separate status for enslaved black women suggests that Cherokee understandings of women's sexual autonomy and their right to protection from sexual assault extended to slaves.[32]

The democratic sexual mores in Cherokee society most likely influenced Shoe Boots's perception of Doll as a sexual being and may have tempered his initiation of a physical relationship with her. Thus, even as we maintain a vigilant awareness of the inherent power imbalance between masters and slaves engaged in sexual affairs, the specific cultural context in which Doll found herself cannot be overlooked. The impenetrable layers of two centuries, cultural difference, culture change, and silence in place of historical evidence make any full understanding of the initiation and continuation of Doll and Shoe Boots's sexual relationship impossible. Perhaps all we can safely assume is that Doll's transformation from slave to slave-mistress must have come with untold costs as well as some benefits. Doll may have engaged in a sexual relationship with Shoe Boots against her will, feeling abused and preyed on, as Harriet Jacobs did, or she may have become involved with Shoe Boots by her own circumscribed "choice," after evaluating her life condition and chances. Doll's ongoing relationship with Shoe Boots may or may not imply complicity in the sexual affair, and we should not assume that she was contented with her lot. If Doll did care for Shoe Boots, it is doubtful that she wished to remain a slave while she lived the next twenty-five years of her life with him. In the words of Hartman, describing a liaison between master and slave: "Do four years and two children later imply submission, resignation, complicity, desire, or the extremity of constraint?"[33]

In her new status as Shoe Boots's mistress, Doll lived in a fundamentally Cherokee world, and more specifically, a Cherokee women's world. The number of African slaves in immediate proximity to Shoe Boots's farm was small. In addition, the organization of Cherokee households around the mother's clan shaped the texture and heft of relationships in Cherokee communities. Shoe Boots was a member of the Wolf clan, as were his mother and sisters, all of whom resided on the farm. Because of their connection through the mother's bloodline, the relationship between brother and sister in the Cherokee kinship structure was deep, stronger than that of husband and wife, who came from different clans. Furthermore, men's frequent activity away from the home—hunting, trading, and meeting in council, often left women to themselves. This meant, first, that Shoe Boots was likely to have had a closer relationship with his sisters than with Doll, and second, that he would have been away from the cabin often enough to leave space for a women's domain of his mother's and sisters' making. This was an arrangement that Doll might have been accustomed to, since women from West and Central Africa also shared gender-specific tasks and lived communal lives often separate from men. But in Africa—or even on a large southern plantation—Doll would have been integrated into that community of women, a member of her own tribe or her own family grouping. In Cherokee country, Doll lived among a circle of women to whom she was not related. If Doll had been Cherokee and married to Shoe Boots, she would probably have lived in her own dwelling, near her own kin.

As the mistress of Shoe Boots's house, Doll played a core role in the Cherokee community. For it was women, in the words of Hill, who "stood at the heart of hospitality. They grew, harvested, gathered, prepared, and served food for guests in households they owned. Each meal and every visit reinforced the strands of relationships and responsibilities that bound Cherokees to one another. The common thread throughout was the identity and work of women."[34] The lines of kinship that crisscrossed from Cherokee town to Cherokee town, the lines that wove inhabitants of disparate villages into a people, originated with women. Doll stood at the portal of this universe, but she could not enter. Clanless, peopleless, and deprived of her freedom, Doll could perform the duties of a Cherokee wife, but she could not become a Cherokee woman—not until or unless she was adopted into a clan, and through this ritual, reborn as a Cherokee.

In the 1800s the occurrence of an African slave woman being adopted into a Cherokee family was rare, but not unheard of. In the late 1700s a black slave named Molly was purchased by Samuel Dent, a white man who had been a trader in Cherokee territory. Before buying Molly, Dent had married a Cherokee woman and beaten her while she was pregnant, causing her death. In an attempt to make amends for his crime, Dent purchased Molly and gave her to his deceased wife's clan, the Deer Clan. The Deer Clan accepted Molly as a family member in place of the deceased wife.[35] Molly, renamed Chickaua by her clan, lived with her new family as a free woman until her liberty and tribal membership were challenged. In 1833 the white daughter of an associate of Dent's claimed ownership of Chickaua and her son, Cunestuta (or Isaac Tucker), and sent agents to the Cherokee Nation to retrieve them. As it happened, before giving Chickaua/Molly to the Deer Clan, Dent had secretly sold her to someone else, a white man whose last name was Hightower. Hightower's daughter, also named Molly, sought to make good on her father's claim. But because they did not want to give up the black woman who was now a member of their clan and thus their relative, the Deer Clan challenged this claim in a case that was heard before the Cherokee Council and Supreme Court. The Deer Clan urged the "Council and authorities of the Cherokee nation" to protect Chickaua and her son: "[We] ask and require of our Council and headmen for assistance and for Council to resist this oppression and legal wrong attempted to be practiced on our Brother and Sister by the Hightower in leasing into slavery two of whom have ever been considered native cherokee. We feel that the attempt is one of cruel greavance."[36] The Deer clan condemned slavery as "oppression" and claimed two former slaves as "brother and sister" and "native Cherokees." To them, Chickaua and Cunestuta's adoption was synonymous with Cherokee belonging and citizenship.

Doll, however, seems not to have been adopted into a clan. There is no notation or indication of any such adoption in the Cherokee records, and the treatment that Doll received over time suggests that she was viewed as a satellite to the community; that is, she was recognized but not accepted into the full circle of kinship. Doll's presence and simultaneous absence in Cherokee life placed her in a strange, purgatorial realm. She stood on the outside looking in, more like a ghost than a person, since "only those who belonged to Cherokee clans—regardless of language, residence, or even race—were Cherokee; only those who had Cherokee mothers were the *Ani-Yun Wiya*, the Real People."[37] A friend of Shoe Boots's, named Nathaniel Fish, remembered an early encounter with Doll that indicates her ambiguous position:

> The time I last saw Shoe Boots he had with him a wife wearing [apparel] generally worn by Cherokees such as ear rings. She was a cold black nigar. Capt. Shoeboots was about my complexion. What caused me to know that it was his wife [was that] while we were at the table eating, Shoeboots and his wife eat on one side of the table. I eat on the other side in front of Shoe-boots and his wife. When they was through eating they got up and went out to another house where they really stayed . . . I do not know how old she was. She was a middle aged woman about 19 or 20 years old. I do not know how long they had been married. She growd up at Shoeboots house.[38]

Fish's account of this meal, which presumably took place in Shoe Boots's mother's cabin, points to Doll's inclusion in Shoe Boots's personal life and her simultaneous exclusion from Cherokee community. Although in this exchange Shoe Boots claims Doll as his spouse, the fact that she is eating at the table with her husband as opposed to eating separately with other women in the household, as was customary for Cherokees, indicates her distance from Shoe Boots's female relatives. The indelible mark of Doll's enslaved status, indicated by her African features and articulated as racial difference by Fish when he recalled the moment decades later, would shadow Doll in all her interactions with Cherokee people. Even as she adorned herself with Cherokee jewelry and became fluent in the language,

Doll would continue to be viewed as an outsider whose presence was open to interrogation.

On the alluvial banks of the Etowah River, and on the rocky ridges of the mountains that cradled it, seasons changed. Black, red, and white oak trees grew and shed their foliage. Masses of clouds formed above the high peaks, shaded the earth, and separated again.[39] Corn was planted, harvested, and shared. Wild grapes were gathered and dried. Cherokee women, dressed in the petticoats and blouses of American women, their hair pulled back and sometimes braided, went about their daily routines.[40] Doll too was caught up in the duties of her household, in autumn collecting hickory nuts and walnuts to combine with corn grits or grind into milk; in the summertime picking strawberries, the fruit that "came from the sun"; and preparing for the birth of her first child.[41] More than a year had passed since the start of Doll's relationship with Shoe Boots, and Doll was now pregnant.

A Cherokee woman with child engaged in certain cultural practices. Her condition was considered so powerful that no one could safely eat the food that she prepared or walk the path she traveled. She regularly drank a mixture of elm bark to aid in her delivery, and every month she went to the sacred rivers to cleanse and pray with the aid of a ritual leader.[42] She avoided certain foods, such as raccoon and pheasant, and feared that eating speckled trout would result in birthmarks on her baby.[43] At delivery, four community women would attend her, along with the medicine person. If complications arose, the healer would intervene and sing "various magical formulas to induce the child to be born."[44] In African American slave communities, where women were separated from the plants and practices of their native land, they depended on the wisdom of older women to carry them through pregnancy. Upon discovering her condition, a young slave woman was likely, "on the advice of older women, to impose dietary restrictions upon herself, to wear some kind of charm, or to perform certain rituals." A slave woman might avoid strawberries, for instance, for fear that her babe would be born with a birthmark.[45] It was difficult for enslaved African American women to take care of themselves during pregnancy, since the economic aim of masters was to expend few resources on pregnant slaves while protecting the lives of the unborn slaves. Pregnant women could thus be worked beyond the limits of safety and beaten for their inadequacies. It is this mind-set that led to the practice of resting the slave mother's belly in a protective trench while she was whipped on the back, illuminating the devaluation of the slave woman and the high value placed on her unborn child, the master's future property.

As an African woman in a Cherokee woman's world, Doll may have felt adrift during her pregnancy. She may have missed the ways of women from her own culture; she may have longed for her mother. She may have felt her exclusion most at this time of ceremonial and spiritual importance, when the centrality of clan membership rose to the fore. On the day in 1806 when Doll's baby came, did Shoe Boots's female family members attend to her? Did an African midwife from Vann's plantation sit by her side? And if her child had trouble dropping or was turned upside down, did someone sing her baby home? One recollection of the birth of Doll's first child survives. A nephew of Shoe Boots described the infant's arrival thus: "At that place was born a child of Shoeboots. It was a girl. In a few days Shoeboots named it Kahuga. . . . Kahuga was the first child of Shoeboots and his negro wife."[46] The baby, Kahuga, was also called by the English name, Elizabeth, perhaps in memory of a mother figure in Doll's family of origin.[47]

A free Cherokee woman, surrounded by kin, would likely feel joy at the birth of a healthy child. For the African woman, though, motherhood was a perilous state that revealed the raw vulnerabilities of bondage. While a slave mother might experience an unending depth of love for her child, she might also suffer a crushing melancholy for having borne that child into slavery. For regardless of the race and status of the father, American slave law dictated that the child would follow "the condition of the mother." This policy, which reversed the patrilineal directive of British common law, served to reward the sexual proclivities of white men while increasing the slave population. Rather than bearing children who would be sold away from them to fatten the master's profit margin, many slave women practiced herbal birth control methods, and some practiced infanticide.[48] Other slave women, forced to bear the children of their masters, had no feelings for their offspring at all, except for the resentment and pain of remembered woundings.

In her narrative Harriet Jacobs describes the cruel contradiction of slave motherhood. For Jacobs, having a child was "a new tie to life" when the abuses of enslavement stole away the will to live, and at the same time, it was passage into a constant state of dread about the fate of that child in the slave system:[49] "I had often prayed for death; but now I did not want to die, unless my child could die too. . . . When I was most sorely oppressed I found a solace in his smiles. I loved to watch his infant slumbers; but always there was a dark cloud over my enjoyment. I could never forget that he was a slave. Sometimes I wished that he might die in infancy. . . . Death is better than slavery."[50] This rare, sustained first-person account of the experience of slave motherhood makes Jacobs's narrative precious to readers today; and yet, because of the social constraints of her time, there was much that Jacobs felt compelled to leave unsaid. The denial of slave women's personhood, the debasement of black women's sexuality, the lack of access to written self-expression for black women, and proscriptions against interracial sex all meant that the evidentiary record, or the documents and testimonies on which historical analyses are based, would echo this silence. Those of us who seek to understand the texture of black women's lives face a dilemma in this case: to what body of evidence do we turn in our effort to remain responsible to historical methods while at the same time drawing as near as we can to the subjective experience of those who have gone before us? It is my belief that imaginative reconstructions of the past, tightly wedded to historical knowledge, can aid us in our quest. While historical fiction cannot supplant the disciplined accounts that historical work produces (just as historical accounts cannot replace the interior depth of fiction), I believe that fiction, as its own form of truth, can bridge the gaps in our evidence and allow us access to the marrow of human feeling.

In her wise and haunting novel, *Beloved*, Toni Morrison lays bare the intersecting currents of life and death in the slave mother's existence in a way that far surpasses what scant historical evidence can illuminate. The protagonist of the novel, Sethe, was born on a large southern plantation, the only child whom her mother let live. Sethe recalls only fragments of this childhood, and it is at the birth of her fourth child, "on the bloody side of the Ohio River," that Sethe remembers recognizing her mother for the first time: "Of that place she was born (Carolina maybe? or was it Louisiana?) she remembered only song and dance. Not even her own mother, who was pointed out to her by the eight-year-old child who watched over the young ones—pointed out as the one among many backs turned away from her, stooping in a watery field."[51] Later, Sethe recalls a singular moment of interaction with her mother: "One thing she did do. She picked me up and carried me behind the smokehouse. Back there she opened up her dress front and lifted her breast and pointed under it. Right on her rib was a circle and a cross burnt right in the skin. She said, 'This is your ma'am. This,' and she pointed. 'I am the only one got this mark now. The rest dead. If something happens to me and you can't tell me by my face, you can know me by this mark.' . . . 'Yes, Ma'am,' I said. 'But how will you know me? How will you know me? Mark me too,' I said. 'Mark the mark on me too.'"[52] In her girlhood longing to share some visible sign of connection with her mother, Sethe does not perceive that this brand, and the connection that it symbolized, marked her for slavery. In response to Sethe's unknowing appeal, her mother slaps her across the face. This interaction indicates a family system contaminated by slavery, in which Sethe could not know her own mother and her mother could not show her proper care. While Sethe is still a child, her mother is hanged for a reason that Sethe never learns. When Sethe attempts to identify the body by looking for the mark, an older slave woman pulls her away and offers a story in solace: "She threw them all away but you. The one from the crew she threw away on the island. The others from more whites she also threw away. Without names, she threw them. You she gave the name of the black man. She put her arms around him. The others she did not put her arms around. Never. Never. Telling you. I am telling you, small girl Sethe."[53]

When she is thirteen, Sethe is sold to Sweet Home, a farm in Kentucky owned by a couple named the Garners and worked by five male slaves: Paul D, Paul F, Paul A, Halle, and Sixo. Sethe chooses Halle as her husband, and together they have three children. The Garners employ what Sethe's mother-in-law, Baby Suggs, calls "a special kind of slavery," in which Baby Suggs's greatest fear, to be knocked down by a white man in front of her children, does not come to pass.[54] Mr. Garner dies suddenly, though, and Mrs. Garner brings in her relative, called Schoolteacher by the slaves, to manage the farm. Under Schoolteacher's reign, Sweet Home becomes a site of overt dehumanization and violence. Sethe, whose later life is propelled by an unending struggle to forget the past, recalls against her will the beauty and terror of that place: "And suddenly there was Sweet Home rolling, rolling, rolling out before her eyes, and although there was not a leaf on that farm that did not make her want to scream, it rolled itself out before her in shameless beauty. It never looked as terrible as it was and it made her wonder if hell was a pretty place too. Fire and brimstone all right, but hidden in lacy groves. Boys hanging from the most beautiful sycamores in the world."[55]

Sethe is pregnant with her fourth child and nursing her youngest, a two-year-old girl, when all the Sweet Home slaves resolve to run away. As evening falls on the night of the planned escape, Sethe suffers an assault at the hands of Schoolteacher's sons, who hold her down in the barn, handling her like a cow or goat, and "[take] her milk."[56] In this mammary rape, the perpetrators not only violate Sethe's body and spirit, but they also drain that sacred substance that symbolizes her motherhood—milk, a conduit and metaphor for family love, the only thing that Sethe alone can give to her baby girl. Sethe tells her mistress about the attack, and in retribution Schoolteacher's boys beat her, "open[ing] her back" in what will become a massive, life-long scar.[57] Sethe learns later that her husband, who disappeared, had witnessed her humiliation and could not survive the fact of it. After the beating, Sethe sends her three children ahead to Cincinnati, where Baby Suggs has settled after having her freedom purchased by Halle.

Unaware of her husband's fate, or of that of the other Sweet Home men, Sethe escapes alone, giving birth to her fourth child, a daughter, on the banks of the Ohio River. Once in Baby Suggs's home, her wounded back and womb tended to, and her children tumbling around her, Sethe enjoys twenty-eight days of blessed freedom. On the twenty-ninth day, Sethe spots Schoolteacher coming up the road, coming to take them back to Sweet Home: "And if she thought anything, it was No. No. Nono. Nonono. Simple. She just flew. Collected every bit of life she had made, all the parts of her that were precious and fine and beautiful, and carried, pushed, dragged them through the veil, out, away, over there where no one could hurt them. Over there. Outside this place, where they would be safe."[58] Sethe rushes her children into the woodshed and tries to take their lives with a saw, injuring her two sons and killing her toddler girl. Her infant is spared from being thrown against the wall when the old man and underground railroad conductor who had carried Sethe and the infant across the Ohio River snatches her from Sethe's hands. This appalling moment, which the novel circles around and back to as it narrates the story of Sethe's life, conveys the supreme corruption and deepest expression of Sethe's love for her children. Sethe would rather see them dead, in a "place where they would be safe," than taken back to slavery.

It is the horror in the shed and all that preceded it that Sethe struggles to disremember for the next eighteen years, but the past and its traumas refuse to be buried. Sethe's murdered baby girl haunts Baby Suggs's house at 124 Bluestone Road, first wreaking havoc as a ghost, then taking on human flesh to rebirth herself into Sethe's life. The appearance of this inhuman, otherworldly child as a gorgeous, glowing twenty-year-old woman draws Sethe, her daughter Denver, and her lover Paul D into a web of corrupted relationships. Sethe stops going to work, begins to waste away from lack of food, and spends every waking hour trying to appease her emotionally insatiable ghost of a daughter, whose name is Beloved. Soon the two exchange places, with Sethe made as malleable as a child, and Beloved, pregnant with

Paul D's child, controlling the course of events. The tainted relationships within the household cannot be set right until the women of the town come to shout Beloved away and Sethe speaks her unspeakable memories, which are the collective memories of all African American slaves.

Beloved is the story of slave mothers: of Sethe, whose milk was stolen; of Sethe's mother, who murdered all her children save one; and of Baby Suggs, who would not love her offspring because "anybody [she] knew, let alone loved, who hadn't run off or been hanged, got rented out, loaned out, bought up, brought back, stored up, mortgaged, won, stolen or seized."[59] This nightmarish story of slave mothers rips back the rough skin of slavery to reveal its bloody heart—the birthing of children into bondage, the denial of the slave mother's freedom to love, the fundamental dishonor to the bonds of kinship that define all human experience. Literary scholar Sharon Holland, in dialogue with literary scholar Hortense Spillers, asks us to dwell on this antebellum reality of the child following the condition of the mother. What, they ask, *is* the condition of the mother?[60] What is the psychic, spiritual, emotional, and ontological condition of the enslaved black "mother," whose relationship to her child will be defined not by the call of kinship but by the prerogatives of property?

This essential crucible in African American women's historical experience, the inability of the slave to mother her child, is imbued with deepening layers of meaning in the cultural context in which Doll conceived her baby girl. Not only did Doll give birth to a slave, she also created a person who reproduced her clanless status. For here, too, the child followed the condition of the mother, in a manner that would forever imperil the offspring of an African woman and a Cherokee man.

FOUR

Property

Were it possible to introduce among the Indian tribes a love of exclusive property, it would be a happy commencement of the business.

HENRY KNOX
United States Secretary of War

The origins of property rights in the United States are rooted in racial domination. Even in the early years of the country, it was not the concept of race alone that operated to oppress Blacks and Indians; rather, it was the *interaction* between conceptions of race and property that played a critical role in establishing and maintaining racial and economic subordination.

CHERYL HARRIS
"Whiteness as Property"

THE EBB AND FLOW OF DOLL'S DAYS began with nursing her newborn child, preparing the hearth, and starting a fire with wood that she herself had collected. In the early morning Doll would have cooked large pots of food for the other slaves and for Shoe Boots to eat during the day—soaking corn and pounding it into meal for bread, boiling corn in lye and water and washing it clean to make skinned corn, roasting pork or deer meat, boiling greens. She also would have worked in her kitchen garden, tending the vegetables that sustained her small household. When she found time in the morning or afternoon, Doll would have spun thread and woven fabric, dying it with Indian mulberry, copperas, and indigo to create brilliant shades of red, green, and blue. And in the cool of evening, Doll would have baked pan bread in the coals of the fire with corn or bean meal, serving it to her family, the other slaves, and any of Shoe Boots's visiting relatives.[1]

But amid these seemingly calm scenes of hearth and home, Doll would have had cause for concern. Though her position as Shoe Boots's partner may have lent her a degree of protection from the realities of being an owned person, the relationships she must have had with other slaves would have kept her keenly aware of the instability of her status. All around her, fellow blacks were facing the vagaries of their enslavement, struggling to free themselves and fighting to resist the inhumanities of bondage. Doll had witnessed one slave ordered away from Shoe Boots's farm, leaving friends and family behind, to accompany the mistress to Kentucky. Doll may even have traveled to nearby farms with Shoe Boots or on her own and developed relationships with other black women and men. The prominent Ridge family, who would own fifty slaves by the 1820s, lived thirty miles north of Shoe Boots, and it is certain that Doll came into contact with their slaves.[2] James Vann, the largest and reportedly cruelest of Cherokee slaveowners, lived in reasonable proximity to Shoe Boots as well. In 1801 Vann had apportioned part of the lands he had occupied for the development of a Christian mission. That mission and its school, run by a Protestant sect of German-speaking immigrants known as Moravians, also retained African slaves. Vann's compound, then, a wide-ranging hilly area sixty miles north of Shoe Boots's farm, housed a relatively large slave population. Leading men from Shoe Boots's town often visited Vann's home, called Diamond Hill, as well as the mission at Spring Place. Moravian records from 1803 report a visit to the mission from "an Indian . . . with his wife, who was white, and another white person and a couple of negroes who live in Hightower."[3] This party may well have been Shoe Boots, Clarinda, and their slaves, suggesting that Doll had visited Spring Place in her early years in Cherokee country. As Shoe Boots's mistress, Doll may have traveled there again and forged lasting relationships with members of the slave community.

Perhaps Doll knew Grace, a free black woman and devout Christian who moved from Virginia because she could not bear to be separated from her husband after he was purchased by Vann.[4] Or perhaps Doll was a confidant of Pleasant, a slave "rented" by the Moravian missionaries, whose repeated rebelliousness, according to her masters, belied her name.[5] Pleasant was constantly battling her owners, so that the missionaries described her as "often ill-humored" and complained that the "Negro woman Pleasant is not as useful to the mission as she probably could and should be; at times she is disagreeable, due to her sulky behavior, and offensive and injurious to others, due to her scolding and swearing."[6]

Vann's slaves were frequently involved in attempts at sabotage and escape, a fact that would have been known to Doll. One man, Isaac, ran away at least twice with a fellow slave and a stolen horse, and then threatened to shoot anyone who tried to capture him.[7] Three slaves also ran away together one autumn, soon followed by a larger group the next summer: "Four of Mr. Vann's negroes ran away from him again last night. Before they went, however, they robbed their master of all the money he had in the house. . . . They also emptied a chest full of silk and cotton scarves and took the things away with them, some of Mrs. Vann's things and clothing from Mr. Vann and 3 pistols." Still another Vann slave committed suicide because, the missionaries speculated, "he was tired of life."[8]

In 1809 Doll would learn firsthand that despite particular intimate relationships, enslavement among Cherokees could be perilous. That year, Doll, her toddler, Elizabeth, and the slaves Frank and Aggy were given away by Shoe Boots. According to John Howard Payne, the traumatic event occurred after Shoe Boots welcomed a white guest onto his land. In Payne's account, Shoe Boots invited the man, John Lecroy, to live on his farm, even offering to build him a house. When Lecroy and his grown daughter moved in, the trouble began:

> She [the guest's daughter] reminded Shoe Boots of the days of the wife [Clarinda], that were gone. He offered himself to his lady guest. She would not be won. "Oh—she right—she right" said Shoe Boots, his voice unshaken, but his eye moistened—"Shoe Boot old—Gal young—But what she do, when Shoe Boot gone?—No body to give she home!—Ho! Old father there—Shoe Boot tell you something—Shoe Boot make will—Give you all him cattle-horses-niggers-all when Shoe Boot die—Shoe boot no let him friend child starve—Bring paper—Write Shoe Boot will."[9]

According to Payne, Shoe Boots's desire for this woman motivated his offer to leave his property, including his lover and child, to the woman's father. But the plan went awry when the father met a devious white man named Wofford, "one of those ferocious adventurers they call Intruders," who encouraged him not to wait until Shoe Boots's death to claim the property.[10] With Wofford promising to "pay the cost" and to "share the profits when old Shoe Boots kicks the bucket," the two men went to a lawyer in Georgia to have a deed of gift drawn up effective immediately. Shoe Boots signed the men's deed, apparently unaware that it would forthwith divest him of his property. In Payne's words, "they persuaded poor Shoe Boots, in a moment of extraordinary good humour, after his manner, to sign and Shoe Boots thought his guest was paying him a great compliment in adopting an Indian's offer, instead of adhering to his own opinion."[11] With the stroke of a pen, Doll, Elizabeth, Frank, and Aggy now belonged to Wofford and Lecroy. When Shoe Boots realized this, he rushed to Cherokee Agent Return Jonathan Meigs for assistance. Meigs dragged a confession out of Lecroy, refunded Wofford two dollars for the deceptive deed, and had Wofford driven out of Cherokee territory.[12]

Payne's account of what must have been a terrifying moment in Doll's young life—the gift of her and her baby to unknown Georgians—is both dramatic and suspect. It is indeed true that Shoe Boots signed all his slaves away in 1809. A copy of the deed of gift still exists in the Habersham County, Georgia, courthouse, worded as follows:

> Know all men by these presents that I Tuskaraga Shoe boots of the State foresaid do hereby in consideration, love and affection which I entertain for John Lecroy of the County and State aforesaid have this day given granted and conveyed . . . in consideration of the premises aforesaid the following negroes to be henceforth the property of him the said John . . . to wit, Doll a woman twenty five years old, Frank a fellow twenty years old, Aggy, a girl twelve years old and Lize a child three years . . . for the proper use and benefit and behoof of him the said John Lecroy his heirs and ofsign to have and to hold the said negroes and their increas unto him the said John Lecroy his heirs and ofsigns forever.[13]

There can be no mistake that Shoe Boots entered into some form of agreement with John Lecroy concerning his slaves, but the romantic compulsion, simple-mindedness, and ingratiating behavior ascribed to Shoe Boots by Payne are questionable, as are the conditions under which the deed was produced.

It is highly unlikely that, as Payne suggests, Shoe Boots would be willing to deed his property to Lecroy because of an attraction to Lecroy's daughter. Besides the fact that Shoe Boots was more likely to have willed his property to his mother's daughters or his sisters' children, court records suggest that he was not given to parting with slaves easily. In 1823 Shoe Boots was sued by another Cherokee over the ownership of an unnamed slave; he fought back and won the case, retaining possession of the slave.[14] Moreover, Shoe Boots's history of attacking white settlements on Shawnee land in Kentucky suggests that he was not especially invested in "great compliments" from white men. Finally, the dialogue in the account by Payne, a playwright, seems to have been embellished or even manufactured, given the stylistic rendering of Shoe Boots's speech and the fact that the event took place at least ten years before Payne visited Cherokee territory.

Subterfuge very likely played a role in the transaction between Shoe Boots and the men. The deed of gift includes a preamble stating that "Lecroy lost the original deed and had a new one drawn up" and that "later, the original was found," which raises questions about the production and reproduction of the document. The involvement of the Wofford family members, notorious squatters on Cherokee land, seems more than coincidental. Shoe Boots's immediate reversal of the agreement indicates his displeasure with the outcome, and the Indian agent's unequivocal interference also suggests the dubious nature of the transaction.

We have no way of knowing exactly what transpired that day, since the only existing records are patently unreliable. Payne's rendition is perhaps clouded by a caricatured view of Shoe Boots; and the court records, written in a language in which Shoe Boots was not literate and recorded by officials of the state of Georgia, are more likely to reflect the intentions and interests of Lecroy and Wofford than those of Shoe Boots. Perhaps Shoe Boots entered into a business venture and ended up signing away all his property because of his lack of English literacy, and not because of any romantic feelings. Perhaps he was intoxicated at the time of the event, since Shoe Boots, as recorded by missionaries, had been a drinker since before the 1820s.[15] Or perhaps Shoe Boots mistakenly thought he was lending out the service of his slaves rather than giving them away. Whatever Shoe Boots's motivations or perceptions might have been, this incident, in which Doll and her daughter were signed away like a horse and buggy, illuminates Doll's extreme vulnerability. She led a life not fully her own, a life in which the X mark of her owner/husband could shift or seal her fate. Shoe Boots's about-face and Agent Meigs's interference meant that Doll and her child would be protected, but only until the next whim or error revealed their status as slaves.

In the early 1800s, when Doll and Elizabeth found themselves at the center of a property dispute between Shoe Boots and two white Georgians, the Cherokee people were under considerable strain. Sustained colonial expansion onto Cherokee lands and U.S. government pressure to adopt Euro-American customs was contributing to a disruption and reformation of Cherokee lifeways. Long-standing social and political patterns were being tested, fractured, and complicated by new and often contradictory modes of thinking and being. Slaveholding among the Cherokees was one of these new patterns that challenged previous customs. The ownership and accumulation of private property was another. Both these practices—slaveholding and acquisitiveness—were closely interlinked and represented a revision of the Cherokee relationships to things, animals, and people.

In the middle 1700s, when the first ethnographic materials written about the Cherokees after the European invasion appear, the Cherokees were not a nation of collectors. They owned land in common, though they worked individual plots, and they placed little value on possessions. Objects such as baskets, woven goods, drinking gourds, and bear skins had utilitarian and sometimes sacred value. They served functional, ceremonial, or artistic purposes, and they could be traded to obtain other items that would be similarly used. Cherokees did not wait until their possessions had enough cumulative value that they could be sold at a profit, thus enabling the purchase of still more things; and they did not display things to reflect their wealth or economic status or tuck them away to ensure future financial stability. The notion of a market economy in which surplus goods were sold for profit did not figure into Cherokee understandings or systems of exchange. Instead, the average Cherokee family operated within a subsistence-based economy in which the usual possessions were "a gun, a tomahawk, and a few horses."[16] Furthermore, Cherokee social and ceremonial structure included built-in systems for redistributing goods to those who did not have enough. The harvest produced from communal fields would be distributed among people in need, and dances would be held to collect items for the poor. In 1761 Henry Timberlake, a lieutenant in the British Army, was assigned to formalize a compact of peace with the Cherokees. During his visit with Cherokees in the Overhill towns along the Tennessee River, Timberlake noted that Cherokees were not possessive of material goods:

> The Indians have a particular method of relieving the poor . . . when any of their people are hungry, as they term it, or in distress, orders are issued out by the headmen for a war-dance, at which all fighting men and warriors assemble; but here, contrary to their other dances . . . one only dances at a time . . . relates the manner of taking his first scalp and concludes his narration, by throwing on a large skin spread for that purpose, a string of wampum, piece of plate, wire, paint, lead, or any thing which he can most conveniently spare . . . then another takes his place. . . . The stock thus raised, after paying the musicians, is divided among the poor.

Timberlake also noted that upon a person's death, Cherokees disposed of possessions along with the body: "Nothing belonging to the dead is to be kept, but everything at his decease destroyed, except these articles which are destined to accompany him to the other world. . . . This custom was probably introduced to prevent avarice, and, by preventing hereditary acquisitions, make merit the sole means of acquiring power, honour and riches. The inventor, however, had too great a knowledge of the human mind, and our propensity to possess."[17] Timberlake assumes here that this burial custom was created to prevent what he views as a shared human trait to accumulate things; however, it is just as likely that the custom developed out of a Cherokee disinterest in materialism. For eighteenth-century Cherokees, possessions did not have a life beyond the user. Thus, the world of possessions was kept in balance with the world of humans; with each new life came the creation of new things needed to assist that life. Ultimately, Cherokees valued the well-being of people in the community over the ownership of things.

Animals in Cherokee life occupied a sphere that was parallel to the human one, and these spheres often intersected. Animals had relatives, towns, and challenges just as humans did.[18] Animals also possessed spirits and purposes, which had to be respected for the animal and human world to be kept in balance. Cherokees accomplished this balance through beliefs, rituals, and prayers that showed respect to their animal neighbors.[19] The heroic and humorous actions of animals are central to the Cherokee oral tradition, and animal names and symbols are assigned to certain Cherokee clans. At the same time, animals played a sacrificial role in sustaining Cherokee lives. Hunting was an important aspect of the relationship between people and animals, since animals were continually asked to give of themselves to provide meat, skins, and sinew. The act of hunting game was integrated into the relationship between people and animals rather than projected outside it, and Cherokee men reaffirmed this relationship during the hunt by addressing and honoring their prey.[20] While Cherokees did track and kill wild game, they did not make a habit of fencing or containing animals. Even when Cherokees acquired livestock such as pigs and cattle from Europeans, they permitted these animals to roam at will and distinguished them by markings or tags.[21]

Cherokees of the eighteenth century and earlier were not without social and political hierarchy. Leading men, and sometimes women, sat on town councils and were considered chiefs at the local level; at times these council members would select their successors based on lineage.[22] However, the form and function of Cherokee hierarchies reflected a society that valued relational harmony, communal goodwill, spiritual practice, respectful negotiation, and accomplishment in warfare rather than material wealth.[23] Regard and political status were conferred on elder men and women who excelled in these arenas, and respected elders did not possess authority over others.[24] English and early American culture, in contrast, often conferred status and influence on those with an impressive lineage combined with wealth.[25] England and other western European nations valued material wealth so highly that they set sail across the oceans in search of lucrative trade routes and natural resources and were willing in that quest to perform a sleight of hand that transformed human beings into capital. The moment of death, which in the Cherokee community meant the burial of things, encapsulated the high value placed on accumulated property in English and Anglo-American culture. Upon death, an Englishman or American would pass down land, possessions, and interest in land to his children and spouse (in England, the eldest son was preferred, but in the American colonies primogeniture was curtailed), ensuring the continuation of family property holdings.[26]

The United States advocated this type of property ownership in its program to civilize the Cherokees. Repeated interactions with Europeans and U.S. government officials started to have an impact on Cherokee people. In the 1790s and early 1800s, some Cherokees began to adopt and adapt Anglo definitions of property, which included categorizing African people as possessions. Many Cherokees took baby steps on the road to material accumulation—accepting a plow or spinning wheel from the federal agent or stealing a single slave to help around the farm, while rejecting the rampant accumulation of things that would lead to personal wealth. But a minority of Cherokees was already poised, through connections with white family members, to inherit large tracts of "improved" land and whole families of slaves. Shoe Boots, a traditionalist Cherokee who owned a handful of slaves and improvements on a sizable plot of land, fell somewhere in between these two groups.

As Cherokees began to value and collect property to varying degrees, they developed a set of ideas, practices, and laws to protect that property. In 1808 the Cherokee Nation passed its first written laws, which regulated the inheritance of property by relatives and mandated the organization of a police force. The 1808 inheritance law allowed for a broad definition of "legal heirs" that included clan members, in keeping with older Cherokee ways of defining family through the mother's line; yet it also included the wife and children of the father, which diverged from clan definitions of family.[27] As Theda Perdue and Rowena McClinton have shown, between 1808 and 1825 Cherokee leaders would steadily refine property law, making patrilineal descent equivalent to matrilineal customs that favored the link between mother, mother's siblings, and child.[28] Whereas kinship codes dictated that a Cherokee derived her or his clan membership and Cherokee identity from the mother and her relatives, legal language began reconstituting the Cherokee family around the patriarchal and nuclear household, in which the significant legal attachments were between father, child, and wife. In the wake of these laws, McClinton argues, "Cherokees evolved into a litigious society," in which family members sued one another over the distribution of property upon the death of a relative.[29] A subset of Cherokee community, particularly wealthy slaveholders, began to appeal to the law to handle disputes that would not have arisen twenty and thirty years earlier.

One highly visible case, brought about by the murder of James Vann in 1809, led to a fracture within Vann's family, since his will called for the extensive estate to be inherited by his eldest son, Joseph. Vann's widow and other surviving relatives contested the will, which was unusual at a time when old patterns of matrilineage, communal land use, and the broad distribution of material goods were in competition with new patterns of patrilineage, individual property ownership, and the narrow inheritance of property. In her analysis of the Vann case, McClinton notes that the Cherokee Council was in the position of having to mediate between venerable customs still followed by many Cherokees and novel customs that the Council itself had legalized. The Council members set aside the Vann will and issued a compromise that still left Joseph the lion's share but directed him to provide for his relatives.[30] A significant portion of the contested Vann property holdings consisted of African slaves, indicating that Cherokees' changing relationship to possessions intersected with their adoption of African slavery. In many of the court cases involving disputes over the last will and testament of the deceased, slaves were at the center of the conflict.

The *Cherokee Phoenix and Indian Advocate* newspaper, published between 1828 and 1834 with the assistance of Christian missionaries, reflects the desire on the part of some Cherokees to protect newly accumulated property. In May 1828 the newspaper reprinted the tribe's first fencing law, passed in 1824, which states: "Resolved by the National Committee and Council that a fence of four inches crack between each rail for two and a half feet up from the ground shall be considered a lawful fence and the hogs of any person whatsoever, breaking into the field of a person having such a fence, the owner or owners of such property shall be responsible for all the damages sustained."[31] In June 1828 the newspaper editor included a warning about theft, titled "Look Out for Rogues." In October of that year, an individual placed an advertisement for a lost "pocket book" that was "stolen out of [his] pocket," for which he was offering a reward of "ten dollars and five for the apprehension of the rogue." In November, a subscriber to the paper offered a reward of ten dollars for any information leading to the whereabouts of a man who "sold [him] a horse, which has since that time proved to be stolen."[32]

Advertisements in the *Cherokee Phoenix* also gave notice of subscribers' intentions to sell and trace human property, indicating that a burgeoning acceptance of the market extended to people of African descent. The first slave-related advertisement appeared in the *Cherokee Phoenix* in February 1829, a period when African slavery was recognized and regulated by the Cherokee government. The advertisement reads: "Notice is hereby given that some time in the latter part of October last a black man came to my house, who says his name is Manuel, and that he belongs to a man on Duck River, in Tennessee, by the name of Joseph M'Connel. This Negro, I should judge, between forty and fifty years old, and upwards of six feet high, square built. The owner is desired to prove his property, pay charges and take him away."[33] Manuel, who had ended up in Shoe Boots and Doll's hometown of Hightower, may have been one of those fabled slaves who sought their freedom in Indian territory. The advertiser, Joseph Wafford, placed this notice seeking Manuel's owner for a month. It is not clear whether Manuel remained in the Cherokee Nation, was finally returned to his former owner, or departed of his own accord. It is clear, though, that the language of the notice defines Manuel in racial terms as "black" and "Negro" and in material terms as "property." Manuel's status as property becomes even more apparent when we compare this notice with another advertisement published in 1830 that describes a lost cow in much the same manner: "A stray cow and yearling have been running with my cattle for more than a year. The cow is of a bright dunn color, marked with an under-bit in both ears. . . . The owner is requested to come forward, prove property, pay charges and take them away." In 1831 an Anglo-Cherokee man named Moses Downing placed an ad offering a twenty-dollar reward for the return of "a mulatto woman" named Eliza who "absconded with a whiteman," was "about thirty years old . . . a likely woman, large and fleshy," and who spoke "the English and Cherokee well."[34] Downing was the owner of five slaves and eleven houses, occupying 115 acres of land along the Etowah River.[35]

The majority of advertisements relating to black slaves that appeared in the *Cherokee Phoenix* were not placed by individual slaveowners but rather by an official of the Cherokee government. Between June 1829 and September 1831, Joseph Lynch, a marshal of the Cherokee Court, placed five notices for the sale of slaves. The marshal's role was to enforce the decisions of the court, including the collection of debts and the calling of witnesses.[36] In this capacity, Joseph Lynch advertised the following sales:

Marshal's Sale. Will be sold to the highest bidder, on the 17th July next, at New Echota, one Negro man named Peter, levied on the property of Edward Hicks to satisfy a bond given by said E. Hicks to the National Treasurer.

Notice. Will be sold to the highest bidder on the first day of December next, at the late residence of James Pettit . . . Corn . . . Fodder . . . Gabriel. All levied on as the property of James Pettit, to satisfy a judgment obtained against said Pettit in favor of Elizabeth Pettit.

Will be sold to the highest bidder on 28th . . . at the town of New Echota, a likely negroe boy named George, levied on as the property of Ambrose Harnage.

Notice. Will be sold to the highest bidder, at the late residence of Thomas B. Adair . . . all the property belonging to the estate of T. B. Adair, deceased, viz: three negroes, Joe, his wife Nelly and child . . . Terms—Twelve months credit for all amounts over five dollars, and for all under five dollars, money paid down.

Will be sold to the highest bidder on a credit of twelve months at the place of holding court in Ahmoah District. . . . Two negro boys, sixteen or seventeen years old, One secondhand carriage, Two horses, One silver Watch, and One Pistol.[37]

This succession of notices placed by Lynch in his official capacity as marshal of the court indicates first that Cherokee citizens were treating slaves as property in contracts made with individuals and the Cherokee government and second that the Cherokee government was actively involved in marketing slave property to benefit its treasury and to resolve legal disputes.

These newspaper advertisements for the sale of slaves, as well as for the return of stolen goods, reflect changes in the ways that Cherokees valued and managed private property in the early 1800s. At the same time, however, the *Cherokee Phoenix* conveyed a continuing ambivalence about such changes. Previous understandings of Cherokee relationships to people, animals, things, and particularly land continued to set limits on how property would be redefined. It is notable that approximately eleven slave advertisements appeared in the newspaper in a run of six and a half years, and that at least three were placed by whites. The same number of slave advertisements might have appeared in a single edition of many white southern newspapers at the time. In addition, the editor of the *Cherokee Phoenix,* Elias Boudinot, reprinted a sampling of controversial articles concerning slavery from other newspapers.[38] Most of these articles documented and criticized international slave trade, with one calling the practice "this horrid and detestable traffic in human flesh."[39] Some of the reprinted articles contained sympathetic portraits of black slaves, with titles such as "Pity for Poor Africans," "The Moorish Prince," and "Letter from an Infant Slave to the Child of its Mistress, Both Born on the Same Day."[40] The third piece, a poem in two parts, was reprinted from the abolitionist newspaper *The Liberator.* In one editorial, the *Phoenix* editor himself inserted an indirect criticism of slavery. Boudinot, who had been educated at Cornwall, a mission school in Connecticut that disapproved of slavery, said sardonically of the state of Georgia: "She will have to overcome one great obstacle before she becomes a great state—slavery."[41] Though advertisers defined slaves as property in the pages of the *Cherokee Phoenix,* the editor of the newspaper presented a dissenting view, indicating a lack of general consensus about the buying and selling of people as merchandise in the Cherokee tribe.[42]

In addition to their reluctance to regard human beings as personal possessions, Cherokees continued to disallow private ownership of the land. Thus, even as Cherokees became wary of thieves and began erecting fences, they rejected a central tenet of the Euro-American understanding of property—that land could and should be owned. What McClinton has described as the two major themes in Cherokee law at the turn of the nineteenth century—the "protection of [shared] Cherokee homeland, 'the common domain'" and the protection of "[private] property in general and inheritance in particular"—reflected competing ideologies regarding property.[43] And for a man like Shoe Boots, this internal conflict hit very close to home. Like other Cherokees who shared his moderately wealthy status, Shoe Boots was engaged in the pursuit and protection of private property in the early 1800s. In 1809 he fought to maintain his farm and slaves, and in 1812 he sought to increase his wealth by participating in the slave economy. After inheriting a number of slaves from a relative living among the

Creek Indians, Shoe Boots sold "chances" to win those slaves in rafflelike fashion to an even wealthier Cherokee, his neighbor The Ridge, who had owned the first plantation in their tribe.[44] By repeatedly acting to protect his investments, Shoe Boots supported the institution of slavery. At the same time, however, he would soon demonstrate a desire to protect his enslaved offspring from a lifetime of servitude. Shoe Boots's contradictory position as both a holder of property and the father of property would lead to unexpected twists in his family's future.

The new interest in accumulating wealth that some Cherokees exhibited connected them to members of neighboring tribes who shared their acquisitiveness and often their mixed-white heritage. Even as a Cherokee elite began to emerge in the early 1800s, a similar class was developing to the south among the Creek (or Muskogee) people, who already shared a number of cultural traits with the Cherokees.[45] The mid-eighteenth century had marked a shift in Creek society that influenced Creek relations with the increasing number of Africans in their territory. A small group of Creeks began to intermarry with European (often Scottish or Irish) traders, and the children of those unions integrated aspects of their white parent's culture into their lives, reshaping and transforming Creek customs.[46] Like Cherokees, well-positioned Creeks began to own black slaves, inheriting them from white relatives and receiving them as gifts from the British during the Revolutionary War.[47] In Creek country, as in Cherokee country, the emerging tribal divisions were regional as well as economic and cultural. Most Creek slaveowners lived in the Lower towns along the Chattahoochie River of present-day Alabama. In the Upper towns near the confluence of the Coosa and Tallapoosa Rivers, the few Creeks who had slaves were more likely to allow them to manage their own homes, tend their own gardens, own property, travel as they wished, and intermarry with Creeks in unions that produced freeborn children.[48]

In the late 1700s and early 1800s the mixed-white, propertied, slaveowning Creeks in the Lower towns increased and consolidated their wealth and political power. As historian Claudio Saunt has found, the growing fondness for private property among some Creeks can be traced by examining their rapid adoption of fences and locks to protect the things they owned.[49] The class stratification that was emerging among the Creeks and Cherokees led to breaches within each tribal group, at the same time that it built bridges between the wealthy of both tribes. In the Creek Nation, this intratribal breach exploded into civil war, and in 1813 Shoe Boots joined that war to preserve the right of slaveholding Creeks to maintain their practice of accumulating property.[50] Before the Creek War, Shoe Boots was known as a courageous warrior and a capable strategist. By war's end, he had gained the reputation of a hero.

The Creek War (or Redstick War, as it is also called) began as a civil war between Creek rebels who were enraged at the widespread adoption of Euro-American ways and moneyed Creeks who had developed close ties of friendship with and dependence on the United States. In 1812 a handful of Creek men from the Upper towns combined cultural conservatism, political protest, and spiritual renewal to build a movement of mass resistance to American intervention in Creek affairs. Like the Cherokees, the Creeks had been pressured by the U.S. government to acquire property and to demonstrate "civilized" behavior and had been forced to suffer the encroachment into their homelands by citizens of Tennessee, Georgia, and the U.S. territories of the Gulf South. Some well-to-do Creeks, like the Cherokees of means, responded to these pressures by making cultural adjustments and political compromises to preserve their land base. In so doing, they adopted certain aspects of American culture, namely, owning property, buying slaves, accumulating wealth, and centralizing political power. Other Creeks who had avoided concessions and rejected the adoption of American ways denounced those Creek leaders who seemed to have made compromises. A convergence of events beginning in 1811 propelled these resisting Creeks into violent protest of the emerging economic and political order in Creek country.

The central conflict of the Creek War was rooted in the early 1800s when the Creek people faced pressure from the U.S. government to overhaul their cultural and spiritual ways, to cede large tracts of land, and to allow white Americans passage through their territory. After the Revolutionary War, as American pioneers settled around the boundaries of Creek territory and clamored for more land, the United States pressed a series of small land cessions on the Creeks. White settlers then spilled over the new boundary lines, hunting and fishing in territory that still belonged to the Creeks.[51] By 1811 it became clear that the federal government would force the Creeks to accommodate white settlers without Creek consent. When the United States wanted to build a road through Creek territory, Hopoithle Miko, a leader of the Upper towns, straightforwardly rejected the request: "You ask for a path and I say no . . . I hope it will never be mentioned again." In response,

Indian Agent Benjamin Hawkins replied: "The period has now arrived when the white people *must* have roads to market and for traveling wherever they choose to go through the United States."[52] This clear dismissal of Creek desires and rejection of Creek authority underscored for many Creeks the veiled intentions of the United States—to override Creek sovereignty and to control Creek landholdings.

This dispute over the new road coincided with a visit by the charismatic Shawnee leader Tecumseh and an accompanying group of shamans, who were traveling through the Midwest and Southeast in the fall of 1811 to urge Indian nations toward spiritual renewal and an intertribal resistance to American colonialism. After years of federal intervention and the fresh insult of the proposed road, Creek men and women in the Upper towns were receptive to Tecumseh's message of revolution. A series of earthquakes in the winter of 1811 and 1812 further convinced some Creek people that the world was in disharmony and that the old order would give way to a new one.[53] Finally, when Creek leaders who were considered friends of the Americans allowed Creek men to be executed for crimes against whites, a small group of Creek rebels emerged. These men claimed to act out of spiritual necessity, and they combined their political resistance with a spiritual revival.

The rebels took revenge on those Creeks who they felt had betrayed their own people. They murdered the leaders responsible for the recent executions and urged other Creeks to adopt violent resistance as well. The Creeks who led and joined this rebellion were known by whites as the Redsticks because they carried red war clubs as symbols of their protest. This prophetic revolt swept through the Upper towns, collecting thousands of converts who cast off and destroyed the accumulated property that they viewed as symbolic of white influence. Religious studies scholar Joel Martin elaborates: "Specifically, the rebels dispensed with ornaments of silver, brass, glass, and beads, implements of husbandry, hoes and axes, and other trade goods. . . . Led by prophets, they killed cattle, hogs and fowl belonging to friendly chiefs and Anglo-American traders. . . . Even more significant, the rebels killed their own livestock and abandoned their cornfields, and rebel women burned fine muslin dresses that they had purchased from traders."[54] Though a handful of towns in the Upper region refused to participate in this violent rejection of American culture, the majority of Creeks who disapproved of the revolt lived in the Lower towns. These towns were largely influenced by federal Indian Agent Benjamin Hawkins, who lived nearby, and by the Georgians on their eastern boundary who had repeatedly threatened violence should the Lower Creeks instigate trouble with white settlers.[55] Over the years these Creeks, as well as some Upper Creeks who were considered tribal leaders by U.S. agents, had received pay and goods from the United States in exchange for their quiet cooperation. They sought American aid in resisting the rebellion that they viewed as an attack on their lives and property.

According to most historians who study the Redstick rebellion and the ensuing Creek War, the rebel Creeks did not originally intend to engage in battle with the United States. Rather, they fought within their own nation to change the course of its history by eliminating treacherous leaders, renewing spiritual devotion, and destroying objects and symbols of American culture. However, Euro-American planters and political leaders in neighboring states desired an all-out war with the Creeks in the hopes that the United States could smother Creek resistance, usurp Creek lands, and redistribute those lands to neighboring states.[56] White settlers exaggerated the scope of the Creek rebellion, insisted that their lives were in eminent danger, and demanded that the federal government intervene. In addition, since the War of 1812 between the United States and Britain was being fought at this time, the settlers claimed (and probably believed) that the Creek insurgence was a plot masterminded by England and Spain to attack America from within. Though the settlers' fears were largely manufactured, the Redsticks did cling to the belief that England would come to their aid if necessary.[57]

In July 1813 American scouts instigated the first major incident that escalated the rebellion into war. They reported the location of a band of Redsticks who, while traveling home from Florida after attempting to collect supplies, had attacked the homes of three Anglo-Creeks.[58] The Mississippi Territory militia responded to the report by attacking the Redsticks at Burnt Corn Creek. In retaliation for that ambush, seven hundred and fifty Redsticks stormed the fortified home of Anglo-American Samuel Mims, where four hundred whites, mixed-race Creeks, Creeks friendly to the United States, and black slaves were sequestered. The Redstick attack, which resulted in the death of almost two hundred and fifty people inside the fort, exposed the rebels to widespread retaliation from the U.S. military.[59]

When Andrew Jackson, then major general of the Tennessee Militia, heard the news of the attack on Fort Mims, his despondency at commanding a dormant post lifted, and he entered what was, according to historian Michael Rogin, "the most decisive eighteen months of [his] life." Before acquiring the approval of President James Madison, Jackson built a force to crush the Creeks, consisting of white volunteers, Creeks allied with the United States, and sympathetic Cherokees and Choctaws.[60] The Cherokees who became involved in the war empathized with the Lower Creeks. Historian R. S. Cotterill points to class stratification among Cherokees as the reason, for it echoed the very conflict at the heart of the Creek War: "Both Choctaws and Cherokees were divided on the same lines as the Creeks, and any intervention in the affairs of their neighbor would possibly result in a civil war at home."[61] Joining forces with members of the wealthy Creek-Irish Grayson family, property-holding Cherokee leaders urged Upper Creeks from the nearby town of Hillaubee not to join the revolt.[62] Thereafter, The Ridge (soon to be known as Major Ridge) pressed the Cherokee Council to join the U.S. military in support of the Creek property holders and gathered a Cherokee military force from Hightower.[63] Shoe Boots was among this force, and, as one Cherokee man informed the Moravian missionaries in July 1813, "four hundred men would be marching under the leadership of the well known warrior, formerly called Shoeboot."[64] Future Cherokee leaders John Ross, Sequoyah, and Junaluska also held positions of authority in the Cherokee regiment. John Ross would later become principal chief of the Cherokee Nation; Sequoyah would develop the syllabary that transformed Cherokee into a written as well as spoken language; and Junaluska, renowned for saving Andrew Jackson's life in battle, became a Cherokee statesman and diplomat.

Commanders of the Cherokee regiment were members of the economic, mixed-race, and political elite whose interests seemed to overlap with those of the Lower or "loyal" Creeks, as the United States came to call them. In a conciliatory address in 1813, Indian Agent Return Meigs informed the Cherokee troops that only a select few could achieve high rank in the Cherokee regiment.[65] Among those few, propertied men like The Ridge, John Ross, and Shoe Boots assumed positions of leadership. More than two-thirds of the Cherokee regiment, thirteen out of nineteen companies, were led by Cherokees who had one white parent.[66] If the "loyal" Creeks were fighting to protect their lives and property from rebel Creeks, the Cherokees were also fighting out of class interests—supporting Creeks who shared their positions of wealth, undergirding friendly relations with the United States to maintain their security, and ensuring that the antimaterialist rebellion would not spread to Cherokee country.

Andrew Jackson would be responsible for the ensuing massacre of hundreds of Redsticks, their families, and even neutral Creeks in the Upper towns before the major battle of the war had even begun.[67] This early destruction of Redstick towns earned national praise for Jackson. One correspondent, whose enthusiasm was typical of many, proclaimed of Jackson: "The victories gained by you against the Indians will hand your name down, to posterity, as the first of patriots."[68] Michael Rogin adds that in tribute to his supporters, "Jackson sent cloth worn by the slain Indians to the ladies of Tennessee." But the catastrophic Battle of Horse Shoe Bend (or Tohopeka), in which Jackson's forces slaughtered almost a thousand Redstick warriors, was the decisive event that would propel Jackson into political prominence. The Battle of Horse Shoe Bend was considered the greatest victory of American forces over American Indians owing to the tremendous number of Native people who lost their lives. According to Rogin, "Jackson's victory over the Creeks was a turning point in his life. He achieved the American army's first dramatic military triumph. In a war largely devoid of American victories, he became a national hero."[69] Jackson's success at Horse Shoe Bend would have been impossible without the contribution of five to six hundred Cherokee allies. The Cherokees who fought with Jackson, though relegated to the rear, had broken ranks, crossed the river, and cut off the Redsticks' only avenue of retreat.

Like Andrew Jackson, Captain Shoe Boots gained prestige for his bravery on the bloody banks of Horse Shoe Bend. In a scene repeated by John Howard Payne and Marion Starkey, Shoe Boots received a fond notice from Jackson himself. After the Cherokees had won the battle, the story goes, the valiant Shoe Boots disappeared, and his fellow soldiers thought him dead. Jackson feared for Shoe Boots's life and paused to lament the passing of the warrior he affectionately called "the Old Cock" because of his habit of crowing in battle.[70] But as Jackson and the soldiers would soon discover, Shoe Boots had survived the battle. Payne supplied a vivid account:

> In the slaughter at the battle of the Great Bend of the Tallapoosie . . . Shoe Boots, who had, as Bonaparte used to say, "covered himself with glory," had also covered himself with wounds, and was nowhere to be found. Numbers of troops, Indian as well as American, were lounging in the forest among the bushes.
> "Poor Shoe Boots," cried one, "I'm sorry the old fellow's silenced at last."
> "Aye," said another, "the old cock has got to the end of his crowing."
> "A brave fellow he was," exclaimed a third.
> "We shall never see a braver," added a fourth.
> And the Indians looked more serious than ever, but were tearless and in the expression of their eyes triumphant.
> "Cock a doodle doo," was uttered from some invisible quarter—

All stood aghast.

"Cock a doodle doo," was uttered more loudly and shrilly than before.

The soldiers started and stared in each other's faces—"Cock a doodle doo!"—was repeated a third time, and lo, upon a stump overtopping some bushes, sprang up Shoe Boots in the midst of the troops, flapping his arms like a rooster.

"Me crow like cock" cried he "but no chicken heart me, and me crow long time yet—Cock a doodle doo!"

And they bore the old warrior off, with shouts of triumph and exaltation.[71]

Starkey recounts this dramatic scene in much the same way.[72] Shoe Boots's alliance with Andrew Jackson, both in battle and in this exchange, positions him unequivocally on the side of colonialist aggression; however, Shoe Boots's position in this mythologized incident was inherently contradictory.

For while the war that Shoe Boots fought to help suppress the rebel Creeks may have been in the economic and political interests of his class, it also opposed the interests of his Afro-Cherokee family. The Redstick vision of a Creek society devoid of American influence implicitly challenged the institution of slavery that elite Creeks were adopting. In battle, the Redsticks acted on their belief that race-based slavery was foreign to traditionalist Creek perspective and categorized Creek traitors and white interlopers, not black slaves, as their enemy. Blacks, in turn, contributed ingenuity, numbers, and support to the Redstick cause. In the battle at Fort Mims, Redstick warriors seem to have taken care not to harm the slaves who were sequestered with their white and Creek masters. According to a black survivor of the attack, "because 'the Maker of Breath . . . ordered [them] not to kill any but white people and half breeds,' they spared many of the fort's African American inhabitants, but they showed no mercy to Anglo-American and metis people."[73] The Redsticks did kill and scalp a small number of African Americans at Fort Mims, but they took 243 slaves with them when they departed.[74] These slaves, who were cognizant of the widespread revolutionary possibilities of the rebellion, joined in the fight. A black man inside the fort, named Siras, cut the fence to allow the warriors access. Other African slaves fought with the rebels and rallied them to continue when their energy flagged.[75] At the Battle of Horse Shoe Bend, black warriors again accompanied their Redstick allies in death and in escape to Seminole country in Florida. Even the ideological underpinnings of the revolt seem to have been influenced by African Americans, whose liberation-theology brand of Christianity spurred Creek spiritual revival.[76]

By battling to suppress this rebellion, Shoe Boots helped guarantee that the future of most black people in the Indian nations of Georgia, Tennessee, and the Carolinas would be bleak. For the death of the Redstick rebellion meant the death of any hope of black equality within the Creek and Cherokee tribes. Indeed, it would not be long before the Cherokee Nation would prohibit black slaves from inheriting property, and thus the right to property that Shoe Boots strove to protect would not extend to his offspring because of their racial status. Though Shoe Boots fought the Creek War in part to secure the class interests of his Creek counterparts, he ultimately worked against his own personal and familial interests. And in a parallel irony, Shoe Boots and other Cherokee warriors soon discovered that Andrew Jackson would break faith with his Indian allies by demanding that they cede millions of acres of land in retribution for the rebellion that they had helped to quell.

While Shoe Boots and men like him strove to protect their property, they participated in a system that would ultimately betray them. In early America, property ownership could not be disentangled from racial categorization and prejudice. Legal scholar Cheryl Harris deftly argues that in colonial and early American history white racial identification (or "whiteness") conferred on its owners a unique status that gave them the right to hold property. In contrast, African and Native people were excluded from the category of whiteness and thus from the right to property ownership. As blackness came to denote enslavement in colonial society, black people themselves became property, and as redness came to denote an uncivilized state, Native people were deemed unworthy of retaining their own land. The investment that members of the Cherokee and Creek elite made in the American system of valuing and racializing property (accepting "improved" land as a signifier of civilization and blackness as a signifier of enslavement), was ultimately an investment in a system that subordinated and excluded them.

Like the African Americans who passed for white to gain access to white status described by Harris, Native people who owned substantial property did so with a temporary "passport" that could be revoked by white America. Thus, the Indian elite who sold and stockpiled slaves were caught in a web of exploitation with those slaves, as both perpetrators and victims. According to Harris, "the hyper-exploitation of Black labor was accomplished by treating Black people themselves as objects of property. Race and property were thus conflated by establishing a form of property contingent on race. . . . Similarly, the conquest, removal and extermination of Native

American life and culture were ratified by conferring and acknowledging the property rights of whites in Native American land. Only white possession and occupation of land was validated and therefore privileged as a basis for property rights."[77] Propertied Cherokees would soon reach a similar conclusion. Although they had amassed significant wealth in the American way, their ascribed "redness" meant that white opportunists could divest them of everything they owned.

Plate 1. The Etowah River, North Georgia,
where the Shoeboots family once lived, 1998.
Author's personal collection.

Plate 2. A model Cherokee house of the early 1800s,
New Echota State Historic Site, Georgia.
Author's personal collection.

Plate 3. Chief Vann House, a Cherokee plantation,
Spring Place, Georgia, 2003.
Courtesy of the Chief Vann House State Historic Site.

Plate 4. (Left) Cherokee statesman John Ridge, 1837.
Plate 5. (Right) *Cherokee Phoenix* editor Elias Boudinot.
Used by permission of the Oklahoma Historical Society Archives and Manuscripts Division.

Plate 6. Arkansas swamp along the removal route.
*Used by permission of the Oklahoma Historical Society
Archives and Manuscripts Division.*

Plate 7. View of the Arkansas River in Webbers Falls, Cherokee
Nation, the town where the Cherokee slave revolt began, 1900.
*Used by permission of the Oklahoma Historical Society
Archives and Manuscripts Division.*

Plate 8. Slave house near Talala, Indian Territory, 1900.
Used by permission of the Oklahoma Historical Society
Archives and Manuscripts Division.

Plate 9. A Cherokee family in front of a cabin, 1890.
*Used by permission of the Western History Collections,
University of Oklahoma Libraries.*

Plate 10. Formal portrait of a Cherokee family, Indian Territory.
Used by permission of the Western History Collections,
University of Oklahoma Libraries.

Plate 11. Cherokee Treaty Party Member and Confederate General Stand Watie.
Used by permission of the Oklahoma Historical Society Archives and Manuscripts Division.

Plate 12. Murrell House, also called "Hunter's Home," a Cherokee plantation, Cherokee Nation, Indian Territory.
Used by permission of the Western History Collections, University of Oklahoma Libraries.

Plate 13. Tahlequah, Cherokee capital, where William Shoeboots lived when he applied for citizenship, 1902.
Used by permission of the Oklahoma Historical Society Archives and Manuscripts Division.

Plate 14. Haskell Shoeboot, a descendant of Shoe Boots and Doll's son William Shoeboots, circa 1986.
Used by permission of the Black American West Museum and Heritage Center.

FIVE

Christianity

But among those Indians of North America, who have not incorporated
the worst vices of civilized life with their own, the preacher of the gospel
has some advantages. They possess not, as do most heathen nations, a
complicated system of false religion, transmitted from their fathers,
which must be overthrown before the gospel can prevail. . . . There is
scarcely any thing among the Indians themselves to oppose the prevalence of the gospel, except their unfortified ignorance and depravity.

Memoir of Catharine Brown: A Christian Indian

SHOE BOOTS EMERGED FROM THE CREEK WAR with a new stature and a
new name. In honor of his reputation for crowing in battle, "the Indian
formerly called Shoeboot," Moravian missionaries recorded, "received the
name Crowing Rooster at the last National Council." Shoe Boots was also
referred to as "Crowing Cock" by one of the warriors under his command.[1]
He took on the title of captain in keeping with his military rank and was
one of nine Cherokee men who received special recognition for their efforts
in the conflict. In 1815, along with Colonel Path Killer and Major Ridge,
Captain Shoe Boots received $956.29 1/2 cents with "sentiments of grati-
tude" from the United States.[2] One year later, Shoe Boots and his colleagues
received a second gift from the federal government: "the present of a good
rifle gun to each of the said warriors with an appropriate inscription."[3] Shoe
Boots's fame as a warrior was so celebrated during his later life that ethnologist James Mooney memorialized him, including a description of Shoe
Boots's war medicine, in a collection of Cherokee history and folklore: "His
war medicine was an uktena scale and a very large turtle shell which he got
from the Shawano. In the Creek war he put this scale into water and bathed
his body with the water, and also burned a piece of the turtle shell and drew
a black line around his men with the coal, and he was never wounded and

never had a man killed."[4] In 1818 Shoe Boots was employed in national service as a Creek-language interpreter for Chief Sour Mush in the first talks between the Creeks and Cherokees following the war.[5] And in 1819 Shoe Boots was referred to by Protestant missionary Daniel Butrick as "the great warrior Shoe Boots."[6]

During Shoe Boots's period of celebrity in the second decade of the nineteenth century, Doll is not mentioned in the documentary record. It is as though Shoe Boots's national acclaim and the fact of his black family could not co-exist in the pages of history. Yet, in the private sphere of their home, Doll continued in her role as Shoe Boots's intimate partner. In 1813 as Shoe Boots entered the war, Doll gave birth to their son, John, and in 1817 she had a second girl, Polly. By the time Polly was born, the eldest child, Elizabeth, was ten years old and mature enough to assist her mother in domestic duties and childcare. The teenage slave who had come to Cherokee country alone two decades before was now thirty-three years old and surrounded by children of her own.

Indeed, Doll's life and the life of the community around her had undergone dramatic changes in those years. With the passage of time and a growing familiarity with her Cherokee neighbors, Doll may have obtained the status of an intimate outsider in Cherokee society. Though she still did not have clan and would have faced limitations in spiritual and ceremonial life, she most likely would have participated in family and social events. There was some precedent for this, since white men who had intermarried with Cherokees also did not have clan but played an integral role in the community, particularly as traders, merchants, and cultural go-betweens. The children of these men were considered Cherokee because they had Cherokee mothers. The status of white intermarried women would be closer to that of Doll, because they too could not birth Cherokee children, and they were unlikely to be engaged in commerce, which carved out a particular space for white intermarried men. However, very few marriages between Cherokee men and white women took place at this time, in part owing to the importance of Cherokee motherhood and clan membership. The two most publicized intermarriages of this sort, that of John Ridge to Sarah Northrup and of Elias Boudinot to Harriet Gold, involved educated Cherokee men and white northern Christian women whose role in the Cherokee community would revolve around keeping model Christian homes and encouraging conversion. The spread of Christian mission schools across Cherokee country and the presence of northern missionaries, both male and female, would have created a ready-made community for these intermarried white women. If other black women were engaged in long-term and public relationships with Cherokee men (with the exception of adopted Deer Clan member Chickaua/Molly), their experiences have not been recorded. Once again, Doll stands alone in her complex positioning. Doll's gender, enslaved status, and increasingly, her racialization as black would continue to limit her role in Cherokee society; but the length of time she had lived among Cherokees, her long-standing relationship with Shoe Boots, her role as mother to children whose father was Cherokee, and the increasing number of other non-Cherokees nearby would likely have carved out a space for her as a marginal member of her Cherokee community.

Doll's position as part of a local African American community may have been more solid, since the number of black slaves in Cherokee country was increasing over time. In 1824 the Cherokee National Council took a census of the population and reported that in Shoe Boots and Doll's district of Hightower, there were 698 Cherokee males, 677 Cherokee females, forty-three "male negroes," thirty-six "female negroes," "four white men married to Cherokee women," and "two Cherokee men married to white women."[7] The census also noted the ownership of "818 horses, 3,170 cattle, 3,777 swine, 298 sheep, 67 goats, 67 looms, 65 ploughs, five blacksmith shops, two mills, 240 wheels, and eleven wagons" by Hightower residents.[8] The reported population numbers combined for a total of 1,375 Cherokees, seventy-nine blacks, and six whites. The census included no category for intermarried blacks and did not distinguish between "negroes" and "slaves" in its terminology, suggesting that the Cherokee National Council was beginning to blur the racial category of "negro" with the class category of "slave" by the late 1820s. Doll was probably counted among the "female negroes" in the census, and she presumably enjoyed the company of other black women in her district.

As these census numbers suggest, the town of Hightower within the district of the same name had grown in population and importance over the years. By the conclusion of the Creek War in 1814, Hightower was a bustling center of activity, large enough to attract the attention of northern missionaries. The impending arrival of those missionaries, and of one man in particular—a controversial and outspoken blacksmith named William Thompson—would shift the fate of the Shoeboots family. In the ensuing ten years, Doll, Shoe Boots, and their children would experience firsthand the interrelated and unpredictable forces of colonization, Christianity, and slavery.

The American Board of Commissioners for Foreign Missions (ABCFM) was an interdenominational evangelical society with abolitionist leanings, headquartered in Massachusetts. With one major mission site called Brainerd already established in the Cherokee town of Chickamauga, the missionaries were looking to expand. In a group letter written by Art Hoyt and others stationed at the Brainerd mission, Hightower is described as "the most important place in the nation for a local school [being] the largest town, containing two hundred or more families and . . . perhaps 30 miles long."[9] In their "List of Places in the Cherokee Nation," the Brainerd missionaries elaborated on their observations, noting that "Hightower lies on the Hightower River, and two roads leaving from Georgia to Alabama. It is watered by a number of beautiful creeks. Good land—large population, perhaps 50 or 60 miles in length."[10] In addition to its fine location and growing population, Hightower also attracted missionary attention because of the willingness of its chiefs to host a Christian school. In 1822 these chiefs, probably including Shoe Boots, invited the Brainerd missionaries to open a school in their town. In a letter to their supervisor in New England the missionaries explained: "Permit us to inform you of another request for a local school. Two chiefs from Hightower town were at Br[other] Hicks a few weeks ago, and he advised them to have a blacksmith, a wheelwright, and a school in their town. . . . On their return they layed the subject before their people, and all were desirous to have the above mentioned mechanics and school."[11] In April 1823 Shoe Boots, a leader in Hightower affairs, visited the Brainerd mission on two occasions and expressed his desire to extend the mission's services to children in his town. The missionaries recorded in their journal: "Shoe Boots, after thanking us for what we were doing for the children here, and assuring us that it gave him great pleasure, took an affectionate leave of us to return home—saying he hoped they should soon have a school at Hightower, and that their children would some day appear like these."[12] As historian Adriane Strenk has argued, Shoe Boots's support of missionary education did not necessarily mean that he considered himself a Christian or that he hoped that Cherokee children would convert to that faith.[13] Rather, he was a pragmatist who wanted the children in his community to be best prepared for any test, even to the point of exposing them to ideas with which he may have disagreed. As Shoe Boots and other Cherokee adults knew, the United States and its citizens were continually plotting to snatch and settle Cherokee lands, and the best defenses against such activity seemed to be literacy in English and technical competency.

Indeed, the instability of the Cherokee future in the Southeast was more than apparent to tribal members by the early 1820s. Andrew Jackson had presided over the cession of Cherokee lands in the wake of the Creek War, and in 1817 the U.S. government had begun transporting mail through the Cherokee territory.[14] Soon thereafter, in 1818, the federal government persuaded a group of Cherokees, led by Chief John Jolly, to relinquish their land and move to Arkansas, prompting the Cherokee Council to pass a law making the unauthorized sale of Cherokee land punishable by death.[15] At the Cherokee Council meeting in July of that year, the governor of Georgia and Indian Agent Return Meigs proposed the exchange of the entire Cherokee territory in the Southeast for western lands secured by the Louisiana Purchase of 1803. In response, a group of Cherokee women entered a petition to the Council urging the men to "hold out to the last in support of our common rights."[16] Chief Path Killer, the principal chief at the time, refused the governor's proposal: "I say again, I love my country where I was raised . . . I hope you have conscience to let me raise my children in my own country." Still, the state of Georgia increased its pressure on the federal government to secure Cherokee land for the state and allowed its citizens to encroach on Cherokee territory and harass and assault Cherokees with impunity.[17] While some Cherokees staunchly resisted Christianity and American education, Shoe Boots and his colleagues believed, as Strenk explains, that "education protected the future of the Nation by endowing Cherokee children with the ability to preserve their homeland and defend themselves."[18]

With the support of Shoe Boots and other local chiefs, the mission school at Hightower was soon operating. In 1822 William Thompson, the blacksmith based at the school, arrived with his family. The missionaries at Brainerd thought highly of Thompson, a white native of Tennessee, and had pressed the board in New England for his appointment: "Should br. Thompson whom we could most cheerfully recommend as believing him to be a persevering, faithful, devoted Christian, and a good workman for this country, be stationed at that place, through a Divine blessing he would perhaps be able to do something towards supporting a small family beside his own."[19] Later, Isaac Proctor, who was to be the head missionary at Hightower, joined Thompson there. By late spring of 1823 Proctor was teaching twenty-five students in a wood school house adjacent to his "dwelling house or rather cabin" that had been built by the townspeople.[20] Proctor wrote that "the school [was] much thought of by the people here especially by some chiefs and headmen."[21] Shoe Boots, who had championed the mission school, seems not to have sent his own mixed-race children there, which could indicate any number of sentiments. Perhaps he feared they would not be accepted; perhaps he felt they were unfit or unworthy; or perhaps he believed that his children already spoke adequate English because of their exposure to their mother and other slaves.[22]

Cherokees in Hightower supported the mission school in a variety of ways: by lobbying for its construction, by helping to build the campus, by enrolling their children, and by attending religious services. One daughter-and-father pair, Mary and Richard Rowe, founded a boarding house for children attending the school, offering to "supply children under twelve years of age, with board and washing for one dollar per week."[23] But just the same, Hightower natives feared that the presence of strangers, especially white strangers, would unsettle and change their community. Early on Hightower residents demonstrated ambivalence toward the Christian newcomers, who were arriving at a time when Georgians were intruding on Cherokee territory and lobbying the federal government for Indian land. Immediately before the missionaries' arrival, the people of Hightower reconsidered hosting the school. The missionaries recorded this change of heart using a tone suggestive of condescension:

> It appears that some of the people of Hightower have had their zeal dampened by reports and sayings of certain white men who occasionally trade among them, and therefore do not proceed with the buildings as fast as might otherwise have been expected. . . . It appears that many from Alabama and Georgia are so sanguine in their expectations that the Cherokee will give up that part of the country that they are exploring it to look [for] the best places for settlement, and some have actually come on with their families supposing the land had been ceded.—While so many white people are grasping for their land it is no wonder if the poor misinformed Cherokees sometimes suspect that missionaries (under cover) have the same object in view.[24]

In an additional challenge to the establishment of the mission in Hightower, an elderly chief interrupted the work of townspeople who were erecting a house for William Thompson. According to missionary reports of the exchange, the chief "reminded the people of the great number of Blacksmiths in the nation who were bad men—and told them if they had not full evidence that this was a good man, they must not strike another stroke for him."[25] The matter was resolved, at least temporarily, when "witnesses then came forward . . . and testified to the character of br. Thompson."

With good reason, the residents of Hightower were suspicious of an institutionalized white Christian presence in their community. From analyses of recent events they must have known, as philosopher Vine Deloria Jr. observed in his 1969 "Indian Manifesto," that "land acquisition and missionary work always went hand in hand in American history."[26] Indeed, the intimate relationship between establishing missions and colonialism was apparent in Cherokee dealings with the United States. The U.S. government program to remake the Cherokee Nation in its own image was, as historian Mary Young has argued, a collaborative project carried out by federal agents and "federally subsidized missionaries." Thus, an institutionalized Christian presence in Cherokee territory served the purpose of "disciplin[ing]" Indian people for their impending colonization.[27] Given the particularities of the ABCFM history in Cherokee country, the missionaries' profession of innocence of this relationship was naive at best. The Brainerd Mission, which was launched to realize the vision of Indian civilization advanced by Secretary of War Henry Knox back in 1789, had been made possible only by the full support and partial funding of the U.S. War Department.[28] In an articulation of the mission's goals, Reverend Cyrus Kingsbury observed that the Christianization of the Indians, in addition to bestowing on them the advantages of civilized life, would be beneficial to national security. Kingsbury noted that religious instruction would be "the most effectual means . . . to give security to our frontier settlements." The partnership between the American Board and the federal government would become obvious in 1817, when an outspoken missionary criticized the government's removal policy. The War Department's disapproval led to a swift retraction on the part of the Church. Rather than jeopardize their governmental support, the American Board warned its members to refrain from involvement in politics and to "withhold themselves sacredly from every colour of interference."[29]

The arrival of these particular missionaries, however, would have different ramifications for the African slaves living in and near Hightower. Unlike the Moravian missionaries based in Spring Place, ABCFM members were New Englanders who opposed the enslavement of blacks.[30] In one example of these missionaries' abolitionist stance, Daniel Butrick of Brainerd passionately criticized slaveowners in an 1825 letter. "I will simply state my views," Butrick wrote. "I believe that all men are born free, and cannot be justly deprived of their liberty but for . . . debt or as hostages of war. . . . I believe therefore that masters are guilty of robbery whenever they command the service of their slaves."[31] In another example, it was reported that missionaries Elizur Butler and Samuel Worcester (who would become renowned in the 1832 Supreme Court case *Worcester v. Georgia*) had been jailed in Georgia in 1829 or 1830 for possessing copies of a fiery antislavery pamphlet, David Walker's *Appeal*, and for teaching black children to read and write.[32]

In *Appeal*, Walker, a black merchant and lay intellectual from Boston, lambasted white Americans, especially representatives of the Christian faith, for punishing slaves who attempted to practice religion: "I have known small collections of coloured people to have convened together, for no other purpose than to worship God Almighty, in spirit and in truth, to the best of their knowledge; when tyrants, calling themselves *patrols,* would also convene and wait almost in breathless silence for the poor coloured people to commence singing and praying to the Lord our God, as soon as they had commenced, the wretches would burst in upon them and drag them out and commence beating them as they would rattle-snakes."[33] While the patrols and ministers that Walker describes denied slaves the right to study the Bible and to engage in communal worship, missionaries of the American Board created a unique opportunity for black slaves in the Cherokee territory. Upon learning of the open-mindedness of these particular ministers, slaves from the surrounding areas attended the Brainerd church. The missionaries recorded the positive reception they received among blacks in their journal: "The African part of our congregation was larger than usual— they came from different directions 10, 12, 17 miles. . . . One of these, who appears to be not more than twenty-five, remembers when he was brought from Africa, and says he is very thankful that God caused him to be brought, though a slave, into the land where he can hear of the Saviour. He says he once thought it hard to be a slave, but now he cares nothing about it if he may be a Christian."[34] But despite sympathetic and strong views among them concerning African American slaves, the missionaries at Brainerd and its satellite missions feared alienating potential Cherokee converts and thus followed a "pragmatic, moderate policy" of cajoling rather than condemning Cherokee slaveholders.[35] As historian Peter Hinks explains, "they considered their position on slavery a delicate one: while they in no way wanted to endorse or foster the institution, they did acknowledge its existence among a number of Cherokees and were concerned to not alienate them or their non-slaveholding brethren by forcing the issue."[36] Along with their fear of alienating converts, the missionaries were lenient in their attitude toward Cherokee slaveowners because they felt that the Indians were not wholly responsible for their participation in this evil. As Butrick noted, the Indians' "opportunities for knowledge [about slavery] have not been as great" as white people's.[37]

Though the missionaries tempered their antislavery feelings in the presence of the Cherokees, they did attempt gentle persuasion through religious teaching. Historian E. D. Graham explains that "the general policy was to treat the slave issue as one on which the Indians were not enlightened, to admit slaveholders to church membership, to show them by reasonable discussion and judicious preaching that slavery was evil and so in time persuade them to sell or free their slaves."[38] Though this approach did not usher in radical change for black slaves of Cherokees, it did foster an environment in which the predominant white southern model of rigid hierarchical relations between master and slave could be challenged and transgressed. The convergence of antislavery sentiment at the mission schools and the Cherokee predisposition toward a flexible system of slavery led to master-slave relations that were uniquely organized and negotiated. Slaves whose Cherokee masters participated in mission life occupied a singular position through which shifts in power were possible, and they used this position to carve out a space for new forms of resistance to slavery.

The most striking particularity of black slave experience in Cherokee missionary towns was the slaves' access to and authority in education. Slaves as well as Cherokees were eligible to attend the schools sponsored by the American Board. Cherokees did not protest the education of blacks and seem not to have feared the independence that literacy could confer on their slaves. In fact, black students were so common in Cherokee schools that they became the majority in some Sunday and primary school classes. Brainerd missionaries Hoyt, Butrick, Chamberlin, and Hall attested to this prevalence of African pupils in the Mission Journal in 1822 and expressed their gratitude at the opportunity to teach black slaves: "There are many of this class of people in bondage to the Cherokees, and they all speak English. Their masters, as far as has come to our knowledge, are all willing to have them instructed, and generally very indulgent in giving them time to attend meeting. If the benefits of our mission could extend no farther than to these depressed sons of Africa, we should have no cause to regret our being sent to labor in this field."[39] Certainly, this high level of educational access for slaves must have been due to ambivalence among Cherokees who were reluctant to accept Christianity and to indoctrinate their children in a foreign value system. However, a noteworthy number of Cherokees valued formal education highly enough to lobby the ABCFM for new schools. And even Shoe Boots, who did not send his own children to school, argued in favor of educational development. The willingness of Cherokees to share this resource with their slaves starkly contrasts with the denial of education to slaves in the white South.

Beyond the opportunity to study at the mission schools, slaves of Cherokees took on the role of translators and instructors in these schools. In a reversal that would have been an anathema in the white slaveholding South, black slaves instructed their masters, who were grateful for the assistance. For unlike slaves in many white households, slaves in Cherokee homes possessed a crucial skill that their masters often lacked—fluency in English. Most slaves of Cherokees had had a headstart over their masters in English language and literacy because they had lived with whites before arriving in Indian country, and many were bilingual—proficient in both English and Cherokee. With this talent, black slaves became indispensable in the education and religious instruction of their masters. The linguistic aptitude of slaves made it possible for Cherokees to understand their missionary instructors and to take the first steps toward learning English.[40]

In numerous examples, black slaves occupied positions of authority over Cherokees in the mission setting. A Cherokee woman who had learned to read parts of the Bible claimed a black person as her teacher when explaining her improvement to her husband. A young Cherokee man applying to the mission school who "was found able to spell correctly in words of four to five syllables" reported that "he had been taught solely by black people."[41] A slave couple who were members of the mission church in 1818 taught their mistress to read, and their efforts were recorded in the Mission Journal: "This man and his wife, who also is serious, have been pretty constant attendants at the Sunday School, and have begun to read in the bible. We are told their mistress (who is one of the late Cherokee converts) is herself learning to read by their assistance."[42] Slaves translated sermons in mission churches, and in one example, a slave occupied the position of "lay officer" while his master was merely an attending church member.[43] In these interactions, slaveowners openly depended on the knowledge of black people and were forced to recognize authority in their slaves, challenging common ideas in the white slaveholding South that slaves were infantile, irrational, intellectually deficient and in possession of few attributes beyond physical strength and reproductive potency.

As slaves instructed their masters on the mission grounds and in some Cherokee homes, Cherokee recognition of and respect for the English skills of African Americans disrupted customary power relations between masters and slaves. This disruption stretched beyond the educational realm, as Cherokee masters continued to rely on the linguistic prowess of their slaves in daily encounters with whites. Theda Perdue writes that "a few conservative Cherokees owned slaves but they seem to have valued their slaves less for labor than for companionship and particularly for the ability to speak English." In one example cited by Perdue, Anglo traveler Ebenezer Newton visited with a respected Cherokee man named Captain Foster in 1818 and reported about his host: "He could not speak a word of English, that I know of, but he had some negroes who could speak very well." In another example, a young female slave fostered communication between her master and his white guests by translating her master's comments into English.[44]

Though these recorded examples of black slaves' role as translators entail friendly and apparently consensual interactions between Cherokees and whites, there must have been times when slaves lent their skills to help manage adversarial encounters. Because Cherokees depended on their slaves for the basic skill of English fluency, African Americans must have played a role in the everyday, individual interactions that were part of the Cherokee struggle to preserve their homelands. Without skills in English, Cherokees had little hope of negotiating with white invaders with clarity and confidence. And without negotiations, Cherokees had no chance of staking a claim that white Americans might respect. For educated Cherokees with white parentage, English proficiency was not an issue, but for Cherokees who spoke only their native tongue, slaves would have been indispensable in their many minute but crucial interactions with white interlopers.

In addition to their ability to tutor their masters in English and aid them in interactions with whites, slaves had practical skills that Cherokees needed in order to demonstrate their level of progress to American officials. Whereas Cherokee men were just beginning to use agricultural machinery like the plow, black slaves had acquired mechanical dexterity in their work for white masters. Similarly, black women arrived at Cherokee households with the ready knowledge of how to spin, weave, and make butter—skills that Cherokee women were just beginning to learn. Scholar Joel Martin describes the interdependent relationship between Creeks and blacks that would have held true for many Cherokee farmers: "African Americans were highly valued as new members of any village for they knew and could teach some of the skills and techniques that the Muskogees deeply desired to learn: 'how to repair guns and traps, to shoe horses, to improve agricultural methods [for new crops], to spin and weave, to make butter, to build houses, barns and wagons.'"[45] The service black slaves rendered as cultural mediators between Native people and whites was noted, if derisively, by John Howard Payne. In an essay about the annual Creek Green Corn Dance (also practiced by the Cherokees), he explained: "The ill-starred red people here are entirely at the mercy of interpreters, who, if not negro-slaves of their own, are half-breeds,—a worse set, generally, than the worst of either slaves or knaves. In the jargon of the border, they are called *linkisters*,—some say because they form, by interpreting, a *link* between the Indian nations and ours; but I would rather regard the word as a mere corruption of *linguist*."[46] Though Payne counts the Indians as unlucky for having to rely on the likes of slaves for important matters, the slaves themselves must have assessed the circumstances quite differently. Black slaves of Cherokees would have quickly ascertained their unique importance to their masters' affairs and recognized that they could barter their indispensable skills for greater flexibility, mobility, and respect. The talents that slaves possessed and the value placed on those talents in Native communities created opportunities for slaves to develop sharper, more persistent, and fresh modes of resistance to their enslavement. In the scenarios played out again and again in the southeastern and western Indian territories, black slaves sidestepped their classification as property and became instead property brokers who negotiated the transmission of language, technical skills, items, and even landholdings between Indians and whites. As one former slave from Oklahoma put it, "sometimes a slave could talk English, in which event the Indian would take him as interpreter when he would go to trade with the horse traders or to Kansas City or other places, because the negro could talk English and also knew the value of an animal."[47]

The role that African Americans played as mediators shifted and reconfigured relations of power between masters and slaves.[48] In these instances, the slave became the knower and agent, while the master became a student and temporary dependent. But while their valuable skills gained the slaves increased autonomy, these disruptions of the status quo were fragmented moments within a context of ever-shifting relations. The power that slaves usurped from their masters was transitory, since they were still chattel by social custom, and increasingly, by law. Furthermore, the very role of cultural mediator that expanded possibilities for black resistance in the long run may have contributed to the American colonization of Native people. Even as the attainment of American linguistic and practical skills seemed necessary in the Cherokees' resistance to American encroachment, embracing these same skills made American cultural ways comprehensible and even admirable to some Cherokees and thus hastened their acculturation. Black slaves, while exercising personal authority and gaining a measure of mobility in their interactions with Cherokee masters, also may have performed a role that amounted to being frontmen and frontwomen for the stealthy advancement of white American culture. The slave who taught her master how to understand the missionary's sermon, for instance, was participating in the transmission of a set of Western ideas, thereby supporting the system that would endeavor to crush them both.

In the short run, however, slaves were wise to take advantage of circumstances that momentarily equalized relations with their masters. And although the American Board missions sometimes participated in the slave system by hiring Cherokee-owned slaves to maintain their farms and buildings, the slaves themselves grasped the opportunities provided by the missionaries' antislavery rhetoric.[49] In one example of slave resistance fostered by the mission presence, a group of slaves abandoned their duties and ignored their master. A Hightower citizen reported the incident in 1824: "Rick Rowe's negroes would not obey him since he had joined the church and himself had to turn in to ploughing his fields."[50] Richard Rowe, proprietor of the boarding house for mission students, had been unaware that exposure to the missionaries would embolden his slaves and undermine his authority. While Graham admits that few Cherokee masters actually freed their slaves as a result of the mission's stance, and the missionaries' subtle challenge to slavery did not "strike down the abstract evil of human bondage," he contends that "considerable improvement was wrought in the living and working conditions of the slaves."[51]

This and more seem to have been true for Doll's family. In 1824, one year after the mission in Hightower was established, Shoe Boots, with the assistance of William Thompson, the missionary blacksmith who wrote the document, petitioned the Cherokee Council for his children's freedom. Though the connection between the antislavery mission and Shoe Boots's attempt to emancipate his children could be coincidence, it seems more likely that it reflects a confluence of serendipity, ideology, and action. Shoe Boots's exposure to abolitionist sentiments, coupled with his awareness of a changing political climate in the Cherokee government, seem to have propelled him into what must have been an unwelcome disclosure, the formal documentation of his sexual relationship with a slave. In one of many surprises that would characterize the conjoined histories of Cherokees and blacks, it was white people who first introduced African slavery to the Cherokees and who later became those slaves' best allies in their pursuit of freedom.

Throughout the first decades of the 1800s, Shoe Boots's best interests and those of his black family seemed at odds. This tension is perhaps best illustrated by the presence of the Hightower mission, which operated as a site for slave resistance even while it collaborated with the federal government's imperialist project of civilizing the Cherokees. Shoe Boots and other community leaders were aware of the danger of having a mission school in their town and thus continually assessed the mission's purpose and performance. In 1824, five months before Shoe Boots relied on the assistance of a mission employee to write his petition, he and seven other Hightower chiefs signed an address to oust the missionaries. The town leaders complained that the mission blacksmith overcharged for his work, that the mission teachers mistreated the children, and that the mission presence disrupted community customs. In a letter written for them by Walter Adair, an educated man of white and Cherokee parentage, they said:

> The blacksmith we had fetched here under high recommendation has not realized the expectation was entertained of him, in first place he is such workman as he ought to be, in next place, he is extravagant man to charge for his work, as for the teachers, they are complained of very much by the young people under their care for edducation, they are trying to do away with our common custom of meeting in our townhouse, other strange rules they are adopting which appears to us ought not to be suffered, it is our wish that the missionaries here should be remaned back to Chickamagu to the Society they belong.[52]

Clearly, in these men's views the town's acceptance of the mission school was conditional. When the missionaries crossed the line from teaching English to dictating and disrespecting cultural norms, local leaders balked. William Thompson seems to have come under particular scrutiny. Brainerd missionaries said of the tension: "Our dear br. Thompson has some troubles. Many of the Cherokees are rather displeased with him. But this is not surprising. He was told when he first went there, that if he would keep a tavern to entertain white men, he must expect opposition from the Cherokees."[53]

The Hightower chiefs who wanted to expel the missionaries were attempting to preserve their culture and customs, of which slavery was now one. Shoe Boots's participation in their action demonstrates again the complexity of his position. If Shoe Boots and his colleagues had been successful in driving out the missionaries, the chain of events that gave his children a chance for freedom might not have materialized. Fortunately for Doll and other Hightower slaves, and perhaps unfortunately for Cherokees in the community, Charles Hicks, a Moravian convert and the second principal chief of the Cherokee Nation, mediated the dispute. Hicks was an educated, mixed-race Cherokee with white ancestry who supported Cherokee "progress" and thus supported the missions. In a letter dismissing the complaint he wrote that the Hightower chiefs were overreacting and misconstruing the situation: "The complaint appears to have risen in consequence of some of our people having joined the Society there, by reason of which they would not attend their all night dances and drinking with them, the religion of which they had embraced forbids them to be at such places—and I am confident that the Society to which they have joined does not forbid our people to Exercise their publick authority. . . . As to the complaint of the Scholars about their Teachers, similar ones have long ago been raised at other missionary schools, but when examined . . . found to be groundless."[54] As a representative of the Cherokee national government, Hicks had done the unthinkable: he had intervened in a local dispute and overruled the wishes of town leaders. Still, his decision stood, and the mission school remained.

The lamentable paradox of this outcome is striking. For in the wake of this heated, internal debate, an outpost of American culture maintained a foothold in Cherokee society, and black slaves in Hightower retained their best allies. The coming of the Christians had led, simultaneously, to the eclipse of Cherokee chiefs' local authority, the undermining of long-practiced community customs, and the pathway to freedom for Doll's three children.

SIX

Nationhood

What time is it? Nation time!

AMIRI BARAKA AND CROWD

National Black Political Association

Nations reel and stagger on their way; they make hideous mistakes; they commit frightful wrongs; they do great and beautiful things. And shall we not best guide humanity by telling the truth about all this, so far as the truth is ascertainable?

W. E. B. DU BOIS
"The Propaganda of History"

We are forever on the improve.

JOHN RIDGE
Letter to Albert Gallatin

WHILE CAPTAIN SHOE BOOTS INVOLVED HIMSELF in the local politics of Hightower, his neighbors and fellow slaveowners, the prominent Ridge family, were embarked on a political project of national import. Shoe Boots and Doll knew the Ridges well, since their homes were relatively close to each other. A slave of the Ridges, named Thomas Ridge, recalled: "I was owned by Major Ridge, Old Capt. Shoeboot lived near Etowah River, I lived about thirty miles from Shoeboots. Capt Shoeboots owned my brother and I often went there. He owned a woman besides my brother . . . I was well acquainted with her and saw her often."[1] Even as Doll developed a relationship with the Ridge slaves, Shoe Boots became a close associate of Major Ridge. He had fought as an officer with Major Ridge in the Creek War and had traded slaves with him. Perhaps even Thomas had been separated from his brother, probably Shoe Boots's slave Frank, as a result of business dealings between Shoe Boots and Major Ridge. By the early 1800s these two Cherokee families—the Ridges and the Shoebootses—were already enmeshed in a complicated, bifurcated relationship that would be tested in the coming years.

Like Shoe Boots, Major Ridge had seen something of value in the early missionary schools. In 1810 Major Ridge and his Cherokee wife, Susannah Ridge, sent their eldest and brightest son, John, to study at the Moravian Mission school in Spring Place, where he could acquire "a white man's education." At just seven years old and weakened by a chronic illness, John lived with strangers thirty miles away from home.[2] He proved himself an accomplished scholar, however, and after successfully learning the basics of the English language, the Christian religion, and Anglo-Protestant values, John, along with his cousin Elias Boudinot, traveled to the ABCFM's Foreign Mission School in Cornwall, Connecticut. John would remain there from 1818 to 1822, receiving the education and training that would lead to his marriage to a white woman as well as his prominent but embattled political career.

In 1819, while a student at Cornwall, John Ridge wrote the poem "Upon a Watch," which foreshadowed a new way of thinking among Cherokee men of his generation:

Little Monitor, by thee,
Let me learn what I should be;
Learn the round of life to fill,
Thou canst gentle hints impart,
How to regulate the heart.
When I wind thee up at night
Mark each fault and set thee right,
Let me search my bosom too,
And my daily thoughts review,
Mark the movements of my mind,
Nor be easy when I find
Lattent errors rise to view,
Till all be regular and true.[3]

As evidenced by his earnest ruminations on the clock, Ridge's formal Christian training had taught him the importance of management, industry, and productivity, as well as a respect for order derived from a central source.

His ode to a life controlled and improved by the careful, regular measurement of time was reflective of his New England education and was in keeping with a new admiration for clock time among other southern slaveholders.[4] As historian Mark Smith has demonstrated, an awareness of time measured by the clock spread among managers and workers in the North with the rise of industrialization in the early 1700s. Clock time became associated with modernity and progress, and as the American South attempted to keep pace with Northern industry, planters introduced a mechanization of slave labor in the late-eighteenth century.[5] John Ridge's emerging time consciousness disconnected him from most Cherokees, who continued to live in accordance with seasonal rhythms, and connected him instead to the tightly organized culture of American reformers and government officials and, increasingly, to southern planters. Along with other educated young men, Ridge would apply this ethos of methodical structure and reform to the dramatic reconfiguration of Cherokee political organization in the 1820s.

A century earlier, Cherokee political life had been structured by a system of widely spread "towns"; sometimes these were single towns, and sometimes they consisted of groupings of smaller villages operating as town units for political purposes.[6] Each town had its own local chief and council of advisors who were independent of any higher authority such as a national government or state religion. Men, women, and children had a place at council meetings and the right to have their views heard by the larger group. Decisions pertinent to the common welfare of the town were reached by consensus rather than coercion, and anyone who refused to give his or her consent could not be bound by the council's decisions. Women seem to have had real, though limited, political power in Cherokee town governance of this period. Though not likely to have been members of the central town council, women enjoyed a formal presence in the council's meetings and the right to voice their opinions through a representative from the women's council.[7] Women also wielded an informal political power, which they could exert by advising male council members and by determining the fate of war captives. The Cherokee towns were self-sufficient and self-governed, sometimes opposing one another in larger political struggles with other tribes or European colonists and sometimes working as allies. Though geographically and politically autonomous, Cherokee towns were connected by the common thread of kinship, since every town included members from each of the seven clans.

Cherokee town governance slowly began to evolve with the settlement of Europeans in the mid-eighteenth century. Because European colonists were familiar and comfortable with centralized governments that held sway over their subjects, they failed to understand or have patience with the Cherokee system of individual and town autonomy that required long and complicated negotiations with any number of town councils. The colonists preferred instead to deal with a central figure, and they sometimes refused to meet with anyone other than a person whom they, often with little reason, deemed a "king." Furthermore, colonists took action against any and all Cherokees for the decisions or behaviors of individuals in one town, in effect making all Cherokees responsible for the actions of a few. In response to this pressure, and because negotiation with white interlopers was becoming a necessity, the Cherokees developed a loosely constructed National Council. The Council was to operate much like a town council, include representatives from each town, and only handle issues pertaining to foreign relations. But by the end of the eighteenth century, the newly formed National Council was receiving criticism from Europeans for its inability to control young warriors accused of harassing white colonists. In an attempt to achieve some semblance of order and authority over these young men, who, in accordance with Cherokee customs could do what they wished, the National Council invited them to become members in the hope that they would then respect the Council's wishes.[8] Shoe Boots, then a young warrior who had just returned from his travels in Kentucky, probably participated in this loosely defined governing body.

The "first chief" of the National Council at this time was an elder named Path Killer. Though a respected advisor, Path Killer did not have power equivalent to that of an American governor or president. Since Cherokee politics was still based on consensus, no single leader had the ability to force his or her will on others. Steadily, though, the Council invested itself with greater authority and began to intervene not only in foreign relations but also in internal tribal affairs like crime. In 1808 the Council adopted a written legal code. In that same year, it created companies of men called the Light Horse, who would act as a police force to put an end to horse theft and to punish horse thieves.[9] In 1810 the Council passed a law annulling the traditional clan responsibility to avenge the deaths of loved ones.[10] And in these matters, it was not the aged Path Killer who took the lead, but the younger, educated men.[11] As Marion Starkey has noted about Path Killer, "though the Cherokees venerated the old man, the missionaries observed that it was usually the well-educated second chief, Charles Hicks, and aggressive young John Ross who carried on the real business of the Nation."[12]

In 1817 the National Council, with Major Ridge as its speaker, passed six articles that would further centralize power and relocate much of the Council's influence in a new and smaller governing body called the National Committee. Streamlined and comparatively efficient, the National Committee evolved into a political inner circle charged with "the overall supervision of the affairs of the nation."[13] The advent of the National Committee corresponded with a new type of Cherokee leader, the John Ridges and John Rosses of the tribe, whose power developed in the national rather than the local arena and whose influence was rooted in personal wealth and the practical skills necessary for dealing with whites. While Shoe Boots, an uneducated, "full-blood" local leader, was typical of National Council members, the National Committee members shared quite a different profile. Many were mixed-race of white parentage, fluent in English as well as Cherokee, educated, and extensively propertied. They were, as sociologist Duane Champagne has described them, "the westernized slaveholders" of the tribe.[14] John Ross, who was president of the National Committee and would later become principal chief for almost forty years, was typical of these rising leaders. With the exception of a half-Cherokee grandmother, Ross came from a family of Scottish traders who had settled in Cherokee territory. Like many privileged young men in the white South, Ross studied with a private tutor before attending an academy in Kingsport, Tennessee.[15] By 1819 Ross owned a two-story home, multiple orchards, a ferry, and nineteen black slaves. Theda Perdue has defined Ross as a "Cherokee founding father," "entrepreneur," and member of a Cherokee "aristocracy."[16] And Starkey, revealing her own prejudices concerning race and "civilization," observed: "There was nothing of the untutored savage about Ross. He had so little Cherokee blood that it is surprising that his enemies did not assail him on this ground."[17]

It would be simplifying matters to correlate white "blood" with personal qualities or particular political perspectives, as Starkey seems to do above. Rather, the young men of the National Committee—often sons of white traders and Cherokee women who had inherited property and slaves from their fathers—were raised in environments infused with Euro-American values and mores in addition to Cherokee ones. As Cherokee statesmen in an increasingly complex political moment, they were influenced and aided by their upbringing in biracial, bicultural families. Relying on this experience, they acted to preserve the Cherokee Nation and its territory—out of a commitment to their tribe, to their families, and to their personal wealth. They believed that the best way to protect Cherokee peoplehood and land was to demonstrate Cherokee progress to American federal and state powers by proving that the Cherokees were a sovereign, civilized nation with rights to be respected and a government to be reckoned with.

To secure the future of the Cherokees in the Southeast and to undergird Cherokee political sovereignty and legal legitimacy, the National Committee propelled the institutionalization of a Cherokee national government modeled after the United States government.[18] Though local town elders, who tended to have a more conservative political outlook, retained some influence over these emerging national leaders, they were also dependent on the judgment of men who had the benefit of education and were rapidly developing institutions that formalized their authority. The result was an uneven and uneasy balance of power between national leaders—the "new political center"—and local leaders who gave their qualified consent to the novel political vision of the National Committee.[19] In a whirlwind of activity between 1820 and 1830, a small group of elite men, including National Committee members John Ross, Charles Hicks, and John Ridge, ordered, monitored, and centralized Cherokee governance. In 1820 the National Committee and Council (together referred to as the General Council) divided the Cherokee territory into eight districts, from which future representatives would be drawn. In 1820 and 1821 the General Council established local courts and a high court, removing responsibility for jurisprudence from clans and town councils.[20] With the appropriation of "one hundred town lots, of one acre square," the governing bodies made plans for the construction of a capital city in 1825. The town of New Echota (or New Town), on the Caunausauga River, included a hewn-log legislative hall, where the General Council would meet, and a two-story brick courthouse with "yellow poplar shingles."[21] In a further attempt to organize and consolidate the dispersed Cherokee people, the General Council authorized the construction of a printing office in New Echota that would house a national press. In February 1828 the national paper, the *Cherokee Phoenix,* released its first issue under the editorship of Elias Boudinot, John Ridge's cousin and classmate. And in a culminating event, the General Council organized and convened a constitutional convention to draft the laws of a new republic. On July 4, 1827, the Cherokee Constitution was ratified.

The twelve drafters of this document, elected by free adult males from each of the regional districts, were a rare group when compared to the majority of Cherokees, yet they were quite similar to one another. Many of them hailed from white-Cherokee families rich in improved land holdings; all but one owned slaves.[22] The presiding officer of the Constitutional Convention was the ubiquitous John Ross. From Shoe Boots's district of High-tower, three men were elected: John Beamer, Thomas Pettit, and Joseph Vann, nicknamed "Rich Joe" because he was the wealthiest man in the Cherokee Nation. Along with numerous slaves, Rich Joe, the son of James Vann, had inherited from his father a two-story brick mansion that rivaled the manors of white plantation owners.[23]

The way these convention representatives were chosen marked an important shift in Cherokee governance. No longer were women and children involved in the official processes of decision-making, and no longer was consensus the preferred method of political discourse.[24] Instead, a select group of the population—free men—elected officials whose decisions were legally binding. In the 1820s Cherokee women saw their political power shift from a public to a private sphere and then lessen altogether as the men in their communities became more entrenched in centralized politics.[25] The consolidation of power in one government and one capital city meant that some Cherokee people, women as well as poor farmers in the outlying districts, would lose access to direct political involvement. The very processes used to organize the new Cherokee government limited the roles that women and most Cherokees would play. And not surprisingly, the political disenfranchisement of these two groups—women and subsistence farmers—coincided with the political exclusion of Afro-Cherokees and black slaves.

Even as the Constitutional Convention was reconfiguring women's roles in Cherokee country, the resulting document defined and revised the place of blacks in the Cherokee Nation. Since the sixteenth century, when Cherokees and Africans first encountered one another, until this period of intense nation-building, relationships between Cherokees and blacks had remained flexible. Cherokees did not share any attitude, either positive or negative, about people of African descent, and they had not sought, through laws or regulations at the town level, to structure and fix racial categories or interracial relationships. Instead, varying familial and community dynamics had shaped individual interactions. Some Cherokees owned slaves; some aided runaways. Some Cherokees avoided blacks; some Cherokees were themselves black people who had become Cherokee through adoption or intermarriage. Often these categories of people overlapped. A Cherokee with an adopted African sister might also trade captured blacks for goods. In sum, Cherokees did not view African Americans categorically or relate to all black people in the same manner. With the construction of the centrally governed Cherokee republic, however, this fluid structure of Cherokee and black interactions would undergo a fundamental shift.

This symbiotic relationship between the development of the republic and of a racially based system of exclusion and slavery is not unique to the Cherokees. This same trajectory is apparent in the birth pains of the United States. When Africans were first transported to Jamestown, Virginia, in 1619, their status was ambiguous. They may have been slaves, or they may have been workers whose labor was contracted for a limited period. Whatever their specific station, they were not viewed as a class of people whose status was racially determined and fixed. In this period Africans were often indentured servants, and as such they labored alongside white workers from whom they were not assumed to be fundamentally different. This relatively open attitude toward racial definitions and the social meanings ascribed to them began to change as English colonists of the emerging planter class saw the need for a large, cheap labor source and suspected a possible danger in interracial class-based alliances. Between 1640 and 1700, Virginians gradually adopted a system of labor that depended on a social and legal category of people who were defined as slaves—a category into which Africans were then said naturally to fit. Thus, the institution of slavery and the ideology of racism grew alongside and into one another.[26]

Slavery not only fattened and expanded the American colonies, it also provided them with an economic means for obtaining their national autonomy. America required foreign assistance to fight the Revolutionary War against England, and that foreign aid could only be secured through the lucrative tobacco trade. As historian Edmund Morgan has argued, "their single most valuable product with which to purchase assistance was tobacco, produced by slave labor. . . . To a large degree it may be said that Americans bought their independence with slave labor."[27] Morgan has contended further that the central paradox of American history may well be the fact that American freedom depended on and converged with American slavery. The Constitution and an emerging set of national laws extended this dialectic by defining the nation racially—reserving citizenship rights only for white inhabitants and denying naturalization to nonwhite immigrants. Even as the American independence movement depended on slave labor for its freedom, the new democracy defined itself through the political exclusion of peoples of color.

A similar paradoxical relationship between slavery and freedom, as well as between state formation and racial formation, was developing in the

Cherokee republic of the 1820s. The leaders of the young government sought to preserve Cherokee independence in part by legislating a fixed and subordinate status for blacks. And Cherokee lawmakers solidified the identity of their republic through the definition and regulation of racial categories. Through the benefit of slave labor, Cherokees could grow surplus crops to increase their wealth and display their participation in the market economy—both viewed as "civilized" endeavors by American officials. Furthermore, by excluding and systematically enslaving blacks, Cherokees could demonstrate the distance between them and this lowly race, thereby exhibiting their unique standing as a civilized tribe and proving their right to be viewed as a sovereign nation. In some ways, this bid for legitimacy worked, since federal Indian agents and white northern reformers proclaimed the Cherokees the most civilized of Indians. In 1859 Indian Agent George Butler linked Cherokee "progress" to slavery: "I am clearly of the opinion that the rapid advancement of the Cherokees is owing in part to the fact of their being slaveholders, which has operated as an incentive to all industrial pursuits, and I believe if every family of the wild roving tribes of Indians were to own a negro man and woman . . . it would tend more to civilize them than any plan that could be adopted."[28] As Butler's statement illustrates, the process of becoming more civilized in the eyes of white federal officials depended on Indians adopting practices of American barbarity, namely, slavery and racism. The Cherokee Constitution of 1827 encapsulated this irony. At the same time that Cherokee leaders created the charter for their new republic in this document, they also defined "blackness" as a racial category and excluded and controlled black and mixed-race Afro-Cherokee people. Cherokee lawmakers, like U.S. statesmen, were defining a nation with particular and exclusionary racial parameters.[29]

The primary purpose of the new Cherokee republic and its constitution was to proclaim and maintain Cherokee sovereignty. This goal is evidenced in the first of six constitutional articles, which lays out the physical boundaries of the nation and declares the Cherokee government's "Sovereignty and Jurisdiction" over that land.[30] Article II divides the new government into legislative, executive, and judicial branches. After first determining the fixed boundaries of the Cherokee nation-state in Article I, the constitution describes a specified people who may legitimately occupy those boundaries as citizens of the nation in Article III. It is in this third article that the state's official position on black people emerges. Article III, Section 4 reads: "The descendants of Cherokee men by all free women, except the African race, whose parents may have been living together as man and wife, according to the customs and laws of this nation, shall be entitled to all the rights and privileges of this Nation, as well as the posterity of Cherokee women by all free men. No person who is of negro or mulatto parentage, either by the father or the mother side, shall be eligible to hold any office of profit, honor or trust under this government."[31] This section states that Cherokee citizenship accrues to two categories of people: children and descendants of Cherokee men and nonblack free women, as well as children and descendants of Cherokee women and all free men. This definition of the Cherokee citizenry effectively disqualifies all black women, slave or free, from being able to produce legally legitimate Cherokee children. It also disqualifies most black men from being able to produce legally legitimate Cherokee children, since few free black men resided in Cherokee territory after the passage of an act to expel free blacks in 1824. The inclusion of this narrow possibility for black men and Cherokee women to produce Cherokee citizens accords with persistent cultural beliefs in matrilineality and the notion that Cherokee women create Cherokee children. However, as the concluding sentence of the section indicates, no black or mixed-race Afro-Cherokee person, regardless of matrilineal descent, would be entitled to run for political office, to serve on the General Council, or to hold any government position such as judge, sheriff, or editor of the national newspaper. The language of this stipulation—that no "negro or mulatto" may be entrusted with "office[s] of profit, honor or trust" not only relegates Afro-Cherokees to a "form of second-class citizenship," as literary scholar Karen Woods has observed, but it also impugns the integrity and abilities of all people of African descent.[32] Article III, Section 7 of the constitution further codifies black exclusion by granting suffrage only to "free male citizens" and by including the parenthetical note "excepting negroes and descendants of white and Indian men by negro women who may have been set free."[33] Freed male slaves, even those of Cherokee descent on their father's side, would not be eligible to vote. And no woman—Cherokee, Afro-Cherokee, black, or white—would have voting rights under this new government.

The Cherokee Constitution mandates that as a general rule, descendants of Cherokees and blacks would not be considered citizens. However, this legal stipulation should have been nonsensical in a society where belonging had been defined in terms of kinship rather than race. How would the Constitutional Committee determine what blackness meant, and who would be considered black in a cultural context in which race and racial difference were foreign categories? To some extent, the groundwork for this new racialized way of thinking had been laid by the duration and intensity of Cherokee interactions with European colonists, American officials, and white slaveholders. Nonetheless, early Cherokee history indicates that for hundreds of years, Africans were not automatically viewed as potential or actual slaves. At some point in the evolution of Cherokee society, Africans and the descendants of Africans began to be lumped together into the category "slave," and the category "slave" became synonymous with, and then subsumed by, the category "Negro." "Negro" at the same time became marked as a tainted, denigrated classification, just as it was in the United States. At the historical moment when the Cherokee national government took shape, the official language of laws and the pecuniary language of newspaper advertisements indicated that slaves were no longer a group of people defined mainly by status and a relational (rather than racial) distance from Cherokees. Now slaves were a subcategory of the fixed and racialized designation "Negro." In Cherokee legal and economic understanding, slaves had become black.

In tandem with this transformation, the Cherokee nation-state had begun the slow process of defining blacks as a separate, racial group with the codification of written laws. In the earliest Cherokee laws referring to blacks, black people are described in terms that recognize a connection between race (blackness) and caste (enslaved status). In 1819 the first law referring to a slave calls the unnamed slave "his [master's] said negro man." In ensuing legislation, blacks are described as "negro slaves," "negro man slave," and "negro woman slave," further linking the categories of race and caste. In 1824 the sole preremoval law that referred to blacks who were not slaves banned "free negroes" from Cherokee territory. By this time, "Negro" had become the base category for unwanted, subjugated African-descended peoples and "slave" or "free" as mere descriptions of kinds of Negroes. Article III, Section 4 of the Cherokee Constitution represents the fullest expression of the Cherokee Nation's racial thinking in this period. In this first instance in Cherokee law when blacks were defined as constituting a distinct racial category, the section refers to an "African race" that is understood to be separate from other "races." Next, in its reference to "negro" or "mulatto" ancestry, the section delineates multiple permutations of "the African race" and indicates that blackness is understood as a biological condition passed down from parent to child, just as clan is passed down from mother to child. In this conceptualization of race, an African is a "Negro," and for all intents and purposes, a "mulatto," or mixed-race Afro-Cherokee person is also a "Negro."

The exclusion of almost all African-descended people from citizenship and suffrage in the Cherokee Constitution set the stage for the systematic subordination of blacks, since they now had no legitimacy or legal standing that the Cherokee Nation was bound to respect. In contrast to the detailed description of black marginalization in Article III, white people were present only in their absence. Cherokee laws passed before the constitution was written had already legalized and regulated intermarriage between Cherokees and whites. Whereas the children of white men and Cherokee women would be Cherokee citizens owing to the customs of clan, the children of Cherokee men and white women held an uncertain position until 1825. In that year, the General Council passed a law stating that "the children of Cherokee men and white women, living in the Cherokee Nation as man and wife, be, and they are, hereby acknowledged, to be equally entitled to all the immunities and privileges enjoyed by the citizens descending from the Cherokee race, by the mother's side."[34] Thus, children of whites and Cherokees were already understood to be citizens by the time the constitutional committee met in 1827. Any ambiguity over the status of white-Cherokees was clarified by the language of this article, which did not expressly exclude descendants of whites, even as it excluded descendants of Africans. Indeed, many members of the Constitutional Convention were themselves the progeny of whites and Cherokees.

The Cherokee nation-state's full acceptance of mixed-race white-Cherokees as citizens did not equate with a full acceptance of non-Cherokee whites. In fact, white people with no Cherokee ancestry were closely regulated by the new government. By 1819 white men married to Cherokee women could claim citizenship rights in the Nation, but they were forbidden to take more than one Cherokee wife, and they could not control their Cherokee wives' property.[35] In addition, white men were allowed to settle and work on Cherokee lands only by official permit. Still, this regulated status for whites differed markedly from the status of free blacks, who were defined by law only as "intruders." Whereas white men could legally remain in Cherokee country, and white women could legally marry into Cherokee families, free black men and women did not have these options. Cherokee law differentiated between Cherokees, blacks, and whites, but it did so in a way that elevated the position of whites in the Nation over that of blacks. In the context of the strategic nationalism of the 1820s, Cherokee leaders used race as a determining factor for deciding who did and did not belong in the Cherokee Nation, and they seared these racialized definitions into law. Whereas black-Cherokees descended from Cherokee mothers or adopted into clans would have been easily integrated into the fabric of Cherokee families and communities in an earlier period, now "black-Cherokee" was almost a contradiction in terms, for the legal definition of Cherokee citizen refused to make fully legitimate anyone of African descent.

The Cherokee Constitution of 1827 does not explicitly legalize black slavery. Neither, for that matter, does the U.S. Constitution of 1787. Instead, both documents take slavery as a given. In the Cherokee Nation, as in the United States, a set of laws regulating the system of slavery and limiting the autonomy of slaves would develop. In the 1820s the Cherokee Nation passed several laws that together amounted to a loose slave code. The General Council approved an act making a slave's owner responsible for that slave's actions, such as selling merchandise or buying alcohol, and they approved an act allowing the formation of patrols to police and punish slaves. They passed an act that made allowances for brutality toward slaves, deeming it legal to kill a slave while engaged in "moderate correction" of him or her. The General Council refused free blacks "under any pretense whatsoever" entrance into Cherokee territory and mandated that they be "viewed and treated, in every respect, as intruders."[36] They also revoked the longstanding right of Cherokee slaves to own property. The list of laws limiting the autonomy and mobility of slaves and sanctioning the exclusion of free blacks was shaping Cherokee slavery in the image of American slavery, so much so that historian Rudi Halliburton has asserted that "slavery in the Cherokee Nation was a microcosm of the 'peculiar institution' that existed in the southern United States."[37]

The amount of attention paid to black people in the constitution and early laws of the Cherokee Nation indicates the historical significance of the African presence within the tribe, while also showing, as Circe Sturm has argued, the imprint of an American nationalism based on (white) racial identity and (nonwhite) exclusion.[38] Clearly the architects of the new Cherokee nation-state could not formulate a government without taking into account black occupancy in Cherokee country, but black people proved to be both a hindrance and a help to Cherokee political leaders as they envisioned their nation's future. At the same time that Cherokee lawmakers felt anxious about the possibility of an infusion of black "blood" into the Cherokee population, they relied on the availability of free, black labor. In this tumultuous political period, black people, when employed as captive laborers, provided a means for Cherokee economic advancement as well as proof of Cherokee acculturation, both of which seemed sure to secure

Cherokee independence within the boundaries of what then constituted the United States. If not for the African slaves in their midst, the Cherokees might merely have been another "wild roving tribe," in the words of Agent Butler, with no hope of progress. At the same time, though, black people, if acknowledged as relatives and defined as free citizens, threatened to undo the very civilizing process that their presence as slaves made possible. African Americans were beneficial to the successful development of the Cherokee Nation as long as they were maintained as outsiders to the national body.

As Sharon Holland has observed, the tendency for various ethnic groups to situate themselves in relation to blacks as a way to elevate their own position within the American nation has long been a pattern in U.S. history. Holland writes that blackness holds a "unique place" as a "paradigm in the quest for achieving the status of 'American.'" She continues: "It is a paradigm so powerful that even some of this nation's first peoples buckled under its discursive weight, taking into their ranks thousands of Africans, and emulating their (white) counterparts."[39] Holland's candid assessment very nearly captures the Cherokee situation of the 1820s, with the exception that the Cherokee lawmakers were not using the discourse of blackness, and indeed, the bodies of black people, for the purpose of becoming more fully American. Rather, in a painful irony, the Cherokee Nation borrowed political systems and racial ideologies from the United States to avoid being colonized by the United States. As cultural critic Priscilla Wald has observed, the growth of the Cherokee republic "signalled a victory for a Cherokee nationalism simultaneously modeled on and opposed to United States nationalism."[40] The Cherokee elite upheld the doctrine of and participated in the practice of antiblack racism, not because they admired Americans but because they wanted to be rid of them. Cherokee leaders were held captive by the colonial power of the United States, even as they legalized their own captivity of African slaves.

This was a hazardous strategy, and for some Cherokees, particularly those who had already been exposed to American values through white relatives and in mission schools, the means became an end in itself. In 1826 National Committee member John Ridge recounted the Cherokees' "state of improvement" in his essay "Sketch of the Cherokee Nation," which he wrote for ethnologist Albert Gallatin, at Gallatin's request.[41] Ridge directed his comments here to a white American audience in an attempt to gain publicity for Cherokee progress and to rally public opinion against removal.[42] Here Ridge comments, almost point by point, on the major goals of the

U.S. civilization program, noting how the Cherokees have advanced. He praises the movement toward individual property holding and the abandonment of the "chase." He insists that men do most of the fieldwork, while women weave textiles that rival those made by New England manufacturers. He notes the development of a new form of government and the numbers of slaves owned by Cherokees: "The African slaves are generally mostly held by Halfbreeds and full Indians of distinguished talents. In this class the principal value of property is retained and their farms are conducted in the same style with the southern white farmers of equal ability in point of property."[43] In this comparison between Cherokees and white farmers, Ridge paints a picture of Cherokee life strikingly different from that of his grandparents' generation. Fifty years earlier, class distinctions between Cherokees would have been minimal, and black slaves would have been few.

Like any people, Cherokees had always adapted to new times and situations, but the Cherokee Nation of the 1820s incorporated change on a grand scale. Against this backdrop, possibilities for Cherokee and black alliances were limited by law and thus erased from the official record. The Cherokee Constitution proclaimed Cherokees of African descent to be noncitizens or second-class citizens. Cherokee laws defined blacks solely as slaves and intruders. The prejudice in these records is so explicit that an interested person reviewing the nineteenth-century laws of the Cherokee Nation would be hard-pressed not to describe Cherokees as stridently antiblack. But in the "hidden transcript" of nineteenth-century Cherokee life, embedded between the letter of the law and the everyday interactions within families and communities, a second record shows a continued complexity in Cherokee and black relationships.[44] Surprising challenges to institutional power, redefinitions of the state's racial meanings, and ruptures in seemingly closed systems lie buried just beneath the surface.[45]

In 1824, when Captain Shoe Boots submitted a petition to the Cherokee national government on behalf of his enslaved children, his action represented a radical challenge to the emerging Cherokee systems of black exclusion and legalized slavery. Shoe Boots's letter to the General Council acknowledged the intimate relationship between him and Doll, named the children of their union, and pleaded for the children's emancipation and Cherokee citizenship. By writing this letter Shoe Boots made himself vulnerable to the criticism of his fellow slaveholders, including his neighbors

Major Ridge, John Ridge, and Joseph Vann, who held key positions on the General Council. Though these men may have engaged in secret liaisons with their own slaves, by 1824 miscegenation between Cherokees and blacks was a shameful and soon to be illegal activity. In his petition, Shoe Boots stated the following:

> To your excellencies the Chiefs in council at New Town—
> My friends and Brothers
>
> It is to you I make my difficulties known, desiring your aid and assistance, knowing it is in your power to give full sanction to this my request. I will here try to give you a full statement; being in possession of a few Black People and being crost in my affections, I debased myself and took one of my black women by the name of Daull, by her I have had these children named as follows, the oldest Elizabeth about the age of Seventeen, the next the name of John about the age of Eleven, the next the name of Polly about the age of Seven years.
>
> These is the only Children I have as Citizens of this Nation, and as the time I may be called on to die is uncertain, My desire is to have them as free citizens of this nation. Knowing what property I may have, is to be divided amongst the Best of my friends, how can I think of them having bone of my bone and flesh of my flesh to be called their property, and this by my imprudent conduct, and for them and their offspring to suffer for generations yet unborn, is a thought of too great a magnitude for me to remain silent any longer.
>
> I therefore humbly petition your honors that you may pass a resolution privileging now to carry into execution my desires, or so direct me by your wisdom, a plea for their freedom, in whatsoever means you may think best.
> this your humble petitioner with every prayer of
> *Captain Shoe Boots.*[46]

Shoe Boots's petition essentially reveals his sexual relationship with Doll, his willingness to claim Doll's children as his own, and his intention to see his children free and vested with Cherokee citizenship rights. The document, reproduced here in its entirety, weaves together the tangled threads of colonialism, nationalism, slavery, and personal intimacies that shaped nineteenth-century life in the Cherokee Nation. Moreover, the emotional tenor of Shoe Boots's plea, shaded by undertones that appear both loving and abashed, reveals the wrenching complexities of race relations among Cherokees, blacks, and whites in this period.

Shoe Boots's letter to the Cherokee Council members is thickly layered with varied cultural and political meanings. If ever a document spoke in tongues—some translatable and some indecipherable to twenty-first-century ears—this one does. An attempt to understand its many layers of meaning might first begin with an analysis of its production. Shoe Boots's letter of petition was originally written in English rather than in Cherokee. John Howard Payne records that the petition was drafted for Shoe Boots by a blacksmith: "The Lothario of the wilderness, when remorse came upon him, went to a blacksmith white friend of his, who was considered a sort of literary man among them, and between them this touching document was indicted."[47] The biblical allusions and moral tone of the petition suggest that the author was Christian as well as literate. Circumstantial evidence makes it nearly certain that William Thompson, the white missionary blacksmith who moved to Shoe Boots's town of Hightower in 1822, wrote the letter. Thompson was part of an abolitionist missionary community and would likely have encouraged the emancipation of Shoe Boots's slaves. Thompson was also clerk of court for Hightower district by 1830, which makes him an even more obvious choice for Shoe Boots to turn to for assistance in such a sensitive matter.[48] Furthermore, Thompson would remain involved in the Shoeboots family's struggle for freedom long after the submission of this first petition.

Originally from Blount County, Tennessee, Thompson joined the American Board missionaries in the Cherokee Nation as a blacksmith for the term of one year in 1821.[49] During that year, the American Board of Commissioners for Foreign Missions determined to open a Christian school in Hightower. Considering that "a missionary blacksmith there might do much towards supporting a school," the missionaries asked Cherokee convert Charles Hicks his opinion of Thompson. Hicks told them that he would "prefer him to any he had thought of sending."[50] Thompson was likewise highly esteemed by the Boston-based evangelists. When he accepted the post at Hightower, the missionaries at the main campus of Chickamauga recorded a glowing send-off in their diary: "Br. Thompson left on this morning with his family to remove to Hightower. He goes to establish a blacksmith shop there at his own expense. . . . His steady habits, faithful Christian conduct, and devotedness to the cause which have been daily manifested since he has been employed in the mission are worthy of our imitation and although he and his family will now conduct secular concerns independent of the mission, we consider them in effect attached." When Thompson arrived at Hightower, soon to be followed by his "aged mother," wife, and sister, he faced several immediate challenges of cultural negotiation.[51] First a local elder discouraged the Cherokee town members from building a house for a blacksmith, who might well have been a "bad man." According to the mission journal, the elder relented after being assured of Thompson's upstanding qualities, and then claimed the house as the symbol of a compact between Thompson and his Cherokee neighbors, saying: "Go on—build him a good house and let this house be between you and him, for a perpetual witness of your mutual friendship." The elder is recorded as turning to Thompson and saying: "This must now be your home—you must live and die and be buried here."

Less than two weeks after Thompson's house was built, the men of Hightower planned to construct his workshop. This too created challenges, since the men had agreed to meet on a Sunday, a sacred day to the missionaries. According to the mission journal, Thompson attempted to avoid bad feelings by speaking to a local chief. Thompson reportedly refused to force his will on the men, but he also refused to participate in any activity that undermined his religious observance: "One man must not think that he would drive to direct them in their business in any aspect—they must do as they pleased; but as he knew the command of God forbidding work to be done on that day, if they came he could not assist them, or even go out to look at the work." After hearing Thompson's reaction, the Cherokee men settled on a different date, saying "they did not know it was the Sabbath."

On the Sabbath in question, Thompson received a visit from several town members who expected to hear a sermon. He informed them that he was not a proper missionary, but then proceeded to read from the Bible, using a Cherokee woman as his interpreter. According to the mission journal, "the woman who interpreted on the Sabbath was herself affected to tears. Among other things she has manifested her regard for br and sis Thompson, by giving them the loan of four acres, with young calves."[52] On the following Monday, the Cherokee men began constructing Thompson's shop. Within six months, a young Cherokee man who had been educated at the Brainerd mission school, Calvin Jones, was studying with Thompson to learn smithery. Soon thereafter, Brainerd supplied Thompson's shop with additional iron and steel.[53] On the whole, the blacksmith's relationship with the Cherokees of Hightower seemed to get off to a beneficent start, with both parties sharing a mutual regard and offering mutual support.

One year later, however, the people of Hightower were not so well pleased with William Thompson. A group of Hightower leaders accused him of overcharging for his work and of being connected to an institution—the

American Board mission—that was attempting to divide Cherokees and destroy their customs. Apparently, Thompson also had opened a tavern and had taken to entertaining white men sometime between 1822 and 1825.[54] By 1830 one influential American Board missionary, Daniel Butrick, also became frustrated with Thompson. In a missionary letter, the two men were said to be having "great and sour difficulties" stemming from "some contracts that have been made with Mr. Thompson" from which "the mission there [had] suffered considerable."[55] Thompson continued to be an active and controversial figure into the 1830s. In the period immediately preceding Cherokee Removal, he wrote angry letters to U.S. Indian agents and to the *Cherokee Phoenix,* publicizing and protesting the treatment that Cherokees were receiving. At times the Cherokee people of Hightower wanted to rid themselves of Thompson, and at other times they relied on him to negotiate on their behalf with white settlers and authorities.

Perhaps this rogue blacksmith was in the right place at the right time when Shoe Boots decided to free his children legally. Or perhaps Thompson, through a personal relationship with Shoe Boots and his family, encouraged or even pressed the decision. Thompson's influence on the creation of Shoe Boots's petition was significant and therefore presents a difficulty in distinguishing between Shoe Boots's "voice" in the letter and that of the blacksmith. Did Shoe Boots dictate the majority of the letter? Did he inform Thompson of his general wishes and leave Thompson to fill in the details? Did the two men discuss the tone of the document? A best guess might be that the letter is the result of some degree of collaboration between Shoe Boots and Thompson, with the shared goal of emancipating Shoe Boots's children.

The final product of this collaboration, a written document that functions both as a confession of illicit behavior and as a plea for leniency, is framed by the conventions of these literary forms. As a genre, the confessional not only *reveals* a person who has transgressed proper codes of behavior, but it simultaneously *constructs* that person by forcing the creation of a certain kind of speaking (or writing) "subject": one who has been "bad," who feels ashamed, and who is often seeking some form of pardon. In addition, as literary scholar David Murray has pointed out, in early American Indian writing in particular, the Indian confession has functioned as a reflection of white American's views of Native people. Giving examples of Christian Indians under the tutelage of Elizur Wheelock, founder of Dartmouth College, Murray explains that Indian confessions, many of them written by Wheelock himself and signed by the Indian in question, act as forms of institutional control and as regulators of the public image of Indians.[56] These confessions, Murray argues, in which Christian Indians admitted to inappropriate behaviors such as drinking and loitering, did double representational duty in American culture, showing Indians to be both naturally degenerate and properly repentant.

Shoe Boots's petition, written for him by a white Christian and submitted to a Cherokee governing body increasingly invested in outlawing behaviors that would be viewed as uncivilized by U.S. officials, functions similarly. To receive the favor he seeks, Shoe Boots must subject himself to institutional authorities by telling all, admitting guilt, and demonstrating contrition. Shoe Boots's petition thus uses the language of institutions—the Christian Church and the new Cherokee government—both of which exert some measure of control over him in this transaction. In the petition, Shoe Boots embodies the figure of the reprobate Indian who shows himself willing, by virtue of his confession, to reform. The confessional form of the letter may well have derived from Thompson's sense of Christian morality; at the same time it may have been used by both Thompson and Shoe Boots as a rhetorical strategy, given their awareness of the Cherokee Council's emerging antiblack political stance. Still, the negative example that Shoe Boots's written confession publicizes serves the Christian mission and Cherokee government as a warning to all others who might be inclined to engage in inappropriate sexual relations as defined by Church and state. The image of Shoe Boots that emerges in this document, then, that of a man who has "debased himself" by having sex with a black woman, displays the influence of Christian proscriptions on Cherokee sexual norms, the growing devaluation of black humanity in the Cherokee Nation, and the Cherokee government's official quest to separate out black community members—in large part because of white American dread of miscegenation and fears about black pollution. This portrait of a man shamed by sexual "sin," rooted in the transgression of racial boundaries, may or may not reveal Shoe Boots's personal views of his sexual relationship with Doll in the twentieth year of their union.

The discourse of sin, shame, and contrition that pervades Shoe Boots's petition is complicated by another discourse with tricultural meanings: that of kinship. The wording of the petition asserts and reasserts familial relationships between Shoe Boots and the Council members, his "friends and brothers," and more particularly, between Shoe Boots and his children: Elizabeth, Polly, and John. The phrase "bone of my bone and flesh of my flesh," which Shoe Boots and Thompson used to describe Shoe Boots's relationship as father to his children, would be culturally resonant and rhetorically powerful to Cherokees, for whom kinship is central, to the black community, in which kinship ties are prized and longed for amid the continual disruption of slavery, and in general to nineteenth-century America, in which a Christian sentimentalism infused popular feeling. It is probable that as a student of the Bible, Thompson advocated biblical language as a means of translating Shoe Boots's concerns about his children to the Cherokee statesmen. The phrase derives from the Christian origin myth described in Genesis, in which God creates Eve out of Adam's rib and Adam then says of Eve: "This is now bone of my bone and flesh of my flesh. She shall be called woman because she was taken out of man."[57] With this incantation, Adam makes Eve into his kin by claiming a relationship to her through a shared bodily substance. As the first man and first woman in creation, in a Christian worldview Adam and Eve are the original human family. By borrowing this language to express Shoe Boots's conception of his relationship to his children, the framers of the letter indicate feelings of deep, even primordial, interconnection and recall the sanctity of kinship within a Christian moral frame.

Though Shoe Boots was not literate in English, he may have been familiar with this biblical story from his visits to various mission churches or from conversations with Thompson or with Cherokee Christians in his community. Shoe Boots may have consented to the biblical language of bone and flesh because he believed its Christian overtones would have purchase with Cherokee leaders engaged in demonstrating how "civilized" they had become. At the same time, this phrasing may have been imbued with a particular Cherokee meaning that made it apt for Shoe Boots's situation and cause. The role of blood in eighteenth- and nineteenth-century Cherokee culture has been of keen interest to anthropologists and ethnohistorians because of its apparent centrality to Cherokee understandings of kinship, gender roles, and social relationships. In the Cherokee creation story, blood is a central theme. The origin myth tells of Selu (the Corn Mother) and Kanati (the Lucky Hunter), whose two young sons begin to wonder how their mother obtains the corn and beans that she feeds them daily. The boys follow Selu to a dwelling and secretly watch as she shakes her arms and produces corn and beans as if by magic. The boys, thinking their mother is a witch who has clouded their ability to see and think clearly, plan to kill her. Selu knows their plan before they enact it and tells her sons that after they kill her, they must drag her body across the ground.[58] Wherever her blood drops, Selu says, corn will grow to sustain her children in the future. Cherokee people as well as scholars of Cherokee life have interpreted this story, in tandem with other stories in the Cherokee oral tradition, as highlighting women's blood as generative, restorative, magical, and also dangerous. Cherokee cultural practices surrounding menstruation, menopause, and pregnancy derive from a belief in the power of women's blood.[59] Women's blood also serves an instrumental function, since it is the necessary element in the creation of Cherokee people. Anthropologists William Gilbert, Raymond Fogelson, and Circe Sturm have argued that the tradition of matrilineage among Cherokees, in which the child becomes Cherokee through his or her mother, rests on more than metaphor. In this period Cherokees believed that the blood of the mother was literally inherited by the child, and therefore that all members of a clan shared the blood of a common female ancestor.[60]

While blood has been the object of in-depth analysis in Cherokee studies, bone as a corporeal substance has attracted less scholarly notice. The reference to bone in Shoe Boots's petition, however, calls attention to a theory about the role of bone in Cherokee understandings of fatherhood. In an article about primary accounts of Cherokee gender norms, Fogelson argues that Cherokee kinship is blood centered: "For the Cherokees, kinship is literally defined as a relationship of blood." Fogelson extends this discussion of blood into a discussion of the role of bone in the moment of conception of a Cherokee child: "The Cherokee theory of procreation holds, in common with the beliefs of other Iroquoians, that the female contributes blood and flesh to the fetus, while the father provides the skeleton through the agency of sperm, which can be considered a form of uncongealed bone. The blood tie of an individual to a mother is thus regarded as a bond of living, procreative substance, not a metaphoric figure of speech."[61] Fogelson suggests here, if briefly, that there exists a physical tie of bone between Cherokee father and child. Circe Sturm cultivates the theoretical seed planted by Fogelson, adding that "the Cherokee incest taboo against marrying within the mother's clan *and the father's clan* provides some evidence that fathers may have been understood as kin, but kin of a different sort. If, as Fogelson suggests, Cherokees believed that fathers provided bone to the developing child in the form of semen, then maybe this was also another 'substance' of Cherokee kinship besides blood."[62] The combined analyses of Fogelson and Sturm indicating that Cherokee fathers may well have been kin to their offspring through bone, even as Cherokee mothers were primary kin to their offspring through blood, lends another layer of interpretation to the biblical allusion in Shoe Boots's petition. In using the phrase "bone of my bone," the letter might be read as a reference to a Cherokee understanding of kinship linking the father to the child. Making this link would have been critical to Shoe Boots's goal of seeing his children become free Cherokee citizens. For the Cherokee custom of matrilineage, combined with a new nationalism that was uneasy about blackness, would have led to a default conclusion that Elizabeth, Polly, and John were Doll's children rather than Shoe Boots's, a position that would curtail their possibilities for liberation and belonging in the Cherokee Nation.

Finally, the phrase "bone of my bone and flesh of my flesh" in Shoe Boots's letter also resonates within the cultural understandings of African American slaves for whom kinship ties were always under assault. The biblical allusion used in the petition to convey an integral relationship between Shoe Boots and his children also appears in the narrative of escaped slave Henry Bibb. When Bibb is being sold away from his wife and baby daughter, he uses the same lyrical language: "She is bone of my bone, and flesh of my flesh; poor unfortunate child. She was the first and shall be the last slave that ever I will father, for chains and slavery on this earth."[63] Bibb's reference to Genesis should not surprise, since nineteenth-century African American writers and abolitionists were well versed in Christian rhetoric and the popular sentimentalism of their day. However, as a male author whose slave narrative is unusual in its focus on familial relationships, Bibb's reiteration of this phrase in declaring his depth of feeling as father to an enslaved child is significant. That Bibb spent time as a slave among Cherokees makes his usage of this phrase all the more intriguing; perhaps his understanding of fatherhood related to bone represents a cultural borrowing or a synergy between Cherokee and African American perspectives.

The discourse of kinship in Shoe Boots's petition sounds multiple echoes, reflecting the cultural complexity of the historical time in which he submitted it as well as the increasing cultural complexity and multiracialism of the Cherokee Nation in the early nineteenth century. A unifying interpretive conclusion that can be drawn from the various uses of this phrase—from the Book of Genesis to Shoe Boots's petition to Henry Bibb's narrative—is the impulse to establish a connection of kinship across some form of culturally imposed or perceived separation. Adam reaches across the distance of sex (an understanding of male and female difference) to claim Eve as part of him. Henry Bibb proclaims his love and compassion for his daughter across the geographical distance growing between them as he is sold away, *and* across the relational distance imposed by the system of slavery that denies black men the right to father their children. And Shoe Boots bridges the distances of blood-based understandings of matrilineal kinship as well as emerging Cherokee definitions of race and blackness to claim Elizabeth, Polly, and John as his children rather than his property.

Shoe Boots's willingness to link himself to his illicit offspring in this official, public forum would have a tremendous impact not only on Shoe Boots's family but also on Cherokee legal history. His unwillingness to so claim Doll would also have lasting ramifications. For even as Shoe Boots's petition calls his children into the circle of Cherokee kinship, it abandons Doll to the margins of family and community. The letter's demeaning and dismissive reference to Doll and the intimate relationship between Doll and Shoe Boots echoes beliefs in broader American culture about black women's debased and polluting sexuality. Though the petition's rejection of Doll coincides with the Cherokee cultural understanding that spouses are not true relatives and that the husband-wife bond is relatively weak when compared to the bond between parent and child, brother and sister, and so on, Shoe Boots's ability to divorce himself rhetorically from the mother of his children signals his enduring privilege, and indeed, power, as a male slaveholder.

The petition that Shoe Boots submitted to the Cherokee governing bodies shows him to be at once advantaged and disadvantaged, entitled and constrained, by the Cherokee Nation's legalization of black exclusion and slavery. Proffering this public statement, which simultaneously maligned and protected his own family, cannot have been easy for Shoe Boots. In doing so, he made himself vulnerable to the criticism and contempt that was sure to follow from the Cherokee leaders who were his peers. Still, Shoe Boots pressed the Cherokee Nation to acknowledge Doll's offspring as free Cherokee citizens, and as it would happen, he was not alone in his challenge of state dictates. Though men like John Ridge may have applauded Cherokee "progress," many other Cherokees resisted acculturation, which in the view of some included the creation of the new republic as well as the adoption of black slavery. On the eve of the Cherokee Constitutional Convention in 1827, a man named White Path orchestrated a rebellion to contest the new government and its laws. Spurred on by the death of Path Killer, the more traditional principal chief, White Path led a group who stormed the Council chambers, denounced the government, and called for a return to previous traditions. Their protest, which was preceded by meetings in the town of Ellijay, led the General Council to pass the following resolution calling for order: "It is therefore Resolved by the undersigned that harmony and unanimity be strongly recommended to the people in supporting the public laws of the nation, and that all meetings of opposition be discouraged and the proper authorities rigidly supported in the suppression of faction and rebellion."[64] This resolution reveals not only the existence of discontent and organized protest among Cherokees but also the radical as well as continuous nature of the new system. Notions of "proper authorities" and "public laws" were departures from long-standing Cherokee customs. At the same time, however, the document shows a retention of Cherokee traditions in the midst of change, since the Council's call for "harmony" and "unanimity" points to central tenets of Cherokee cosmology.

White Path's popular resistance movement condemned the American values that the Cherokee republic seemed to accept. And according to legal historian Rennard Strickland, some proponents of the movement disavowed the legalized subjugation of blacks in the Cherokee Nation: "While the retention of tribal lands was clearly a national goal, on some issues there were wide discrepancies between the statutes enacted by the committee and council and the policy followed by the nation as a whole. Such instances illustrated the situation in which tribal values were not adequately reflected in the statutes passed by the legislative branch. There was no better example of this than the series of regulations concerning the conduct of Negro slaves owned by Cherokee Indians."[65] Strickland asserts here that the laws of the state, especially those regulating slavery, differed from the beliefs and actions of many Cherokee people. The notes of Sophia Sawyer, Protestant missionary to the Cherokees, support Strickland's assertion and even suggest that some Cherokees spoke out directly against slavery. Sawyer quoted a Cherokee interpreter as saying: "God cannot be pleased with slavery" and emancipating the slaves would be "doing right."[66] The argument that tribal values and behaviors conflicted with the state's categorization of blacks as slaves is supported by census figures. Out of the 16,542 Cherokees in the Nation in 1835, only 7.4 percent owned slaves, and the majority of these slaveowners lived in mixed-race, white-Cherokee families.[67] These census numbers are an indication both of the widening economic gap between Cherokee planters and small farmers and of most Cherokees' separation from and rejection of slavery.

Nineteenth-century Cherokee records reveal not only challenges from outside the institution of the state but also weaknesses within the system. Though Cherokee leaders in this period were diligent in their attempts to forestall Cherokee-black marriages and to exclude people of African ancestry from citizenship, they sometimes violated their own laws. A striking example is the case of Chickaua, or Molly, the black woman discussed in chapter 3 who had been adopted by the Deer Clan in the place of a murdered daughter. Chickaua's legal white owner had come to claim her, but local members of the Deer Clan refused to let her be taken, submitting a petition that asked the Cherokee government "to resist this oppression and legal wrong."[68] The clan's accusation of a "legal" wrong here seems at first unclear and unfounded, since Chickaua was indeed a black slave owned by a white woman. She did not fall into the narrow category of descent from a Cherokee woman and free black man that granted citizenship and state protection to some Afro-Cherokees. Nonetheless, the Deer Clan appealed to a long-standing tribal custom that persisted despite the apparent primacy of the Cherokee nation-state; they referenced the laws of kinship, which obligated Cherokees to protect and aid clan members in need. Regardless of constitutional law, the petitioners claimed these two slaves as relatives to whom they had an unspoken duty.

The National Council sent the case to the Cherokee Supreme Court, which on October 18, 1833, accepted an affidavit swearing to Chickaua's adoption and emancipation within the Deer Clan. Among others, the affidavit was signed by White Path, the leader of the 1827 rebellion. The court concluded, as summarized by historian William McLoughlin, that "the slave, Molly, had become a Cherokee, had always been treated as a Cherokee, and still retained the rights of Cherokee citizenship by virtue of her adoption into the Deer Clan, regardless of her race, complexion, or ancestry. By this same right, her son was also a Cherokee citizen."[69] In the end, a branch of the Cherokee government charged with upholding the constitution instead violated it, protecting the freedom and Cherokee citizenship of two black slaves. Even as Cherokee political leaders strove to exclude and subordinate people of African descent, they were bound by Cherokee tradition to make an exception in this instance. The Supreme Court judged Chickaua's case not racially, as Cherokee law dictated, but culturally, as the code of kinship required. The values of Cherokee kinship persisted beneath the overlay of race, disrupting exclusionary practices and renewing the Cherokee conscience.

The Cherokee government's willingness to act on behalf of Cherokee citizens and their black relatives can be seen in another example, which begins with a bill of sale for "a Certain boy (said to be a mulatto) slave named Moses, about ten or eleven years of age, for in consideration of the sum of one hundred and fifty dollars."[70] The purchaser was George (or

Oowanahtekiskee), Moses's Cherokee father. In a second document, dated November 11, 1822, George explained his wishes to the General Council:

> Know ye that I, George or Oowanahtekiskee, have this day appeared before the National Committee and Council, and by my own free will and choice; and actuated from the impulse of paternal affection, do hereby declare my earnest desire to emancipate the boy, Moses, which I have this day bought . . . and further do hereby claim and acknowledge the aforesaid boy to be my true and begotten son, and for the purpose of effectually securing to him the blessings and happiness of freedom, I hereby quit claim and forever relinquish all interest and demand for the sum of money which I paid for said boy, and will forever defend his freedom against the claim of myself, my heirs, and etc.[71]

The General Council accepted George's assertion of "paternal affection" and approved the emancipation of Moses.

Two years later the General Council heard a similar request from Captain Shoe Boots, and their answer reflected a continued commitment to the ethos of kinship obligations. On November 18, 1824, the Council answered Shoe Boots's petition as follows:

> The National Council has taken into consideration the petition of Captain Shoe Boots, purporting to grant freedom to his three children which he had by his *slave,* the Council therefore has no objections to recognizing their freedom, as well as their inheritance to the Cherokee Country.
>
> But it be ordered that capt. Shoe boots cease begetting any more Children by his said slave *woman* provided the National Committee will concur in this decision . . .
>
> *Concurred by the National Committee.*[72]

This disdainful reply to Shoe Boots's petition, in which the Council underlined the words "slave" and "woman" to emphasize Doll's doubly debased status, continues the objectification and ostracization of Doll—the now nameless slave mother—evident in the original petition. In vehemently forbidding the continuation of the sexual relationship, the Council indicates in no uncertain terms the seriousness of Shoe Boots's transgression. The statesmen seem to have used the occasion of Shoe Boots's petition as an opportunity to publicize its contempt for black and Cherokee "race mixing" and to single out black womanhood as a lowly identity; but despite their disapproval, the General Council members capitulated to Shoe Boots's request. The government's favorable response was in no small part due to the Council members' regard for Shoe Boots as a fellow warrior and local leader, but just as important was their shared respect for kinship responsibilities. Shoe Boots's petition reminded them of this obligation by addressing the Council members as his "friends and brothers." This idiomatic expression repeated at the beginning of many Cherokee letters to the Council was more than formula and symbolic rhetoric. Given the large size of Shoe Boots's clan (Wolf) and the tendency for every clan to be represented on the Council, some of the men who sat in judgment of Shoe Boots would have been his clan brothers. Thus, the General Council members, many of them relatives of Shoe Boots, were compelled by tribal values to act on behalf of Shoe Boots's children.

They did not, however, wish to continue granting citizenship to black slaves, even those of Cherokee ancestry. In an attempt to foreclose future possibilities for Cherokee and black "intermarriage" that might place them in a similarly awkward position, the General Council passed the following act on November 11, 1824, three weeks after receiving Shoe Boots's petition and one week before ruling on it:

> Intermarriages between negro slaves and indians, or whites, shall not be lawful, and any person or persons, permitting and approbating his, her or their negro slaves to intermarry with Indians or whites, he she or they, so offending, shall pay a fine of fifty dollars, one half for the benefit of the Cherokee Nation; and . . . any male Indian or white man marrying a negro woman slave, he or they shall be punished with fifty-nine stripes on the bare back, and any Indian or white woman, marrying a negro man slave, shall be punished with twenty-five stripes on her or their bare back.[73]

Given that the Cherokee General Council passed an act banishing free blacks from the Cherokee Nation on the same day, this law in effect outlawed all black-Cherokee marriages. The few exempted from this law would have been individuals like Elizabeth, Polly, and John and Chickaua/Molly—all of whom had received freedom and citizenship rights through special acts of government. Despite the best attempts of Cherokee lawmakers to limit Cherokee intermarriage with blacks, these individuals would marry non-black Cherokees, and they and their children would be among the first to occupy a new legal status of free Afro-Cherokee people who enjoyed full citizenship rights.

The surprising outcome of Shoe Boots's appeal shows the continuing contradictions that characterize the history of this family. Elizabeth, John, and Polly could not claim Cherokee clan membership, and therefore citizenship, through the traditional means of asserting maternal clan or being adopted. For them the ironic merger of Cherokee traditions and Anglo-American cultural ways is what made acceptance possible. The children were granted Cherokee citizenship not through the recognition of matrilineal descent but through the recognition of their Cherokee patrilineal descent. As it happened, the same body of laws that had narrowed the definition of Cherokee citizenship when it came to black people had broadened that definition when it came to patrilineality. In a revision of matrilineal kinship norms, the Cherokee Constitution had included the children of Cherokee men and nonblack, free women as members of the Nation. This shift in legal categorization, together with Shoe Boots's assertion of a kinship of the bone (or father as kin to child), converged to benefit his offspring. The children of Shoe Boots and Doll slid into citizenship through a loophole within a loophole, claiming a right to Cherokee belonging at the crossroads of culture change. This dialectic of race and kinship would continue to influence the family's future, even as it reflected a broader pattern of transformation and contestation within the Cherokee populace, as women and men, planters and hunters, red and black, recalled and reenvisioned what it meant to be Cherokee.

SEVEN

Gold Rush

The beautiful and beloved country of the Cherokees is now passing to the occupancy of the Georgians. The drawing of the lands and Gold mines of the Cherokee continues to be prosecuted with vigour, under the authority of the enlightened and christian Governor of Georgia. . . . The Cherokee country is now wedged with settlers, and droves of land hunters, to which the Indians cry daily, and it is literally Robery! Robery!

ELIJAH HICKS
Cherokee Phoenix (1833)

The Georgians are coming, oh ho! oh ho!
The Georgians are coming, oh ho! oh ho!
The Georgians are coming
With roaring and humming
And cruiskin's with rum in, oh ho! oh ho!

Cherokee song (1830s)

SHOE BOOTS HOPED TO PROTECT HIS OFFSPRING in the event of his death by appealing to the General Council for their freedom. And five years after altering the course of his children's lives, Shoe Boots did die, "at the Thompson Ferry on the Hightower River."[1] The announcement of his passing was published in the *Cherokee Phoenix* newspaper on November 11, 1829, by John Ridge and Thomas Woodard, a mixed-race Cherokee of white ancestry and a nephew of Shoe Boots.[2] As executors of Shoe Boots's estate, Ridge and Woodard announced the procedure for all claims and debts: "Notice, To all whom it may concern, that, the undersigned having been appointed Administrators on the estate of Shoe Boots deceased, we hereby notify all persons indebted to the estate to come forward and make payment, and all persons having claims against the estate to present them for payment within twelve months."[3]

Shoe Boots's three eldest children were legally free and no longer considered part of their deceased father's estate, but their mother was still enslaved, as were the newest additions to their family, little brothers William and Lewis, who had been born just a few years earlier. Because these two boys had not been listed in Shoe Boots's petition of 1824, they were not protected by the Council's act of emancipation and citizenship. And so it seemed that the fate Shoe Boots had feared for his eldest children, that they would be "divided among the Best of [his] friends," could befall instead his youngest sons.[4] A statement made by John Howard Payne indicates that Doll herself led the charge to fight the impending sale of her children: "The dark faced one (the servant woman daull) endeavoured to make interest with the general council for the emancipation of twins, born after the death of their imputed father." (Though Payne says the twins were born after Shoe Boots's death, a nephew of Shoe Boots's later testified that the boys were born well before Shoe Boots passed away.)[5] However, the Cherokee legislature's proceedings on the twins' case lists only two people as the initiators of the freedom suit: Shoe Boots's two sisters, Peggy and Takesteskee.[6] We cannot know what happened behind the scenes when the frightful news of the twins' fate reached the women on Shoe Boots's farm. It is quite possible, as Payne indicates, that Doll initiated the challenge and enlisted the aid of Cherokee citizens to speak on her behalf. It is also possible that Peggy and Takesteskee were outraged at the turn of events and needed no urging to become involved. Whatever the women's discussions entailed that day, the result was a bold plan. The two sisters, probably with Doll's backing, took the family's case straight to the Cherokee lawmakers.

Cherokee records provide scant information about Shoe Boots's sisters. At least one, and possibly both of them, lived on Shoe Boots's farm and would likely have worked with Doll ever since her arrival thirty years prior. The sisters would also have known their brother's children well and would have seen William and Lewis grow from infants to boys of approximately five to six years—their age at Shoe Boots's death. Beyond the real likelihood of loving attachment between the aunts and their young nephews, Peggy and Takesteskee's willingness to act on behalf of their brother's children would have been in accordance with Cherokee cultural understandings. Brothers and sisters shared an extremely close tie in Cherokee families. The kinship responsibilities between paternal aunts and their nieces and nephews were therefore strong; in the absence of the father, it became the duty of his sisters to protect his children. Breaking down Cherokee kin relationships, anthropologist William Gilbert explains: "The paternal aunt is always accounted a person to whom the highest respect is paid [by her nieces and nephews]. She is just like a father. She protects and looks after her brother's offspring whenever necessary. She accounts her brother's children just as important as her own children."[7] Peggy and Takesteskee must have taken this cultural prescription to heart, leading them to intervene on their nephews' behalf.

The moment when the aunts petitioned the Cherokee government to free their young nephews is one of the most arresting in this family's saga. Not only did three women cross boundaries of race and caste to work together in an imminent crisis, but they also brought what they knew would be an unpopular issue to a governing body controlled by male slaveholders. In a period when Cherokee women had circumscribed political power and black people had none at all, it is remarkable that Peggy, Takesteskee, and Doll almost succeeded in their attempt. The National Council voted to free the boys, but the National Committee refused to concur. It may not surprise that the town-elected National Council supported the request while the small, select governing body of the National Committee rejected it. The National Committee wrote in their succinct response: "The Petition of Peggy and Ta, ke, ste, skee—sisters of the late Capt. Shoe Boots, of High Tower, praying the General Committee to grant the freedom of two boys, Billy and Lewis, said to be children of the said Capt. Shoe Boot, by a black woman of his, and granted by the Council, was received and read. After some enquiry and remarks by the members, the question was taken whether the house should concur with the Council and decided in the negative, Timson only in the affirmative."[8] Though the Committee's rejection does not detail the content of their "enquiry and remarks" or the reasoning behind their decision, it seems likely that they considered their 1824 order that Shoe Boots end the affair with Doll and their 1824 law outlawing Cherokee-black intermarriage fair warning of their views. In addition, the petition submitted by Cherokee women at a time when no woman could serve as a political representative or hold public office would be less compelling than that of a male military captain and local chief. In his interpretation of the Committee's response, Payne sympathizes with the lawmakers and attributes their rejection to their desire to protect the memory of one of their own: "The

National Committee refused to entertain the petition, and would not suffer any more of such black spots to rest upon the memory of their departed and lamented Warrior and Friend."[9]

While John Ross, John Ridge, and other members of the National Committee acted, in Payne's estimation, to preserve Shoe Boots's memory, Doll, Peggy, and Takesteskee struggled to safeguard his children's future. And soon the women would discover that the emancipation of William and Lewis was just one of many worries; for in the space of a year, the fate of the older children had shifted from one of security to one of alarming vulnerability. The legal emancipation of Elizabeth, John, and Polly had been a tribal action, sanctioned and preserved by the Cherokee national government. But in 1829 the episode that has been called the first gold rush in American history erupted in Cherokee country. After the discovery of gold in Cherokee territory, the governor of Georgia, already incensed at the Cherokee adoption of a constitution, made the unprecedented move of extending Georgia's legal jurisdiction over the Cherokee Nation and annulling all Cherokee laws. As far as Georgia was concerned, the Cherokee government no longer existed, and Cherokee people were subject to the mandates of the southern state. This action would be challenged and legally overturned by the United States Supreme Court in 1832, but in the meantime, Georgia politicians enforced the takeover with military might. Cherokee country was now occupied territory, patrolled by officers of the Georgia militia and peopled by an influx of white settlers and gold seekers.[10]

In the midst of Georgia's occupation, the Cherokee Nation spun into chaotic disarray. Once-powerful leading men found themselves powerless to protect their country; ordinary men and women were threatened, attacked, and expelled from their homes; and missionaries who protested Georgia's action were arrested and jailed by the state militia. The *Cherokee Phoenix* reported regularly on the extreme levels of disruption and injury. In Shoe Boots and Doll's hometown of Hightower, the Georgia Guard stormed the mission and arrested William Thompson when he "refus[ed] to relinquish his houses into the hands of the guards." Editor Elias Boudinot explained in his dispatch: "It was very currently reported that the Guard intended to seize the property of such white men as would not take the oath of allegiance [to the state of Georgia]. . . . Now possession has actually been taken of a missionary station. . . . We know not what is to come next." Around the same time, also in Hightower, a Cherokee youth named Joseph Beanstick was arrested under false pretenses in the "war-like irruption into Hightower of a band of Militia."[11] Cherokee women were especially vulnerable in the presence of the state military. The *Phoenix* warned: "Cherokee Women, Beware. It is said the Georgia Guard have received orders, from the Governor we suppose, to inflict corporeal punishment on such females as shall hereafter be guilty of insulting them."[12] Two years after this warning was posted, a Cherokee woman brought suit in the Georgia courts against a Georgian sheriff and colonel, David Duke, for battery and attempted rape against her and her friend. The judge refused to rule on the case, since it was illegal for Cherokees to offer testimony in the Georgia courts.[13] When the *Cherokee Phoenix* reported the incident, Boudinot was placed under house arrest on the charge of libel, leading to the suspension of the paper and a turnover in editorship.

In addition to arresting and harassing members of the Cherokee populace, the Georgia Guard raided for slaves. For black people, the most unprotected class in the Cherokee Nation, the terror must have been raw. They were as valuable to the Georgian invaders as land and gold, and just as likely to be stolen. Many of them had lived with white masters before entering Cherokee territory, and although wealthy Cherokees had virtually replicated American slavery by 1830, these slaves would have dreaded returning to their previous owners. One ex-slave of Creeks recalled years later in a WPA interview: "I was eating out of the same pot with the Indians while they [slaves owned by whites] were still licking their masters' boots in Texas."[14] Blacks viewed enslavement by Indians as the lesser of evils, and for slaves who were related to Cherokees and who could expect some protection from their kin, the evil was lesser still. For the marauding Georgians, though, all blacks were fair game, whether they were slaves, free, or Cherokee citizens.

In the early summer of 1830, Elizabeth, Polly, John and their mother, Doll, found themselves running for their lives as Georgia guardsmen hunted them down. On June 12 of that year, the *Cherokee Phoenix* reported: "We are told three Georgia officers were the other day about Hightower, hunting some negroes, Belonging to Shoe Boot's estate, but they were obliged to return without a booty. A forged deed of gift is the foundation of the claim."[15] And so it seemed that the suspicious deed of gift signed by Shoe Boots back in 1809 had resurfaced after his death to sink his family back into slavery. Though the federal Indian agent had invalidated that deed, and the children had since been emancipated by the Cherokee government, Georgia's takeover had voided those actions. Any challenge to the deed of gift would now have to be launched in the Georgia state courts, in which neither blacks nor Cherokees could testify. With excellent timing, the white intruder named Wofford, who had masterminded the original scheme, reemerged to claim his "gifts." Though Wofford's first attempt to seize the family was unsuccessful, he later captured and enslaved them. According to Payne, "Wofford found that by this the resolution of the Council freeing the slave children of Shoe Boots was of no effect. He came back to the nation, armed with the authority of his deed. . . . The emancipated children were kidnapped and taken to Georgia. One of them (John) escaped, but the rest remained in the clutches of the Adventurer."[16]

In written historical accounts of Shoe Boots's life, this is where the story ends. Shoe Boots is dead, and all but one of his children are enslaved. Even William and Lewis, who had gone to live with Peggy and Takesteskee, are said to be the slaves of the aunts who had tried to free them. William McLoughlin closes his account of Shoe Boots's story thus:

> The boys remained the slaves of Shoe Boots' sisters. Shortly after this, a white man appeared in the nation and claimed that Chulio [Shoe Boots] had given him a deed for all his property. He took the three oldest children by Daull away with him, saying that by state law their black ancestry made them slaves for life no matter what the Council had voted. One boy, John Shoeboot, escaped and returned to the nation. Chulio's sisters brought suit for return of the other two, but there is no evidence that their release was ever obtained.[17]

This tragic conclusion to the tale is contradicted, though, by the second act in the Shoeboots family drama that began in the tumultuous 1830s and extended into the eras of Cherokee Removal and the American Civil War. This second act is the story of Shoe Boots and Doll's children, who continued to resist enslavement with the aid of relatives and friends and continued, through the creation of new families, to test the meanings of Cherokee kinship and citizenship.

At the end of 1830 Doll and her daughters were living among the slave population in Georgia, and their future looked bleak. The girls had lost their freedom, Doll had lost the relative security that being Shoe Boots's "wife" had afforded her, and all three had lost contact with the boys in the family. John had run away from his would-be captor, and the twins, who had once seemed safe with their aunts, were now separated as well. At the age of sixty-seven William Shoeboots would recall that he was separated from his elder siblings and that his twin brother was snatched away from him, never to be seen again: "Lewis, my brother, had been stolen and carried off. I don't know what ever became of him after that."[18] Dispersed and lost to each other, Doll and her children had little hope of gaining their freedom and returning home to the community of Hightower. Not only had the Cherokee Council banned escaped slaves from Cherokee territory, but Shoe Boots's cabin and land would have been inaccessible to his black family. As Rennard Strickland explains, in the Cherokee Nation of the nineteenth century, "illegal Negro-Indian marriages prevented inheritance by children of such unions, since property could only descend to 'lawful children.' Negroes were considered property and were generally prohibited from inheritance of other property."[19] Despite the fact that their father owned a comfortable farm, Shoe Boots's children, if defined as the offspring of an illegal union, could be homeless if they returned to Cherokee country.[20] Indeed, during their short absence, another family had settled on Shoe Boots's homestead: in 1832 a Cherokee couple named Edward and Elizabeth Bean lived there briefly before eventually emigrating to Arkansas.[21] And in a further complication, Cherokee territory was no longer governed by Cherokees in the chaotic 1830s. It had been commandeered by the state of Georgia in the takeover of Cherokee affairs that had made the family vulnerable to reenslavement in the first place.

Doll and her children must have felt utterly abandoned, powerless in their position as slaves in exile. But soon they would discover loyal allies in the Cherokee Nation. Though information about Doll and her children in the 1830s is scanty, it is clear that their friends and relatives did not desert them. After kidnapping the family, Wofford was compelled to appear in court to verify the validity of his deed. The catalyst behind Wofford's subpoena seems to have been a suit brought by William Thompson, the missionary blacksmith who had probably assisted Shoe Boots in writing the petition for his children's freedom in 1824. It is likely that Shoe Boots's sisters, Peggy and Takesteskee, were involved in contesting the theft of their brother's family as well, and may even have requested Thompson's aid in the matter. According to Payne, "to confirm his title, Wofford went to law. He lost his cause, but appealed. If he gains in the appeal, he swears he will possess all the family, even the one that escaped. The case is still before the Georgia Courts."[22] In the repeated challenge to Wofford's claim, Shoe Boots's family and community members demonstrated a commitment to fighting for their loved ones' welfare. Wofford apparently became so overwhelmed with the legal battle that he sold the family members off.

While the neighborhood blacksmith came to the aid of Doll and the children, one of the administrators of Shoe Boots's estate, Thomas Woodard, played a lamentable role in the sale and dispersal of the family. His duty was to protect Shoe Boots's interests, which in an emerging paradigm of patrilineal inheritance would include securing the welfare of Shoe Boots's nuclear family. But the task of defining Shoe Boots's family, along with greed buoyed by prejudice, presented Woodard with a dilemma. Shoe Boots's "black" family was now deemed "illegal," a fact that he could easily take advantage of. And Woodard, Shoe Boots's own nephew, chose to define Doll and the children as property rather than kin. He acquired his cousin Elizabeth from Wofford and later sold her to another Georgia citizen named George Lavender.[23] He also obtained possession of little William, one of the twins.

Elizabeth, now a mother, had passed through the hands of three masters, two of them white, one of them Cherokee. She was a slave for nearly five years before Thompson was able to secure her freedom. By February 1837, Thompson had reached an agreement with Lavender to purchase Elizabeth, called Lizza, and her small child for the price of $2,000. The stated purpose of the agreement was "to put her in possession of her freedom."[24] Meanwhile, Doll and William found themselves back in the Cherokee Nation, occupying peculiar positions in the home of John Ridge, the second administrator of Shoe Boots's estate. In the account of a Cherokee man who knew the Ridges, there was a "black woman who board[ed] with Maj[or] or Jno Ridge by the name of 'Dolly.'" William Shoeboots said of his own history: "I stayed with Jno Ridge after my father died—No others of my brothers or sisters stayed with Mr. Ridge."[25] Through an unrecorded chain of events, Ridge obtained the release of Doll and William and installed them in his home. Though certainly a better advocate than Woodard had been, Ridge seems not to have known how to handle a case in which the estate's property and the deceased's beneficiaries were one and the same. Rather than freeing Doll and William outright, he took on the role of pseudoguardian, allowing them to live with him while maintaining the distinctions of race and status. Doll seems to have played a role akin to slave in the Ridge household, charged as she was with the care and service of Ridge's elderly mother. A former slave of the Ridges remembered that "the mother of [William] Boots lived with old Mrs. Ridge."[26] Another Cherokee man attested: "I always understood that she [Doll] was a slave of Mrs. Ridges; that was the common report."[27] William, however, seems to have enjoyed a more privileged status in the Ridge home, probably because of his Cherokee parentage, youth, and gender. Those who knew the Ridges did not label William a slave, and his stay with John Ridge was understood to be temporary. According to the Ridge slave quoted above, "John Ridge taken William Shoeboots to keep until he was of age."[28]

Thus, Elizabeth's mother and younger brother were living within the borders of the Cherokee Nation when Elizabeth managed to return home, a free woman once again. Despite antimiscegenation laws that did not recognize Afro-Cherokees as Cherokee citizens, Elizabeth seems to have received a warm welcome. The promise that Shoe Boots had obtained from Council members guaranteeing his children's "inheritance to the Cherokee Country" was literally realized, and Elizabeth inherited the family farm.[29] Her boon was certainly in part due to the fact of her Cherokee citizenship, which would still have been respected by Cherokees, despite Georgia state's attempt to nullify the Cherokee Nation. Perhaps her paternal aunts or family friends like William Thompson or even John Ridge had intervened on Elizabeth's behalf.[30] However it came to pass, in 1836 "Lizza Shoeboot" was listed as head of household of a sizable farm on the Etowah River.[31] Elizabeth was now worth more than $1,000, an amount that could have purchased her freedom while she was a slave in Georgia. Though $1,000 is modest in comparison to the vast wealth of some Cherokee slaveholders, it was a small fortune next to the poverty of many Cherokees and black women in Cherokee country. At the age of twenty-nine, Elizabeth could claim ownership of the following property, recorded by agents of the Bureau of Indian Affairs:[32]

Dwelling House	$200
kitchen	$30
Stable	$20
[Corn]crib	$10
35 acres of imp[roved] land @$10	350
21 peach trees @1.50	31.50
17 apple $3.00	51.00
	$692.50
Rent Out 35 acres imp[roved] land 3yrd @$4	$420

Elizabeth's ability to inherit marks a continuity of tribal and geographical belonging between Cherokee father and Afro-Cherokee child. At the same time, it marks her difference from most other black women in Cherokee territory, including her mother, Doll. In comparison to them, Elizabeth was fantastically privileged: free, propertied, and a Cherokee citizen. And yet her capture, enslavement, and untold sufferings must have remained open wounds for Elizabeth, who continually moved between privilege and disadvantage. In an increasingly well-defined hierarchy of race in the Cherokee Nation, Elizabeth's position was unstable; she was Shoe Boots's child, but also Doll's, and she lived out the legacies of both.

Elizabeth Shoeboots's complicated state of affairs invites comparison to free women of color in the white slaveholding South. Cases like hers, in which a mixed-race slave child benefits materially from her master/father's status, are not restricted to Indian country. Most notable in the white South is the story of Amanda America Dickson, a slave conceived through the rape of her mother by the master's son. Amanda's mother, Julia, is said never to have forgiven the rape by David Dickson, even as she became involved in a long-term sexual relationship with him. Amanda, the offspring of that union, was her father's only child and the "pet" of his household.[33] Despite the legal protest of white relatives, Amanda became the richest woman in Hancock County, Georgia, when she inherited the bulk of her father's $700,000 estate in 1887. Though miscegenation was prohibited in Georgia and called into question the legality of Amanda's very existence, she retained her father's property by verdict of the Georgia Supreme Court.

Amanda Dickson was shielded from the full impact of her racial status by her relationship with a rich and powerful white man. As her biographer, Kent Leslie, puts it, "her personal identity was ultimately bounded by her sense of class solidarity with her father, that is, by her socialization as David Dickson's daughter."[34] Though Dickson took care publicly to obfuscate his relationship with his black slave and their child, in the privacy of his home he ensured that his daughter enjoyed the privileges of her economic class. While a young child and legal slave, Amanda's duties were slight. She tended to the needs of her white grandmother, to whom she was close. After her grandmother's death Amanda studied with tutors, dressed like a southern lady, and married a white Confederate soldier—her father's nephew.

Sexual liaisons such as the one between David Dickson and his slave, Julia, were grudgingly tolerated in white southern society, but open acknowledgment of familial relationships between white parents and "mulatto" children was deemed socially unacceptable. It was one thing to have a black sex partner whose inferior status was clearly maintained, but quite another to welcome black offspring into the privileges of white society. Still, for slaveholding men in the South, the power to write rules in accordance with their will also gave them the power to bend those rules to their desire. As long as David Dickson was discreet and publicly upheld the values of white manhood and supremacy, he could sire a black child, raise her in his home, and make her rich with virtual impunity. Leslie explains: "A person who had the legal power to beat another human to death, to sell other human beings, to separate husbands from wives, and to separate mothers from children might be motivated by lust, affection, or his or her own ego to transcend the South's ethical code of honor. These autocrats were sometimes able to use personal relationships in an organic society and a web of economic obligations to confound the very system that had empowered them."[35] Of the many white men who fathered children by slave women, a minority provided for their offspring, setting those children apart from the majority of slaves who enjoyed no privileges of wealth, status, or racial indeterminacy that would mitigate their oppression. In the white South, as in Cherokee country, exceptions were made to the sanctioned rules of race.

If the rare enslaved woman of color in white society could at times enjoy this type of privilege, how unique was it, in the broader context of American slavery, for exceptions to be made to the racial order in Indian country? Does Elizabeth's inheritance and the experience of Shoe Boots's children say anything qualitatively different about slavery in America, or does it merely confirm that slavery was unpredictable in any location and, in Leslie's words, that "boundaries of race were unsustainable"?[36] The relationship of Amanda's and Elizabeth's mothers to the racial status quo in their respective communities suggests an uncomfortable correlation between the white South and Cherokee South. In both cases, a black woman remains enslaved and vulnerable, even as she engages in a long-term sexual relationship with her master. Neither Julia Dickson nor Doll were freed along with their children, and neither mother had legal claim to their late partners' estates. In both the Euro-American and Native American contexts, sexual relations between nonblack free men and black slave women, disparaged though quietly tolerated, were transgressions of the status quo. In both communities, black women retained a subjugated status complicated by the limited and discreet privileges that accompanied concubinage. The experiences of Elizabeth and Amanda seem alike as well in that they were exceptions to the racial status quo. Despite their race, both daughters were recognized by their fathers' communities as eligible to inherit the family's property.

As similar as these scenarios may seem, however, cultural particularities embedded in each render them distinct. The bases on which these women could claim a unique status from other blacks differed markedly. Amanda America Dickson won her case to receive the inheritance spelled out in her father's will because of the centrality of property rights in Euro-American culture. David Dickson, being of sound mind, had dictated who should fall heir to his property. In a nation built on the sanctity of private property rights as a core component of citizenship, this was a sacred act. Though Amanda's white relatives charged that antimiscegenation laws rendered her claim invalid, the court refused to dismiss the importance of her father's legal decree. The judge in the first case instructed the jury: "To set aside a will because it is capricious or unreasonable, or because the testator may have selected an unworthy object for the bestowal of his bounty would be to deprive him of the right secured by law to dispose of his estate by will in such a way as may seem good in his own eyes. . . . Every man in this state has the right to will his property to whom he pleases." The Georgia Supreme Court supported this decision on appeal, relying on the Fourteenth Amendment to conclude that "no state interest had primacy over property rights, not even the issue of 'racial purity.'"[37]

As indicated by the courts' interpretation of the case, the close paternal relationship between David Dickson and his daughter was not a decisive factor in the rulings. In fact, Dickson's special care of Amanda and long-term sexual relationship with Julia jeopardized Amanda's chances. Her lawyers, the administrators of her father's estate, argued that Dickson had *not* shown special favor to Julia or Amanda and that he had always treated them as slaves, because familial affection had to be *disproved* for Amanda to be successful. Ironically, to achieve a favorable outcome in this case it was better for Amanda to have been conceived through rape than through an intimate relationship between her white father and black mother. For if the white family members had proven that David Dickson showed affection to a black woman and her child, he would be judged unsound of mind and unduly influenced by (treacherous) Negro women, thus rendering his will invalid. In essence, to care for black people was thought to be so unnatural for a white man that evidence of such behavior would indicate insanity or lack of self-possession. As Amanda's lawyers made their case for a relationship of apathy between Dickson and his black family, they called to the stand prominent members of white society who had visited Dickson's home to prove that the visitors had witnessed no racial misconduct. In one exchange the lawyer asked:

Had you known that David Dickson was living with a negro strumpet who not only permitted him to have access to her person but negroes and white men, and that he was in the habit of kissing and hugging this negro strumpet, and that he was in the habit of kissing and hugging those negro children, would you have carried your wife to visit his house if you had known these things?

Well, sir, I don't think I would.[38]

To be considered sane in the eyes of whites, David Dickson had to have been a cold-hearted man who used a black woman for sex and then discarded her and her child. Sentiment and the value of familial relationships had to be put aside for Amanda to secure her father's estate. Amanda prevailed not because she was an accepted member of the Dickson family, but because a white man had written a will that was upheld by the courts.[39]

In contrast, Elizabeth Shoeboots's inheritance rested on an enduring Cherokee respect for kinship ties and recognition of familial obligation across racial lines. Shoe Boots's petition for his children's freedom, in which he openly claimed Elizabeth as daughter, was the foundation of her successful inheritance. The National Council's response that granted freedom and citizenship to Elizabeth and her siblings recognized that with Cherokee citizenship came a communal right to the Cherokee homeland, or "inheritance to the Cherokee Country." Though Shoe Boots's will is not on record among the documents of the Cherokee Nation or Cherokee Indian Agency, his desire to have Doll's offspring recognized as his children and as Cherokees was respected even after his death. The question of individual property rights was not the issue of weight. Rather, the key to Elizabeth's inheritance was the acknowledged relationship between father and child. Because Shoe Boots claimed her as kin, Elizabeth was Cherokee. Because Elizabeth was Cherokee, she and her siblings were entitled to their father's home in the Cherokee Nation.

In Cherokee country kinship mattered, even as racial designations wended their way into law. As Strickland has argued, Cherokees did not simply and wholly reproduce laws that originated in white culture. Instead, they shaped, interpreted, and enforced the laws in (sometimes veiled) accordance to Cherokee values: "The Cherokee legal experience illustrates that it was, in fact, possible to create Indian versions of white ways. The result, however, was not what 'civilizers' had expected."[40] Historian Mary Young has contended similarly that Cherokees were "subjects, rather than objects, of cultural change."[41] Indeed, one unexpected dimension of slavery in

Cherokee country was the propensity of long-standing family norms to disrupt the legalized slave system. Native people in the Southeast viewed kinship, not freedom, as the antithesis of slavery.[42] In the Cherokee understanding, to be kin meant being human, and to be human meant being free.

After her release from bondage in the mid-1830s, Elizabeth Shoeboots sought to restore her ravaged family. She gathered those siblings she could locate and became, according to a Cherokee man who knew her, "the head of the family." In the words of this witness, "Lizzie Boots, Polly Boots, John Boots, [William] Boots the above named family all lived together previous to the emigration."[43] Elizabeth must have visited with her mother and brother William often, since she lived just thirty miles from the Ridge estate. John, who had escaped from Wofford in 1830, may have lived down the road from Elizabeth. Though John Shoeboots's exact whereabouts are unclear from the records, a man named John is listed in the Cherokee Census of 1835 and described as owning eight acres on the Etowah River in 1836.[44] By this time, John Shoeboots was married to a Cherokee woman called Conmenoula, who was described by an associate and former slave as a "full blood Indian," "dark skinned" with "long black hair."[45] The couple had one child, whom they named Mary.[46] The Shoeboots family continued to grow as Elizabeth married a "fullblood" Cherokee man named Ferguson (or Ohkilunakah) and had her second child with him.[47]

It seems that life should have been good for Elizabeth, or at least better than it had been. In a sharp reversal of fortune, she had moved from being counted as property to owning property herself. And as a free, propertied woman in the Cherokee Nation, Elizabeth enjoyed privileges that enslaved African Americans did not. Being Afro-Cherokee in the microcosmic world of Cherokee life was a decided advantage over being a black slave in that world. At the same time, though, being Indian in America, and especially in the Southeast of the 1830s, was a sure disadvantage. Elizabeth had escaped slavery in the white South only to find herself ensnared in a morass of anti-Indian prejudices and policies. In effect, as a woman of both African and Cherokee descent, Elizabeth lived between a rock and a hard place. The multiple racial categories that described her in nineteenth-century Georgia made her vulnerable to exploitation and abuse, though often in varying degrees and in differing ways. Georgia sentiment and law assumed that the natural and morally defensible state of black people was slavery, which perpetually exposed Elizabeth and other free people of color to reenslavement. At the same time, Georgians defined free people of color as a threat to the slave system and attempted to legislate their political impotence and eviction. Fearful that free blacks would incite those still enslaved, the state regulated the manumission of slaves, required free blacks to register and later expelled them, and supported the colonization movement that would send them "back" to Africa. At the same time, Georgia resented Indians and their occupancy of valuable lands and ridiculed the right of Cherokees to govern their own nation. The state of Georgia had acted on this conviction by illegally assuming jurisdiction over Cherokee territory, a maneuver that had devastating effects on Elizabeth as a Cherokee and as a black woman.[48]

Elizabeth could be alternately defined as black, Cherokee, or a free person of color to suit the needs of the state and its white citizens. In the trial for Elizabeth's emancipation, the Georgia courts described her both as "a yellow girl" and "the above niggra Lizza."[49] Her Cherokeeness and Cherokee citizenship went unnoted, presumably because her evident blackness and state of enslavement negated those aspects of her personhood. Furthermore, since southerners no longer systematically enslaved Indians, acknowledging her Cherokee citizenship could have caused additional legal problems for her enslavers. However, in the evaluations of Cherokee property conducted by the War Department's Bureau of Indian Affairs as a precursor to Removal, Elizabeth is listed along with other Cherokees. Here her blackness is neither noted nor alluded to. In this context, if she had been identified as black, ejecting her with the Cherokees might have posed logistical problems that could have slowed the Removal process. The varying labels used to describe Elizabeth in government records of the period point to the manifold political and economic aims that were served by classifications of racial difference. Positioned within and between multiple oppressed identities, Elizabeth Shoeboots was vulnerable to the very worst of state and federal mandates, including the loss of home and land that she would soon suffer on the Cherokee Trail of Tears.

PART TWO

———

Of Blood and Bone

Freedom, Kinship, and Citizenship——West

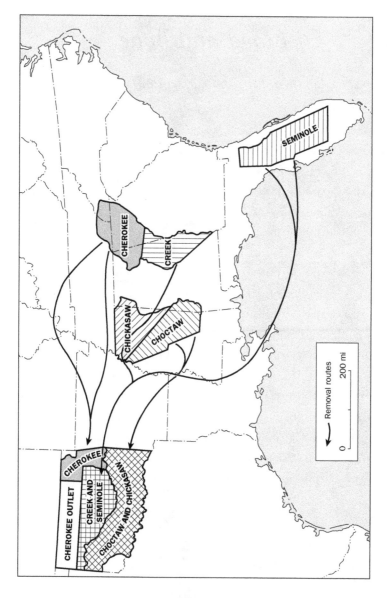

Map 3. Locations of the Five Tribes before and after removal, from Theda Perdue, *Nations Remembered* (Norman: University of Oklahoma Press, 1993). Used by permission of the University of Oklahoma Press.

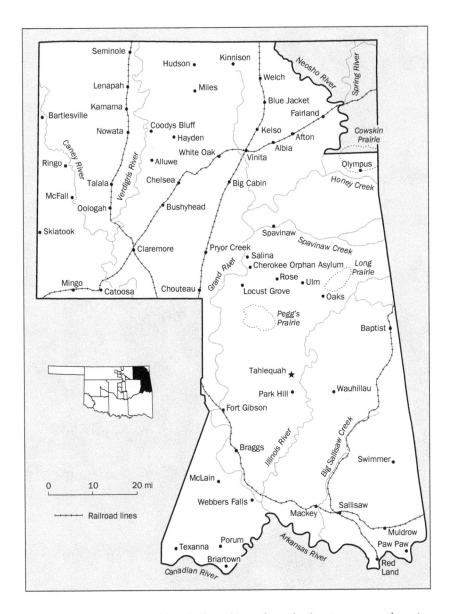

Map 4. Honey Creek, Webbers Falls, Tahlequah, and other important places in the Cherokee Nation, Indian Territory, from John W. Morris, Charles R. Goins, and Edwin C. McReynolds, *Historical Atlas of Oklahoma,* 2d ed. (Norman: University of Oklahoma Press, 1986). Used by permission of the University of Oklahoma Press.

EIGHT

Removal

Baby Suggs grew tired, went to bed and stayed there until her big old heart quit. Except for an occasional quest for color she said practically nothing—until the afternoon of the last day of her life when she got out of bed, skipped slowly to the door of the keeping room and announced to Sethe and Denver the lesson she had learned from her sixty years a slave and ten years free: that there was no bad luck in the world but white-people. "They don't know when to stop," she said.

TONI MORRISON
Beloved

The people of the United States permitted their President to sink the Cherokee ship at one blow of his mighty breath to its fly-colors, regardless of the Government laws, expressly enacted for their protection, but the bane did not stop here: we ask the American reader where is the stopping place.

ELIJAH HICKS
Cherokee Phoenix

ELIZABETH SHOEBOOTS WAS THE HEAD OF HER HOUSEHOLD, the mother of small children, and a survivor of enslavement. She was also among the thousands of Cherokees who faced the rude awakening of Indian Removal. Twice she was forced out of her home, made to recover and rebuild, first at the hands of slavecatchers and then at the hands of American soldiers. The expulsion of the Cherokees from the Southeast had its foundation in an illegal compact. In 1802 the U.S. government entered into an agreement with the state of Georgia, promising to expel the Indians in the state's territory in exchange for Georgia's relinquishment of particular lands in the West. Over the ensuing twenty-five years, Georgia argued that the federal government was failing to fulfill this compact. Though the Cherokees did cede thousands of acres during these years, they still occupied lands that Georgia claimed. The ratification of the Cherokee Constitution in 1827 further incensed Georgia officials, who insisted that the notion of a sovereign Cherokee republic violated the state's rights to certain lands. Georgia then extended its jurisdiction into Cherokee territory, annulled Cherokee laws, and insisted that any white people in the Cherokee counties of the state of Georgia must seek the state's permission to remain there. The U.S. Supreme Court cases *Cherokee Nation v. Georgia* (1831) and *Worcester v. Georgia* (1832) developed in response to Georgia's action of incorporating the Cherokee Nation. The Supreme Court decided in favor of Cherokee semisovereignty, defined as "domestic dependent nation[hood]" and deemed Georgia's action illegal. However, the outcome of the 1828 presidential election, won by celebrated Indian fighter Andrew Jackson, would render the Supreme Court decisions ineffectual.

A longtime and vehement proponent of Indian relocation, Jackson refused to enforce the Supreme Court's rulings and instead defended the state of Georgia. Jackson's first State of the Union address in December 1829 outlined a plan for Indian "removal" and urged Congress to enact it through legislation. This would be a national policy, affecting not only the Cherokees and other southeastern nations but also nations in the Midwest. Jackson argued in his address that the fact of American progress was to be commended, not regretted: "Philanthropy could not wish to see this continent restored to the condition in which it was found by our forefathers. What good man would prefer a country covered with forests and ranged by a few thousand savages to our extensive Republic, studded with cities, towns, and prosperous farms, embellished with all the improvements which art can devise or industry execute, occupied by more than 12,000,000 happy people, and filled with all the blessings of liberty, civilization, and religion?"[1] In Jackson's view, the removal of eastern Indians to a region west of the Mississippi was "not only liberal, but generous." They would be isolated and protected from the white man's influence, and their cultures would be better preserved. In the end, Jackson argued, this move West would be beneficial to the Indians, the impetus and opportunity for positive development:

> Doubtless it will be painful to leave the graves of their fathers; but what do they [do] more than our ancestors did or than our children are now doing? To better their condition in an unknown land our forefathers left all that

was dear in earthly objects. Our children by thousands yearly leave the land of their birth to seek new homes in distant regions. Does humanity weep at these painful separations from everything, animate and inanimate, with which the young heart has become entwined? Far from it. It is rather a source of joy that our country affords the scope where our young population may range unconstrained in body or in mind, developing the power and faculties of man in their highest perfection. . . . Can it be cruel that this Government when, by events which it can not control, the Indian is made discontented in his ancient home to purchase his lands, to give him a new and extensive territory, to pay the expense of his removal, and support him a year in his new abode? How many thousands of our own people would gladly embrace the opportunity of removing West on such conditions![2]

Jackson's address launched heated debates in the House and Senate. Supporters of the Cherokees and Indian tribes, such as missionary Jeremiah Evarts (whose pen name was William Penn) and journalist John Howard Payne, vehemently protested removal. In one of his famous William Penn essays, Evarts argued: "The American Indians, now living upon lands derived from their ancestors, and never alienated nor surrendered, have a perfect right to the continued and undisturbed possession of these lands. . . . These rights of soil and sovereignty are inherent in the Indians, till voluntarily surrendered by them; and cannot be taken away by compacts between communities of whites, to which compacts the Indians were not a party."[3] Nevertheless, the final votes in Congress favored the Indian Removal Act, with numbers as close as 28 to 19 in the Senate and 102 to 97 in the House. On May 28, 1830, Jackson signed the act into law.

Cherokee political leaders followed these developments closely, reprinting the congressional debates in the *Cherokee Phoenix* and writing articles in defense of Cherokee sovereignty. Cherokee people without official positions of leadership also protested and debated the issue. In October 1831 a delegation of Cherokee women appeared before the National Council to urge resistance to the new law. They asserted in their petition: "We believe that the present plan of the General Government to effect our removal West of the Mississippi, and thus obtain our lands for the use of the State of Georgia, to be highly oppressive, cruel and unjust. And we sincerely hope there is no consideration which can induce our citizens to forsake the land of our fathers of which they have been in possession from time immemorial, and thus compel us, against our will, to undergo the toils and difficulties of removing with our helpless families hundreds of miles to unhealthy and unproductive country."[4] John Ross, principal chief of the Cherokee Nation, agreed with the women, as did the majority of Cherokees. By 1833, however, a minority faction of Cherokee leaders began to advocate removal. They argued that it could not be prevented, and thus it was in the best interest of the Cherokee people to accept the inevitable and negotiate a favorable treaty with the United States.

The leaders of this proremoval group were Major Ridge, his son John Ridge, and his nephews, Elias Boudinot and Stand Watie, friends and business partners of Shoe Boots. As internal dissension grew among Cherokees, the United States and the state of Georgia increased their pressure. In 1834 the federal government ceased payment of monies to the Cherokees that were their right by treaty, and in 1835 the state of Georgia enlisted the Georgia Guard to seize the Cherokee printing press and thus disable the publication of the *Cherokee Phoenix*. In the autumn of 1835, U.S. officials took advantage of the opportunity that Cherokee discord presented. They met with members of the minority faction and their supporters, numbering almost two hundred in all, in the capital town of New Echota. There the members of this faction, that came to be known as the Treaty Party, signed the Treaty of New Echota, a document that sanctioned Cherokee removal in accordance with the Indian Removal Act and established that removal must occur within two years of the treaty's ratification. The Treaty of New Echota was blatantly fraudulent, since it bypassed the recognized channels of Cherokee government and lacked the support of the majority of the Cherokee population, numbering almost sixteen thousand. However, despite vehement Cherokee protests that included a petition of fifteen thousand signatures, the treaty was ratified by the U.S. Congress in 1836.[5] Most Cherokees refused to believe that this was their fate: to be moved West, the direction that signified darkness and death in Cherokee culture, and to be forced into an unknown land against their will. For the next two years the majority of Cherokees continued to fight removal through political protest and the defiant act of living in their homeland. In 1838, when the designated two-year period had ended, they were pressed to abandon that land by force of arms.

If slavery is the monumental tragedy of African American experience and the trauma of continual return in the memory of black people, then removal plays the same role in American Indian experience. The theft and destruction of lives, lands, and cultures link these events as holocausts, and in the specific context of Cherokee history, slavery and removal are intimately connected. The expulsion of Cherokee people cleared the way for the expansion of American slavery into those abandoned lands; the expansion of slavery then contributed to the rapid growth of cotton production that would dramatically boost the U.S. economy. At the same time, the presence of black slaves during removal made it possible for their Cherokee masters to survive the ordeal and to rebuild efficiently in the West. The institution of American slavery depended on Cherokee removal, even as the "success" of removal depended on slavery. The experience of Elizabeth Shoeboots and her family members, then, for whom slavery and removal were conjoined forces, in fact reflects a broader phenomenon. Ironically, or perhaps not, this historical moment, which so clearly revealed the interdependence of white supremacist systems, marked a negative turning point in relations between blacks and Cherokees. Removal would open a seemingly unbridgeable gulf between Cherokees and blacks because it exacerbated preexisting tensions and prejudices even while eliminating the historical bases of communication and negotiation.

Forced removal was carried out summarily by the U.S. military and the local Georgia militia, with little regard for Cherokee dignity or life. On May 10, 1838, General Winfield Scott, the executor of removal, issued a warning to the Cherokee people: "My troops already occupy many positions . . . and thousands and thousands are approaching from every quarter to render assistance and escape alike hopeless. . . . Will you, then by resistance compel us to resort to arms . . . or will you by flight seek to hide yourself in the mountains and forests and thus oblige us to hunt you down?"[6] Women, children, and the elderly were rousted out of their cabins and directed at gunpoint by soldiers. Men were yanked from the fields, with many unable to locate and join their disheveled families. Forced to leave most of their possessions behind, the Cherokees were sometimes present as white Georgians immediately took ownership of their cabins, looting and burning cherished objects. Daniel Butrick, a missionary of the American Board, summarized the scene in his journal: "Women absent from their families on visits, or for other purposes, were seized, and men far from their wives and children were not allowed to return, and also children being forced from home, were dragged off among strangers. Cattle, horses, hogs, household furniture, clothing and money not with them were taken and left."[7] One Georgia militiaman who was present reported: "I fought through the civil war and have seen men shot to pieces and slaughtered by thousands, but the Cherokee removal was the cruelest work I ever knew."[8]

According to a high-ranking officer, by June 1838 the fields and hills, valleys and riverbanks that Georgia claimed were now free of Cherokees. General Charles Floyd, a Georgia militia member in command of Cherokee expulsion from the state, reported to the governor on a job well done: "Sir: I have the pleasure to inform your excellency that I am now fully convinced there is not an Indian within the limits of my command, except a few in my possession, who will be sent to Ross' Landing tomorrow. My scouting parties have scoured the whole country without seeing an Indian, or late Indian signs. If there are any stragglers in Georgia, they must be in Union and Gilmer counties, and near the Tennessee and North Carolina line; but none can escape the vigilance of our troops. Georgia is ultimately in possession of her rights in the Cherokee country."[9] Being captured and commanded against their will were only the first traumas of the Cherokees' removal experience. Like captive Africans awaiting the slave ships or Japanese Americans during World War II, Cherokee people, numbering almost fifteen thousand, were loaded into "stockades," or concentration camps, until the appointed time of their departure.[10] There, crowded together in makeshift shelters in the moist summer heat, many fell ill. Though General Scott had planned for the expulsion of the Cherokees by steamboat in the summer, the heat was intolerable, and Chief John Ross requested permission for the remaining Cherokees to organize their own removal in the cooler autumn weather.

That next fall, the Cherokees divided into thirteen groups of nearly one thousand people, each with two appointed leaders.[11] They set out on multiple routes to cross Tennessee, Kentucky, Illinois, Missouri, and Arkansas at ten miles a day with meager supplies. Among these groups were black people and black-Cherokees, slave and free, who traveled with the Cherokees to remain near relatives, to escape enslavement in the white South, and to serve their masters. Whites who had married Cherokees as well as white missionaries like Butrick also made the journey. At certain points along the way, the straggling bands of travelers were charged fees by white farmers before they could cross privately owned land. The few wagons available to them were used to carry the sick, infants, and the elderly. Most walked. They walked through the fall and into the harsh winter months, suffering the continual deaths of loved ones to cold, disease, and accident. White Path, leader of the Cherokee rebellion against the new constitution back in 1827, became deathly ill during the march. According to an article in the

Kentucky Gazette, dated November 1838, "White Path ha[d] been in the last stages of sickness for many days and ha[d] to be hauled and [was] helpless." He died on the Trail at the age of seventy-five.[12] Quatie Ross, wife of Principal Chief John Ross, also lost her life en route to Indian Territory. Rebecca Neugin, a small child at the time of removal, recounted her family's experience to historian Grant Foreman in 1932:

> When the soldiers came to our house my father wanted to fight, but my mother told him that the soldiers would kill him if he did and we surrendered without a fight. They drove us out of our house to join other prisoners in a stockade. . . . My father had a wagon pulled by two spans of oxen to haul us in. Eight of my brothers and sisters and two or three widow women and children rode with us. My brother Dick who was a good deal older than I was walked along with a long cow whip. . . . My father and mother walked all the way also. . . . There was much sickness among the emigrants and a great many little children died of whooping cough.[13]

Butrick, who continued to keep a journal during the march, also recorded in entry after entry the increasing rates of illness and death.

For those Cherokees who owned or had access to black women and men, the harsh impact of removal was blunted. In addition to bearing the hardships of the journey, slaves were enlisted to do the additional work of hunting for their masters, nursing the sick, preparing meals, guarding the camps at night, and hiking ahead of the group to ensure passable roads.[14] Butrick recorded in his journal the labors and deaths of a handful of blacks in his detachment. One elderly black woman, whose children had recently purchased her freedom, "died in the camps." Her son, Peter, and his wife were then sold to slave speculators. Along the Trail, one black man "cut some wood for the night," and a black woman, "our kind Nancy," was "employed . . . to wash and [dry] our clothes in the evening by the fire." An unnamed black man died on a February day that also took four Cherokee lives: "During this time five individuals have died, viz. one old Cherokee woman, one black man, and three Cherokee children, making in all since we crossed the Tennessee River 26 deaths."[15] Many people lost their lives during the Cherokee removal, and scholars attempting to count those deaths have estimated four thousand. Historian and demographer Russell Thornton has argued that this figure is much too low. He in turn has offered his own estimate, which takes into account not only actual deaths but also the loss in population that resulted from a decline in the birthrate. Thornton estimates that the total Cherokee population loss due to forced removal was more than ten thousand people.[16]

Describing Cherokee removal by way of miles and deaths captures the quantitative hardship of the incident but misses its psychological and spiritual reverberations. In her novel *Pushing the Bear,* Cherokee poet Diane Glancy has reframed this event by imagining the inner journeys of those who walked. Glancy constructs a multivoiced history by weaving together the threads of diverse experiences. She balances the voices of Maritole, a young Cherokee woman and the main character of the novel, with Maritole's family members, Cherokee Christians, traders, elders, and spirits. Excerpts from historical documents such as property claims and government reports are also woven into the text, creating a narrative that is layered and expansive. Unlike Andrew Jackson's representation of removal as an improving exercise, Glancy depicts the affair as a nightmare. In Glancy's portrayal the walk West is a life-stealing march, which Maritole describes in the bleakest of terms: "We were marching west toward darkness, toward death. . . . The cold sat upon my bones. It was as though I had no clothing. It was as though I had no skin. I was nothing but a bare skeleton walking the path." Maritole's brother, Tanner, renames the Trail of Tears to express the reality of spiritual and physical death, saying, "Behind us for a hundred miles stretched the trail of ghosts of our dead ones."[17]

Glancy articulates the injustice of removal by underscoring the significance of place for the Cherokees, the relationship between land and identity. For at the center of the removal tragedy is the deep and life-sustaining relationship between Cherokee people and their land. So central is the land to this story that it becomes a character in Glancy's rendering, materialized by the maps that begin each chapter and by the words of the Cherokee characters. The use of maps in the book that trace the route of departure allows for the visual reenactment of displacement, even as it unmasks the force behind removal, since early maps were both expressions and tools of European colonialism. The conceptualization of the natural world as voiced by the characters emphasizes the importance of the land base depicted in the early maps, the homeland that is being left behind. In one instance while the people are walking the Trail, a holy man tries to comfort them by reciting the cure for lost voice: "These (five barks) cure them with: Cherry, a small acorn oak, flowering dogwood, bitter apple, big (white) willow." The other characters respond anxiously: "'What if those trees don't grow outside Cherokee land?'" and "'What if the words only work on land where we were born?'"[18] The intimate relationship, even union, of land and people is reiterated in a recurring and mutating phrase spoken by various characters in the novel: "we were the land."

As the families, friends, and neighbors of Glancy's imagination drag themselves across an unforgiving country, they consistently invoke their homeland, its places and stories. While Maritole tries to soothe an ailing friend, she whispers, "The old land won't leave us, Luthy. We carry it within us wherever we're going."[19] But even as the characters invoke their old home, they are desperately aware of their loss. One woman thinks to herself, "I felt a grief so deep it was nearly silent. We were the land. The red clay people with mouths that would talk. Sometimes I even thought I could hear the hens cackle on my farm. I looked over my shoulder. If only I could listen hard enough." The alienation the characters feel as they travel further from their homeland is exemplified in Maritole's dream of an empty landscape: "In the nights my spirit walked a slick road. I dreamed all the land was white as the inside of an apple. It would never be anything but white."[20]

As the characters in *Pushing the Bear* march from their home place to an unknown place, they wonder how a people can survive apart from their land when the people *are* the land. The conceptual framework introduced in Glancy's novel allows us to understand that Indian Removal was more than the relocation of bodies and possessions. It was the tearing of the flesh of the people from the same flesh of the land, a rupture of soul and spirit. This rupture contributed to the deterioration of tribal well-being, as factionalism and civil war fractured the Cherokees in the West. Concurrently, removal created a legacy of detachment between Cherokees and blacks that would lessen potential for cross-racial alliances and narrow the possibility of subverting racial hierarchies. In the Cherokee Nation West, the treatment of slaves became harsher and more rigid, since much of the flexibility that had endured in the East was extinguished by law.

Key to making sense of the decline in relations between Cherokees and blacks in the West is Glancy's paradigm of place. For Cherokees and other Native peoples, place was paramount in maintaining cultural values and moral relationships. Displacement, therefore, was likely to weaken those values and relationships. Removal separated Cherokees and blacks from the ground where they first encountered one another and developed bonds, and thus it damaged ties of connection that were inscribed and reinforced in the landscape. In their studies of place and its meanings for human societies, geographers David Lowenthal and Kenneth Foote have addressed the meaning and resonance of homeland. Lowenthal notes, in exploring the phenomenon of homesickness, that the intensity of a people's relationship to their homeland is due in part to the fact that the history of the people is tangible in the terrain.[21] Similarly, Foote explains that "the physical durability of landscape permits it to carry meaning into the future so as to help sustain memory and cultural traditions."[22]

Deriving meaning and tradition from the land is especially important to American Indian people, the only population indigenous to the United States. Land, specifically homeland, sustains Native identities and values, not just because it is the place where the people eat and sleep, but because it is a repository of the people's cultural ways, beliefs, and histories. Laguna Pueblo writer Leslie Marmon Silko explains in an essay titled "Interior and Exterior Landscapes: The Pueblo Migration Stories" that tribal stories hold the people's communal identity and are themselves held in place by the land. Each story is connected to a specific location in the Pueblo homelands, and a story is recalled when a person comes across a geographical marker that corresponds with that tale. In this intimate relationship between story, identity, and place, the earth itself sustains and reinforces who the people are.[23] N. Scott Momaday intimates a similar relationship in his personal, family, and tribal memoir, *The Way to Rainy Mountain*. Here he journeys through Kiowa history and culture in fragmentary episodes that intertwine landmarks, stories, and personal revelations. In his introduction to the book Momaday captures the ability of a geographical feature, in this case Rainy Mountain, to mark and contain the history of a people and thereby to restore personal and community life. Toward the conclusion of the book Momaday dwells on the indescribable and boundless power of place and the necessity for people to be in close relationship with the land: "Once in his life a man ought to concentrate his mind upon the remembered earth, I believe. He ought to give himself up to a particular landscape in his experience, to look at it from as many angles as he can, to wonder about it, to dwell upon it. He ought to imagine that he touches it with his hands at every season and listens to the sounds that are made upon it. He ought to imagine the creatures there and all the faintest motions of the wind. He ought to recollect the glare of noon and all the colors of the dawn and dusk."[24]

Anthropologist Keith Basso also explores this relationship to homeland illustrated by Silko and Momaday. In his work with the Western Apache, Basso has found that landscape plays a profound role in reinforcing their identity and regulating group morality. Basso explains that one category of

Western Apache stories, which he terms "historical narratives," are told to discourage unacceptable behavior and to set the listener on a path of self-correction and self-renewal.[25] These stories, cautionary tales that depict a person doing something wrong and that warn of the negative consequences of his action, are always tied to a location where the original event is said to have taken place and always include the name of that place within the narrative structure. The listener, the target of such a story, is moved to change through the sting and shame of rebuke. When a person who has been the target of an historical narrative passes by the location where that story took place, she is reminded of her mistake and encouraged again to live right. Often historical narratives are imparted to a younger person by an older relative, so that the stories are imbued not only with the lesson and location of the original event but also with the spirit and memory of the teller: "Apaches view the landscape as a repository of distilled wisdom, a stern but benevolent keeper of tradition, an ever-vigilant ally in the efforts of individuals and whole communities to put into practice a set of standards for social living that are uniquely and distinctively their own."[26]

In a sense these stories live in the land, since the landscape holds them steady and brings them to mind in the service of the people. It follows, then, that Western Apaches view the land as an enduring protector of community values. As Basso puts it, "grandmothers and uncles must perish but the landscape endures, and for this the Apache people are deeply grateful." One Western Apache man, Nick Thompson, made a blunt and evocative statement: "The land looks after us . . . the land keeps badness away." For Western Apaches, memories of community values are embedded in the land, and separation from that land leads to forgetfulness, transgression, and trouble. As Basso explains, "losing the land is something the Western Apache can ill afford to do, for geographical features have served the people for centuries as mnemonic pegs on which to hang the moral teachings of their history." The power of homeland and consequences of separation from it are not unique to Western Apaches. For Native people across a range of tribes, epistemologies and moral codes are tied to landscapes and places.[27]

Indian Removal disrupted the relationship between Cherokees, their homeland, and the stories that lived there. As a result, the cultural values embedded in those stories could no longer be reinforced through the visible markers of place. The two hundred years of history that Cherokees had shared with Africans in the Southeast would also have been inscribed in the landscape. Family and community memories involving black friends and relatives would have been marked and recalled by the locations where significant events happened; a Cherokee story about the effects of displacement serves as a metaphor for this connection between human relations and terrain. In "The Removed Townhouses," Cherokee people are separated from their relatives, first by the spirit world and then by federal removal policy. This story was recorded by ethnologist James Mooney between 1887 and 1890 in his meetings with Cherokee oral traditionalists in North Carolina:

> Long ago, long before the Cherokees were driven from their homes in 1838, the people on Valley river and Hiwassee heard voices of invisible spirits in the air calling and warning them of wars and misfortunes which the future held in store, and inviting them to come and live with the Nunnehi, the Immortals, in their homes under the mountains and under the waters. . . . The people were afraid of the evils that were to come, and they knew that the Immortals of the mountains and the waters were happy forever, so they counciled in their townhouses and decided to go with them. . . . They are there now, and on a warm summer day, when the wind ripples the surface, those who listen well can hear them talking below. When the Cherokees drag the river for fish the fish-drag always stops and catches there, although the water is deep, and the people know it is being held by their lost kinsmen, who do not want to be forgotten.
>
> When the Cherokees were forcibly removed to the West one of the greatest regrets of those along the Hiwassee and Valley rivers was that they were compelled to leave behind forever their relatives who had gone to Nunnehi.[28]

"The Removed Townhouses" tells of the sad end to a relationship that was already compromised by difference—the difference between the human world and the spirit world. The people on the Hiwassee and Valley Rivers were separated from their relatives because those relatives had joined the immortals. Still, the two groups were able to communicate through the river that linked them across that difference. Leaving the Cherokee homeland during removal meant severing that connection. In the new place, there would be no Hiwassee River, no historical landmark to serve as a repository of memory and a medium of communication.

The deterioration of relations between Cherokees and blacks postremoval can be understood in similar terms. Cherokees and blacks were already separated in the Southeast by the breach of race, as Cherokees began to own slaves and to codify racial definitions and hierarchies. At the same time, though, individuals belonging to these groups were connected through the places where they lived together. Like the river in the story, those places could serve as channels for connection and negotiation. Removal meant tearing the people—Cherokee, black, and Afro-Cherokee—away from those places, thus cementing the distance between them. History has not recorded the many events, weighty and whimsical, that took place between Doll, her children, and other Cherokees who lived on the Etowah River. We do know, however, that the river would have served as a marker of those events, a reminder of the relationships that were born and nourished there. Relationships, like stories, belonged to places and were held fast by them. With the loss of those places, fragile relationships were left vulnerable to deterioration.

The despair that characterized the new western communities in 1840, along with an emerging culture of disconnection from the past, made it easier for some Cherokees to adopt Euro-American values to the detriment of the black people living among them. The ties of kinship, respect, and affection between Cherokees and individual blacks who had survived the early stages of slavery were weakened by the division of Cherokees from their homeland. The places where blacks and Cherokees had raised families together were now behind the state lines of Georgia and Tennessee. In a new landscape devoid of embedded mutual memories, the people were separated by a cavernous divide of race and caste.

The beleaguered Shoeboots family, along with many others, made this journey of no return. Doll went West before her daughters, transported by flatboat and steamship, with Major and Susannah Ridge and their slaves. In 1838 Elizabeth and her sister, Polly, walked the Trail of Tears with their young children and relatives. All crossed into another world. The Drennen Roll of 1851, which catalogs the Cherokees who emigrated during forced removal, lists Elizabeth and Polly side by side, each followed by the names of their dependents:

Lizzy Boot, Ail-se, Sally, Lotty, Morrison, Dahsegahyahge

Polly Boot, Mireah, Eliza Hammer, Louisa, Lizzy, Mary, Chahwahyoocah[29]

Uprooted from the Etowah River in the Cherokee Nation East, what would become of their family in the Cherokee Nation West?

NINE

Capture

While they generally accepted as citizens of their nations those blacks who were related to them by blood, they refused to give them full rights and privileges, such as holding public office. Those not related by blood were tolerated but legislated against, and for the most part, the Indians would rather have been rid of them.

DANIEL F. LITTLEFIELD AND MARY LITTLEFIELD
"The Beams Family"

I was born after the War, about 1868, and what I know 'bout slave times is what my pappa tole me. . . . Pappa named Charley Nave; mamma's name was Mary Vann before she marry, and her pappa was Talaka Vann, one of Joe Vann's slaves down around Webbers Falls. My father was born around Tahlequah just about where the colored church stands on depot hill. . . . I wasn't scared of them Indians for pappa always told me his master, Henry Nave, was his own father; that make me part Indian.

CORNELIUS NEELY NAVE
Cherokee freedman

IN THE WINTER AND SPRING OF 1839, Elizabeth and Polly Shoeboots dragged themselves into present-day Oklahoma with other Cherokees who had resisted removal. The land they entered was not empty, nor was it solely theirs, since two groups of Cherokees had previously settled in the northeastern corner of Indian Territory. To avoid white encroachment, a band known as the Old Settlers had traveled from the Southeast to present-day Missouri, Arkansas, and finally Oklahoma between 1794 and 1820.[1] This group, which came to be called the Western Cherokee Nation, governed itself by a loosely constructed ethical code that bore little resemblance to the elaborate constitution developed by the Eastern Cherokees. Cherokees who had been members of the Treaty Party were also settled in, having moved West soon after the ratification of the Treaty of New Echota. These families had chosen the fertile lands alongside waterways, leaving the leftovers to the straggling new arrivals. Political order began to disintegrate as Cherokees from the West and East, the Treaty Party and the Ross Party, wrestled over jurisdiction and authority. The Western Cherokee Nation, which had the support of the Treaty Party, and the Eastern Cherokee Nation, which opposed the Treaty Party, convened in uneasy councils to declare the need for unity, only to separate again into vitriolic factionalism.

Amid political instability, the last Cherokee emigrants took up residence within the prescribed four thousand square miles, east and north of the Creeks, Choctaws, and Seminoles, who also had been removed. Previously a nation with territory spanning several states, the Cherokees now occupied the northeast corner of a single Territory. Though the federal government had set aside 5 million acres for the tribe, most of that land was off-limits to settlement and unsuitable for farming. A significant portion of the new territory was open, arid prairie land, a stark contrast to the lush hills and ample rivers of Georgia, Alabama, North Carolina, and Tennessee. Federal Indian Agent John Jones filed this report: "At least two-thirds [of the 5 million acres set aside] are entirely unfit for cultivation. A large share of the tillable land is of an inferior quality. Most of the tillable land is entirely worthless, even for timber, as it consists of stony ridges and valleys covered with a scrubby growth."[2] If the western land seemed ungenerous to the new arrivals, so too did the U.S. government. The payments the Cherokees were due to receive for their eastern lands held in common and for their individual improvements of those lands were slow in coming. The sojourners were destitute, with little means of feeding themselves or of providing shelter for their extended families. With weary bodies and sparse supplies, they strung together shacks, cleared fields, and planted seeds in the bristly ground. They waited for the crops to grow while begging provisions from Arkansas traders, promising to repay their debts with future government money. Poor, hungry, sick, and mournful, most struggled to survive.

Their material poverty was only one facet of the emigrants' misery. They were also battered by psychological upheaval, engulfed by emotional despair. Their familiar homes, beloved lands, and guiding principles seemed far away, and relations between community members were steadily deteriorating. The anchors of place, morality, and custom that previously had regulated social behavior were giving way to turmoil. In the assessment of Theda Perdue, "the Cherokees no longer felt that they controlled their own destiny, and a sense of rootlessness and the feeling that life had little meaning pervaded the Nation."[3] The tribe was coming undone.

In this vacuous West, economic divisions and class resentment intensified. Here the poor were very poor, and the rich very rich, since personal advantages made all the difference in people's early success. The upwardly mobile Treaty Party members had moved West first, settled on the richest lands alongside waterways, and ensured the growth and consolidation of their wealth. The affluent slaveowning Cherokees, including supporters of removal as well as dissenters, had at their disposal a portable labor force with which to rebuild and reinvest their fortunes. John Ridge, a principal Treaty Party leader, had moved his family and slaves in 1837. His improvements were worth almost $20,000 before removal, and he safeguarded his assets by choosing to resettle near his father in the fertile Grand River valley nestled below the foothills of the Ozark Mountains.[4] While many late-removing Cherokees faced "scrubby growth" upon arrival, John Ridge and Major Ridge settled on Honey Creek, a beautiful and abundant site. Ridge's biographer, Thurman Wilkins, says of their arrival: "The Ridge's party arrived in time to see the bottomlands aflame with redbud that ranged from pink through crimson on to purple. Dogwood, too, bloomed in cascades gleaming white, and fragrant wild plum blossoms glowed along the courses of small streams. Honey Creek, they found, was aptly named."[5]

While their compatriots struggled to eat, these families flourished in a market economy driven by slave labor. Their robust crops, salt mines, and trading posts quickly appeared as if out of thin air.[6] For Major Ridge, whose preremoval improvements were valued at $24,000, transforming the new land for productive use simply meant directing his eighteen slaves. Wilkins writes of Major Ridge's early success in the Indian Territory: "The Ridge put his blacks to work, bought stock and farming equipment, and soon had the beginnings of a splendid farm." These well-positioned Cherokees quickly learned to expand their application of slave labor, making the herding of livestock a profitable endeavor and investing in the purchase and operation of steamboats.[7]

Within five years of removal, nearly three hundred moneyed, mixed-race Cherokee-white families constituted an elite and distinguished class. Of this group William McLoughlin writes:

> Some of them had plantations 600 to 1,000 acres and cultivated wheat, cotton, corn, hemp, and tobacco; most had large herds of cattle and horses. They owned 25 to 50 slaves; several owned over 100. . . . Some in this elite

were merchants, traders, or businesspeople with important sources of credit. Several owned steamboats that carried surplus cotton, corn or tobacco to markets in St. Louis and New Orleans and brought back manufactured goods—iron, cook stoves, farm machinery, dry goods, rugs—which they advertised for sale in the *Cherokee Advocate*. Some became horse traders or supplied cattle for eastern cities, and some were slave dealers.[8]

According to a former slave owned by Cherokee elites, the steamboats that McLoughlin describes as delivering cotton to New Orleans returned from those trips with "lots and lots of slaves from Louisiana."[9] The contrasting poverty of most Cherokees fueled internal resentment, which had at its root a criticism of the apparent ethos of the elite. Many Cherokees disparaged the rampant accumulation of wealth and the exploitation of slave labor exhibited by the propertied and the rich, defining these behaviors as antithetical to traditional Cherokee values.[10]

These economic and cultural divisions created an ironic situation for the Shoeboots family. Elizabeth and Polly, free Cherokee citizens, were likely impoverished and struggling in the West. Like other Cherokees forced to remove, they would have been unable to bring many of their possessions with them and awaited the payment of federal annuities. Meanwhile, their mother, Doll, and younger brother, William, who had not been freed by Shoe Boots or accepted as Cherokee citizens, had their basic needs met while occupying an ambiguous position in the households of Major and John Ridge. William, who had lived with John Ridge since Shoe Boots's death, had also traveled West with him: "I came to this country with the Ridges as did my mother 'Dolly' . . . my mother and myself remained with Jno Ridge, on Honey Creek."[11] While William was apprenticed to John Ridge's brother-in-law "to learn the carpenters trade" and then to another man "to learn the blacksmith trade," Doll worked as a personal servant to Mrs. Ridge.[12] Their circumstances, though unenviable because of their lack of free choice, would have been materially superior to Elizabeth and Polly's, both of whom had children of their own and few resources in those early postremoval years.

Even as the gap between rich and poor was widening in the West, old political conflicts were erupting. Supporters of John Ross felt betrayed by the members of the Treaty Party who had sanctioned removal, and they set out to punish the prominent treaty signers one by one. The avengers met in secret council, tried the accused in absentia for breaking an 1829 law against the sale of tribal lands, and dispatched vigilante posses. Fanning out across the dusty territory, the tightly organized bands located John Ridge, Elias Boudinot, and Major Ridge at their homes, businesses, and on the roads. On June 22, 1839, the avengers struck, executing the accused men in full view of family members and passersby.[13] Doll and William Shoeboots may well have been among the witnesses, since they were living and working in the Ridge home at the time of the attacks. William wrote of this episode: "My mother and myself remained with Jno Ridge on Honey Creek . . . until he was killed—I was about grown when Jno Ridge was killed."[14] Though distressing to Cherokee community members, the vengeance murders were not unexpected. John Ridge and his father had predicted that the people's rage would be directed against them. Back East, John Ridge had said of himself, speaking in the third person: "You say John Ridge signed his death warrant when he signed that treaty, and no one knows it better than he."[15]

Stand Watie, a Treaty Party member who had been warned in time to escape, emerged as the new leader of the party. The younger brother of Elias Boudinot, Watie was a wealthy man in his own right, and he would later emerge as the only Indian general of the Confederate forces and the second-to-last southern general to lay down arms in the Civil War. Though Watie successfully escaped his would-be assassins, the murder rate multiplied in Cherokee country as Treaty Party members sought revenge against Ross's supporters. Before long, focused political violence spawned random violence as gangs of outlaws began terrorizing communities. The Cherokee Nation West was riddled with dissension, studded with violence, and sickened by communal decay. Even the general election of 1843, which brought the Ross Party into the majority as political office holders, could not quell the disquiet. Outlaws and vigilantes continued to act at will, killing thirty-three people between 1845 and 1846.[16] Black slaves were often caught in the crossfire of political conflict when opposing party members targeted one another by stealing or killing the slaves of their enemies.

As geographical, social, and moral boundaries fluctuated, the task of making distinctions between Cherokees and blacks became important to Cherokee political leaders. Not only had the U.S. War Department issued a directive that the Cherokees not allow their territory to become a haven for escaped slaves, but there was also a deepening acceptance of slavery as a justifiable and profitable institution.[17] The value of slaves had increased markedly in this new context, resulting in a harsher, riskier, and more restricted existence for all black people. Cherokee leaders reinstated and strengthened the Eastern Cherokee slave code, once again outlawing Cherokee-black intermarriage and property ownership by slaves. The Cherokee rape law that had once included equal protection for all women and equal punishment for all men now distinguished between Cherokees and blacks, adding to the original clause: "Upon the conviction of any negro for the aforesaid offense against any free female, not of negro blood, he shall suffer death by hanging."[18] Now black male slaves could be put to death for rape—unless the victim was a black woman. The revised slave code also included new prohibitions. It forbade teaching slaves to read and write, required slaves to carry a pass while traveling, and discouraged the emancipation of slaves by making former owners responsible for freed people's actions.

As new uses for slave labor increased the hunger for human capital, slave trading became a lucrative business. The desire for slaves was so insatiable in Indian Territory and in Arkansas Territory to the south, that any black person, slave or free, became fair game for capture and sale. The illegal theft of black people proliferated in the unstable political environment, putting free blacks and Cherokee people of African descent in perpetual jeopardy.[19] Black children were especially vulnerable to abduction by roving criminals and traders. Madison Gerring, an infamous white outlaw who went by the nickname "Mat," was seen with his Cherokee associates, members of the Starr family, as they "pushed themselves into the negro houses of Elizabeth Peck, and kidnapped a couple of negro children, and stole two mules." Reports like this one appeared regularly in the *Cherokee Advocate* of the 1840s, and letters between wealthy slaveholders depicted their anxious desire to recoup stolen slaves or to replace them with newly purchased bondspeople.[20]

Even as the Cherokee elite acquired more and more slaves, they worried about the increasing number of blacks in their midst over whom they had no control. Runaway slaves from the American South were making their way to Indian Territory, believing it to be a sheltered location. Nearby Seminole slaves enjoyed a remarkable degree of autonomy and traveled into the Cherokee territory at will, setting what was viewed as a negative example of license and brazenness for Cherokee slaves.[21] The *Cherokee Advocate,* which began publishing in 1843, deplored the inundation of loose blacks: "Our country is traversed by a number [of slaves] who have escaped from their rightful owners; either of the Nation or the State or the Creek country, we have every reason to believe. Some of these have become associated with the band of Seminole slaves under the guardianship of Gen. Jessup— and the mere fact of being thus protected, has infused into them a spirit which leads them with the most bare faced impunity to trespass upon peaceable Cherokees."[22] The newspaper urged slaveowners to control their slaves, advocating stringent measures. In 1853 the editors advised: "We would take this time to say to all slave-holders in our country, to draw the reins of government over the slaves with a steady and firm hand. The permitting of our slaves at any and all times without our consent to run about over the country generates a spirit of insubordination. They forget their stations and become impertinent and insulting."[23] If the need to take blacks in hand was self-evident, so too was the simple, unchanging fact that some Cherokees were themselves of African descent.

Cherokees had long wrestled with the presence of black people among them. Their categorization and treatment of blacks had fluctuated through the years, all the while showing an imperfect but persistent pattern of acceptance and care for blacks who were relatives. In keeping with this pattern, a loophole was written into the Cherokee black codes, making room for exceptional treatment of blacks who were also Cherokee. The intent of this exception echoed that of the Cherokee Constitution of 1827, which allowed citizenship, though in a limited form, for blacks descended from Cherokee mothers. In these new codes regulating the behavior of black people in the Cherokee Nation, Afro-Cherokees, indicated indirectly through the phrase "not of Cherokee blood," were granted preferential treatment. The phrase appeared frequently in the new legislation, offering a measure of protection for blacks of Cherokee descent. Cherokee law forbade "any free negro or mulatto, not of Cherokee blood" to own property. The law required that free blacks or mulattos "not of Cherokee blood" receive thirty-nine lashes for selling liquor. The law mandated that teaching literacy to free blacks "not of Cherokee blood" was punishable by a $500 fine.[24] Furthermore, "amalgamation," which was against the law, was defined as "intermarriage . . . between a free male or female citizen with any slave or person of color not entitled to the rights of citizenship under the laws of this Nation."[25] Afro-Cherokee citizens, a designation derived from legally recognized Cherokee blood relations, were excluded from the harsh treatment that black noncitizens suffered.

The safeguard for blacks "of Cherokee blood" written into these laws was a blessing for blacks who were Cherokees, even as it dismissed blacks who were not, marooning them outside the protected circle and abandoning them to slavery. Indian Territory, while perilous for all black people, provided loopholes of retreat for some.[26] As a result, Afro-Cherokees and blacks without Cherokee ancestry received vastly differential treatment from the Cherokee state, a fact that becomes apparent in the juxtaposition of two episodes that took place in the 1840s: an attempted mass escape known as the "Cherokee slave revolt" and the heroic rescue of Shoe Boots and Doll's grandchildren from outlaw slave traders.

Webbers Falls, the original site of the "Cherokee slave revolt," was a prosperous town in the Canadian District, in the southwest corner of Cherokee territory near the Choctaw border. Stand Watie's son, Watica Watie, described the town as follows in a school essay: "Webbers Falls is situated about twenty-five miles below Fort Gibson on the south side of the Arkansas River . . . [it] has a beautiful view both up and down the river . . . in the summer when the grass is grown there is no place [more] beautiful. . . . It is also shaded by large trees and on account of the richness of the soil it is the most productive portion of the Cherokee Nation."[27] Joseph Vann must have discovered long before young Watica Watie had that Webbers Falls was a lovely spot with fine soil for planting. After losing his brick home in the Southeast to white marauders in the early 1830s, Vann had rebuilt his plantation house in Webbers Falls. Vann owned at least five hundred acres and between three and four hundred slaves in the Cherokee Nation West.[28] A former slave of Martin Vann, named Henry Henderson, recalled the widespread landholdings of the Vann family: "I was born with the Vanns until the war come along and I went with the soldiers. . . . The slaves was all divided among the Vanns; Joe, Martin, Sena and Clarena was some of their names. Altogether the Vanns owned hundreds of slaves and thousands of land acres all over the country from Webbers Falls to Tullahassee on to the North around Bible's Prairie near Vinita."[29] Joseph Vann, the eldest son, also owned a steamboat ferry called the *Lucy Walker* that he dispatched from a dock on the nearby Illinois River. Henderson said of the Vann family's line of work: "They bought and sold slaves, raised corn and cotton and run the steamboat." In the early 1840s, to Joseph Vann's dismay, his dock was frequented by a group of newly arrived residents: Seminole blacks who refused to behave like slaves. In the absence of black codes in the Seminole Nation, these men and women dressed in Seminole apparel and carried weapons at their sides. They farmed land and raised livestock of their own and seemed to have a lax relationship with their masters.

The slaves of Joe Vann, positioned as they were between an exacting master and a community of bold black men and women, determined to escape. While most historians who have written about this uprising pinpoint the cause in more restrictive slave laws, Daniel Littlefield and Lonnie Underhill speculate that the rebellion was primarily influenced by the proximity of black slaves who were living like free people.[30] Both these circumstances probably affected the slaves' action, which has been viewed by some as an aberration in Cherokee history but was actually a continuation of slave resistance. While certainly the most spectacular act of rebellion against slavery in the Cherokee Nation, the 1842 revolt was not the first. As historian Celia Naylor-Ojurongbe has argued, the long-standing contention that Indians were kinder masters has diverted attention from the history of slave defiance among Cherokees and other tribes.[31] Even back East, Cherokee-owned slaves had escaped as individuals and in pairs, refused to perform tasks, and manipulated their masters. Naylor-Ojurongbe has documented a similar range of resistance activities in the Cherokee Nation West, including the 1842 slave revolt as well as an apparent second plot in 1846 that was foiled by slaveholder Lewis Ross, who found that his slaves "had been collecting ammunition & guns."[32] Perhaps not surprisingly, the most extensive evidence of slave resistance before and after removal comes from the extensive Vann plantations of "Rich Joe" and his father, James.

The dramatic story of the Cherokee slave revolt of 1842 stunned Cherokees and nearby whites. A report of the event printed more than fifty years after the fact in the *Fort Smith Elevator*, an Arkansas newspaper, reads like a legend:

> The people of Webber's Falls, Cherokee Nation, awoke one Spring morning in the year 1842 to find themselves abandoned by their slaves. Not a negro could be found on any of the farms in the bottom or in the surrounding neighborhood. At that time there were several hundred of them there or thereabouts. Joe Vann alone had brought out from Tennessee [*sic*], two years before, more than two hundred of them and settled on the rich alluvial lands of that section of the nation. The owners were for a time in a state of consternation. Men rode about the adjacent country to ascertain what had become of the runaways. In a short time it became apparent that they had abandoned their owners and when the trail was found the conclusion arrived at was that they were seeking to escape from bondage by making a desperate effort to reach New Mexico. How these ignorant people came to learn of such a country was never known.[33]

The mass escape described in the article actually began on November 15, 1842. Before sunrise on that day, a group of twenty slaves from the Vann plantation and surrounding farms met close to town to carry out their plan. First they raided a local store and stole supplies: weapons, horses, mules, and ammunition. Then they set a course for Mexico, heading southwest.[34]

Though the *Fort Smith Elevator* reporter was surprised that slaves had heard of the Southwest, we should not be. Not only did slaves participate in an underground network of communication, which kept them apprised of local and national events, but they also, of necessity, were conscious of geography. Novelist, cultural critic, and Oklahoman Ralph Ellison has observed that for African American slaves, "geography was fate." The location of the slaves profoundly shaped their experience, since the boundaries that separated regions also marked the line between bondage and possibilities for liberation. Ellison explains: "The Mason-Dixon Line had taught them the relationship between geography and freedom. They knew that to be sold down the Mississippi River usually meant a harsher form of slavery. And they knew that to escape across the Mason-Dixon Line northward was to move in the direction of a greater freedom."[35] Finding free spaces did not always mean following the North Star, the now-mythic paradigm familiar to students of slavery. Slaves in the West saw their star to the south, in the free territory of Mexico. The Cherokee slaves who escaped in 1842 would not be the last to seek a Mexican reprieve. In 1859 a band of Black Seminoles led by the war heroes Wild Cat and John Horse rejected the indignities of the Indian Territory to found a black Seminole community in Coahuila, Mexico.[36]

As they traveled south through Creek country, the Vann slaves and their compatriots encountered Creek slaves, who joined the escape. Their Cherokee and Creek owners followed in pursuit, and soon the Creek contingent came upon the refugees. Numbering almost thirty-five, the slaves fought their pursuers, losing fourteen of their party to death and recapture. The survivors continued on their route and came upon a family of Choctaw slaves who were being taken back to their owners by a Delaware Indian and a white man. The runaways killed the captors and freed the slave family, who joined the fleeing group.[37] Meanwhile, in the Cherokee capital of Tahlequah, the National Council addressed the emergency. They authorized the organization of a special company of Cherokee men to capture the runaways:

Whereas, the National Council have this day been informed, by good authority, that certain Negroes, belonging to Joseph Vann of Canadian District, and other citizens of the Nation, have plundered their owners, bid defiance to the laws of the country, and absconded: thereby making their way to the Creek Nation,

Be it therefore resolved . . . That Captain John Drew be, and he is, hereby appointed to command a company, which shall consist of *One Hundred* effective men, to pursue, arrest, and deliver over said negroes, to the commanding officer at Fort for safekeeping.[38]

The appointed captain, John Drew, was a fitting choice for leader of the regiment. A prominent Cherokee businessman and slave trader, he owned a salt works business in Webbers Falls. The Council agreed that the national treasury would pay Drew and the enlisted men for their service and that the men would not be held responsible for the death of any slave who resisted arrest.[39] Without equivocation, the government of the Cherokee Nation sanctioned and financed the recapture of slaves, demonstrating its support of slavery and its commitment to the protection of Cherokee "property."

Thirteen days after the escape, the search party led by Captain Drew overtook the runaways. Drew later reported in a statement to the Cherokee Council that his company of ninety men found the slaves "about 280 miles from Webbers Falls . . . being in an almost starving condition."[40] Exhausted and hungry, the slaves surrendered, with the exception of two who were out hunting. Thirty-one of the runaways were returned to Webbers Falls on December 7, 1842. Five were jailed for the murder of the Delaware Indian and white man.[41] According to the *Fort Smith Elevator,* their recapture was a source of joy for the slaves: "Men, women and children were scarcely able to drag themselves along and were overjoyed on the approach of their pursuers, whom they regarded rather as friends come to rescue them from death from starvation than as taskmasters certain to drag them back to bondage."[42] Doubtless the runaways would have disagreed with this observation. For the configuration of race and caste in 1840s Cherokee country meant that the power of the Cherokee nation-state would be brought to bear against them. The architects of their so-called rescue were in league with their enslavers and had every intention of "dragging them back to bondage." Betty Robertson, a former slave once owned by Joseph Vann, gave an account of her father's participation in the revolt: "My pappy run away one time, four or five years before I was born, mammy tell me, and at that time a whole lot of Cherokee slaves run off at once. They got over in the Creek country and stood off the Cherokee officers that went to git them, but pretty soon they give up and come home. Mammy say they was lots of excitement on old Master's place and all the negroes mighty scared, but he didn't sell my pappy off. He jest kept him and he was a good negro after that. He had to work on the boat, though, and never got to come home but once in a long while."[43] Betty Robertson's father, whose punishment for attempted escape seems to have been separation from his family, was killed in an explosion on the steamboat in 1844. The accident also claimed the life of Joseph Vann, his master.[44]

Like the fleeing Vann slaves, Shoe Boots and Doll's grandchildren would find themselves at the mercy of slavecatchers in the 1840s. In their case, however, Cherokee officers would represent true salvation. The grandchildren's blackness would make them vulnerable to enslavement, but their "Cherokee blood" would distinguish them from other blacks.

During the period of the Cherokee slave revolt, Elizabeth Shoeboots was in her late thirties, residing near the Grand River in the Delaware District, in the northeast portion of the Cherokee Nation West. She had separated from her first husband by this time and was living with a Cherokee man named Morton. She now had four children—two boys and two girls—named Claude, Ailsey, Sally, and Morrison. Her sister, Polly, lived nearby with a Cherokee man named Joe and had at least three children: Maria, Lewis, and Joe.[45] Despite their mixed-race parentage, Elizabeth and Polly seem to have faced no difficulties in marrying Cherokee partners. Their Cherokeeness—defined by family belonging, citizenship, community ties, and cultural identity—served to anchor them within Cherokee society. Of Shoe Boots and Doll's five children, only William (and perhaps Lewis) seems to have married a non-Cherokee, black partner.[46]

It may not be coincidental that the three oldest children, Elizabeth, Polly, and John, were accepted into Cherokee social life, as evidenced by their marriages to Cherokee spouses. As the only children in the family who had grown up with their father on the Etowah River, these three would have been remembered by other Cherokees as being present in the Cherokee community over a long time period. In contrast, William and Lewis were born just before their father's death, at the time of the Georgia takeover of Cherokee government. The twins did not grow up ensconced in a Cherokee family and community but rather shuttling between slaveowners and guardians.

The legal citizenship in the Cherokee Nation that Elizabeth, Polly, and John could claim not only marked their legitimate participation in the polity, but it also identified them as members and makers of the community, distinguishing them from other blacks who were not legally recognized as Cherokee—including their own brothers.

The children of Elizabeth and Polly—the third generation of the Shoeboots family—could also claim Cherokee citizenship, derived from both their family lines. Elizabeth's and Polly's daughters were reared by mothers who had lived in the Cherokee Nation most of their lives and were racially mixed but culturally and legally Cherokee; in addition, the children were nurtured by Cherokee fathers and extended kin. As a result, Elizabeth's and Polly's little ones must have identified as Cherokee, just as most of the relatives and friends around them did. At the same time, the children of Elizabeth and Polly would have realized that their family was different from many others. Their grandmother, though certainly fluent in Cherokee culture, was African in descent and a slave. In addition, one of Elizabeth's children had herself been enslaved while young and may have retained memories of that experience. The children of Elizabeth and Polly Shoeboots, therefore, were most likely aware of their complicated position—anomalous in relation to other Cherokees, privileged in relation to other blacks. And if for some reason they had remained sheltered from the racial realities of their lives, the events of 1847 would have shattered their illusions.

The crime took place on the banks of the Grand River, at the home either of Elizabeth or Polly. In the early fall of 1847, a trio of infamous outlaws led by Madison Gerring barged into the household, tied up two girls, and carried them away. On October 7, just days after the attack, the *Cherokee Advocate* printed an announcement detailing the course of events:

Kidnapping

We have been informed that on Tuesday night of last week, two mulatto children were kidnapped from their mother on the Grand River, and ran off into the State. The children are girls, both free, and of Cherokee mixture, and were taken by three men, two of whom were recognized as white men. The wretches entered the house, enquired of the mother where her children were, tied them while in bed in her presence and took them off—one of them representing himself as the sheriff of the Delaware District.

This outrage is a very gross and daring one, and some measure should be adopted by those in authority to restore the unfortunate victims to freedom.

It is quite probable that that notorious villain, Mat. Gerring, and some of his associates were the perpetrators of the outrage.[47]

The girls, probably Elizabeth's daughters Ailsey and Sally, or Polly's daughter, Maria, were in the hands of these men for more than a month. During that time, the girls were dragged east into Missouri, where they were then advertised for sale. Once sold, the children were likely to have been enslaved in a southern state like Louisiana, where they might have been forced into the "fancy trade" that favored lighter-skinned black women for sexual slavery and concubinage.

The visibility of the Shoeboots family's African ancestry made them a target for attack. Slave stealers and traders traversed the Indian country at will in the mid 1800s, seeking booty to sell in neighboring tribal communities and states. Their search for potential slaves was rampant, their behavior unregulated, since many of them roamed with gangs of outlaws. As historian Katja May has observed, because of these conditions, accounts of happy and well-preserved free black families in the Cherokee territory are few and far between. In her words, the "harsh reality" was that "free blacks were in constant danger."[48] The mainly white traders from Arkansas, Missouri, and Texas would buy claims to black people who were actually free and then attempt to capture them. And in many other cases, no pretense of a legal claim was offered. The traders would simply break in and steal people from their homes. In this treacherous situation, the only saving grace for a free black person might be his or her kin relationship to Native people in the community.[49]

The incomprehensible horror of the kidnapped Shoeboots girls' experience was a reality shared by thousands of black slave women. These girls, however, were Cherokee by blood, Cherokee by citizenship, and freeborn. Though we will probably never know the inner trauma that the girls and their families suffered, we do know how the Cherokee community and government responded to the attack, revealing the complexity of the children's position in Cherokee society. The *Cherokee Advocate*'s stance on the crime is indicative both of the girls' acceptance as Cherokee community members and of their alienation as part-black, mixed-race people. The editor of the *Advocate*, William Ross, was clearly outraged by the crime and wielded the force of public opinion to compel the Cherokee state to action. At the same time, Ross was careful to denote the girls' racial background, and he did this immediately, in the first line of the article. The girls are "of Cherokee mixture," and more particularly, "mulatto" rather than simply "Chero-kee." It is true that the girls' mixed-race ancestry is pertinent to under-standing the motivation behind their kidnapping. But it is also the case that by 1847 the Cherokee Nation was a place where race mattered. Race de-marcated and maintained not only the division between the free and un-free, the citizen and the noncitizen, but also between the legitimate and nonlegitimate, the valued and the devalued. The kidnapped girls straddled the dividing line between these categories, likely producing anxiety among their Cherokee peers. The *Advocate* editor thus maintained a sense of so-cial order by marking and announcing the girls' racial difference. In doing so, he echoed the division between blacks and Cherokees maintained at the level of Cherokee law and governance.

The subtle suggestion that these girls were a different sort of Cherokee citizen is also apparent in the *Advocate's* follow-up report on the crime:

> Recovered.—We mentioned some time ago that a couple of free mulatto girls were kidnapped at their mother's on Grand River. . . . Some time after-wards, Mr. Charles Landrum, Sheriff of Delaware District, received infor-mation as to the course they had been taken, and set out in pursuit of them in company with a Cherokee and a white man. About twelve miles beyond Warsaw, Missouri, he came upon the two girls at a house at which they had been left for sale and has brought them back to the Nation and restored them to their freedom.
>
> Mr. Landrum deserves great credit for interesting himself in this affair and for recovering these two girls, who had been kidnapped and run off by that notorious wretch, Matt Guering, and one of the Starrs.[50]

The *Cherokee Advocate's* continued attention to this episode bespeaks the community's genuine concern for the girls' welfare. But even while cele-brating their recovery and lauding the lawmen involved, the newspaper again indicates the girls' tenuous position within their community. The ed-itor commends the sheriff of Delaware District for "interesting himself in this affair," suggesting that the sheriff's involvement was a special favor rather than his duty. The kidnapping of these Delaware residents, it would seem, lay outside the official scope of local law enforcement.

In the end, the *Advocate* editor was correct in his assessment that the Shoe-boots girls garnered attention that most Afro-Cherokee and African-Amer-ican women could not expect from Cherokee officers. The girls received special treatment from Sheriff Charles Landrum, who was aided in his search by Pigeon Halfbreed, an old neighbor of their grandfather's from back on the Etowah River. Though these girls were vulnerable to violent attack and to being marginalized within the Cherokee community because of their race, they were blessed with a measure of protection by virtue of their kin relationship to other Cherokees. The girls' clear blood relationship to Cherokees in Delaware District and to the famous Shoe Boots prompted swift action on their behalf. On the national level, the girls' rescue was sanctioned fiscally. On November 12, 1847, the National Council passed an act to reimburse the rescuers: "Be it enacted by the National Council, That the sum of twenty-three dollars, Le, and the same is hereby allowed, out of the National Treasury, for the benefit of Charles Landrum and Pigeon Halfbreed. That amount having been expended by them in pursuing into the state of Missouri and recovering the two grand-daughters of Shoe Boot, deceased, who had been kidnapped on the night of the 27th of September last, from their mother in Delaware District, Cherokee Nation, for the purpose of being sold into slavery."[51] In this official record, the girls' relation to Shoe Boots is key evidence of their place in the Nation and a clear indication of the treatment they should receive. Because they are both black and female, neither the names of the girls themselves nor that of their mother are noted. It is Shoe Boots's name that serves to justify the children's restoration to freedom at the expense of the Cherokee government. Nevertheless, the most salient fact in the outcome of this episode is that the girls *were* saved, despite their complicated racial position. Unlike the black runaways who were hunted down as property and returned to their owners after the Cherokee slave revolt, these children were considered part of the greater Cherokee family and worthy of rescue.

The liberation of Shoe Boots and Doll's granddaughters bears out the contention that Cherokees and other slaveholding Indians made special allowances for kin of African descent. At the same time, this incident, as well as the Cherokee slave revolt, raises the disturbing question of what became of slaves whom Cherokees did not recognize as relatives—a question complicated by the fact that in a period of political turmoil and race-based injustice, all relatives may not have been accounted for. If the personal testimony of former slaves of Cherokees is to be believed, an unknown number of people relegated to slave status and defined as "Negro" were themselves of Cherokee descent. The Cherokee government's official sanction of slavery and segregation in the West obscured this reality and threatened kinship ties that extended across race and caste. Indeed, the way that Cherokee belonging and citizenship came to be defined over time—according to legal dictate and racial designation—denied acceptance to some black-Cherokee people who would have been included in previous understandings of family and tribal belonging.

Once cut off from the lifeline of tribal membership, Afro-Cherokees were especially vulnerable to expulsion and enslavement. Some Cherokees continued to dismiss the racial definition of citizenship and held their mixed-race relatives close to the bosom of family and community, while others released their relatives, knowingly or unknowingly, into the civic and social death of slavery. The daughters of Elizabeth and Polly, like their mothers before them, were spared a life of bondage because they were claimed as kin. But other girls, African American and Afro-Cherokee alike, would take their place in the auction house in Warsaw, Missouri, and on the vast plantations of the Ridges and the Vanns.

TEN

Freedom

What for? What does a sixty-odd-year-old slavewoman who walks like a three-legged dog need freedom for? And when she stepped foot on free ground she could not believe that Halle knew what she didn't; that Halle, who had never drawn one free breath, knew that there was nothing like it in this world.

TONI MORRISON
Beloved

Be it enacted by the National Council, that all Negroes and other slaves within the limits of the Cherokee Nation, be, and they are hereby Emancipated from Slavery. And any person or persons who may have been held in slavery, are hereby declared to be forever free.

"An Act of Emancipation of the Slaves in the Cherokee Nation"

THE 1850S ARE OFTEN CALLED THE "GOLDEN AGE" of Cherokee history. In this period after removal and the political turmoil of its immediate aftermath, Cherokees managed to rebuild shining communities in the West, studded with farms, plantations, schools, salt mines, ferries, and mercantile shops. Though the harsh predicament of most slaves owned by Cherokees belied this new model, for Doll the 1850s proved to be among the best decades of her life. Doll had been transported West with the Ridge family in 1837. She had come into the hands of John Ridge at the death of Shoe Boots and was installed in Ridge's mother's home as a personal servant. In 1849, ten years after the executions of Major and John Ridge, Doll's mistress, Susannah Ridge, died. The inventory of the estate of Major and Susannah Ridge, taken on October 26, 1849, begins with a list of twenty-nine slaves, valued at a total of $8,560. Doll appears as number twenty-six on this list and is described as follows: "1 Negro woman Doll about 70 years old 000."[1] Unlike the other slaves ranging in age from one to thirty-eight whose names are followed by a dollar amount, Doll's name is followed by a set of zeros. An elderly woman whose capacity for hard work had diminished over time, Doll was no longer of value to the Ridge estate, and the Ridge family emancipated her following Susannah Ridge's death.[2] At the age of approximately seventy, Doll was free at last.

With her hard-won freedom in hand, Doll went to live with her eldest daughter, Elizabeth, who resided in the Delaware District close to the Ridge estate. In 1852, fourteen years after removal, Elizabeth received her federal reimbursement for property in the East, amounting to $456.25. Her sister, Polly, received an annuity that year as well.[3] Elizabeth and Polly then acquired home sites side by side on the west bank of the Grand River, near the juncture of Honey Creek. Their homesteads are numbered 233 and 234 in an anonymous account book in which Elizabeth's plot is valued at $344.00 and marked "paid," and Polly's plot is valued at $529.75.[4] John Shoeboots, who had started a family in the East after eluding slavecatchers almost twenty years earlier, had departed from Georgia alone in 1845 and traveled West "to hunt his folks."[5] Soon thereafter, he rejoined his sisters in the Delaware community of the Cherokee Nation West.[6]

The region where Elizabeth, Polly, and John made their home might seem an odd choice for an Afro-Cherokee family descended from slaves. Delaware District, particularly the vicinity of Honey Creek, was settled by prominent slaveowning Cherokees who were also members of the Treaty Party. A Cherokee man who lived near Honey Creek as a child recounted to an interviewer: "The bend in the Grand River, south of Bernice, was known as the Watie Bend, and was first settled before the Civil War by General Stand Watie, Elias Boudinot and Col. James M. Bell." Another Cherokee resident of the area remembered, "The people brought their negro slaves with them and settled on Honey Creek."[7]

Indeed, the future Confederate hero Stand Watie built his first home on the east side of the Grand River on Honey Creek and later built several homes on both sides of the river.[8] Before his death, John Ridge had operated a profitable trading post and general store south of his Honey Creek home, near the Arkansas border. And Charles Landrum, the former sheriff of Delaware District, owned a blacksmith shop on the Grand.[9] The success of more than a few of these Honey Creek residents was built on and sustained by slave labor. The papers of Stand Watie and his close associates attest to this fact, peppered as they are with transactions involving slaves:

bills of sale, plans for trade, and complaints about black people stolen or lost. In one example, John Rollin Ridge, son of John Ridge, wrote to his cousin Stand Watie in 1850: "Dear Cousin, I find it necessary at this time to dispose of Grigg. Having waited for some time to hear if you would buy him yourself, and heard nothing, I have bargained with Mr. Bryart, or Cardwell, who will pay you the amount of the mortgage (533 dollars) and take him." John Rollin Ridge wrote again to his elder cousin: "I need money, or what can be converted into money right away. I might sell the negroes, or I might hire them out as it suited."[10] Stand Watie's wife, Sarah Watie, wrote the following to her husband in one of several letters that mentions slaves in passing: "Mr. Russel offered me that house that Mr. Tol lives in if you could get a black man for the rent."[11]

The families of Honey Creek were quite economically successful, and yet they did not comprise the upper crust of Cherokee slaveholding society. That designation fell to the Vanns, the Rosses, and to the Murrell family from the town of Park Hill. The Murrell family estate, called Hunter's Home, still stands as an emblem of the lifestyle of the Cherokee ultraelite. Operated by the state of Oklahoma as a historic site, the Murrell mansion is described in informational literature as the "showplace of a golden age."[12] The home was the second estate of George Murrell, a white planter and merchant who had married Minerva Ross, the niece of Principal Chief John Ross. The Murrells had forty-two slaves, whom they housed in nine slave cabins. They decorated their home with French and Italian furnishings and fine imported linens. One visitor to the Murrells described the decor as follows: "We thought it beautiful because it had red plush furniture and prisms on the chandeliers. There were large mirrors over the curved mantles and the andirons and fixtures for the fireplace were burnished brass." Another wrote: "Between the parlor and the sitting room there were a hundred canaries in there among the flowers. It was a beautiful sight."[13] Few Cherokee families could afford to live in such luxury. The Waties and Ridges of Honey Creek, though not extravagantly moneyed like the Murrells, were comfortably situated and even wealthy in comparison to most Cherokees. Stand Watie owned at least a handful of slaves and styled himself a southern gentleman, dressing in Irish linen and black silk cravats. Upon the death of Susannah Ridge, the Ridge estate was worth a total of $20,135.25.[14]

Honey Creek was a thriving community of avowed slaveholders. Nevertheless, Elizabeth and Polly, and later John, had reason to settle in close proximity to it. It is likely that the sisters immigrated there after removal to be close to their mother and younger brother, William, who were living with the Ridges. Perhaps Elizabeth and Polly also sought to renew their relationships with old companions. Their father, after all, had been a slaveowner as well, and many of his neighbors had relocated to Honey Creek. The place where the Grand River spilled into Honey Creek became, in some ways, a reconstitution of the community in which Elizabeth and Polly had been born along the Etowah River. The slaveowners of Honey Creek had been their father's friends and would prove to be unexpected allies to Elizabeth, Polly, and even Doll during the Cherokee "golden age."

Elizabeth and Polly, as well as their brother John, seem to have been active participants in the life of the Delaware District community. Letters between the Watie, Ridge, and Boudinot families do not mention the Shoeboots by name, but anonymous account books in the papers of the Ridges and the Waties indicate their presence. In an account book dated circa 1852, John Shoeboot owed $40 for goods and $5 for a loan of cash. His older sister, Lizzy Shoeboot, is noted a second time for having paid off her home site. Polly is noted as having paid $430 of the total she owed for her home. In another account book, Lizzy owed $145.95. In a third, Polly had paid $22 and Lizzy had paid $24 for unrecorded purchases, possibly from the Ridge general store.[15] In the summer of 1860, Elizabeth and a child of Polly's apparently fell ill, as Stand Watie recorded in his accounts to Dr. J. E. Spencer a payment of $12 for "treatment of Lizzy Boot and niece."[16] Though the Shoebootses were unlikely to have wielded significant political or economic influence in Delaware District, they were within the hub of community life, paying for and receiving their coffee and calico just like other Cherokees and likely attending social and ceremonial events.

William Shoeboots, one of the twins whose freedom and Cherokee citizenship had not been petitioned for by his father in 1824, was not so well integrated. He spent his adolescent years under the guardianship of John Ridge, learning carpentry and blacksmithing. When he came of age, William was free to set out on his own, but his lack of legal Cherokee citizenship and his young age at the time of removal limited his opportunities. Unlike his sisters, he owned no property before removal for which he might seek federal reimbursement. He noted that in 1852, when his sisters received payment for their losses in the East, he "drew no money."[17] Disillusioned with life in the Cherokee Nation, William decided to try his luck elsewhere and struck out for the California gold mines discovered in the aftermath of the U.S. war with Mexico. He traveled in the company of two other men, William and Calvin Holmes. It may not have been a coincidence that John Rollin Ridge, son of John Ridge, left for California as well in the early 1850s. William Shoeboots and his companions may have traveled with Ridge, whom William would have known from his early years, or William may have journeyed West in Ridge's wake. John Rollin Ridge became an editor of several California newspapers as well as a noted poet and author in the state. William Shoeboots, however, did not realize his California dream and returned to the Cherokee Nation three years after his departure. He would later move to Kansas, become a farmer, marry an African American woman, and start a large family before returning to Cherokee territory.[18]

In the same year that Elizabeth and Polly came into their money and William drew none, Doll applied to the federal government for free land to which, she argued, she was entitled. In 1850 Congress had passed an act guaranteeing "bounty land" to the widows of military officers. In 1852 Doll submitted her application to an Arkansas court, stating that Shoe Boots had been an officer in the Creek War, and that she had been his wife. Details about Doll's life, such as her age in 1852, which is given as sixty-five, and her place of residence, which was the Delaware District of the Cherokee Nation, are included here. But most important, the file makes explicit Doll's claim of having been married to Shoe Boots in keeping with Cherokee custom. Doll stated, as summarized by a court reporter, that "she was married to said Captain Shoe Boots about the year 1802 in the Cherokee Nation according to the then existing Laws and Customs of the Cherokee Nation and continued to live together as man and wife upto his death which took place about the year 1825. And that she has remained a widow ever since upto this date, that she has no record of said marriage."[19] Doll's explanation of her relationship with Shoe Boots must have been convincing to the court, since she received a warrant for forty acres of land. When Congress passed an act in 1855 allowing all veterans to receive up to one hundred and sixty acres, Doll again demonstrated her astuteness by destroying her first warrant and applying anew, this time in Missouri. She swore in this second statement that she and Shoe Boots "were married in the old Cherokee Nation now the state of Georgia. They were married by the laws of the Cherokee nation, the dates she cannot recall. Before marriage was her name Dolly. That her said husband died in the state of Georgia many years since she cannot recollect." This time the processing of Doll's application was postponed for lack of marriage documentation. By 1858, however, the Missouri court was apparently satisfied and issued a warrant for one hundred and twenty acres to "Dolly Shoeboots, widow of Shoeboots, a Cherokee Indian."[20]

This was a momentous outcome for Doll, who now possessed significant property of her own. Nevertheless, Doll's silence on the subject of her enslavement in her testimony begs further questions. Was Doll forthright about her life? Were there things she had forgotten, things she refused to remember, things she had come to believe as truth? And how many of her spoken words were accurately recorded in the court reporter's standardized version of events? Doll's narrative of a marriage to Shoe Boots and a conventional Cherokee family life may be more revealing of her political acumen than of her actual affair with him. For to secure the bounty land, Doll was under pressure to portray a conjugal relationship that would be acceptable to the white court.

But at the same time that omissions and exaggerations are present in Doll's account, perhaps this testimony, the only extant document from Doll's perspective, reveals the genuine spirit of the couple's life together. Though a legal slave while she was with him, Doll considered herself Shoe Boots's wife, and in the privacy of home and family, Shoe Boots seems to have thought of her in much the same way. Certainly Doll's security in Shoe Boots's household increased over time. The longer she was with him, the more influence she had in family affairs and the more regard she garnered from Cherokee community members. This process of transformation from a relationship of coercion or convenience to one of intimacy was not unusual in early American communities. In fact, historian Ann Plane points out that the term *marriage* can mislead us in our attempt to understand unions of the past, especially in Native America, since "many forms of marriage often co-exist, each with different implications about the rights and responsibilities of the parties."[21] It is quite possible that in the long course of their relationship, Doll and Shoe Boots were indeed "married by the laws of the Cherokee nation," which, in the early 1800s, would have meant an informal but meaningful ceremony often constituted by an exchange of gifts between the couple and sometimes their parents.[22] A gradual evolution from concubine to wife, with the backdrop of enslavement ever present but fluctuating in intensity, may be the closest we can arrive at characterizing Doll's experience. By the time she was an elderly woman, Doll felt justified in staking her claim as Shoe Boots's rightful widow, and she strategically deployed the language of matrimony to secure the land she believed was her due.

The story Doll told about her life with Shoe Boots was the abridged version, carefully edited to reflect the elements that she wanted the court officials to hear. This being the case, then members of the Cherokee community also shared in this narrative construction, since three of them submitted affidavits offering the same account. Pigeon Halfbreed entered a statement in 1852, stating that "Dolly is his [Shoe Boots's] widow, that they lived together upto his death as man and wife." In two additional attachments, witnesses from the Delaware District, Stand Watie and Wilson Loowaga, also swore that "they [were] personally acquainted with the claimant Dolly Shoeboot and [knew] her to be the widow of Capt. Shoeboot deceased."[23] That Doll and Shoe Boots's relationship could be described by other Cherokees in such straightforward, unequivocal terms is suggestive of the standing that Doll had attained in Cherokee community. Not only had Doll marshaled the support of Cherokee men in a period when blacks were treated as slaves or aliens, but she also had lived in the community long enough and deeply enough to share in a common understanding of her place there. By attesting to Doll's "marriage" to Shoe Boots, these men were in effect claiming her, linking her to the broader body of the Delaware District community. Doll's race did matter, and its absence in the narratives told at this pivotal moment suggests how disruptive race would have been to the official story of Doll and Shoe Boots's relationship. At the same time, the willingness of each witness in this case to mask the racial dynamics that were so deeply embedded in Doll's situation further underscored her multifaceted position in Cherokee society. She and the Cherokee witnesses shared the tacit understanding that her former slave status was not to be revealed in the state court. Together they participated in the construction of a "critical fiction," an act that is itself expressive of interconnection and relationship.[24]

By 1860 Doll Shoeboots, known also by her Cherokee name, Congeeloh, was a free, propertied woman.[25] A census of free inhabitants living among the Five Tribes of the West lists her as an eighty-year-old "housekeeper" in the Delaware District of the Cherokee Nation.[26] Not long after this census was completed, Doll passed away. She had lived sixty years among Cherokees as a sister-outsider of that community, linked by relationships, separated by race.[27] She would die in a place far from home in the midst of armed conflict. Her son, William, said of her passing: "Dolly my mother died during the [Civil] war, in the Choctaw Nation."[28] A Cherokee man who knew her also described Doll and her death, speaking these fittingly incongruous words: "Dolly Shoeboot was a Black negro. She has a Cherokee name. . . . I think that she died on the Kiamichi River during the war."[29]

Doll's long, portentous life is a testament to the intricacies of the past, as is her death during the clash that tore the American and Indian nations asunder.

By 1860 the Cherokee emigrants had settled into their western home, learning to love the beauty of contrasts that spilled open prairies into blue lakes and wooded hills. The halcyon days of the Cherokee golden age would be short-lived, however, since the mounting contest of the Civil War punctured this period of stability and prosperity and devastated Indian country in the West. Government appointees in the Confederate states saw the Indian Territory as crucial to the South's success, positioned as it was between Arkansas and Texas. They pressured Indian nations to join them in political and military alliance, arguing that as fellow slaveholders the Indians shared a culture with the white South. With a vow to uphold the sovereignty of Native nations should they win the war and a cautionary reminder that Indian annuities were invested in bonds held by the southern states rather than by the federal government, the Confederacy secured the loyalty of four of the Five Tribes. By 1861 only the Cherokees had not signed a treaty of alliance with the South. Principal Chief John Ross, a major slaveholder, was adamantly against taking sides in the conflict and insisted on neutrality, urging his constituency to remain united and to avoid the affairs of the United States. But the Cherokee Nation was already splintering once again under the pressure of this new conflict. The slaveholding elite had organized themselves into a secret society called the Knights of the Golden Circle, which pledged to protect slavery in the nation. A coalition of white missionaries, Cherokee Christians, and Cherokee traditionalists organized in opposition, forming the Keetoowah secret society, whose mission it was to put political control of the nation in the hands of conservative "full-bloods." The Keetoowahs opposed the "whitening" of Cherokee culture and the political influence of mixed-race white Cherokees. They insisted on a return to what they viewed as traditional Cherokee values, which preceded and rejected the ownership of black slaves.[30]

An ideological civil war soon erupted in Cherokee country, between pro-Confederate Cherokees and proneutrality Cherokees, who would soon redefine themselves as pro-Unionists. The lines of dissent were familiar. Members of the Treaty Party who had favored removal also supported slavery and a Confederate alliance. Stand Watie, leader of the Treaty Party since the deaths of the Ridges, was a vocal proponent of secession. Cherokee traditionalists and missionaries who had resisted removal also resisted an alliance. As tensions increased between these factions and their constituencies, John Ross feared for Cherokee unity. Meanwhile, the absence of federal aid left the Cherokees bereft of support and vulnerable to external and internal pressure to join the Confederates. The National Council called a mass meeting in Tahlequah for the Cherokee people to debate the issue, and those in attendance passed a series of resolutions underscoring the principles to which they ascribed. The convention, chaired by Second Chief Joseph Vann, resolved in part:

> That we proclaim unwavering attachment to the constitution and laws of the Cherokee Nation, and solemnly pledge ourselves to defend and support the same, and as far as in us lies to secure to the citizens of the nation all the rights and privileges which they guarantee to them.
> That among the rights guaranteed by the constitution and laws we distinctly recognize that of property in negro slaves, and hereby publicly denounce as calumniators those who represent us to be abolitionists, and as a consequence hostile to the South, which is both the land of our birth and the land of our homes.[31]

The document linked sovereignty and slavery, indicating that central to Cherokee rights as an independent nation was the right to possess black people. As the Keetoowahs had feared, slavery, an institution of white America, had become critical to the Cherokees' conception of their own national identity. Following the passage of these resolutions, the Cherokees signed a treaty of alliance with the Confederacy, which surpassed previous treaties with the United States in its preservation of Cherokee independence.[32] Soon thereafter, Stand Watie and John Drew, leader of the hunt for the Cherokee runaways in 1842, organized and commanded the first Confederate Cherokee regiments.[33] Though Chief John Ross later severed his alliance with the South, a portion of the Cherokee populace was already wedded to the Confederate cause.

The Cherokee Nation's choice, made in the direst of circumstances, proved disastrous. William McLoughlin writes of the Civil War's end: "All the prosperity of the year 1861 had disappeared; the Cherokees were back virtually where they had been in 1839 when they were dispossessed, divided, and driven from their ancient homeland. Counting the losses from battle, guerrilla action, disease, and related causes, the Cherokee Nation had lost over 4,000 persons in the war years."[34] Historian Daniel F. Littlefield describes the situation in similarly bleak terms: "When the war ended, the Cherokee Nation was in ruin. Crossed and recrossed by both Union and Confederate military units and raided by foraging parties, guerrillas, bushwackers, cattle thieves, and border bandits, the Cherokee country suffered more destruction than did any of the other Indian nations that comprised the Indian Territory."[35] With the Confederate defeat came a Cherokee defeat that would deepen Cherokee subjection to the federal government. The Cherokees had been the first of the Five Tribes to free their slaves in 1863, but the Treaty of 1866 between the Cherokee Nation and the United States forced the Cherokees to go one step further and accept these former slaves as full citizens. The treaty also required that the Cherokee government cede more than a million acres for the settlement of whites and other Indians as well as for railroad development.[36] As a result of their actions in the Civil War, the Cherokees forfeited not only control over their national borders but also discretion over the makeup of their citizenry.[37]

While the end of Radical Reconstruction in 1877 would reinvest the white southern elite in their land and political power, it ushered in a political nadir for Cherokees and others of the Five Tribes. White secessionists regained their property, but Native people in Indian Territory, many of whom had remained loyal to the United States, lost jurisdiction over tribal lands. By 1907 Indian Territory would enter the Union as part of the new state of Oklahoma. As a separate and independent political entity, the Cherokee Nation no longer existed.[38]

The Cherokee elite and architects of the Cherokee nation-state who had adopted slavery to demonstrate their level of civilization lost nearly all in their fight to maintain it. Slavery had opened the door to internal strife and political co-optation among Cherokees and had led to a final conflict that divided the Cherokee Nation against itself. Enslaving people of African descent proved a miserable and ineffectual strategy for protecting tribal sovereignty. Nevertheless, the marginalizing of former slaves, commonly referred to as freedmen and freedwomen, continued in Cherokee society.[39]

The legacy of this complex and compromised history would forever challenge families like the Shoeboots, whose Cherokee citizenship and African heritage had come to be viewed as irreconcilable. A testament to this family's enduring "in-betweenness" can be found at the start of the Civil War. In 1861 Elizabeth's son, Doll and Shoe Boots's grandson, joined the army of the slaveholding Confederacy. Enlisting with the First Cherokee Mounted Volunteers and serving under Colonel John Drew, Morrison Shoeboot was described as follows in his military record: "Age 18, height 5ft, complexion dark, eyes black, born in [the] Cher[okee] Nat[ion]."[40]

Citizenship

ON THE CUSP OF THE TWENTIETH CENTURY, as the period known as the Reconstruction era slid into the Dawes Allotment era, the descendants of Shoe Boots and Doll were fading from the Cherokee record books. The Dawes Roll of 1898–1914 and the Guion-Miller Roll of 1909–1910, major censuses of Cherokees compiled by U.S. government officials, do not include any people named Shoeboots.[1] There are myriad reasons for the family's disappearance. The daughters of Shoe Boots and Doll, Elizabeth and Polly, married Cherokee men whose full names are not given. It is likely that the children of these unions took the surnames of their fathers and thus were listed by unidentifiable last names in the Cherokee rolls.[2] The eldest son of Doll and Shoe Boots, John Shoeboots, had one child named Mary. Mary, who was born in 1839, spent many of her childhood years with her mother in Georgia and barely knew her father. She married two African American men in succession, applied for Cherokee citizenship in 1887, and was rejected because she could not prove to the satisfaction of the committee that John Shoeboots, probably deceased by this time, was in fact her father.[3]

William, one of the youngest sons of Shoe Boots and Doll, had relocated to Kansas by 1860. There he married an African American woman named Dicey Downing, whose last name indicates that she may have been a Cherokee freedwoman from Indian Territory. William and Dicey had several children who, though they carried on the Shoeboots surname, would never appear on the Cherokee Nation rolls. William returned to Indian Territory before the final Dawes lists were compiled, but he, like Mary, was denied Cherokee citizenship in a controversial case that spanned nearly a decade. Lewis, William's twin, vanished from the Cherokee records, and apparently, from his family's lives, after he was sold into slavery in the 1830s.

Though some Shoeboots descendants, namely, the offspring of Elizabeth and Polly, may indeed be included in the Cherokee rolls under various last names, it might be said that the Shoeboots family fell victim to the "pencil genocide" of the Dawes Allotment era.[4] The construction of Dawes Rolls, declared to be the final say on who was considered Cherokee, erased the Shoeboots, and other African-descended families like them, from official tribal memory. The youngest children of Shoe Boots and Doll, William and Lewis, were the most vulnerable to this process, since they had never received acknowledgment from the Cherokee government, and they had never appeared on any Cherokee roll. Long-term separation from their family and community of birth may also have contributed to the twins' exclusion.[5] In addition, in a period when racial divisions were hardening among Cherokees, William's marriage to an African American woman rather than to a Cherokee woman, may have negatively influenced his chances for acceptance. Finally, it might be said that in keeping with traditions of matrilineality, Elizabeth and Polly's status as recognized Cherokee women may have given their children an added advantage in their quest for citizenship.

In the decades after the Civil War, the Cherokee Nation struggled to rebuild itself and fought to maintain its political independence in the face of increasing pressures. The postwar Treaty of 1866 with the U.S. government had already infringed on the rights of Cherokees to maintain their land base and determine their citizenry. With the opening of portions of Cherokee land to non-Cherokee settlement, the construction of two railroads that snaked one hundred feet through Cherokee territory, and a provision allowing for a future Territorial Government that could potentially supersede individual tribal governments, American settlers hungered for more of what rightfully belonged to the Cherokees.[6] Travelers seeking new homes and business opportunities in the West pushed their way beyond the borders of the Cherokee Nation. Thousands of newcomers, both white and black, settled illegally in Cherokee territory.[7] Leaders of the Cherokee governing Council were ill equipped to stem the tide and turned to the United States to control its wayward citizens. At the same time, these same citizens were lobbying the U.S. government to abolish Indian title and legally open Indian lands. The intensity of these circumstances not only tested the fortitude of Cherokee officials but also strained the already tense relations between Cherokees and the people of African descent who had lived among them for generations.

As more and more outsiders of various racial backgrounds crossed Cherokee borders, distinctions between former slaves of Cherokees, Afro-Cherokees, and newcomer blacks began to blur. The overwhelmed Cherokee government seized on a strategy that would strictly determine who had the right to settle on Cherokee land and practice the privileges of citizenship. Despite the Treaty of 1866, which stipulated that "all freedmen who have been liberated by voluntary act of their former owners or by law, as well as all free colored persons who were in the country at the commencement of the rebellion, and are now residents therein, or who may return within six months, and their descendants, shall have all the rights of native Cherokees," some Cherokee leaders now sought to remove blacks from the Nation.[8] And Cherokee public opinion was also being swayed in this contentious moment. Daniel F. Littlefield has noted that articles and editorials in the *Cherokee Advocate* expressed the following sentiment: "STILL THEY COME. The Nigger in the Woodpile is Sticking his Head Out Farther than Ever. And Even the Cloven Foot too Can be Easily Identified" and urged its readers: "Be men, and fight off the barnacles that now infest our country in the shape of non-citizens, free Arkansas niggers and traitors."[9]

To regain authority over people living within its borders, including people of African descent who had long resided among Cherokees, the Cherokee government inaugurated a new process to evaluate and regulate citizenship in the Nation. In 1869 the National Council passed an act authorizing the Cherokee Supreme Court to judge citizenship claims. Almost ten years later, the Council convened a special committee, then created an independent citizenship court, to serve the same purpose. Those who failed to meet the requirements for citizenship would be categorized as unlawful intruders and would lose any land they occupied as well as the value of any improvements they had made to that land. Black freedmen and freedwomen who had been former slaves of Cherokees but had not returned to the Nation within six months following the Treaty of 1866 were especially vulnerable to rejection. Many of these individuals had lived in the Nation all their lives but were transported south to Choctaw territory, Chickasaw territory, and Texas during the Civil War by masters who did not want to free them.[10] Others had fled Cherokee territory in the chaos and destruction of battle and settled in Union camps. Some of these freedpeople were not informed of their emancipation; others did not learn that they were eligible for Cherokee citizenship until the deadline had passed, and still others were unable to return to the Cherokee Nation in time. The threat of expulsion from Cherokee territory for these former slaves meant not only a loss of property but also an impending separation from family members who had received citizenship and would remain in Cherokee country.[11]

But even as the Cherokee Nation instituted a system to identify its citizenry and expel illegal settlers, the U.S. government was developing a policy that would further disempower the Cherokees and other Native nations. In 1887 Congress passed the General Allotment Act, which was intended to dissolve Indian tribalism and foster assimilation into American society. Instead of living on communal property to which individuals did not have ownership rights, Native peoples would be forced to subdivide their tribal landholdings into personal plots ideal for farming. "Surplus" lands that remained unassigned after this process could be sold to nontribal members. Retired Massachusetts senator Henry L. Dawes was selected to chair the congressional commission that would carry out this work. The Cherokees, Creeks, Choctaws, Chickasaws, and Seminoles of Indian Territory adamantly protested the Allotment Act and were thus exempted from the legislation for the first six years.[12] However, in 1894 Henry Dawes, Archibald McKennon, and Meredith Kidd, fellow members of the Dawes Commission, traveled to Indian Territory to assess conditions there. And in 1898 Congress passed the Curtis Act, which officially granted Dawes and his commission the power to allot the tribal lands of Indian Territory without the consent of the governments of the Five Tribes.

To divide and assign the landholdings in question, the commission had first to construct accurate lists of tribal members.[13] The compilation of these lists, which would be referred to as the Dawes Rolls, withdrew the authority to determine tribal membership from the Cherokee government and other governments of the Five Tribes, investing that authority in U.S. federal officials, the Indian Office of the Department of the Interior (later called the Bureau of Indian Affairs), and Congress.[14] Everyone who wished to be considered a citizen of the Cherokee Nation—Cherokees, freedpeople, and whites who had married into the tribe—had to make a formal application to the Dawes Commission. The applications were judged by the commission, sometimes appealed to the U.S. Court in Indian Territory, and reviewed by the Department of the Interior. Thereafter, an enrollment list of "Cherokees by Blood" was compiled that indicated (with a regular lack of accuracy) the ratio of Cherokee "blood" of the applicant; a list of "Intermarried Whites" was compiled that cataloged white Americans who had married Cherokees (there was no like category for intermarried blacks); and a list was compiled of "Freedmen" that included former slaves of Cherokees, Afro-Cherokees, and free blacks who had lived in Cherokee territory at least since the start of the Civil War.

The process was arduous, inconsistent, and contested on multiple fronts. Cherokee leaders denounced the right of the Dawes Commission to determine who was Cherokee and appointed a tribal attorney to record the Cherokee Council's dissent in almost every application for citizenship.[15] Some traditionalist Cherokees refused to comply with the commissioners, rejecting the notion that they should submit to an external power for membership in their own nation. People of both black and Cherokee descent would later protest that they were restricted in the way they could be listed, since the Dawes Rolls were organized by racial designation. Though a significant number of blacks in the Nation claimed and could demonstrate Cherokee ancestry and identity, the vast majority would not be listed on the "Cherokee by Blood" roll. Because they appeared "black" to Dawes commissioners and because they were usually identified as former slaves, Afro-Cherokees were listed on the "Freedmen" roll, which did not record degree of Cherokee "blood." After years of challenges, congressional fine-tuning, and further review of applications, the Dawes Rolls were declared complete in 1914. In the Cherokee Nation, which would later base its own internal criteria for tribal membership on lineal descent from a person on the Dawes Rolls, Afro-Cherokees would be forever handicapped by this paper segregation, unable officially to demonstrate the fact and degree of their Cherokee bloodlines.

The citizenship court established by the Cherokee National Council in 1879 was charged with the responsibility of protecting the legitimate Cherokee populace as well as the Cherokee land base from illegal settlers. Their predisposition, therefore, was to ferret out fraud through the careful review of received applications. Still, for members of African-descended families like the Shoeboots, this official process may have seemed a rare opportunity for the lost and expelled to be gathered back into the fold. Perhaps William

Shoeboots felt exactly this way. For in the spring of 1887, William submitted his application to the Cherokee Commission on Citizenship, seeking legal belonging and full rights in the community and nation of his birth.

At the age of sixty-four, William may well have been the last surviving child of Shoe Boots and Doll. And like his father before him, William engaged in a public action that challenged the Cherokee Nation's limited definition of the relationship between race and citizenship. Rather than viewing African heritage as a special circumstance or a barrier to Cherokee acceptance, William made a statement that reveals a notion of Cherokee-ness based not on racial designation but on family lines and kinship circles. William's petition, structured as a narrative of personal and family history, suggests an alternative yet culturally rooted measure of Cherokee belonging, one that emphasizes the creation and preservation of families over divisive governmental dictates.

In 1888 William Shoeboots had his day in court and made his case for citizenship. He opened his testimony first by stating that he was a resident of the Cherokee Nation and then by naming his closest relatives. The court record begins:

> William Shoeboot being duly sworn upon his oath says . . . I live in Tahlequah district Cherokee Nation. I am the party who has this application on file for citizenship in the Cherokee Nation—I have seven children, named: Lizzie Davis Shoeboot about 32 years old, Willie Shoeboots about 28 years old, Rufus Shoeboots age 23 years, Flora Shoeboots age 19 years, Jno [John] Shoeboots aged 17 years, Jim Shoeboot aged 14 years, and Sophia Shoeboots aged 13 years. . . . My mother was "Dolly"—a black woman—she had six [sic] children by Tarsekayahke—My brothers and sisters named as follows— Lizzie Shoeboots, Jno [John] Shoeboots, Polly Shoeboots, Lewis Shoeboots, William Shoeboots (myself). Lewis and myself were twins.[16]

In a lengthy application that includes an opening statement and additional details elicited during cross-examination, William Shoeboots recounts his version of the Shoeboots family saga. The story that William relates about himself and his relatives not only discloses missing pieces of the family's experience but also reveals William's own engagement in the process of constructing a particular narrative about his family's history. High stakes were involved in William's appearance in court that day. The outcome of his case would influence not only his right to Cherokee citizenship, as well as the rights of his offspring, but also the way that his family of origin would be remembered. William's own account then, taken together with the compiled affidavits that the court collected from witnesses, says as much about *how* one tells a story of racial complexity in the Cherokee Nation as it does about the content of the story itself.

Many of the details disclosed by William mirror the general outlines of the family's history as it was recorded in other sources. However, a crucial disjuncture between William's account and other versions coalesces around the question of the family's status as enslaved or free, which stems from the position of their mother. While William openly states Doll's race as "black," he never intimates that his mother was a slave. In fact, the word *slave* does not appear in William's statement. He says of his family: "Myself and brother and sisters were free people and born of a free woman." In addition, he indicates nothing of the legal battle to free his siblings in the early 1830s or of the kidnapping of his nieces in 1847. When discussing the strange and traumatic separations his family endured, William's language becomes evasive. He says obliquely about his sister Elizabeth, who was sold by Tom Woodard: "Lizzie stayed at Tom Woodard's." He states that his brother Lewis was "stolen and carried off" but does not specify how this occurred or why it was permitted. He says simply of his move West with the Ridge family, under whose guardianship he remained and for whom his mother worked as a slave: "I came to this country with the Ridges as did my mother."[17]

It was customary in citizenship cases for the court to include testimony from individuals who were acquainted with the applicant. Each of the witnesses in William's case affirmed that he was indeed the son of Shoe Boots and Doll. However, one of these witnesses, a former slave named Thomas Ridge, whose brother was owned by Shoe Boots, paints a different picture of William's childhood than does William himself. While William is silent about the issue of slavery, he is direct. According to Ridge, William experienced slavery firsthand: "I am well acquainted with the applicant, have known him from his childhood—after the death of his father old man Shoeboot, he was taken by a man name Thomas Woodard, to take care of him. He Woodard commence selling them. Sold his sister first. John Ridge and Wm Tompson got them back." Another witness in William's case, a Cherokee man named Ed Carey, was similarly clear about the Shoeboots family's history of slavery. In his statement, Carey says about Doll's status: "I always understood that she was a slave of Mrs. Ridges, that was the common report. . . . It was the common report in the neighborhood that at the death of Mrs. Ridge she gave Dolly her freedom."[18]

Although William Shoeboots was surely aware of these unsettling events in which he played a part, he excludes them from the statement that he makes to the court. William resists articulating the legacy of slavery in his family, which shaped so many of their experiences and hardships. Instead he attempts to portray the image of a free Cherokee family that happened also to be black. William's version of his family's experience was likely motivated both by strategy and conviction. Like his mother, who failed to mention a history of slavery in her application for bounty land as Shoe Boots's widow, William may have thought that the specter of enslavement would weaken his case. He also may have believed just as strongly that for all intents and purposes, his family should be viewed as free. William's careful sidestep around the issue of slavery is echoed in his treatment of race. Although William does describe his mother as "a black woman" early in his statement, he never mentions race again and attaches little importance to it as an aspect of his history and personhood. William's diminishment of the impact of race, like his erasure of the fact of slavery, likely stemmed from strategy as well as conviction. Perhaps he felt that emphasizing the racial categorization of his family would reify his blackness at the expense of his Cherokeeness and thereby undermine his bid for Cherokee recognition. Perhaps he also believed, as his father seems to have felt, that race should not be a determining factor in his right to Cherokee citizenship.[19]

Through his own statement and the testimony of others, William Shoeboots's application made a strong case for his claim of citizenship rights. He amply demonstrated that he was the son of Shoe Boots, who was described time and again in the testimony as a "full-blood Cherokee." However, the Cherokee Commission on Citizenship was conflicted in their assessment of William's claim. In their response they expressed that they were bound by an Act of Council to make a determination based not on whether a claimant was Cherokee by kinship but on whether that claimant could trace his or her lineage to particular Cherokee rolls beginning in 1835. Their decision would thus be guided by restrictive governmental codes that were more reflective of a legalistic, even colonial, apparatus than of the complexities of Cherokee relationships. Shoe Boots died in 1829, never making it onto these official rolls. His eldest children, who had been freed and admitted to citizenship by petition, did appear on the census of 1835 (John) and the Drennen roll of 1851 (Elizabeth and Polly). However, their enrollment was not considered relevant to William's case because they were not his lineal antecedents.

And so it happened that William Shoeboots's right to Cherokee citizenship would be evaluated in a vacuum of lists and paperwork, outside the context of his familial relationships. Though his blackness was not the obvious reason for William's tenuous standing (white Cherokees could be rejected on the same grounds), race did play a subtle part.[20] The majority of Cherokee and black couplings took place in the eighteenth and early nineteenth centuries, long before the 1835 roll was taken. And while intermarriage between Cherokees and black slaves was outlawed in 1824, intermarriage between Cherokees and whites was legalized in the same period. Many black people of first-generation Cherokee descent would have been William's age or older, which means that their Cherokee parents and grandparents would have been deceased before the 1830s. The simple (or perhaps not so simple) issue of timing meant that it would be especially difficult for Afro-Cherokees to prove their Cherokee lineage to the satisfaction of the law.

The Cherokee Commission on Citizenship seems to have recognized the irony of William's case and thus wrestled with their decision. Henry Barnes, a member of the Commission, testified after the fact that

the decision of the Commission was that the evidence produced before the Commission proved to the satisfaction of the Commission and beyond all doubt that the claimant, William Shoeboot, was the son of old Shoeboot, well known as a prominent citizen of the Cherokee nation while he lived, and that therefore the claimant was entitled to citizenship. But that Capt. Shoeboot having died before the roll of 1835 was made in connection with the Cherokee nation in the West, and the law or Act of Council vesting the Commission with jurisdiction over claims for Cherokee citizenship, confirming readmitting only those claimants who should prove themselves to be lineally descended from Cherokees whose names were enrolled on some one of certain designated Rolls of Cherokees commencing with the Roll of 1835 in point of time, the Commission decided that they could not declare Wm Shoeboot entitled to Cherokee citizenship as the evidence showed he deserved.[21]

The commissioners thus recognized William Shoeboots as a Cherokee man deserving of Cherokee citizenship. And yet, by dictate of law, William and his descendants would be denied their place in the Cherokee Nation.[22]

Unable to reconcile the facts of the case, the Cherokee Commission on Citizenship declined to make an official judgment. Their inaction might be viewed as an act of resistance, an unwillingness to enforce an unjust law at the expense of the logic of kinship. At the same time, the commission's indecision brilliantly captures the paradoxical position of the Shoeboots family, from century's beginning to century's end. At the time of William's death in 1894, seven years after he had submitted his application, his case was still pending.

The status of Doll and Shoe Boots's youngest child continued to hang in the balance until William Shoeboots's own children, Rufus and Lizzie Shoeboots, protested the commission's inaction. In the intervening years between William's case and his children's appeal, the Dawes Commission, an external committee authorized by Congress, had made inroads into usurping the Cherokee Nation's citizenship process. Although the Dawes Commission was deemed illegitimate by the Cherokee government and by many Cherokees, for Afro-Cherokees and black freedpeople who had not received citizenship from the tribe, a Dawes application may have seemed an alternative route to recognition and rights. In a letter to the Dawes Commission dated 1896, Rufus Shoeboots and his sister, Lizzie Shoeboots, voiced their frustration and requested that their father's case be reconsidered and settled: "Our allegation is that if he, William Shoeboots, was entitled to the rights of Cherokee citizenship we his children and grandchildren are entitled also. Wm Shoeboot, our ancestor, having died while his application for citizenship was pending, we his children, respectfully submit the evidence presented by him." They further argued, intimating foul play, that testimony on their father's behalf by "John Thompson Adair and Allen Ross, two very prominent and respected Cherokee citizens" was missing from the record.[23] Rufus and Lizzie entered into evidence all the documents from their father's case that they could obtain from the Cherokee government, in addition to their own statements and new testimony from a host of witnesses. They tried to prove that William Shoeboots had been entitled to Cherokee citizenship, that they were William Shoeboots's children, and that they and their offspring were entitled to Cherokee citizenship as well. As in their father's case, Cherokee neighbors testified on the applicants' behalf. In a group statement, three Cherokee men described their acquaintance with William Shoeboots, who "for some time acted as a street supervisor in the employ of the town corporation and thus became well known to many of the residents." They also reported that the claimants, Rufus and Lizzie, were "recognized, acknowledged and treated as his children."[24]

Still, the children's appeal, which rested on the application of their father, was denied. This time, the officials evaluating the case, white men of the Dawes Commission, showed no ambivalence. They stated in a standardized form letter that "Wm Shoeboots, through whom the petitioners claim to derive their right to citizenship in the Cherokee Nation, is not now and has not been a citizen of the Cherokee Nation, since the removal of said Nation, west to the Indian territory." Further, the Dawes Commissioners added in a handwritten note at the bottom of the form: "That Wm Shoeboots mother was pure blood African who was never married to his father an Indian. That said applicants are negroes and not entitled to citizenship in this Nation."[25]

If William Shoeboots had avoided the quagmire of race and slavery in his personal testimony, the Dawes Commissioners seized on it in their response to his children's appeal, much more so than the Cherokee commissioners had eight years earlier. The Dawes Commission specified and emphasized Doll's race as "purely" African and represented the relationship between Doll and Shoe Boots as illegitimate. Underlying their rejection was the prejudiced conviction that William and his children were black, not Cherokee, and that these two categories were mutually exclusive. In an afterthought scribbled at the bottom of a page, the commissioners invalidated three generations of a family's history, expunging them from the political body of the Cherokee Nation.

But in William's case the word of the Dawes Commission was not final. Because it was the policy of the Cherokee National Council to reject the authority of Henry Dawes and his colleagues, the Council charged Cherokee Nation attorneys with reviewing Dawes Commission proceedings and recording an official response on behalf of the Cherokee government.[26] The tribal attorneys made such a reply in the appealed case of William Shoeboots. However, rather than rejecting the Dawes decision, attorneys for the Cherokee Nation reinforced and clarified it, eliminating any lingering doubt about the historical relationship of black people to the Cherokee Nation:

They failed to prove a lineal descendant on any of the authenticated rolls of the Cherokee Nation; but there was a weakness in their proof not then discovered. For prior to the war, descendants of Cherokee men by women of the African race were not considered by the Cherokees as members of the Tribe: Section 5, Article 3 of the Constitution of the Cherokee Nation. These applicants may be entitled under the Treaty of [18]66, though the difficulty in the way is, that they attempted to establish by their proof that their ancestors, though of the negro race, were free at the time of the birth of William Shoeboots, from whom they claim descent. And they probably were.[27]

The Cherokee lawyers' response tolerates little ambiguity. It maps out two straightforward routes to Cherokee citizenship, one for "Cherokees," and one for "Negroes." A Cherokee could trace his or her lineage to a parent or forebear on the "authenticated rolls." A black person formerly owned by Cherokees could appeal to the Treaty of 1866, which granted citizenship to freed slaves who had returned to the Cherokee Nation within six months. The Cherokee lawyers indicated that because the Shoeboots claimed to be free-born Cherokees, they could not appeal to the Treaty of 1866, and because they were also descended from a black mother, they were ineligible for Cherokee citizenship through routes external to that treaty.[28] A family like the Shoeboots that was black *and* Cherokee and had been both enslaved *and* free had no place within the streamlined, race-conscious categories designated by the Cherokee and American governments. William Shoeboots's strategy of deemphasizing slavery had failed. The very freedom that he claimed for his Afro-Cherokee family made that family inconceivable in the view of the Cherokee Nation. To be a black citizen of the Cherokee Nation, the attorneys seemed to say, required always having been a slave. For reasons of clarity and expediency, and in keeping with the Cherokee Nation's fixed definitions of racial categorization and tribal belonging, no other possibility would be entertained.

And yet the story of the Shoeboots family is at its roots one of possibility. For centuries of Cherokee history, it was possible for Cherokees and Africans to negotiate the color line that now seems immutable. It was further possible for children of Cherokee and black unions to find pockets of protection within the increasingly menacing contexts of legislated racism and state-supported slavery. The tension between the Cherokee government's ideas about race and the Cherokee people's ideas about kinship continued into the late 1800s and beyond. Just as they always had, Cherokee neighbors, relatives, and friends spoke on behalf of the Shoeboots family, claiming them as members of the tribal community, while acknowledging the contradictions of their inclusion. In his testimony supporting William Shoeboots's bid for citizenship, John Cochran, a great-nephew of Shoe Boots, offered the following story: "When I first saw Capt. Shoeboots and his negro wife they came to my Grandmother's house where I and my mother stayed. When they went to the table to eat the question was asked:

Shoeboots, have you got this woman for a wife or a slave? Shoeboots answered: no, I have her for a wife . . . Kahuga was the first child of Shoeboots and his negro wife. The twins were both boys . . . Capt. Shoeboots was a Cherokee by blood. Shoeboots was my mother's uncle. Shoeboots was in the wolf clan."[29] John Cochran was more than likely the grandson of Peggy or Takesteskee, the two sisters of Shoe Boots who had once fought for William and Lewis's freedom before the Cherokee Council. In his statement, Cochran reclaims relational ties that the women in his family had long held dear, offering memories of kinship to mediate the ravages of racial separation. He names Shoe Boots's nation and clan, links Shoe Boots to his own mother, and connects all this information to the births of Shoe Boots and Doll's children. In doing so, Cochran weaves Shoe Boots and his family into a web of familial, clan, and tribal relationships. He indicates, in words both plain and insightful, that long before the Cherokees became a race-conscious nation, Shoe Boots was a Cherokee. And in accordance with the logic of kinship, so too were his children.

The Shoeboots Family Today

The Shoeboots family story does not conclude with William's children's failed attempt to achieve Cherokee citizenship. Nor does the Shebootses' struggle for community belonging and integrative identity reach closure in successive generations.[1] The continually complex and ambiguous position of this family is revealed yet again in the recent life of Haskell James Shoeboot, a latter-day descendant who became well-known as a respected cowboy, physician, and police officer in mid-twentieth-century Oklahoma and Colorado.

For instance, during a remarkable run for election to the governorship of Colorado in 1966, Haskell Shoeboot stressed his identification as a Native American but not as an African American. When the *Rocky Mountain News* described him as "black" in an article about the campaign, Shoeboot "took offense at the reference to his racial identity as Black, and drafted a letter regarding [the] same, demanding a retraction."[2] Twenty years later Haskell Shoeboot again emphasized his Cherokee identity in a book ironically titled *Black Cowboys* (a project of the Black American West Museum and Heritage Center). In a biographical sketch based on interviews, Haskell Shoeboot reported that "his father and mother were full-blood Cherokees" and said about his family's history: "He was born the year the whites made the run on the Cherokee Strip and took the land from the Cherokees at that time. His people were never slaves on either side, they were Cherokees who lived in Georgia."[3] And in this same publication, Haskell Shoeboot is pictured wearing a feathered headdress in the tradition of Plains Indian tribes. This image, reminiscent of Wild West shows and the public performance of "playing Indian" described by Native scholars, could lead some to question Haskell Shoeboot's personal motivation and cultural authenticity. And his seeming denial of black ancestry and affiliation could lead others to challenge his level of critical race consciousness. However, these arresting words and actions might be viewed in another way. Rather than nullifying his claims to Cherokeeness and denigrating his blackness, perhaps Haskell Shoeboot's studied self-representation reveals the legacy of a tumultuous racial past.

In 2004, as this book goes to press, descendants of Haskell Shoeboot who trace their lineage to Rufus Shoeboot, William Shoeboots, and Captain Shoe Boot, are commemorating and continuing their forebears' quest. They are searching for William's lost gravesite and seeking inclusion in the Cherokee Nation of Oklahoma.

Research Methods and Challenges

The main challenge of a book such as this, which seeks to unearth a subaltern story in the context of the histories of people of color and women in the United States, is the unpredictability of source materials. In early-nineteenth-century America, accounts of Native and black life were often written by white men. In the best-case scenarios these men had limited access to the guarded, inner experiences of the people of color about whom they wrote.[1] In the worst-case scenarios, white ethnographers, missionaries, travelers, and intellectuals abused their disproportionate power and entered self-serving, distorted information into the historical record. And yet, in the fields of early Native, black, and women's history, often the best source one can hope for is one of these same white men who wrote a journal, kept a slave schedule, or left a will.

The context for Cherokee Studies is somewhat unique but still problematic. In addition to white men's reports on Cherokee life, Cherokees themselves kept a variety of early records. Because Cherokees were the first Native people in America to write down their language and to establish a republic governed by a constitution, and among the first to welcome white missionary educators, they have produced written materials in the form of personal journals and letters, laws and court records, and tribal newspapers. The perceived acculturation of Cherokees and the historical circumstances that placed Cherokees at the center of a debate about Indian Removal attracted U.S. officials and lay scholars in the nineteenth century, who recorded additional aspects of Cherokee life. The plentiful production of written materials by and about Cherokees has had a cumulative effect, attracting scholarly attention to Cherokee Studies. As a result, Cherokees are one of the most studied tribes in U.S. history with a vast archive of primary and secondary materials housed in various federal, state, tribal, and private holdings around the country.

As historian Liza Black has noted, the existence of the Cherokee archive contributes to an illusion of transparency, supporting the fallacy that historians can penetrate and perceive the essence of Cherokee life through the written sources.[2] But in fact the Cherokee archive masks as much as it seems to reveal. Not only do the Cherokee voices represented tend to emanate from particular subsets of the Cherokee community—educated mixed-white people who were intellectuals and political leaders—but these voices were also edited at the time of their inscription toward particular political ends. Historians who have used these materials to develop a narrative of the Cherokee past have often duplicated the biases of the archive, focusing on the Cherokee male elite and accepting the strategic self-representation of individual Cherokees as historical truth. In addition, the Cherokee archive presents the problematic aspects of its own existence. As ethnohistorian James Axtell has observed, scholars know about the American Indian past through the practices of invasion, usurpation, and surveillance that positioned white individuals and U.S. government agents in positions to observe, collect, and record Indian life.[3] The Cherokee materials are so rich in part because Cherokees were one of the first Native tribes to be collared by the colonizing apparatus of the United States. Likewise, material on blacks among Indians is most prevalent in the Cherokee Nation because Cherokees owned more black slaves than any other tribe.[4] The available material on Cherokees and black people among them is shaped by the brutalities of captivity and skewed by the over-representation, under-representation, and strategic representation of particular individuals and experiences.

The historiography of Shoe Boots's life reflects not only the biases of the archive but also the ideological uses to which the Cherokee materials have been put. As a lauded war hero, Shoe Boots is a notable figure in Cherokee history. His first biographer was John Howard Payne, a dramatist, journalist, lay historian, and celebrated author of the song "Home, Sweet Home," who traveled to the Cherokee Nation in the 1830s. Payne's notes on Cherokee historical figures and sociopolitical life are widely made reference to as valuable primary source materials in Cherokee Studies. In these notes, Payne describes Shoe Boots as a man who had a "love of display in dress" and wore signature "hessian military boots with tassels" and "long red feathers in his hat."[5] Payne says of Shoe Boots's appearance: "On his Indian hunting shirt he wore a military coat and epaulettes; he was always caparisoned with a long sword and a belt sustaining horsemen's pistols at each side, with a grim looking knife, and his tall, gaunt figure was surmounted with a vast-cocked hat and a towering military plume." Payne also observes that Shoe Boots was "fond of music and of dancing," that he played the blait (a flutelike instrument) to imitate fawn and cock calls, and that he was given to "moments of hilarity."

Payne records that after Shoe Boots joined a band of Shawnees in an attack on a Kentucky town, he took captive "a white girl of eleven, said to have been the natural daughter of Governor Shelby, the Governor of Kentucky." Payne writes that Shoe Boots's kindness to the young woman led to an eventual consensual marriage: "He grew into greater consequence than ever by his important services, and ingratiated himself by his devotedness and delicacy and decorum still more and more with his captive, whose charms, it may be conjectured, had already made a captive of her captor. She accepted his hand, and they had two sons and one daughter."[6] Additional evidence does not corroborate this tale of Shoe Boots's kidnapping of and marriage to a daughter of the governor of Kentucky. The identity of Shoe Boots's captive was Clarinda Allington (or Ellington), a common Kentucky settler who is not connected to the governor in alternative accounts.

Other aspects and interpretations of Shoe Boots's biography as recorded by Payne are also imperfect. This shortcoming can be attributed to the frailties of human error, the inability of any scholar to always be correct. And added to these causes is the fact that those who wrote about Shoe Boots, like all historians, were engaged not only in historical writing but also in the project of history making. They were shaping history as well as recording it, in accordance with their own political affinities and personal ideologies.[7] A dramatist and Cherokee sympathizer, Payne was re-creating the story of the Cherokees in a moment of imminent doom. In 1835, when Payne first entered the Cherokee Nation, the Cherokee people were embroiled in political struggle. The state of Georgia's attempt to push them West had the force of the Georgia National Guard, the greed of white settlers and gold miners, and the tacit consent of President Andrew Jackson behind it. Despite attacks on their lives and homes, the majority of Cherokees vehemently resisted removal. Payne journeyed from New England to write a series of articles about the conflict for a new periodical he planned to publish. In the course of his research, he befriended Principal Chief John Ross, attended Council meetings, and began writing petitions to Congress and the American public on behalf of the Cherokees.[8] In the words of Gabriel Harrison, who published a study of Payne's life and work in 1885: "We soon find Mr. Payne not only talking with the red man in the depths of the forest, but eating at his table, sleeping in his hut, and advising chief Ross what to do, and how to act with the United States government. . . . Always eager for adventure, and fond of the marvelous, he must have enjoyed greatly these strange people, and the wild, beautiful scenery that surrounded them."[9] Though Payne abandoned his serial publication owing to a lack of subscribers, he continued his research and involvement in Cherokee affairs, copying tribal documents for the Council and recording "the literature and the anecdote of the nation" for a future monograph.[10]

Payne's unspoken aim here seems to have been to write a book that would continue the work of his articles and public letters—to represent the Cherokees as an earnest, improving, and heroic people, wronged by the United States. Shoe Boots was just the kind of figure who could illuminate and enrich this historical narrative. He was an Indian warrior of heroic proportions who nevertheless represented no threat to white Americans. Andrew Jackson himself had bestowed honors on Shoe Boots, and a white woman had consented to be his bride. Shoe Boots epitomized the romantic, vanishing Indian whose mythic image was becoming popular in the mid-nineteenth century. There was, however, one exception to this idealized characterization—Shoe Boots's sexual affair with his African slave. This was an aspect of Shoe Boots's story that would detract from his otherwise symbolically appealing life. Thus Payne's representation of Shoe Boots's history is redemptive, seeking to overcompensate for the "black spots on Shoe Boots's memory" by overdramatizing the stories of Shoe Boots's romantic love for a white woman and his service for the U.S. military. As a playwright whose work has been compared to that of Washington Irving and Mary Wollstonecraft Shelley, Payne would have been fit for the task. Said Harrison about Payne's penchant for drama: "Mr. Payne, in all his dramatic writings, shows a superior knowledge of the human passions. . . . The passions are immediately presented to intensify the situation, which affords the actor a full opportunity to express his dramatic power, and thereby to grasp the sympathy and attention of his audience."[11]

Payne's personal view of the Indian reinforced his political project of humanizing the Cherokees for a white public. In a letter to his sister describing the Green Corn Festival, a renewal ceremony practiced by tribes of the Southeast, Payne expressed the sentiment that American Indians were both exotic and disappearing: "It was strange to see this, too, in the midst of my own land; to travel, in the course of a regular journey, in the new world, among the living evidences of one, it may be, older than what we call the old world. . . . And it was a melancholy reflection to know that these strange people were rapidly becoming extinct."[12] Payne's sentimental feelings about Native people and his belief in the myth of the vanishing Indian made for a particular kind of history—paternalistic and picaresque. Payne's account, written in narrative form, describes Shoe Boots as a "Lothario of the forest," a swashbuckling adventurer, "fond of a carouse." In Payne's account, the unruly Shoe Boots rises to the heights of civilized behavior for the love of a white woman, and dies in regrettable infamy for the lust of a black woman. Payne's rendition, filtered through the cross-cutting lenses of racial ideology, gender ideology, and political purpose, presents Shoe Boots as a noble savage turned tragic hero, his white wife as an angel, and his black lover as a stain on his life record. In Payne's narrative, Shoe Boots is more a character than a man, one whose life is represented for propagandistic purposes.

The various mythical and mistaken components of Shoe Boots's life, as Payne renders it, contribute to the construction of narratives with a particular public aim. Though I have attempted to document my findings and make my modes of interpretation transparent, I do not wish or claim to escape from the personal, political, and cultural urgencies of historical work. It is these very urgencies, in fact, that led me to take as my central focus the slave woman whom Payne relegated to the sidelines of his account. I have situated Doll at the heart of this story to commemorate her life as well as to mark her experience as historically valuable. And I have traced the legacy of kinship in the Shoeboots family history in part to show that in an earlier time, Native and African Americans related to one another around, under, and over the constriction of race.

Antebellum African American experience has perhaps been more accessible to scholars than Native American experience of that period, in large part because black slaves produced hundreds of accounts of their enslavement in published slave narratives and conversion narratives, oral slave narratives, and historically based fictionalized accounts of slavery. The experience of blacks among Indians, however, has been less frequently documented. Far fewer Indians than whites owned slaves, decreasing the pool of slaves who could write about this history, as well as the number of slaveowners who would leave records. In addition, many small-scale Indian slaveholders, including Shoe Boots, were not literate and did not keep slave schedules and purchase records. Fewer Indians than blacks wrote personal narratives in the nineteenth century, and none of these extant narratives describes Indian slaveholding. Not surprisingly, then, the details of Doll's life have proven the most evasive. Not only was she a black slave in a Native American context, in which slave life went largely unchronicled, but she was a black woman in a context in which records were kept by white and Cherokee men who did not view a life such as hers as noteworthy. As a man, war hero, and political leader, Shoe Boots's name continually appears in Cherokee Nation records and general histories of the tribe. Doll, in contrast, has held little interest for record keepers or scholars.

Capturing the texture of black slave women's lives has been the beloved labor of black women intellectuals. Angela Davis, bell hooks, Paula Giddings, and Deborah Gray White, among others, have devoted their early works to African American women in slavery.[13] Often these scholars had little to go on—the biased records of white men and sometimes women invested in the slave system, the male-centered histories that dominated the field into the 1980s, and interviews with former slaves shaped in part by the charged racial dynamics of white interviewers and black interviewees. In *Ar'n't I A Woman: Female Slaves in the Plantation South*, the first full-length study of its kind, White points to the lack of sources as a major obstacle to contemporary understandings of black slave women, writing: "Source material on the general nature of slavery exists in abundance, but it is very difficult to find source material about slave women in particular. Slave women were everywhere, yet nowhere." She confronts this scarcity of sources in her own research by approaching the materials she does possess in innovative ways. She depends on inference to make connections and engages in comparative analyses to better understand her subject.[14] Using this method of cross-referencing sources, White and other students of African American women's history have mapped out a landscape of slave women's experience. Scholars who study black slave women have had to combine their knowledge, skills, and creativity in unexpected ways owing to this lack of available sources. In the end, though certainly to a greater extent, historians of black women do the same work as all historians—combining imagination and documentation, envisioning how things might have been, and reshaping that vision in accordance with the evidence.

In my reconstruction of Doll's experience, I borrow this method and rely on the composite picture of black slave women's lives sketched by scholars who have written before me. In addition, because much of the data about Doll's day-to-day life is elusive, I often incorporate material from slave narratives written by black women as well as interviews with former slaves of Native Americans that were conducted as part of the Federal Writers' Project during the Works Progress Administration of the 1930s.[15] I also intertwine fictional representations of the trauma of slavery (as well as of Indian Removal), because I believe that fiction uniquely captures the texture of the subjective experience, leading us to revelations that can lend depth and feeling to historical understanding. In telling the stories of Doll and her family, I reveal the difficulties and treacheries of my evidence base, attempting to treat historical documents to the critical readings that are more often reserved for literary texts. The account that I offer here rejects the aesthetic of a seamless narrative, retaining the gaps, ambiguities, and inconsistencies that reflect the nature of this subject.

My use of the John Howard Payne Papers in reconstructing Doll's life has perhaps been the greatest test of this method. Payne mentions Doll in the context of his biography of Shoe Boots, yet he did not well regard people of African descent, a fact that compromises the dependability of his observations for a history that highlights the experience of blacks among Cherokees. While Payne romanticized Indians to the point of idolizing a Creek girl whom he called "my beautiful princess" and whose "carriage" he described as "graceful and *distingué,* and quite European," he disparaged blacks. He considered American Indians noble, if unlucky, but saw blacks as degenerate.[16] Payne's feelings are apparent in a description of African women of Muslim and Jewish faiths, included in an 1842 letter to his sister after his appointment as the United States Consul at Tunis:

> What are those waddling masses of draperies, gowns, one would say, and
> shawls, of every hue and texture hung around the sides of a huge barrel, with
> a black masked head thrust through its top, and a pair of thick legs through

its bottom? "Foregad!" as the old nurse says in "Romeo and Juliet," "how every part of it quivers!" Behold! Another, and yet another of these monsters! Some unmasked! Hush, man! These are Moorish women! The one or two with their broad faces bare are Jews. That fourth one so carefully muzzled with a black silk scarf, as if nature had mixed her Indian ink inadequately, is a she-nigger![17]

Payne describes Doll with a subtler disdain. The first time she appears in his narrative, Payne refers to her as "the dark faced one (the servant woman daull)," designating her by color and caste and including her name as an afterthought. Later Payne describes Doll and her children as "black spots to rest upon the memory" of Shoe Boots, attributing these sentiments to the Cherokee Council while at the same time revealing his own beliefs that association with blackness breeds ignominy.[18] Despite his grievous perspective, the fact remains that Payne's is the most detailed and thorough account of Shoe Boots and Doll's life together. To exclude his notes would mean the end of Doll's story, and to trust them would mean to distort her character. I have tried to forge a path between this Scylla and Charybdis by reading Payne with skepticism—questioning the structure and emphases of his account and sifting out the information that can be corroborated by other primary sources.

Key sources for this project have been the John Howard Payne Papers housed at the Newberry Library, veterans' records and Bounty Land files of the National Archives, and Cherokee citizenship applications found at the Oklahoma Historical Society and the National Archives–Southwest Region in Fort Worth, Texas. In addition, I have uncovered fragments of information about Shoe Boots and Doll in diaries of missionaries of the American Board of Commissioners for Foreign Missions located at the Houghton Library of Harvard University and the Moravian Missionary journal and letters, housed at the Moravian Archives in Winston-Salem, North Carolina. I have also pieced together evidence from Cherokee Nation Supreme Court records, Georgia state court records, records of the Cherokee Agency in Tennessee in the Tennessee State Library and Archives, the Cherokee Nation Papers of the Western History Collections at the University of Oklahoma, and the Cherokee Letters Collection of the Georgia State Archives. Remnants of the lives of Doll and Shoe Boots's children have surfaced in Cherokee property evaluations, census and removal rolls, Bureau of Indian Affairs records, as well as articles in the *Cherokee Phoenix* and *Cherokee Advocate* newspapers. Oral history also played an important role in my identification of invaluable primary sources. By informing me of key figures in the Shoeboots family social circle, a descendant of Shoe Boots and Doll pointed the way to a cache of evidence in the Stand Watie Papers at the University of Oklahoma.

Definition and Use of Terms

In the period when Doll and Shoe Boots lived, their family would have been alternately described by a list of animal husbandry–like terms: "mustee" (black and Indian), "mulatto" (black and white, sometimes black and "other"), or "halfbreed" (Indian and white, sometimes Indian and "other"). Slave records of the period tended to refer to people of Native and African ancestry as "Negro," distinguished from non-Native "Negroes" by references to their skin color, hair type, or Indian relatives. The nineteenth-century Cherokee censuses included a category for "Mixed Negroes" (which was adjacent to categories for "Mixed Spanish" and "Mixed Catawbas," a neighboring tribe).

In public scholarship and discussion today, the most commonly used term to describe people of African and Native descent is "Black Indian," popularized by William Loren Katz in his book of the same title. Though straightforward, this term evades specific tribal communities and locations. To call the children of Shoe Boots and Doll "Black Indians" would mean little in the context of their particular experience, for being black and Cherokee was worlds apart from being black and Seminole or black and Lakota. Still, the phrase sometimes serves well as shorthand, as a broad brushstroke for painting this particular mixed-race formation. Tribally specific terms, such as black-Cherokee or Afro-Cherokee, come closer to capturing a more accurate meaning. However, placing "black" or "Afro" in advance of the tribal nation implies a relationship of priority, so that black/Afro becomes the more significant of the two markers. In a society where blackness is viewed as a racial category that subsumes and even invalidates all others, this is an imperfect effect. Furthermore, for mixed-race families who spent their entire lives in Native communities, emphasizing their blackness over their tribal identity would be an inaccurate representation of their experience.

Amid the confusion and inadequacy of these various terms, I attempt below to offer some schema for the ways I employ racial, cultural, political, and geographical terminology in this book. I often use "African American" and "black" interchangeably to describe black people in general. However, when discussing people of African descent who lived in Native nations, I prefer "black," a more flexible descriptor that allows for non-American black identities within the borders of the United States. I call Native American people in the United States "Native," "American Indian," and "Indian" interchangeably. When referring to a broad configuration of Cherokee community, I use "Cherokees," "Cherokee country," "Cherokee territory," or "Cherokee people." At other times, particularly when marking economic and/or cultural distinctions among Cherokees, I use the term "Cherokee elite" to refer to the minority of Cherokees who were wealthy, and a variety of transparent terms to refer to the majority of Cherokees who were subsistence farmers. I call Cherokees who were positioned in between these two groups a middle, or propertied class. When I refer to the "Cherokee Nation" or "Cherokee nation-state," I mean the particular governmental formation that evolved in the early 1800s in the Southeast and was reinstated in the West after Cherokee removal, noninclusive of Cherokee groups who moved West earlier or who remained in the East after removal and developed separate communities and governments. When I use the term "Indian Territory," I am indicating the land of present-day eastern Oklahoma to which Southeastern Indian nations, including the Cherokee, were relocated in the 1830s.

The term "mixed blood" is often used unreflectively in histories of Native America to indicate people of Indian and white descent, a usage that renders invisible people of Indian and black descent. I attempt to specify the particular configuration I point to when using the term "mixed blood," and I often prefer the term "mixed-race" with an accompanying descriptive phrase. I have alternated between calling the children of Doll and Shoe Boots "blacks," "slaves," "black-Cherokees," or "Afro-Cherokees," terms that accurately describe their condition in some moments, such as when their blackness propelled a shift in their circumstances but squarely miss the point most of the time when their experience as mixed-race people cannot be organized into clean linguistic compartments.

By its nature this book defies the precision and limitations of fixed terminology. The Shoeboots family members seem to have been racially mixed and culturally Cherokee, having lived in Cherokee communities throughout most of their lives. They spoke Cherokee, lived Cherokee, and probably dreamed Cherokee, even as their experience of being racialized as black set them apart, texturing and modifying what being Cherokee meant for them.

Cherokee Names
and Mistaken Identities

In keeping with the Cherokee practice of taking on new names at certain stages of life, on special occasions, and in honor of respected persons and benefactors in his time, Shoe Boots was known by a number of names. To complicate matters further, English writers often ascribed multiple spellings to Cherokee names and invented their own English monikers to refer to particular people. Additionally, white visitors to the Cherokees sometimes mistook different people for one another and recorded these mistakes in their personal letters and accounts. The primary and secondary Cherokee records refer to Shoe Boots as Shoe Boot, Shoe Boots, Tuskingo, Tuskaraga, Tarsekayahke, Tah-see-key-yar-key, Chulio, Chulioa, Gentleman Tom, Crowing Cock, and Crowing Rooster. They refer to Doll as Doll, Daull, Lucy, and Lilcy. The long list of names for Shoe Boots in particular has been a source of confusion in Cherokee studies.

William McLoughlin, a prolific scholar and leading authority on Cherokee history, asserted in his book *Cherokee Renascence in the New Republic* (1986) that Shoe Boots was the same man as a person called "Chulio," a prominent and radical Cherokee political figure of the early nineteenth century.[1] Using this assertion as a framework for his reading of primary sources, McLoughlin attributed the actions of the man called Chulio to the man called Shoe Boots. McLoughlin's reasoning for interpreting the records this way is sound—the person or people called Shoe Boots and Chulio often occupy the same pages of the records, turning up in the same town, fighting in the same war, visiting the same mission schools. The two names even have similar meanings. The derivation of Shoe Boots is fairly straightforward; it was a descriptive name for someone who wore shoes that came above the ankle. And according to Cherokee linguist Durbin Feeling, *chulio* can be translated as "he has on socks."[2] To make matters even more confusing, Chulio was called "The Boot" in some missionary records, and Shoe Boots was called "Boots" in Cherokee Agency records. In subsequent histories of this time period, scholars of Cherokee studies have assumed McLoughlin's framework and merged Shoe Boots with Chulio. However, a close reading of previously cited and new evidence suggests that Shoe Boots and Chulio were in fact different people.

In the records of the Cherokee Agency, where Chulio's political feats are chronicled, he is never referred to as Shoe Boots. Moreover, when the agency records refer unequivocally to Shoe Boots, they never mention Chulio and instead give his second name as Tuskingo. In the Moravian missionary records, which include several entries on Chulio (also called Gentleman Tom), who is described as the father of Tommy Acura, one document lists Chulio and Shoe Boots separately. The record, a letter from the Hightower headmen, is signed by the following men, with an X marked by each name: "Colenawai x, Canullahee x, Cachetause x, Nantatagu x, Chulioa x, Shoe boots x, Cahnetohee x, Esaunoot x."[3] Again, in the American Board of Commissioners for Foreign Missions (ABCFM) records, Chulio and Shoe Boots are referred to as though they are different men. A recent publication of the ABCFM journal, edited by Joyce Phillips and Paul Gary Phillips, includes a note to this effect:

> The Brainerd missionaries seemed to make a distinction between The Boot and Shoe Boots. . . . Butrick smoked a peace pipe with The Boot, and The Boot requested that Butrick call his wife and him "mother" and "father.". . . Just three weeks after this visit with The Boot at Turkey Town, Butrick wrote that he visited Hightower at The Feather's, and The Feather sent for the other nearby chiefs. Butrick went on to say that br. John [Arch] spent some time in conversing on the evil of drinking. . . . The great Warrior Shoe Boots, said he was determined to drink no more." In a period of just three weeks, Butrick identified that The Boot was from Turkey Town, and that Shoe Boots lived in Hightower.[4]

Furthermore, military records from the Creek War differentiate between Shoe Boots and Chulio. Shoe Boots is listed as a captain in Colonel Morgan's regiment, and Chulio is listed in a separate file as a lieutenant in Morgan's regiment.[5] Likewise, they were paid for their military service at different times and in different amounts. Shoe Boots was paid $956.29 1/2 in 1815, while "Chulio alias The Boot" protested in 1819 that his payment of $192 had not been sufficient.[6]

Chulio was a frequent companion to Chief Sour Mush and often interpreted for him in negotiations with whites. The observations of General John Coffee concerning Sour Mush's interpreter is additional evidence separating Shoe Boots from Chulio. Coffee posed a concern about "the statement of Governor Mitchell, giving the substance of a talk delivered to him by the Cherokee chief, Sour Mush, by his interpreter, Shoe Boot, in 1818." Coffee further stated: "There must be a mistake in that . . . it is charged that Shoe Boot could not speak the English language so as to interpret the talk alleged to him. See the statement on oath of six persons, on the back of Governor Mitchell's certificate, who knew Shoe boot, and say that he could not speak English intelligibly."[7] This record suggests that even in the 1820s observers confused Shoe Boots with Chulio. This was perhaps because in addition to living in the same town, frequenting the same places, and having similar names, both men were known to wear unusual adornments in their hair. John Howard Payne writes that Shoe Boots wore a "vast-cocked hat and a towering military plume," while the Moravian missionaries recorded that Chulio wore distinctive "red feathers in his cap."[8]

Because Doll has not been considered an important figure in Cherokee history, scholars have taken fewer pains to ascertain her identity. It is the rare history that calls Doll by the correct name and rarer still that attempts to describe her beyond the label-turned-epithet "Shoe Boots's slave wife." Historians William McLoughlin, Theda Perdue, and Adriane Strenk are among the few who consider Doll's personhood and trace the outlines of her experience.[9] In her book *The Cherokee Nation* (1973), Marion Starkey refers to Doll by another name and cites Payne as her source: "The famous warrior Shoe Boots, being deserted by his white wife and their two children, took to wife his negro slave Lucy."[10] Several historians repeated the mistake, referencing Starkey in their footnotes.[11] I have been unable to locate any primary source that refers to Doll as "Lucy." It is possible that these scholars confused Doll with one of Shoe Boots's sisters, who was called Takesteskee and may also have been known as Lucy.[12] Confusion in this case may have been exacerbated by the Cherokee matrilineal kinship system in which Shoe Boots's sisters would have been his social intimates and their children like his own.

My conclusion at this writing is that Shoe Boots and Chulio/Gentleman Tom were two different people who both resided in the town of Hightower. Though Shoe Boots was sometimes called Boots and Chulio was sometimes called The Boot, there seems also to have been a third man, named The Boot, who lived in Turkey Town. Shoe Boots also had a Cherokee name that has been recorded with different spellings. The most reliable of these spellings are probably the versions given by his son William and John Howard Payne as Tarsekayahke and Tah-see-key-yar-key, respectively.[13] Shoe Boots was also known by the war name Crowing Cock or Crowing Rooster. Doll went by the nickname Dolly and also by a Cherokee name spelled differently by two of her contemporaries as Cob-cob-lol and Con-gee-loh.[14] William Shoeboots listed the Cherokee names of his siblings as follows: Lizzie (Kayuka), Polly (Wahlie), John (Ahtasa), and Lewis (Anustrung).[15] Doll and her children took or were accorded Shoe Boots's first name as their surname. In the records, their last name is rendered as Shoeboots, Shoeboot, and the abbreviated versions, Boots or Boot.

Primary Sources for Further Study

The sources reproduced here sometimes include variations in spelling and errors in grammar. These have not been altered from the original or indicated by *sic*.

CHAPTER ONE. CAPTIVITY

Treaty with the Cherokee, 1791 (Treaty of Holston)

The Treaty of Holston was contracted between the president of the United States, George Washington, and the undersigned chiefs and warriors of the Cherokee Nation in the aftermath of the American Revolutionary War. Although a very small number of individual Cherokees owned black slaves in the middle 1700s, often inherited from European fathers or captured in raids on European colonial settlements, the Treaty of Holston spurred the spread of slaveholding in Cherokee society. Article 14 held Cherokee people to a promise that they would strive to attain a level of "civilization" as defined by white American cultural values. This included, among other things, a focus on intensive agricultural production that could be achieved through the use of slave labor.

A Treaty of Peace and; Friendship made and concluded between the President of the United States of America, on the Part and Behalf of the said States, and the undersigned Chiefs and Warriors, of the Cherokee Nation of Indians, on the part and Behalf of the said Nation.

The parties being desirous of establishing permanent peace and friendship between the United States and the said Cherokee Nation, and the citizens and members thereof, and to remove the causes of war, by ascertaining their limits and making other necessary, just and friendly arrangements: The President of the United States, by William Blount, Governor of the territory of the United States of America, south of the river Ohio, and Superintendant of Indian affairs for the southern district, who is vested with full powers for these purposes, by and with the advice and consent of the Senate of the United States. And the Cherokee Nation, by the undersigned Chiefs and Warriors representing the said nation, have agreed to the following articles, namely:

ARTICLE I.

There shall be perpetual peace and friendship between all the citizens of the United States of America, and all the individuals composing the whole Cherokee nation of Indians.

ARTICLE II.

The undersigned Chiefs and Warriors, for themselves and all parts of the Cherokee nation, do acknowledge themselves and the said Cherokee nation, to be under the protection of the said United States of America, and of no other sovereign whosoever; and they also stipulate that the said Cherokee nation will not hold any treaty with any foreign power, individual state, or with individuals of any state.

ARTICLE III.

The Cherokee nation shall deliver to the Governor of the territory of the United States of America, south of the river Ohio, on or before the first day of April next, at this place, all persons who are now prisoners, captured by them from any part of the United States: And the United States shall on or before the same day, and at the same place, restore to the Cherokees, all the prisoners now in captivity, which the citizens of the United States have captured from them.

ARTICLE IV.

The boundary between the citizens of the United States and the Cherokee nation, is and shall be as follows: Beginning at the top of the Currahee mountain, where the Creek line passes it; thence a direct line to Tugelo river; thence northeast to the Occunna mountain, and over the same along the South-Carolina Indian boundary to the North-Carolina boundary; thence north to a point from which a line is to be extended to the river Clinch, that shall pass the Holston at the ridge which divides the waters running into Little River from those running into the Tennessee; thence up the river Clinch to Campbell's line, and along the same to the top of Cumberland mountain; thence a direct line to the Cumberland river where the Kentucky road crosses it; thence down the Cumberland river to a point from which a south west line will strike the ridge which divides the waters of Cumberland from those of Duck river, forty miles above Nashville; thence down the said ridge to a point from whence a south west line will strike the mouth of Duck river.

And in order to preclude forever all disputes relative to the said boundary, the same shall be ascertained, and marked plainly by three persons appointed on the part of the United States, and three Cherokees on the part of their nation.

And in order to extinguish forever all claims of the Cherokee nation, or any part thereof, to any of the land lying to the right of the line above described. beginning as aforesaid at the Currahee mountain, it is hereby agreed, that in addition to the consideration heretofore made for the said land, the United States will cause certain valuable goods, to be immediately delivered to the undersigned Chiefs and Warriors, for the use of their nation; and the said United States will also cause the sum of one thousand dollars to be paid annually to the said Cherokee nation. And the undersigned Chiefs and Warriors, do hereby for themselves and the whole Cherokee nation, their heirs and descendants, for the considerations above-mentioned, release, quit-claim, relinquish and cede, all the land to the right of the line described, and beginning as aforesaid.

ARTICLE V.

It is stipulated and agreed, that the citizens and inhabitants of the United States, shall have a free and unmolested use of a road from Washington district to Mero district, and of the navigation of the Tennessee river.

ARTICLE VI.

It is agreed on the part of the Cherokees, that the United States shall have the sole and exclusive right of regulating their trade.

ARTICLE VII.

The United States solemnly guarantee to the Cherokee nation, all their lands not hereby ceded.

ARTICLE VIII.

If any citizen of the United States, or other person not being an Indian, shall settle on any of the Cherokees' lands, such person shall forfeit the protection of the United States, and the Cherokees may punish him or not, as they please.

ARTICLE IX.

No citizen or inhabitant of the United States, shall attempt to hunt or destroy the game on the lands of the Cherokees; nor shall any citizen or inhabitant go into the Cherokee country, without a passport first obtained from the Governor of some one of the United States, or territorial districts, or such other person as the President of the United States may from time to time authorize to grant the same.

ARTICLE X.

If any Cherokee Indian or Indians, or person residing among them, or who shall take refuge in their nation, shall steal a horse from, or commit a robbery or murder, or other capital crime, on any citizens or inhabitants of the United States, the Cherokee nation shall be bound to deliver him or them up, to be punished according to the laws of the United States.

ARTICLE XI.

If any citizen or inhabitant of the United States, or of either of the territorial districts of the United States, shall go into any town, settlement or territory belonging to the Cherokees, and shall there commit any crime upon, or trespass against the person or property of any peaceable and friendly Indian or Indians, which if committed within the jurisdiction of any state, or within the jurisdiction of either of the said districts, against a citizen or white inhabitant thereof, would be punishable by the laws of such state or district, such offender or offenders, shall be subject to the same punishment, and shall be proceeded against in the same manner as if the offence had been committed within the jurisdiction of the state or district to which he or they may belong, against a citizen or white inhabitant thereof.

ARTICLE XII.

In case of violence on the persons or property of the individuals of either party, neither retaliation or reprisal shall be committed by the other, until satisfaction shall have been demanded of the party of which the aggressor is, and shall have been refused.

ARTICLE XIII.

The Cherokees shall give notice to the citizens of the United States, of any designs which they may know, or suspect to be formed in any neighboring tribe, or by any person whatever, against the peace and interest of the United States.

ARTICLE XIV.

That the Cherokee nation may be led to a greater degree of civilization, and to become herdsmen and cultivators, instead of remaining in a state of hunters, the United States will from time to time furnish gratuitously the said nation with useful implements of husbandry, and further to assist the said nation in so desirable a pursuit, and at the same time to establish a certain mode of communication, the United States will send such, and so many persons to reside in said nation as they may judge proper, not exceeding four in number, who shall qualify themselves to act as interpreters. These persons shall have lands assigned by the Cherokees for cultivation for themselves and their successors in office; but they shall be precluded exercising any kind of traffic.

ARTICLE XV.

All animosities for past grievances shall henceforth cease, and the contracting parties will carry the foregoing treaty into full execution with all good faith and sincerity.

ARTICLE XVI.

This treaty shall take effect and be obligatory on the contracting parties as soon as the same shall have been ratified by the President of the United States, with the advice and consent of the Senate of the United States.

In witness of all and every thing herein determined between the United States of America and the whole Cherokee nation, the parties have hereunto set their hands and seals, at the treaty ground on the bank of the Holston, near the mouth of the French Broad, within the United States, this second day of July, in the year of our Lord one thousand seven hundred and ninety-one.

William Blount, governor in and over the territory of the United States of America south of the river Ohio, and superintendent of Indian Affairs for the southern district,

Chuleoah, or the Boots, his x mark,

Squollecuttah, or Hanging Maw, his x mark,

Occunna, or the Badger, his x mark,

Enoleh, or Black Fox, his x mark,

Nontuaka, or the Northward, his x mark,

Tekakiska, his x mark,

Chutloh, or King Fisher, his x mark,

Tuckaseh, or Terrapin, his x mark,

Kateh, his x mark

Kunnochatutloh, or the Crane, his x mark,

Canquillehanah, or the Thigh, his x mark,

Chesquotteleneh, or Yellow Bird, his x mark,

Chickasawtehe, or Chickasaw Killer, his x mark,

Tuskegatehe, Tuskega Killer, his x mark,

Kulsatehe, his x mark,

Tinkshalene, his x mark

Sawntteh, or Slave Catcher, his x mark,

Auknah, his x mark,

Oosenaleh, his x mark,

Kenotetah, or Rising Fawn, his x mark,

Kanetetoka, or Standing Turkey, his x mark,

Yonewatleh, or Bear at Home, his x mark,

Long Will, his x mark,

Kunoskeskie, or John Watts, his x mark,

Nenetooyah, or Bloody Fellow, his x mark,

Chuquilatague, or Double Head, his x mark,

Koolaquah, or Big Acorn, his x mark,

Toowayelloh, or Bold Hunter, his x mark,

Jahleoonoyehka, or Middle Striker, his x mark,

Kinnesah, or Cabin, his x mark,

Tullotehe, or Two Killer, his x mark,

Kaalouske, or Stopt Still, his x mark,

Kulsatche, his x mark,

Auquotague, the Little Turkey's Son, his x mark,

Talohteske, or Upsetter, his x mark,

Cheakoneske, or Otter Lifter, his x mark,

Keshukaune, or She Reigns, his x mark,

Toonaunailoh, his x mark,

Teesteke, or Common Disturber, his x mark,

Robin McClemore,

Skyuka,

John Thompson, Interpreter.

James Cery, Interpreter.

Done in presence of—

Dan'l Smith, Secretary Territory
United States south of the river Ohio.

Thomas Kennedy, of Kentucky.

Jas. Robertson, of Mero District.

Claiborne Watkins, of Virginia.

Jno. McWhitney, of Georgia.

Fauche, of Georgia.

Titus Ogden, North Carolina.

Jno. Chisolm, Washington District.

Robert King.

Thomas Gegg.

Additional Article To the Treaty made between the United States and the Cherokees on the second day of July, one thousand seven hundred and ninety-one.

IT is hereby mutually agreed between Henry Knox, Secretary of War, duly authorized thereto in behalf of the United States, on the one part, and the undersigned chiefs and warriors, in behalf of themselves and the Cherokee nation, on the other part, that the following article shall be added to and considered as part of the treaty made between the United States and the said Cherokee nation on the second day of July, one thousand seven hundred and ninety-one; to wit:

The sum to be paid annually by the United States to the Cherokee nation of Indians, in consideration of the relinquishment of land, as stated in the treaty made with them on the second day of July, one thousand seven hundred and ninety-one, shall be one thousand five hundred dollars instead of one thousand dollars, mentioned in the said treaty.

In testimony whereof, the said Henry Knox, Secretary of War, and the said chiefs and warriors of the Cherokee nation, have hereunto set their hands and seals, in the city of Philadelphia, this seventeenth day of February, in the year of our Lord, one thousand seven hundred and ninety-two.

H. Knox, Secretary of War,

Iskagua, or Clear Sky, his x mark (formerly Nenetooyah, or Bloody Fellow),

Nontuaka, or the Northward, his x mark,

Chutloh, or King Fisher, his x mark,

Katigoslah, or the Prince, his x mark,

Teesteke, or Common Disturber, his x mark,

Suaka, or George Miller, his x mark,

In presence of—

Thomas Grooter.

Jno. Stagg, jr.

Leonard D. Shaw

James Cery, sworn interpreter to the Cherokee Nation.

Indian Affairs: Laws and Treaties, vol. 2, *Treaties*, edited by Charles J. Kappler (Washington, D.C.: Government Printing Office, 1904), 29–33

CHAPTER TWO. SLAVERY

Records from the Case of Nancy, an Enslaved Cherokee Woman

Cherokee chiefs' account of Nancy's capture: "Testimony of Two Cherokee Chiefs Relating to Nancy, a Cherokee Woman," October 28, 1808, Records of the Cherokee Agency in Tennessee. Accessed in microfilm publication 504, reel 5 (1810–12), Center for Research Libraries, Chicago.

Nancy's bill of sale: William Kennedy to John Fulton, April 2, 1778, bill of sale, Records of the Cherokee Agency in Tennessee. Accessed in microfilm publication 504, reel 5 (1810–12), Center for Research Libraries, Chicago.

This related set of documents provides another example of slavery in the Cherokee Nation at the time when Doll was acquired and owned by Shoe Boots. In this case, Nancy, a Cherokee woman with probable African ancestry, was held as a slave by whites, showing that in addition to being slaveholders, some Cherokees were in danger of being enslaved themselves and racialized as "black" in the tumultuous period of the American Revolution. Nancy was a girl when soldiers captured her and her mother, most likely in 1776. She was held by three different owners as a slave in Virginia until, in 1801, she claimed a Cherokee identity and protested her enslaved status at Fort Southwest Point in Tennessee. Although several Cherokee chiefs claimed Nancy as Cherokee and the Virginia Supreme Court proclaimed all Indians in the state to be free in 1806, these documents do not indicate that Nancy, a mother and grandmother, ever secured her freedom. For more on this case, see Tiya Miles, "The Narrative of Nancy, a Cherokee Woman," *Frontiers: A Journal of Women Studies* 29, nos. 2–3 (2008): 59–80.

Another example of a Cherokee woman enslaved in the nineteenth century appears in the research of historian Arika Easley-Houser. Easley-Houser has surveyed newspaper reports that detail the case of Lucy, a teenager imprisoned in Columbia, South Carolina, in the 1850s because of a question about her racial identity. A white man named Mr. Darby had placed a runaway slave ad for Lucy and tried to reclaim her. However, Lucy identified herself as a Cherokee, which threw Darby's rightful ownership into doubt. Lucy remained in jail from 1851 to 1854, when Cherokee chief Junaluska claimed her as Cherokee and told her story of capture in 1837. See Arika Easley-Houser, "The Indian Image in the Black Mind: Representing Native Americans in Antebellum African American Public Culture," PhD diss., Rutgers University, 2014; "An Interesting Trial," *Frederick Douglass' Paper*, September 4, 1854; *Daily Globe*, November 29, 1854; *Alton Weekly Courier*, November 30, 1854.

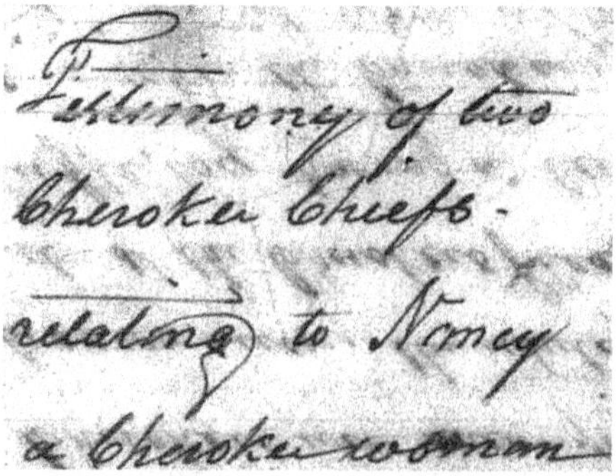
Testimony of two
Cherokee Chiefs -
relating to Nancy
a Cherokee woman

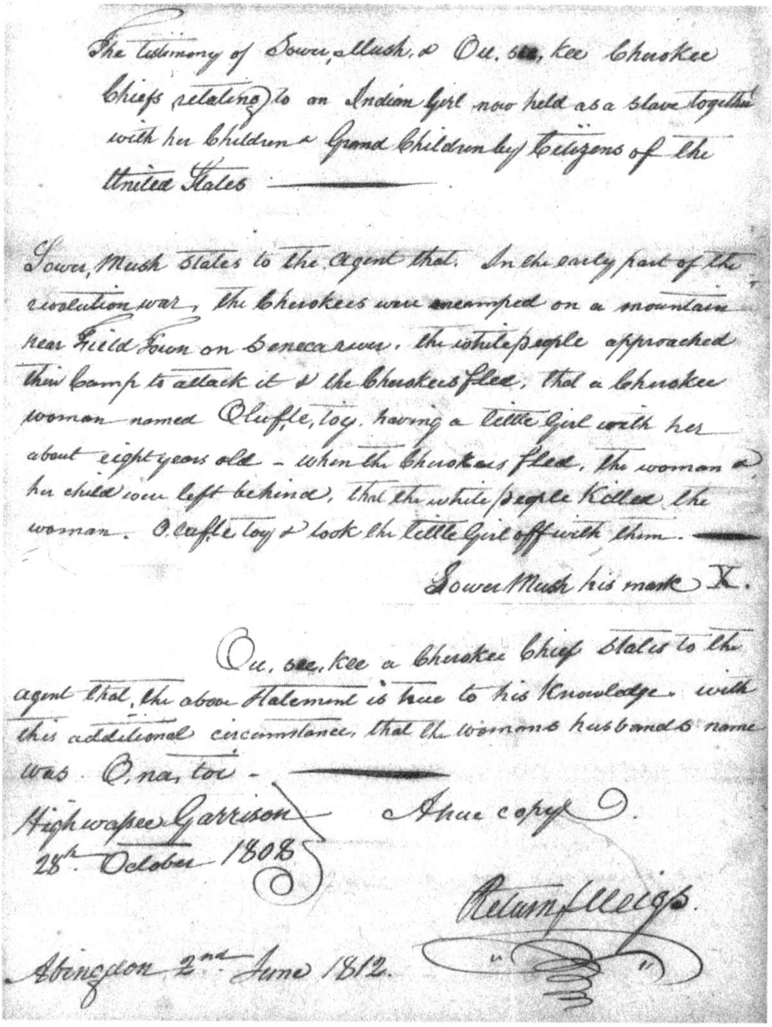
The testimony of Sower, Mush, & Ou, sa, kee Cherokee Chiefs relating to an Indian Girl now held as a slave together with her Children & Grand Children by Citizens of the United States ——

Sower, Mush states to the Agent that. In the early part of the revolution war, the Cherokees were encamped on a mountain near Field Town on Seneca river. the white people approached their Camp to attack it & the Cherokees fled, that a Cherokee woman named Olufle, toy. having a little Girl with her about eight years old — when the Cherokees fled, the woman & her child were left behind, that the white people Killed the woman. O.cufle toy & took the little Girl off with them. ——

Sower Mush his mark X.

Ou, sa, kee a Cherokee Chief states to the agent that, the above statement is true to his Knowledge. with this additional circumstance, that the womans husbands name was O, na, toi ——

Highwassee Garrison
28th. October 1808

A true copy

Return J Meigs.

Abingdon 2nd June 1812.

Figure 1. Account of Nancy's capture, "Testimony of Two Cherokee Chiefs Relating to Nancy, a Cherokee Woman," October 28, 1808, Records of the Cherokee Agency in Tennessee. Images courtesy of the Center for Research Libraries, Chicago.

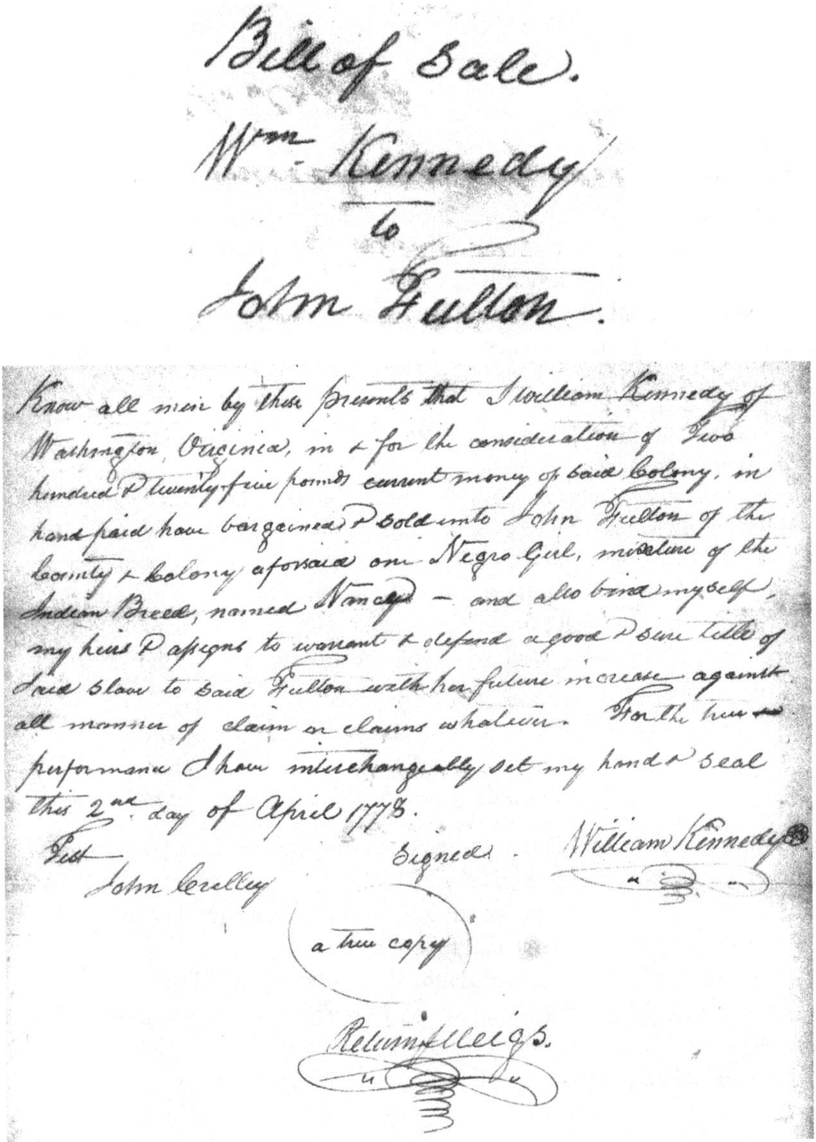

Bill of Sale.
Wm. Kennedy
to
John Fulton.

Know all men by these presents that I William Kennedy of Washington, Virginia, in & for the consideration of Two hundred & twenty-five pounds current money of said Colony, in hand paid have bargained & sold unto John Fulton of the County & Colony aforesaid one Negro Girl, mixture of the Indian Breed, named Nancy — and also bind myself, my heirs & assigns to warrant & defend a good & sure title of said slave to said Fulton with her future increase against all manner of claim or claims whatever. For the true performance I have interchangeably set my hand & seal this 2nd day of April 1778.

Test
John Kelley

Signed. William Kennedy

a true copy

Return J. Meigs.

Figure 2. Bill of sale for Nancy from William Kennedy to John Fulton, April 2, 1778, Records of the Cherokee Agency in Tennessee. Images courtesy of the Center for Research Libraries, Chicago.

Virginia Slave Statute, 1662

As one of the first American colonies to legislate slavery, Virginia attended closely to the status of black women. In 1662 it passed Act XII, requiring that "all children borne in this country shalbe held bond or free only according to the condition of the mother." Although the law also stipulated that "any christian" would pay a fine for "ffornication with a negro man or woman," it ensured that children resulting from sexual relations between free white men and enslaved black women would be slaves, thus barring these mixed-race children from access to the privileges of whiteness and contributing to the wealth of male slaveholders.

> December, 1662. Act XII. *Negro womens children to serve according to the condition of the mother.*
>
> Whereas some doubts have arrisen whether children got by any Englishman upon a negro woman should be slave or ffree, *Be it therefore enacted and declared by this present grand assembly,* that all children borne in this country shalbe held bond or free only according to the condition of the mother, *And* that if any christian shall committ ffornication with a negro man or woman, hee or shee soe offending shall pay double the ffines imposed by the former act.
>
> William W. Hening, *The Statutes at Large; Being a Collection of All the Laws of Virginia,* vol. 2 (New York: R. and W. and G. Bartow, 1823), 170

Molly's Case in the Cherokee Nation Supreme Court

The oft cited 1662 Virginia law and records of a Cherokee Supreme Court case from 1833 show how both American slavery and Cherokee slavery linked the categorization of the child to the "condition" or status of the mother. While American law stated that the child would follow the mother's status, Cherokee cultural practice dictated that the child would inherit the mother's clan. This parallel worked to the detriment of Doll. She was a slave without clan status in Cherokee society, which customarily would have meant that her children inherited both dimensions of her marginal status. In contrast, the example of Molly, another woman of African descent in early nineteenth-century Cherokee country, shows a different possible outcome for black women in this context. Because she was adopted by the Cherokee Deer clan and hence emancipated and accepted as kin, her mixed-race children became free Cherokee citizens.

The Deer Clan's Defense of Molly

Cherokee Nation North Carolina
 This will certify that we under sind Cherokee of the state of North Carolina were Residents of the Nation of the time that a white man and an

Indian trader who had a Cherokee woman for his wife but who by his usage of her in Beating and other wise mistreating of her when in a state of pregnancy died the clan or tribe to whom she belonged determined to kill the said white man by the name of Sam Dent who to appease them and satisfy said tribe or clan went off to augusta georgia and did then purchase a female slave by the name of molly and brought female unto the cherokee nation and did offer her to the clans remuneration for the wrongs he had done, a Town Council and Talk was then had at Chota old town at Tennessee River and the said female was then and there Received by D clan and by the authorities agreeable to the indian Law and usage in the place of the murdered wife of said Sam Dent and has . . . herself and descendants been ever since Recognized by said nation or clan as a cherokee . . . The only descendants of said molly has been and are claimed to be the property of one Molly Hightower who has come into the said nation and set up a claim by Bill of sale for said Sam Dent to . . . Hightower's father who was also an Indian trader and who lived many years near the Decendants of said and. . . . Set up any claim to the Law Defendants that the pursuit petitioner Chunestutat Alisa Isaac Tucker, and his mother, Chickaua . . . were off in therefore mentioned native as [we have ever considered] the Council and authorities of the Cherokee nation as also we the subscribers members of the same clan ask and require of our Council and headmen for assistance and for Council to resist this oppression and legal wrong attempted to be practiced on our Brother and Sister by the Hightower in leasing to slavery two of whom have ever been and considered native cherokee we feel that the attempt is one of cruel greavance to us and ask of your Honorable bodies Redress in the protection and defense of the two afore mentioned members of our clan and your petitioner will ever pray.

  . . . the doctor
[chianistitualias]
Isaac Tucker his x mark
Chickaune molley her x mark
Charles Buffinton
The old thigh his x mark
Buck Horn his x mark
[Chicked] his x mark

Cherokee Supreme Court Docket 1833, Cherokee Collection, microfilm publication 815, Tennessee State Library and Archives, Nashville

Testimony Regarding Molly's Adoption
This day appeared before me:
  Daniel McCoy one of the judges of the Supreme Court of the Cherokee Nation of the Big Half Breed Jms Watts the Tiger and the White Path who being duly sworn and saith that to the best of their knowledge and belief that the mother of Edward and Isaac Tucker Molly was surrendered and delivered

up when a girl some time previous to the Revolutionary War by a white man named Samuel Bend to the authorities of the Cherokee Nation for certain important considerations and that said Molly was then emancipated and adopted into the clan composing the Deer family arguably to the then existing usages and customs of said nation. Since that time she has continued in the nation and enjoyed the liberty of freedom and that her two sons Edward and Isaac Tucker were born at the beloved town called Echota on the Tennessee River and have ever been free and resided in the Nation sworn to and subscribed before me at Red Clay this 18th Oct. 1833.

Daniel McCoy
[J.S.] Court
. . . Big Half Breed his x
White Path his x
James Watts his x
Tiger his x

Cherokee Supreme Court Docket 1833, Cherokee Collection, microfilm publication 815, Tennessee State Library and Archives, Nashville

CHAPTER FOUR. PROPERTY

Letter to Protect Cherokee Lands

Letter from five Cherokee chiefs (Shoe Boots, Sour Mush, Standing Turkey, Jobbers Son, and Dreadful Water) to Josiah Tatnall, March 27, 1802, MS 606, Folder 14, Box 1, Hargrett Library, University of Georgia, Athens.

Shoe Boots's Deed of Gift

Tuscarora Shoe Boots deed of gift for personal property, April 24, 1835, Clerk of Court and Probate Court, Book N, Habersham County, Clarksville, Ga.

These sources show Cherokees making claims to land in a manner that resisted white encroachment yet also asserting the right to sell blacks as property in the manner of white slaveholding society. In the first source, a letter not cited in the first edition of *Ties That Bind*, five Cherokee chiefs write to Governor Josiah Tatnall of Georgia by way of General John Clark. They are protesting the arrival of white settlers and attempting to protect the Cherokee communal land base. In the second source, a deed of gift, Shoe Boots gives away Doll and their children along with his other slaves to a white man in the area. When read together, these sources demonstrate that Cherokee people at this time both rejected and adopted aspects of Euro-American views of property. While many repudiated the idea that land should be subdivided and held privately, some accepted the notion that people of African descent could be treated as privately owned movable goods. Individuals such as Shoe Boots held both views simultaneously. He is a signatory to both documents here.

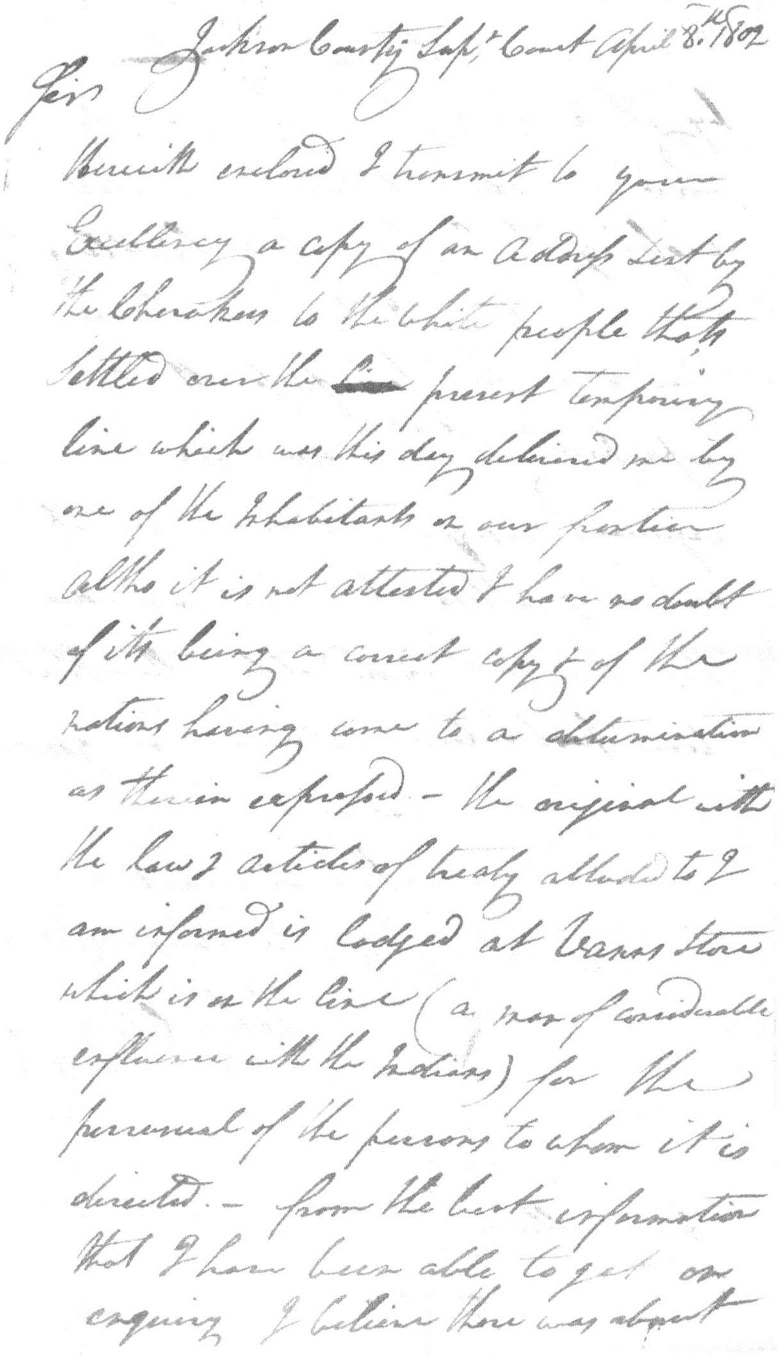

Jackson County Supr Court April 8th 1802

Sir

Herewith enclosed I transmit to your Excellency a copy of an Address sent by the Cherokees to the white people that settled over the ~~Line~~ present temporary line which was this day delivered me by one of the Inhabitants on our frontier altho it is not attested I have no doubt of its being a correct copy & of the nations having come to a determination as therein expressed — the original with the last 2 articles of treaty alluded to I am informed is lodged at Vanns store which is on the line (a man of considerable influence with the Indians) for the perusal of the persons to whom it is directed. — from the best information that I have been able to get on enquiry I believe there was about

Figure 3. Letter from five Cherokee chiefs to protect Cherokee lands, March 27, 1802, with Shoe Boots's signature. Held at and images courtesy of Hargrett Library, University of Georgia, Athens.

thirty five families cut off ~~the~~
by the running of the line, seventy
moved over line & that they are daily
crossing it for the purpose of settling

Such as I have seen here
I have endeavoured to impress with the
impropriety of the measure and the
injurious consequences that would with
certainty attend it I recommended
their returning immediately within the
line particularly those that have gone
over since it was run. —

with much respect
I am Sr Your Excellency's Ob Servt

John Clark Maj Genl

His Excellency
The Governor

Cherokee Nation March 27th 1802

To the White people that is improving
and Settling on our lands over the line
a Counceil was held at Eastanaulee and
it was resolved that there should be no
Crops raised on our Lands and we
take this opportunity to acquaint you
of the same, and that we wish for peace
and are in hopes you will quit your proceedings and go off peaceably and if you
do not we are Determined to come and destroy
all the improvements made on the same
We have also sent you the Law and Articles
of Treaty which may convince you that we
are doing of ourselves Justice and you not
an injury   From your friend & brothers

Signed

Shoe Boots
Sour Mush
Standing Turkey
Jobbors son
Dreadful Water

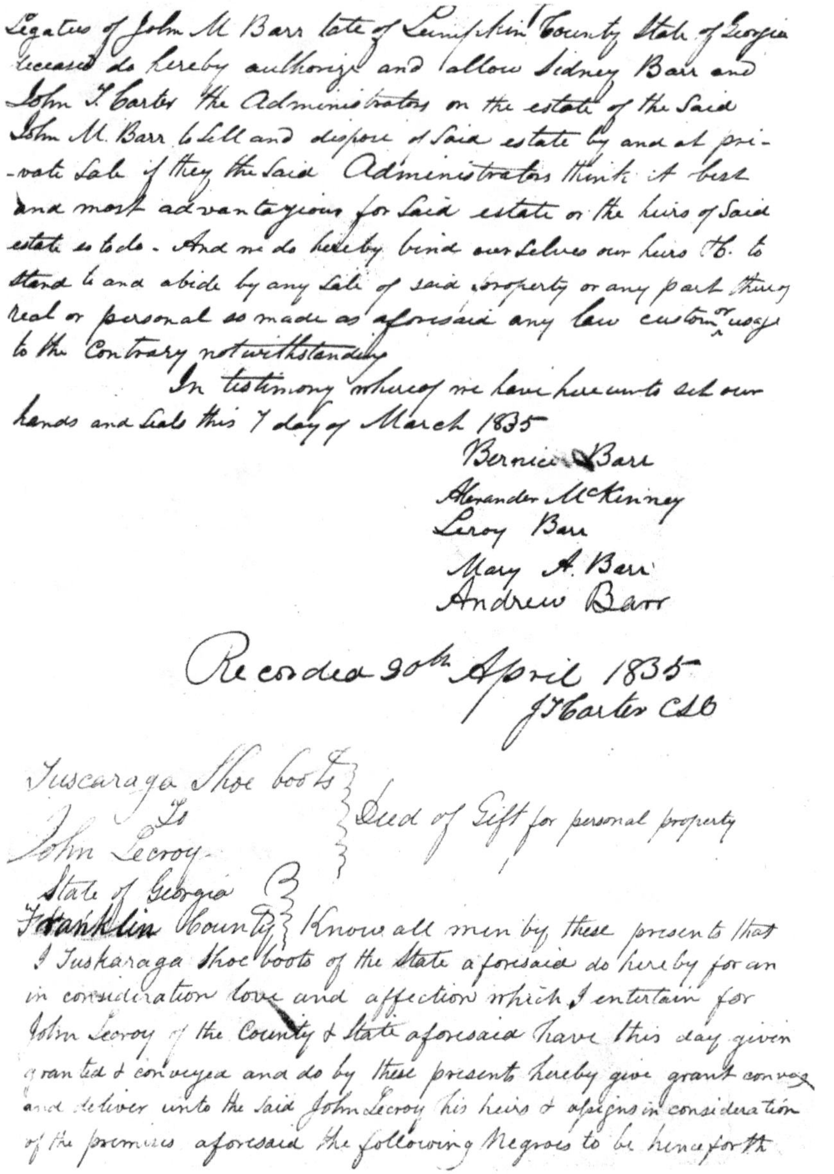

Legatees of John M Barr late of Lumpkin County State of Georgia deceased do hereby authorize and allow Sidney Barr and John T Carter the Administrators on the estate of the said John M. Barr to sell and dispose of said estate by and at private Sale if they the said Administrators think it best and most advantageous for said estate or the heirs of said estate to sell. And we do hereby bind ourselves our heirs &c. to stand to and abide by any sale of said property or any part thereof real or personal so made as aforesaid any law custom or usage to the Contrary notwithstanding

In testimony whereof we have hereunto set our hands and seals this 7 day of March 1835

Bernice Barr
Alexander McKinney
Leroy Barr
Mary A. Barr
Andrew Barr

Recorded 20th April 1835
JT Carter C&c

Tuscaraga Shoe boots }
To } Deed of Gift for personal property
John Lecroy }

State of Georgia }
Franklin County } Know all men by these presents that I Tuskaraga Shoe boots of the State aforesaid do hereby for an in consideration love and affection which I entertain for John Lecroy of the County & State aforesaid have this day given granted & conveyed and do by these presents hereby give grant convey and deliver unto the said John Lecroy his heirs & assigns in consideration of the premises aforesaid the following Negroes to be henceforth

Figure 4. Tuscarora Shoe Boots's deed of gift for personal property, April 24, 1835. Held at and images courtesy of the Clerk of Court and Probate Court, Habersham County, Clarksville, Ga.

the property of him the said John his heirs and assigns to wit, Doll a woman twenty five years old, Frank a fellow twenty years old, Aggy a girl twelve years old & Lize a child three years old & do hereby covenant and agree with the said John Lecroy in consideration of the natural love and affection which I entertain for him as aforesaid that the said negroes so by me given granted conveyed & delivered to him the said John & to & for the proper use benefit and behoof of him the said John Lecroy his heirs & assigns to have and to hold the said negroes & their increas unto him the said John Lecroy his heirs & assigns forever

In witness whereof I have hereunto set my hand and affixed my seal this 1st day of Sept. 1809

Nathaniel Wofford   Tuscarag   his X Shoeboots
Saml Bright   mark
Wm Lecroy

Recorded 24th April 1835
J.T. Carter C.H.

L. B. Burnett }
    To   } Deed for part of Lot No 99 = 3rd Dist
Robt. H. Patton }
             1/4

Georgia
Habersham County } This Indenture made this twenty ninth day of April (1835) eighteen hundred and thirty five between L.B. Burnett of the County and State aforesaid of the one part and Robert H. Patton of the County of McMinn and State of Tennissee of the other part Witnesseth that the said Burnett for and in consideration of the Sum of five hundred dollars to him in hand paid at and before the dealing and delivery of these presents the receipt and payment of which is hereby acknowledged hath bargained granted & sold and by these presents doth bargain grant sell and convey unto the said Robert H. Patton his heirs executors administrators and assigns the undivided one-fourth part of a piece or parcel of land hereinafter described being a part of Lot number twenty two in the third district of said County begining on a large poplar on the North Bank

CHAPTER FIVE. CHRISTIANITY

Moravian Mission Diary, Springplace, Cherokee Nation

These diary entries were written by missionaries from the Moravian Church in Salem, North Carolina, who settled in the Cherokee Nation near the wealthy slaveholder James Vann. Their arrival in the early 1800s and the development of their Springplace Mission brought change and opportunity to African American slaves. Blacks attended worship services and performed the intellectual labor of translating between the missionaries and Cherokee slaveholders. They also attempted to harness skills that the missionaries brought, such as literacy, for themselves. The missionary presence was both a benefit and a detriment to Cherokee people. While the missionaries taught Native children how to read and write in English, a skill that Cherokee leaders sought for the youth in their community, they also insisted upon the truth of their Christian religious faith. These diary entries illustrate a number of themes: the influence of Christian missionaries on the experience of slaves, black slaves' roles as translators and mediators between missionaries and Cherokees, black slaves' ability to take advantage of missionary activities for their own ends, and Cherokee criticism of the cultural change that the missionaries encouraged. Isaac, an enslaved man who studied English with the missionaries and ran away from Vann three times, appears frequently in these excerpts. Shoe Boots visited the Springplace Mission during the earthquakes of 1811–12 and indicated his suspicion that a shift from old Cherokee ways was incurring natural disaster. One of the excerpted diary entries refers to him by another name: Chuleoa. Researchers should note that the compilation of Springplace Mission materials edited by Daniel Crews and Richard W. Starbuck, released by the Moravian Archives Southern Province and cited here, includes letters with descriptions of enslaved African Americans that were not available at the time of the first edition of *Ties That Bind*.

> *May 28.* The Overseer had corn sown on the planted fields, because the birds often ripped out what had been planted. It did not help, though, because the birds let the hard grain lie and preferred to take the tender sprouts. This afternoon all the Negroes went home, so that it was very quiet all around us. The Negro Isaac enquired from Br. Byhan what he would have to give if he gave him instruction in reading. Br. Byhan replied that he would not expect anything from him, except that in return he should give him instruction in the Cherokee language, which he promised to do.
>
> *Sun., May 30.* It was very quiet at our place since we did not get to see any people. We wanted to visit our neighbors but did not find them at home.
>
> *May 31.* Three Indians came to us. They asked us for some salt, for which they promised us venison. In the last day, the weather has been so cool that we could stand a good fire at night.

June 1. An Indian came to us and soon after that 2 women who had earthenware bowls for sale, which we bought from them. A Negro was our interpreter for this.

June 2. All the Negroes came to work here again. An Indian also stopped at our place on his way to Estenally, sat down very quietly for a while, and then went on his way.

Records of the Moravians among the Cherokees, edited by C. Daniel Crews and Richard W. Starbuck, vol. 2 (Tahlequah, Okla.: Cherokee National Press, 2010), 427–28

Sun., Sept. 16.

1. Br. Wohlfahrt reported that he had an opportunity last week to speak to one of Mr. Vann's Negroes, named Isaak, regarding the necessity of our yielding ourselves to become the property of the Saviour. Br. Wohlfahrt also read aloud to him from the Periodical Accounts regarding the Lord's work among the Negroes in the West Indies, which the Negro himself had desired to hear. Br. Wohlfahrt told him that we had come to this country for the same purpose: to proclaim the Word of God to the Indians, but that since it appears that the Indians do not as yet have ears to hear the Word of God we intended to try all the more to speak with the blacks about their souls' salvation. For the Saviour had come into the world for *all* men out of *love* for them and had shed His blood for them, and had died for all men, etc. It appeared that this had not left him untouched.

Records of the Moravians among the Cherokees, edited by C. Daniel Crews and Richard W. Starbuck, vol. 2 (Tahlequah, Okla.: Cherokee National Press, 2010), 779

Early in the third hour *on the 16th,* two shocks from an earthquake were felt. The houses shook and everything in them moved. The chickens fell to the ground from their resting places and caused a frightful crying. At eight o'clock another smaller shock was felt.

On the 17th Chief Bead Eye, his brother The Trunk, and two other Indians came to get information from us about the earthquake. They all seemed very upset and said that the earth is very old, would it soon fall apart? We explained to them what causes earthquakes, with the comment that the all-powerful God who made the earth and everything on it and to this day has maintained it, also had the power and force to punish in various ways humans who live in sin, and the He often had used such earthquakes for such a purpose.

The residents of this country had reason to thank Him that He was so merciful to them this time and should see it as a warning to stop serving sin and to obey His voice. It was certain that God had determined a day in which He would judge all humans and each one would be rewarded according to his works. Then the earth would be consumed by fire, and so on.

They hung their heads and seemed to be deep in thought. During a heavy rain in the evening, we had the joy of seeing our former pupil Tommy arrive here with his father, our friend Chuleoa, and his wife. They were also deeply concerned about and horrified by the earthquake. Chuleoa brought us a letter from Mr. Charles Hicks, in which, among other things, he reported the following: "I cannot describe the great consternation that we felt last night.

"Our living quarters were moving so much that they seemed close to falling down. Just before this a loud noise was heard from the north-north-west and some people saw a flash of light from right where the noise in the air had begun. This morning, between seven and eight o'clock, we felt two shocks again, but not as strong as the earlier ones and without the slightest noise. Our house, however, shook a lot and the roof was moved.

"All the trees were also moving without the slightest wind." "Oh!" Mr. Hicks added, "may we honor merciful God for His protection from day to day and call to Him for help in improving our lives in the future." Mr. Hicks had directed this company to us, as with the above-mentioned, for more exact instruction in the matter. We spoke with them in a similar manner as with the former ones, and our Tommy translated our words with the greatest seriousness.

Our Peggy, who was at neighboring Indians today on business, could not describe in what consternation she found the poor people everywhere. Some of them attributed the event to conjurors and some of them to a great snake who must have crawled under their house, and some of them to the weakness of the earth which, because of its age, would soon fall in. Our Sister took advantage of this opportunity to extol to them the love and the seriousness of God and to advise them to take the salvation of their souls seriously.

The Moravian Springplace Mission to the Cherokees, edited by Rowena McClinton, vol. 1 (Lincoln: University of Nebraska Press, 2007), 460–61

CHAPTER SIX. NATIONHOOD

Cherokee Nation Constitution, 1827

Cherokee Nation, *Laws of the Cherokee Nation: Adopted by the Council at Various Periods, 1808–35* (Tahlequah, C.N. [Okla.]: Cherokee Advocate Office, 1852), 118–30.

This source and the next demonstrate the role of race and the exclusion of blacks in the formation of Cherokee governance shaped in the 1820s and 1830s. As was the case with the United States Constitution, many of the architects of the Cherokee Constitution were slaveholders. Article III, Section 4 of the Cherokee Constitution denies the rights of citizenship to the offspring of Cherokee men and black women while allowing citizenship to the offspring of Cherokee men and nonblack free women. The citizenship of the offspring of Cherokee women is assumed, given the predominance in the nation of a matrilineal clan system. This article also prohibits "mulattoes" of any parental combination from holding governmental office in the Cherokee Nation, indicating a lack of public trust in Afro-Cherokee people. The constitution does not limit white residents in the same manner. Article III, Section 7 secures voting rights for "free male citizens" while prohibiting free blacks, free Afro-Cherokees, and all women from voting. For an in-depth look at the legislation of interracial marriage and the legal place of mixed-race progeny in the Cherokee Nation over the course of the nineteenth century, which followed a similar pattern of black exclusion, readers should see the work of historian Fay Yarbrough, *Race and the Cherokee Nation: Sovereignty in the Nineteenth Century* (Philadelphia: University of Pennsylvania Press, 2007).

Shoe Boots's Petition to Free His Children

Captain Shoe Boots to the Chiefs in Council, October 20, 1824, no. 6508, roll 46, Cherokee Nation Papers, Western History Collections, University of Oklahoma, Norman.

This is the first document of significance uncovered during the research for this book. Shoe Boots's emancipation petition shows his attempt to circumvent new Cherokee ideas and laws about black marginalization on behalf of his Afro-Cherokee children. In the petition, he seeks to legally free his children and asserts their citizenship rights. Note that Doll's name appears in the original cursive script as Daull. Her name is spelled as Doll or Dolly in other primary documents and throughout *Ties That Bind*.

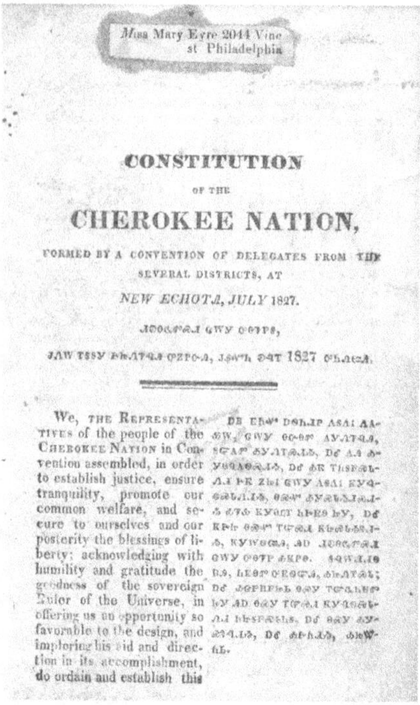

Figure 5. Articles 1 through 3 of the Cherokee Nation Constitution, 1827, in English and Cherokee, from Cherokee Nation, *Constitution of the Cherokee Nation, Formed by a Convention of Delegates from the Several Districts, at New Echota, July 1827* (New Echota, Ga.: Isaac H. Harris and John F. Wheeler, 1828). Held at and images courtesy of the Newberry Library, Chicago.

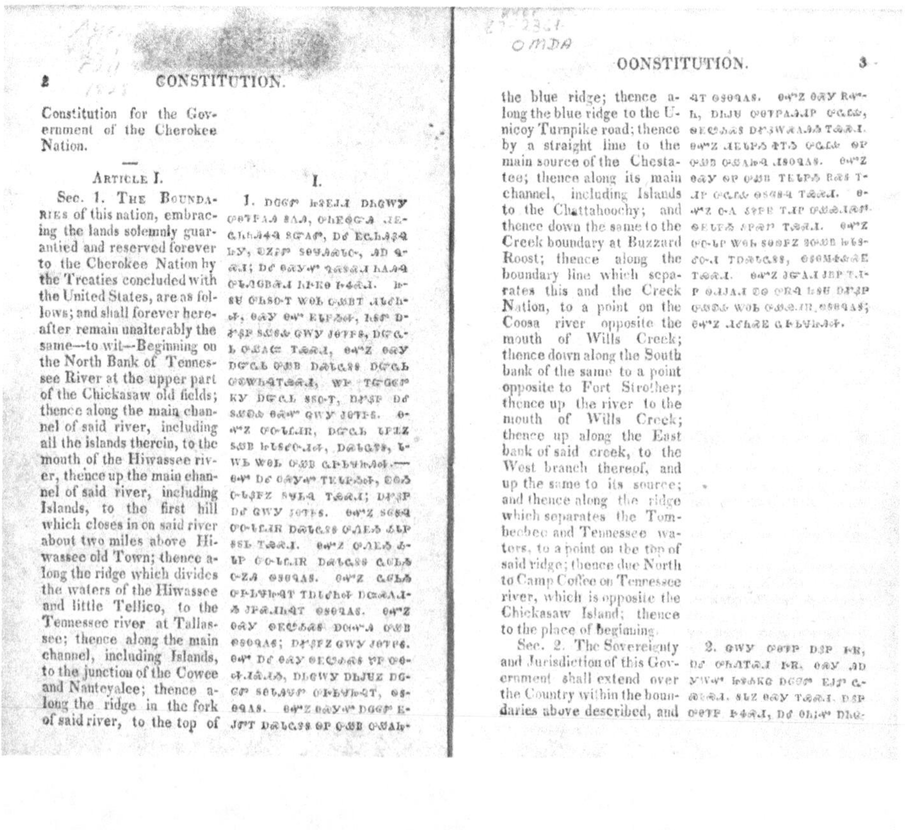

CONSTITUTION
OF THE
CHEROKEE NATION,
FORMED BY A CONVENTION OF DELEGATES FROM THE
SEVERAL DISTRICTS, AT
NEW ECHOTA, JULY 1827.

We, THE REPRESENTA-
TIVES of the people of the
CHEROKEE NATION in Con-
vention assembled, in order
to establish justice, ensure
tranquility, promote our
common welfare, and se-
cure to ourselves and our
posterity the blessings of liberty; acknowledging with
humility and gratitude the
goodness of the sovereign
Ruler of the Universe, in
offering us an opportunity so
favorable to the design, and
imploring his aid and direction in its accomplishment,
do ordain and establish this

CONSTITUTION.   2

Constitution for the Gov-
ernment of the Cherokee
Nation.

ARTICLE I.

Sec. 1. THE BOUNDA-
RIES of this nation, embracing the lands solemnly guar-
antied and reserved forever
to the Cherokee Nation by
the Treaties concluded with
the United States, are as follows; and shall forever hereafter remain unalterably the
same—to wit:—Beginning on
the North Bank of Tennes-
see River at the upper part
of the Chickasaw old fields;
thence along the main channel of said river, including
all the islands therein, to the
mouth of the Hiwassee river, thence up the main channel of said river, including
Islands, to the first hill
which closes in on said river
about two miles above Hi-
wassee old Town; thence a-
long the ridge which divides
the waters of the Hiwassee
and little Tellico, to the
Tennessee river at Tallas-
see; thence along the main
channel, including Islands,
to the junction of the Cowee
and Nanteyalee; thence a-
long the ridge in the fork
of said river, to the top of

CONSTITUTION.   3

the blue ridge; thence a-
long the blue ridge to the U-
nicoy Turnpike road; thence
by a straight line to the
main source of the Chesta-
tee; thence along its main
channel, including Islands
to the Chattahoochy; and
thence down the same to the
Creek boundary at Buzzard
Roost; thence along the
boundary line which sepa-
rates this and the Creek
Nation, to a point on the
Coosa river opposite the
mouth of Wills Creek;
thence down along the South
bank of the same to a point
opposite to Fort Strother;
thence up the river to the
mouth of Wills Creek;
thence up along the East
bank of said creek, to the
West branch thereof, and
up the same to its source;
and thence along the ridge
which separates the Tom-
beebee and Tennessee wa-
ters, to a point on the top of
said ridge; thence due North
to Camp Coffee on Tennessee
river, which is opposite the
Chickasaw Island; thence
to the place of beginning.

Sec. 2. The Sovereignty
and Jurisdiction of this Government shall extend over
the Country within the boundaries above described, and

the lands therein are, and shall remain, the common property of the Nation; but the improvements made thereon, and in the possession of the citizens of the Nation, are the exclusive and indefeasible property of the citizens respectively who made, or may rightfully be in possession of them; *Provided*, That the citizens of the Nation, possessing exclusive and indefeasible right to their respective improvements, as expressed in this article, shall possess no right nor power to dispose of their improvements in any manner whatever to the United States, individual States, nor to individual citizens thereof; and that, whenever any such citizen or citizens shall remove with their effects out of the limits of this Nation, and become citizens of any other Government, all their rights and privileges as citizens of this Nation shall cease; *Provided nevertheless*, That the Legislature shall have power to re-admit by law to all the rights of citizenship, any such person or persons, who may at any time desire to return to the Nation on their memorializ-

ing the General Council for such readmission. *Moreover*, the Legislature shall have power to adopt such laws and regulations, as its wisdom may deem expedient and proper, to prevent the citizens from monopolizing improvements with the view of speculation.

ARTICLE II.

Sec. 1. THE POWER of this Government shall be divided into three distinct departments;—the Legislative, the Executive, and the Judicial.

Sec. 2. No person or persons, belonging to one of these Departments, shall exercise any of the powers properly belonging to either of the others, except in the cases hereinafter expressly directed or permitted.

ARTICLE III.

Sec. 1. THE LEGISLATIVE POWER shall be vested in two distinct branches; a Committee, and a Council; each to have a negative on the other, and both to be styled, the General Council of the Cherokee Nation; and the style of their acts and laws shall be,

"RESOLVED by the Committee and Council in Gen-

eral Council convened."

Sec. 2. The Cherokee Nation, as laid off into eight Districts, shall so remain.

Sec. 3. The Committee shall consist of two members from each District, and the Council shall consist of three members from each District, to be chosen by the qualified electors of their respective Districts, for two years; and the elections to be held in every District on the first Monday in August for the year 1828, and every succeeding two years thereafter; and the General Council shall be held once a year, to be convened on the Second Monday of October in each year, at New Echota.

Sec. 4. No person shall be eligible to a seat in General Council, but a free Cherokee Male citizen, who shall have attained to the age of twenty-five years. The descendants of Cherokee men by all free women, except the African race, whose parents may been living together as man and wife, according to the customs and laws of this Nation, shall be entitled to all the rights and privileges of this nation, as well as the

posterity of Cherokee women by all free men. No person who is of negro or mulatto parentage, either by the father or mother side, shall be eligible to hold any office of profit, honor or trust under this Government.

Sec. 5. The electors, and members of the General Council shall, in all cases except those of treason, felony, or breach of the peace, be privileged from arrest during their attendance at election, and at the General Council, and in going to, and returning from, the same.

Sec. 6. In all elections by the people, the electors shall vote *viva voce*. Electors for members to the General Council for 1828, shall be held at the places of holding the several courts, and at the other two precincts in each District which are designated by the law under which the members of this Convention were elected; and the District Judges shall superintend the elections within the precincts of their respective Court Houses, and the Marshals and Sheriffs shall superintend within the precincts which may be assigned them by the Circuit Judges of their respective Districts, together with one other person, who shall be appointed by the Circuit Judges for each precinct within their respective Districts; and the Circuit Judges shall also appoint a clerk to each precinct.—The superintendents and clerks shall, on the Wednesday morning succeeding the election, assemble at their respective Court Houses, and proceed to examine and ascertain the true state of the polls, and shall issue to each member, duly elected, a certificate; and also make an official return of the state of the polls of election to the principal Chief, and it shall be the duty of the Sheriff's to deliver the same to the Executive; *Provided nevertheless,* The General Council shall have power, after the election of 1828, to regulate by law the precincts and superintendents and clerks of elections in the several Districts.

Sec. 7. All free Male citizens, (excepting negroes and descendants of white and Indian men by negro women, who may have been set free,) who shall have at-

tained to the age of eighteen years, shall be equally entitled to vote at all public elections.

Sec. 8. Each House of the General Council shall judge of the qualifications, and returns, of its own members.

Sec. 9. Each House of the General Council may determine the rules of its proceedings, punish a member for disorderly behaviour, and, with the concurrence of two thirds, expel a member; but not a second time for the same cause.

Sec. 10. Each House of the General Council, when assembled shall choose its own officers; a majority of each house shall constitute a quorum to do business, but a smaller number may adjourn from day to day, and compel the attendance of absent members in such manner and under such penalty, as each house may prescribe.

Sec. 11. The members of the Committee shall each receive from the public Treasury a compensation for their services which shall be *two dollars and fifty cents* per day during their attendance at the General

Council; and the members of the Council shall each receive *two dollars* per day, for their services during their attendance at the General Council:—*Provided,* That the same may be increased or diminished by law, but no alteration shall take effect during the period of service of the members of the General Council, by whom such alteration shall have been made.

Sec. 12. The General Council shall regulate by law, by whom and in what manner, writs of elections shall be issued to fill the vacancies which may happen in either branch thereof.

Sec. 13. Each member of the General Council, before he takes his seat, shall take the following oath, or affirmation; to wit: "I, A. B. do solemnly swear (or affirm as the case may be) that I have not obtained my election by Bribery, Treats or any undue and unlawful means used by myself, or others by my desire or approbation, for that purpose; that I consider myself Constitutionally qualified as a member of ; and that, on all questions and measures which may

come before me, I will so give my vote, and so conduct myself, as may, in my judgment, appear most conducive to the interest and prosperity of this Nation; and that I will bear true faith and allegiance to the same; and to the utmost of my ability and power observe, conform to, support, and defend the Constitution thereof."

Sec. 14. No person who may be convicted of felony before any court of this Nation, shall be eligible to any office or appointment of honor, profit or trust, within this Nation.

Sec. 15. The General Council shall have power to make all laws and regulations, which they shall deem necessary and proper for the good of the Nation, which shall not be contrary to this Constitution.

Sec. 16. It shall be the duty of the General Council to pass such laws as may be necessary and proper, to decide differences by arbitrators to be appointed by the parties, who may choose that summary mode of adjustment.

Sec. 17. No power of suspending the laws of this Nation shall be exercised,

unless by the Legislature or
its authority.

Sec. 18. No retrospective law, nor any law impairing the obligations of contracts shall be passed.

Sec. 19. The Legislature shall have power to make laws for laying and collecting taxes, for the purpose of raising a revenue.

Sec. 20. All bills making appropriations shall originate in the Committee, but the Council may propose amendments or reject the same.

Sec. 21. All other bills may originate in either house, subject to the concurrence or rejection of the other.

Sec. 22. All acknowledged Treaties shall be the Supreme law of the land.

Sec. 23. The General Council shall have the sole power of deciding on the construction of all Treaty stipulations.

Sec. 24. The Council shall have the sole power of impeaching.

Sec. 25. All impeachments shall be tried by the Committee:—when sitting for that purpose, the members shall be upon oath or

18. ᎠᏎ ᏗᎵᎬ ᎥᏍ ᎥᏣᎥᎢ ᏍᏛᏣᎥᎢ, ᎠᏎ ᎲᏏ Ꮓ Ꮞ�125Ꮫ ᎥᏍ ᎥᎲᎦᎥᎢ ᎠᏈ4ᎥᎢ.

19. ᎤᎵᎪ– ᏎᏫᏍᎢ ᎤᎵᏪᎥᏐ ᎥᎲᎽᏔᎥᎢ Ꮘ4ᎥᎢ ᎢᏎᎿ9ᎲᎶ– ᎥᎵᏍ ᎠᏐ ᎤᎤᏣᏘᎥᎢ, ᎠᏎ Ꭴ– ᎣᏏᎵᏍ.

20. ᎠᏎ ᎠᏔᎥ ᎢᎠᏣᎳᎯᎥᎢ ᎲᏍᎶᏛᎯᎠᏣᎥᎢ, ᎠᏎ ᎠᏍᏐ–Ꭼ ᏍᏴᎥᏓᏍᎶᎶᎢ Ꮘ4ᎥᎢ; ᎤᎲᏪ– ᎤᏴᎥᏯᎲᏐ– ᎡᏣᎵᎠᎬᎥᎢ ᎠᏈ ᎡᏣᎵᎠᏣᎥᎢ Ꮘ4ᎥᎢ.

21. ᎵᏏᎤᎵᎠᏘᎥᎢ Ꮘ4ᎥᎢ ᎢᎢ– ᎤᎳ, ᎠᏈ4ᎥᎢ ᏣᎴᎾ, ᎢᎡᎠᎵᎠᎬᎯ– ᎣᎵᎢ ᎠᏈ ᎠᎡᎡᎵᎠᏣᎵᎢ Ꮘ4ᎥᎢ.

22. ᎲᏍᎶ ᏎᏭᎵᎢ ᎢᎤᎯᎡᏍᏛ–Ꮆ, Ꮞ49ᎥᎢ ᎢᎠᏐᎡᎶᎵᎥᎢ ᎡᎲᏍᎲ Ꮘ4– ᎡᎥᎢ.

23. ᎤᎵᎪ– ᏎᏫᏍᎢ ᎥᎲᎽᏔᎥ ᎥᏓᎵᎢ Ꮘ4ᎥᎢ ᏣᎶᏛ ᎤᎶᏣ ᎲᏏ ᏍᏯᏐᏛ ᎢᎤᎯᎡᏍᏛ–Ꮆ.

24. ᎤᎵᎳ ᎢᎡᏍᎩ ᎥᎲᎽᏔᎥ ᎣᎾ Ꭳ–Ꭱ ᎣᎶᏍᏔᏈᎵᏣᎥᎢ Ꮘ4ᎥᎢ, ᎢᎤᏃ ᎤᎲ ᎠᏎ ᎠᏈᎥᏔᏈᎾ ᎢᏓᎡᎬᏈᎥᎢ.

25. ᎤᏯ ᎠᎲᎵ3ᎢᏈᎥᎢ ᎲᏏᏈ– ᎥᎵᎠᎥᏈ4ᎥᎢ, ᎠᏎ ᎠᏍᏐ–ᏓᏯ Ꭳ– ᎣᏍᏔᏈᎥᎢ Ꮘ4ᎥᎢ, ᎠᏈ ᎠᎮ ᎵᏈ– ᎣᎾ Ꮘ4ᎥᎢ; ᎠᏈ ᎢᎡ ᎤᏯ ᎣᎴᏐ– ᎣᎬ ᎢᏌᎵᎢ ᎥᏍ4ᎥᎢ, ᎡᎵ ᎡᎩ

affirmation; and no person shall be convicted without the concurrence of two thirds of the members present.

Sec. 26. The Principal Chief, assistant principal Chief, and all civil officers, under this nation, shall be liable to impeachment for any misdemeanor in office; but Judgment, in such cases, shall not extend further than removal from office, and disqualification to hold any office of honor, trust or profit, under this Nation. The party whether convicted or acquitted, shall, nevertheless, be liable to indictment, trial, judgment, and punishment, according to law.

ARTICLE IV.

Sec. 1. The Supreme Executive Power of this Nation shall be vested in a Principal Chief, who shall be chosen by the General Council, and shall hold his office four years; to be elected as follows,—The General Council by a joint vote, shall, at their second annual session, after the rising of this Convention, and at every fourth annual session thereafter, on the second day after the Houses

ᎢᎤᎤᏔᏒ ᎳᏈ ᎥᎲᎵᎠᎥᎢ ᎠᎲᎵᏈ– ᎥᎢ.

26. ᎤᎬᎬᏣᏐ, ᎠᏈᎠᏎ ᏎᏯ ᎤᎬᎬᏣᏐ, ᎠᏈ ᎣᎲᎵ ᎠᏎᏈ ᏈᎮᏔᏖ– ᎥᎢ, ᏈᎲᎶᏔᏈᎵᎾᎢ Ꮘ4ᎥᎢ, ᎢᎤᏃ ᎠᏎᏈ ᏈᎲᎵᏔᎿᏔ ᎠᎲᎲᏐ–ᎾᎥᎢ, ᎢᎤᏃ ᎤᎲᎠᏐᎬ ᎥᏎᎵᎲᎿᏣᎥᎢ, ᏈᎲᎤᎶᎾ–ᎵᎸᎢ Ꮘ4ᎥᎢ ᎠᏈ ᎠᏎᏈ ᏎᎲᎵᏔᎥᎢ ᎲᏈᎡᎠ ᎢᎤᏈᎵᎵᎢ Ꮘ– 4ᎥᎢ. ᎠᎴᎵᎥᏓ5Ꭰ– ᏎᎲᎶᎢ Ꮘ– ᎥᎢ ᎲᏍᏈᎵᏔᎵᎠᏈᎥᎢ ᎢᎠᎵᎠᏯᎥᏐ, ᎠᏈ ᎣᏍᏐᏈᎵ ᎲᏎᏔᏖ ᏖᎬᏐ– ᏈᎵᏔᎵ ᎡᎵᎲᎲᏔᎥᎢ ᎲᏈᎵᎵᎠ– ᎠᎵᎠᎵ, ᎢᎤᏃ ᎠᏈᎶ ᎤᎲᎶᎢ Ꭳ– Ꭸ ᎣᎲᏍᎩᎶᏐᎬ ᎣᎲᏐ– ᏧᏯ ᎠᏎᏈ ᎠᏍᏐ–ᏔᏯ.

IV.

1. ᎤᎵᎳ– ᎤᎬᎬᏣ ᎢᎡᏍ ᏎᏯ Ꮘ4ᎥᎢ, ᎠᏈ ᎤᎵᎪ– ᏎᏫᏍᎢ ᎤᎲ– ᏪᎩ ᎣᎤᏯᏣᎥᎢ Ꮘ4ᎥᎢ, ᎢᎤᏃ Ꭳ–Ꭹ4– ᎥᏔᎵᎲᏈ ᎢᏍᎣᏍᎵᎠᎢ Ꮘ4– ᎥᎢ, ᎠᏈ ᎠᏘ ᎢᎤᏈᎡᎵᎢ ᎠᎡᏐᎠᎢ ᎥᎢ. ᎤᏍ ᎣᎲᏍᎶᎶ–Ꭼ ᎵᎠᏪᎶ–Ꭰ ᎠᏈᎾ, ᎣᎥᎽ ᎠᏈ ᎡᎶᎡ– ᏥᎵ ᎣᎶᏍᏣᎥᎢ Ꮘ4ᎥᎢ; ᎤᎵᎪ– ᏎᏫᏍᎢ ᎤᎲᏪᎩ ᎣᎥᎤ ᏔᎬᎶ–Ꭰ ᎵᎠᏪᎶ–Ꭰ ᎠᏈᎾ, ᎣᎥᎽ ᎠᏈ ᎡᎶᎡ– ᎤᏐ ᎣᏍᏔᏣᎥᎢ Ꮘ4ᎥᎢ. ᎣᎥᏃ ᎢᎤᎲᎵᎠᏐ ᎣᎵᎳᎠᏈᎥᎢ Ꭳ– Ꭹ ᎠᏒᎵᎲ ᎣᎲᏐᎵᎢ ᎲᏈᎵᎠᎡᏔ– ᏈᎥᎢ. ᎠᏎᏈᏯᎲ ᏖᎤ ᎥᎲᏪᎶ–Ꭰ ᏈᎵ ᏈᎥ ᎣᎲᏍᏔᎵ Ꮘ4ᎥᎢ ᎤᎬᎬ– ᎬᎶ.

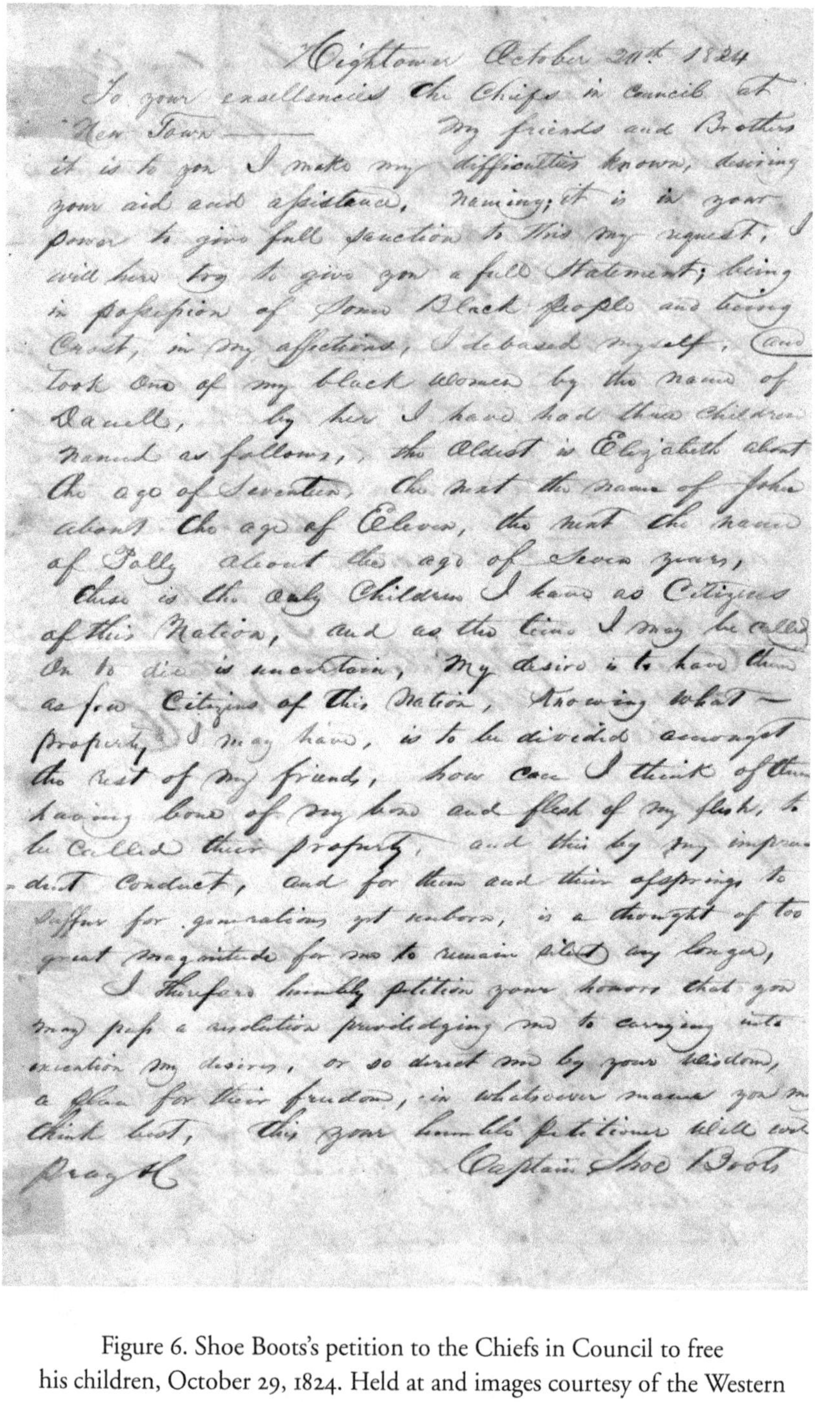
Hightower October 29th 1824
To your excellencies the Chiefs in Council at New Town — My friends and Brothers it is to you I make my difficulties known, desiring your aid and assistance, knowing; it is in your power to give full sanction to this my request, I will here try to give you a full Statement; being in possession of Some Black people and having Crost, in my affections, I debased myself, and took One of my black Women by the name of Daull, by her I have had three Children named as follows, the Oldest is Elizabeth about the age of Seventeen, the next the name of John about the age of Eleven, the next the name of Polly about the age of Seven years,
these is the only Children I have as Citizens of this Nation, and as the time I may be called On to die is uncertain, My desire is to have them as free Citizens of this Nation, Knowing what property I may have, is to be divided amongst the rest of my friends, how ever I think of them having bone of my bone and flesh of my flesh, to be called their property, and this by my imprudent Conduct, and for them and their offsprings to suffer for generations yet unborn, is a thought of too great magnitude for me to remain silent any longer,
I therefore humbly petition your honors that you may pass a resolution privilidging me to carrying into execution my desires, or so direct me by your wisdom, a plan for their freedom, in whatsoever manner you may think best, this your humble petitioner will ever pray &c
Captain Shoe Boots

Figure 6. Shoe Boots's petition to the Chiefs in Council to free his children, October 29, 1824. Held at and images courtesy of the Western History Collections, University of Oklahoma, Norman.

I do Certify the above to be a true Copy
of the Original

New Town 6th Novr 1834 —   A. McCoy
                                   Clerk Nl Committee

The National Council have taken into Consideration the petition of Captain Shoe Boots,
purporting to grant freedom to his three Children
which he had by his Slave, the Council therefore
has no Objections to recognizing their freedom, as
well as their inheritance to the Cherokee Country,

But it is ordered that Capt Shoe Boots
Cease begitting any more Children by his said
Slave Woman provided the National Committee
will Concur in this decision

                                   Major Ridge
6th Novr 1834 —   Speaker of the Council
Concured by the National Committee
A. McCoy Clk   John Ross Prest
Nl Committee   Nl Committee

I do Certify the above to be a true Copy of
of the Original   A. McCoy Clk
                                   Nl Comte

I A. McCoy do Certify that the forego is
is a true Copy of record from the Book of
record now in the possession of Mr John Ross
This 4th day of February 1837 —
                                   A. McCoy
I do Certify that I was present and saw A. McCoy
take the foregoing from the Original acts of the Committee
and Council
Red Clay 4th February 1837   Saml K. Weird

I do Certify that I am acquainted with the hand writing of A. McCoy & know that his signature is in this paper and given & are in his hand writing

New Echota 8th Feby 1837   John Ridge Prest
                                                          Committee

Resolved that we consider Lizzy John & Polly Children of Capt. Shoe Boots & are Free persons according to the act of the Cherokee Council in Nov. 6. 1824. as per Copy of the above document

New Echota 9 Feby 1837   John Ridge Prest
                                                  Committee

I do Certify the foregoing petition together with the annexed artifices to be true Copies of an original proof handed me for transcription by Mr William Thompson acting agent for the three Children herein before named, for their proper benefit, Transcribed Ross Landing Tennessee

8th March 1837.   A. True Copy Teste

                                    A. M. Rawlings

Georgia State Land Grant, Land Tickets, and
Survey Map for Cherokee Lands

Cherokee County plat, 1832, and land grant, 1834, issued to Stephen Carter, Head-
right and Lottery Loose Plat File, Survey Records, Surveyor General, RG 3–3-
26, and Land Lottery Grant Books, Lottery Records, Surveyor General, RG
3–5-29, Georgia Archives, Morrow.

Land lottery ticket, 1832, Land Lottery Administrative Records, General Administrative Records, Surveyor General, RG 003–01–020, Georgia Archives,
Morrow.

Mapping of Cherokee County Section 1, District 10, District Plats of Survey,
Survey Records, Surveyor General, RG 3–3-24, Georgia Archives, Morrow.

The first American gold rush can be said to have occurred on Cherokee lands in
1829. After the discovery of rich gold deposits in the Appalachian Mountains, the
state of Georgia, led by Governor Wilson Lumpkin, took measures to seize these
valuable lands. Declaring the extension of its jurisdiction over Cherokee territory, the state annulled Cherokee laws, then usurped Cherokee land and redis-
tributed parcels, inclusive of homes, to white settlers. The land lottery tickets and
land grants reproduced here represent part of the paper trail of Georgia's actions,
which the U.S. Supreme Court deemed illegal in 1832. Georgia gold mining and
minting ended in 1849, just as the California gold rush was surging forward.

These sources—a land grant, a lottery ticket, and a district map—indicate
the process of Georgia's redistribution of Cherokee land after the gold rush. They
also show the multifaceted nature of colonialism, which involves both extractive
practices (such as the removal of gold) and the acquisition of land for settlement
(referred to in recent indigenous studies literature as "settler colonialism"). These
sources further point to mapping as a tool for claiming authority over land and
for making land more amenable to commercialization through surveys and sales.
Visitors to Georgia can learn more about at the gold rush at the Dahlonega Gold
Museum.

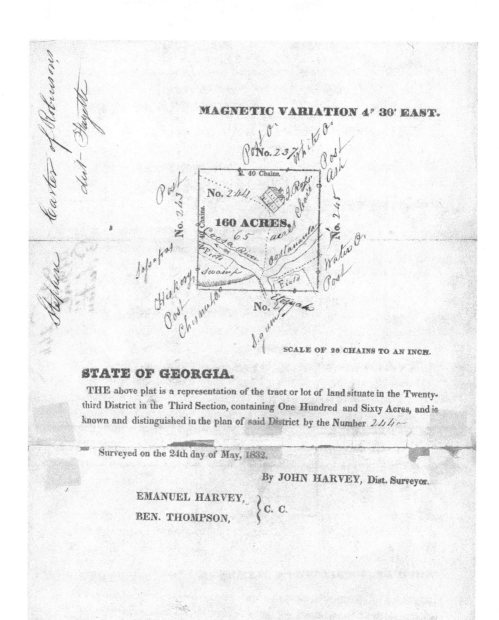

MAGNETIC VARIATION 4° 30' EAST.

No. 237

No. 244

N. 40 Chains.

160 ACRES

No. 243

No. 245

No. 2

SCALE OF 20 CHAINS TO AN INCH.

STATE OF GEORGIA.

THE above plat is a representation of the tract or lot of land situate in the Twenty-third District in the Third Section, containing One Hundred and Sixty Acres, and is known and distinguished in the plan of said District by the Number *244*

Surveyed on the 24th day of May, 1832.

By JOHN HARVEY, Dist. Surveyor.

EMANUEL HARVEY, } C. C.
BEN. THOMPSON,

Figure 7. Cherokee County plat and land grant issued to Stephen Carter. Held at and images courtesy of the website (www.georgiaarchives.org) of the Georgia Archives, Morrow.

State of Georgia.

By his Excellency *Wilson Lumpkin* Governor and

Commander in Chief of the Army and Navy of this State, and of the Militia thereof.

TO ALL TO WHOM THESE PRESENTS SHALL COME, *GREETING*:

KNOW YE, that in pursuance of the several Acts of the General Assembly of this State, passed the 21st of December, 1830, and the 22d of December, 1831, to authorize the survey and disposition of the lands within the limits of Georgia, in the occupancy of the Cherokee tribe of Indians, and all other unlocated lands within the limits of said State, claimed as Creek lands, and forming the County of Cherokee, I HAVE GIVEN AND GRANTED, and by these presents DO GIVE AND GRANT, unto *Stephen Carter*

of *Robinson's* District *Fayette* County *his* heirs and assigns forever, all that TRACT OR LOT OF LAND, containing *One Hundred and Sixty Acres*, situate, lying and being in the Twenty-third District of the Third Section, in the County of Cherokee, in said State, which said Tract or Lot of Land is known and distinguished in the plan of said District by the number *two hundred and forty four* having such shape, form and marks as appear by a plat of the same hereunto annexed :

TO HAVE AND TO HOLD, the said Tract or Lot of Land, together with all and singular the rights, members and appurtenances thereof, whatsoever, unto the said *Stephen Carter his*

heirs and assigns ; to *his* and their own proper use, benefit and behoof forever in fee simple.

GIVEN under my hand and the Great Seal of the said State, this *fourteenth* day of *February* in the year eighteen hundred and *thirty four* and of the Independence of the United States of America the *fifty eighth*

Signed by his Excellency the Governor, this *14* day of *Feby* 18*34*

Wilson Lumpkin

D. Buckner S. E. D.

Registered the *14* day of *Feby* 18*34*

53

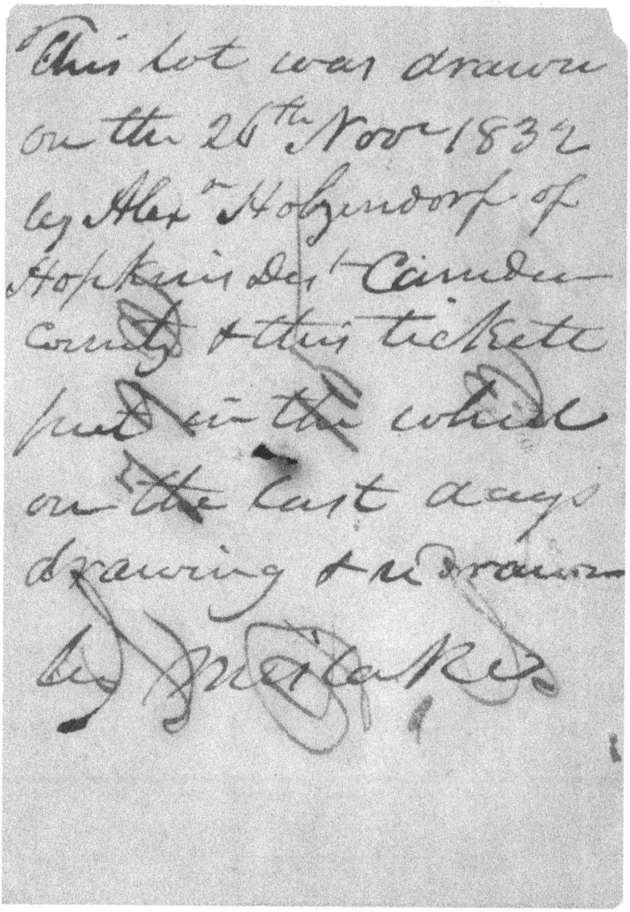

Figure 8. Example of a land lottery ticket from 1832. Held at and image courtesy of the Georgia Archives, Morrow.

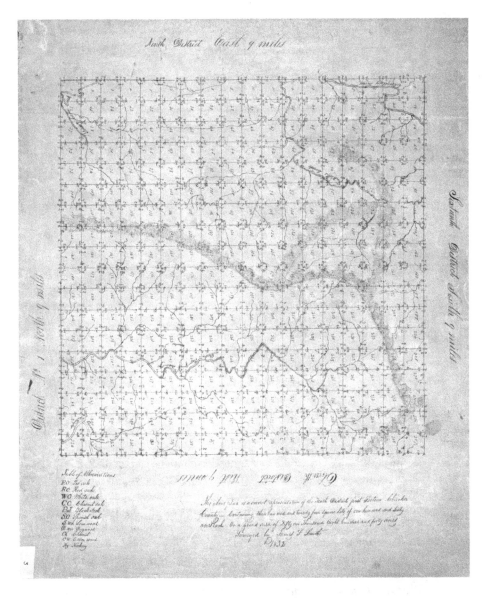

Figure 9. Mapping of Cherokee County Section 1, District 10. Held at
and image courtesy of the website (www.georgiaarchives.org) of
the Georgia Archives, Morrow.

CHAPTER EIGHT. REMOVAL

Indian Removal Act, 1830

The United States government's policy of Indian Removal devastated Cherokee people and the black slaves living among them. The Indian Removal Act, approved by Congress in 1830, is reproduced here. It sanctioned, indeed mandated, the expulsion of indigenous peoples, affecting not only Cherokees and other southeastern nations but also Native nations in the Midwest.

UNITED STATES CONGRESS
Indian Removal Act
May 28, 1830
Chapter CXLVIII

An Act to provide for an exchange of lands with the Indians residing in any of the states or territories, and for their removal west of the river Mississippi.

Be it enacted by the Senate and House of Representatives of the United States of America, in Congress assembled, That it shall and may be lawful for the President of the United States to cause so much of any territory belonging to the United States, west of the river Mississippi, not included in any state or organized territory, and to which the Indian title has been extinguished, as he may judge necessary, to be divided into a suitable number of districts, for the reception of such tribes or nations of Indians as may choose to exchange the lands where they now reside, and remove there; and to cause each of said districts to be so described by natural or artificial marks, as to be easily distinguished from every other.

Sec. 2 *And be it further enacted,* That it shall and may be lawful for the President to exchange any or all of such districts, so to be laid off and described, with any tribe or nation of Indians now residing within the limits of any of the states or territories, and with which the United States have existing treaties, for the whole or any part or portion of the territory claimed and occupied by such tribe or nation, within the bounds of any one or more of the states or territories, where the land claimed and occupied by the Indians, is owned by the United States, or the United States are bound to the state within which it lies to extinguish the Indian claim thereto.

Sec. 3 *And be it further enacted,* That in the making of any such exchange or exchanges, it shall and may be lawful for the President solemnly to assure the tribe or nation with which the exchange is made, that the United States will forever secure and guaranty to them, and their heirs or successors, the country so exchanged with them; and if they prefer it, that the United States will cause a patent or grant to be made and executed to them for the same: Provided always, That such lands hall revert to the United States, if the Indians become extinct, or abandon the same.

Sec. 4 *And be it further enacted,* That if, upon any of the lands now occupied by the Indians, and to be exchanged for, there should be such improvements as add value to the land claimed by any individual or individuals of such tribes or nations, it shall and may be lawful for the President to cause such value to be ascertained by appraisement or otherwise, and to cause such ascertained value to be paid to the person or persons rightfully claiming such improvements. And upon the payment of such valuation, the improvements so valued and paid for, shall pass to the United States, and possession shall not afterwards be permitted to any of the same tribe.

Sec. 5 *And be it further enacted,* That upon the making of any such exchange as is contemplated by this act, it shall and may be lawful for the President to cause such aid and assistance to be furnished to the emigrants as may be necessary and proper to enable them to remove to, and settle in, the country for which they may have exchanged; and also, to give them such aid and assistance as may be necessary for their support and subsistence for the first year after their removal.

Sec. 6 *And be it further enacted,* That it shall and may be lawful for the President to cause such tribe or nation to be protected, at their new residence, against all interruption or disturbance from any other tribe or nation of Indians, or from any other person or persons whatever.

Sec. 7 *And be it further enacted,* That it shall and may be lawful for the President to have the same superintendence and care over any tribe or nation in the country to which they may remove, as contemplated by this act, that he is now authorized to have over them at their present places of residence: Provided, That nothing in this act contained shall be construed as authorizing or directing the violation of any existing treaty between the United States and any of the Indian tribes.

Sec. 8 *And be it further enacted,* That for the purpose of giving effect to the provisions of this act, the sum of five hundred thousand dollars is hereby appropriated, to be paid out of any money in the treasury, not otherwise appropriated.

The Cherokee Removal: A Brief History with Documents, edited by Theda Perdue and Michael D. Green (Boston: Bedford / St. Martin's, 2005), 123–24

Cherokee Women's Writing in Protest of Removal

Cherokees of both sexes vociferously protested the Indian Removal Act via multiple means: from petitions and direct lobbying through personal letters to individuals with influence to newspaper editorials in the *Cherokee Phoenix.* Cherokee women were outspoken and active in their protest, as the sources reproduced here illustrate. One leader of the women's protest movement was Nancy Ward, a Cherokee Beloved Woman, which meant a woman who was revered by the members of her community and called upon to make important decisions such as determining the fate of war captives. Another leader was a wealthy Cherokee plantation mistress, Peggy Scott Vann Crutchfield. These sources again indicate a long-standing attachment to homeland among Cherokees of various economic classes, in contrast to an emerging American value of relocating to access new lands; they also show the prominence of slaveholders in Cherokee political life. For more on Cherokee women's activism, see Tiya Miles, " 'Circular Reasoning': Recentering Cherokee Women in the Antiremoval Campaigns," *American Quarterly* 61, no. 2 (June 2009): 221–43.

Cherokee Women's Petition, May 2, 1817

The Cherokee ladys now being present at the meeting of the chiefs and warriors in council have thought it their duty as mothers to address their beloved chiefs and warriors now assembled.

Our beloved children and head men of the Cherokee Nation, we address you warriors in council. We have raised all of you on the land which we now have, which God gave us to inhabit and raise provisions. We know that our country has once been extensive, but by repeated sales has become circumscribed to a small track, and [we] never have thought it our duty to interfere in the disposition of it till now. If a father or mother was to sell all their lands which they had to depend on, which their children had to raise their living on, which would be indeed bad & to be removed to another country. We do not wish to go to an unknown country [to] which we have understood some of our children wish to go over the Mississippi, but this act of our children would be like destroying your mothers.

Your mothers, your sisters ask and beg of you not to part with any more of our land. We say ours. You are our descendants; take pity on our request. But keep it for our growing children, for it was the good will of our creator to place us here, and you know our father, the great president, will not allow his white children to take our country away. Only keep your hands off of paper talks for its our own country. For [if] it was not, they would not ask you to put your hands to paper, for it would be impossible to remove us all. For as soon as one child is raised, we have others in our arms, for such is our situation & will consider our circumstance.

Therefore, children, don't part with any more of our lands but continue on it & enlarge your farms. Cultivate and raise corn & cotton and your mothers and sisters will make clothing for you which our father the president has recommended to us all. We don't charge any body for selling any lands, but we have heard such intentions of our children. But your talks become true at last; it was our desire to forewarn you all not to part with our lands.

Nancy Ward to her children: Warriors to take pity and listen to the talks of your sisters. Although I am very old yet cannot but pity the situation in which you will here of their minds. I have great many grand children which [I] wish them to do well on our land.

Cherokee Women's Petition, June 30, 1818

Beloved Children,

We have called a meeting among ourselves to consult on the different points now before the council, relating to our national affairs. We have heard with painful feelings that the bounds of the land we now possess are to be drawn into very narrow limits. The land was given to us by the Great Spirit above as our common right, to raise our children upon, & to make support for our rising generations. We therefore humbly petition our beloved children, the head men & warriors, to hold out to the last in support of our common rights, as the Cherokee nation have been the first settlers of this land; we therefore claim the right of the soil.

We well remember that our country was formerly very extensive, but by repeated sales it has become circumscribed to the very narrow limits we have at present. Our Father the President advised us to become farmers, to manufacture our own clothes, & to have our children instructed. To this advice we have attended in every thing as far as we were able. Now the thought of being compelled to remove the other side of the Mississippi is dreadful to us, because it appears to us that we, by this removal, shall be brought to a savage state again, for we have, by the endeavor of our Father the President, become too much enlightened to throw aside the privileges of a civilized life.

We therefore unanimously join in our meeting to hold our country in common as hitherto.

Some of our children have become Christians. We have missionary schools among us. We have hard the gospel in our nation. We have become civilized & enlightened, & are in hopes that in a few years our nation will be prepared for instruction in other branches of sciences & arts, which are both useful & necessary in civilized society.

There are some white men among us who have been raised in this country from their youth, are connected with us by marriage, & have considerable families, who are very active in encouraging the emigration of our nation. These ought to be our truest friends but prove our worst enemies. They seem to be only concerned how to increase their riches, but do not care what becomes of our Nation, nor even of their own wives and children.

The Cherokee Removal: A Brief History with Documents, edited by Theda Perdue and Michael D. Green (Boston: Bedford / St. Martin's, 2005), 131–33

CHAPTER NINE. CAPTURE

Cherokee Newspaper Article on the Kidnapping of Shoe Boots and Doll's Grandchildren

"Kidnapping," *Cherokee Advocate*, October 7, 1847.

Newspaper publication was an important strategy of Cherokee nationalism, education, and self-defense in the face of American colonialism. Elias Boudinot became the founding editor of the first Cherokee newspaper, the *Cherokee Phoenix*, in 1827. He intended the paper to demonstrate Cherokee progress, civilization, and literacy. The publication ran until 1834, the eve of the signing of the 1835 Treaty of New Echota, which cemented Cherokee removal from the Southeast.

The National Council established the *Cherokee Advocate* newspaper in 1844, with William Potter Ross selected to be its first editor. Created within a decade of Removal, the *Advocate* assumed an informational and educational purpose. The Cherokee press proved to be important to the Shoeboots family in Indian Territory. The *Advocate* provided information to the public on the kidnapping of Shoe Boots's mixed-race grandchildren. This notice, as well as the successful effort to save the girls, indicates that these children were seen as Cherokee citizens whose welfare was a matter of official concern.

Newspaper coverage in this period also indicates that Cherokee editors were concerned with crime linked to slavery, with catching slaves on the run, and with the presence of free blacks in Cherokee territory. The lack of newspaper coverage of the Cherokee slave revolt, a significant event in 1842, illustrates the scholarly cost of a temporal gap in the Cherokee press. The revolt occurred in the multiyear lapse between the publication of the *Phoenix* and the publication of the *Advocate*. An account of the slave revolt in a Cherokee publication would have been revealing. For more on the Cherokee press, see James W. Parins, *Literacy and Intellectual Life in the Cherokee Nation, 1820–1906* (Norman: University of Oklahoma Press, 2013), 51–151; Phillip H. Round, *Removable Type: Histories of the Book in Indian Country, 1663–1880* (Chapel Hill: University of North Carolina Press, 2010), 123–49. For a review of stories on Native Americans in African American newspapers, see Hannah Gourgey, "Poetics of Memory and Marginality: Images of the Native American in African-American Newspapers, 1870–1900 and 1970–1990," in *The Black Press: New Literary and Historical Essays*, edited by Todd Vogel (New Brunswick, N.J.: Rutgers University Press, 2001), 104–20.

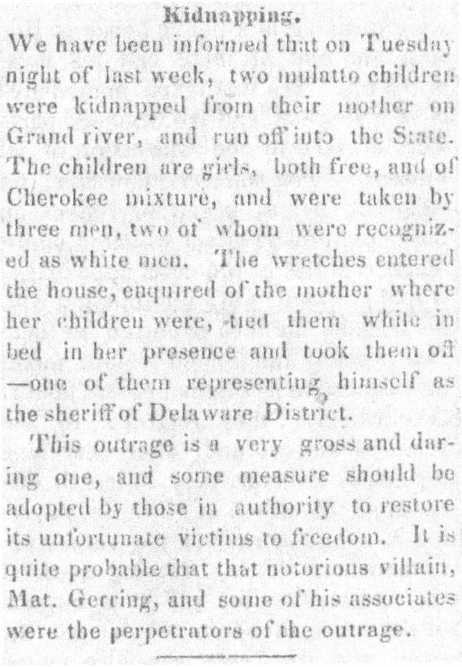

Kidnapping.

We have been informed that on Tuesday night of last week, two mulatto children were kidnapped from their mother on Grand river, and run off into the State. The children are girls, both free, and of Cherokee mixture, and were taken by three men, two of whom were recognized as white men. The wretches entered the house, enquired of the mother where her children were, tied them while in bed in her presence and took them off—one of them representing himself as the sheriff of Delaware District.

This outrage is a very gross and daring one, and some measure should be adopted by those in authority to restore its unfortunate victims to freedom. It is quite probable that that notorious villain, Mat. Gerring, and some of his associates were the perpetrators of the outrage.

Figure 10. Article in the *Cherokee Advocate* of October 7, 1847, on the kidnapping of Shoe Boots and Doll's grandchildren.

CHAPTER TEN. FREEDOM

Ridge Estate Inventory

Inventory, Etc. of Estate of Major Ridge & Wife, October 26, 1849, Cherokee Nation Papers 46:6541, Western History Collections, University of Oklahoma, Norman.

Doll's Land Warrant and Land Patent

Bounty land files, file 838:39 (Shoeboots), Military Service Records, Veterans Records, National Archives and Records Administration, Washington, D.C.

Patent for land sale from Dolly Shoeboots to David B. Cumming, November 1, 1860, Document No. 93063, General Land Office Records, United States Bureau of Land Management, Automated Records Project, Federal Land Patents, State Volumes, www.glorecords.blm.gov/ (Springfield, Va., Bureau of Land Management, Eastern States, 2007).

After the death of Shoe Boots, Doll was relocated to the Ridge family household by means that are unclear in the extant record. She was owned until late in life by Susannah Ridge, the widow of the Cherokee leader Major Ridge. The first source reproduced here, the Ridge estate inventory, lists Doll as an item of human property in her elder years. In addition to showing Doll's status and location in the antebellum period, this source demonstrates the productive use of estate inventories for researching individual slaves in Native as well as Euro-American households. The next two documents evidence Doll's acquisition of land toward the end of her life. After great persistence over several years, she received land as the widow of Captain Shoe Boots, a Cherokee Volunteers veteran of the War of 1812. Cherokee citizens who knew Doll and her family supported her in this assertion of her relationship with Shoe Boots. These records not only show Doll's achievement of a relatively happy ending to her story but also point to the possibility of black women's becoming landowners in the Cherokee Nation. Once held as property by the father of her children, Doll, referred to as Doll and Dolly in these documents, became the holder of property in land.

Amt brought over	$8560
6 mules @ $50	300
1 Horse (grey) (Sanchal)	75
1 Sorrel Horse	50
1 Old Horse	5
1 Small Pony	15
1 Jack	75
1 Wagon	100
3 Yoke oxen	
130 Head cattle (Supposition)	
1 Pr French Burrs & Irons of Grist Mill	25
1 " Saw Mill irons	150
1 Large pr timber wheels	50
1 Cash on Hand	922.25
1 Lot Hogs	30
29 Head Sheep	29
Debts due said Estate, some good, bad & desperate upon	
which it is supposed that there will be realized	1000
	$12256.25
Amount of advances made by Major Ridge and Susannah	
Ridge in their lives to Geo. W. Paschal and Sarah Paschal his	
wife, to wit:	
1837 May Cash	$500
" June Do May. Ridge pd note to Jno. Ridge executed	
by Geo. W. Paschal as per letter to J.B.S.R.	800
1838 Cash advanced by Susannah Ridge	500
1838 Apl Cash recived of Susannah Ridge	120
1 Mule	
1 Negro boy Isaac	600
1 Pleasure Carriage	60
	$3710

Figure 11. Estate inventory of Major and Susannah Ridge. Held at and images courtesy of the Western History Collections, University of Oklahoma, Norman.

The undersigned heirs and representatives of the heirs of the Estate of John Ridge, and Walter Ridge, by his Guardians Stand Watie, and Geo. W. Paschal and wife, have proceeded to inventory the effects of the Estate of Major Ridge and Susannah Ridge, as per the above statement, whereby it appears that Geo. W. Paschal, and his wife, have received over and above their pro rata share the sum of $1452. which they duly agree to appropriate to the payment of the debts contracted by Major Ridge and John Ridge during their lives. The sum of $2722.25/100 is left in the hands of the administrator for the purpose of paying all just demands against said Estate of Major Ridge and Susannah Ridge, any residue of which last mentioned sum (should there be any) is to be divided among the heirs according to their respective rights. The sum of Four Thousand One Hundred and Thirty two dollars apportioned divided and set apart to the said heirs as per statement above made as their separate and independent property.

 In testimony that the above is a correct statement of the Inventory and Division by the mutual agreement of said heirs, we hereunto set our hands this 27th day of October 1849.

Herman Ridge by
David Walker his Guardian &
Aeneas Ridge by
David Walker his Guardian
Andrew J. Ridge by
J. M. Tibbetts, the attorney
J. H. Sturman Guardian of said so
Flora C. Ridge by
J. M. Tibbetts, the attorney of
J. H. Sturman Guardian of said Flora
Walter Ridge by his Guardian
Stand Watie

(over)

Copy of the Inventory and division among the
Heirs, of Major and Susannah Ridge.

An Inventory and valuation of the assets of the
Estate of Major Ridge and Susannah Ridge, taken by
appraisement on the 26th day of October, A.D. 1849, and
also a thief, to wit:

1	Negro boy Oliver, about 22 years old				$600
1	" woman Milly " 28 " "				46
1	" boy Aug " 8 " "				
1	" child of Milly " 4 " "				2
1	" Woman Eliza " 26 " "				500
1	" girl Mary " 14 " "				400
1	" child of Eliza " 2 " "				125
1	" Woman Dinah " 38 " "				350
1	" " Lydia " 30 " "				450
1	" " Peggy " 38 " "				425
1	" " Betsey " 23 " "				500
1	" boy Stephen " 18 " "				550
1	" " Henry " 17 " "				450
1	" " Jesse " 11 " "				350
1	" " Robson " 10 " "				300
1	" girl Lucy " 14 " "				375
1	" " Itly " 12 " "				275
1	" " Martha " 8 " "				250
1	" boy Solomon " 7 " "				225
1	" " Thomas " 4 " "				200
1	" girl Charity " 1½ " "				12
1	" boy Wiley " 6 " "				2
1	" girl Maria " 4 " "				18
1	" boy Joe " 4 " "				200
1	" girl Margaret " 1 " "				100
1	" Woman Doll " 70 " "				000
1	" Man Tom " 42 " "				300
1	" boy Eli " 2 " "				125
1	" girl Ellen " 1 " "				100
	Am't Carried over				$8560

The undersigned heirs and representatives of the heirs of the Estate of John Ridge, and Walter Ridge, by his Guardian Stand Watie, and Geo. W. Paschal and wife, have proceeded to inventory the effects of the Estate of Major Ridge and Susannah Ridge, as per the above statement, whereby it appears that Geo. W. Paschal, and his wife, have received over and above their pro rata share the sum of $1452, which they hereby agree to appropriate to the payment of the debts contracted by Major Ridge and John Ridge during their lives. The sum of $2722 25/100 is left in hands of the administrator for the purpose of paying all just demands against said Estate of Major Ridge and Susannah Ridge, any residue of which last mentioned sum (should there be any) is to be divided among the heirs according to their respective rights. The sum of Four Thousand One Hundred and Thirty two dollars apportioned, divided and set apart to the said heirs as per statement above made as their seperate and independent property.

In testimony that the above is a correct statement of the Inventory and Division by the mutual agreement of said heirs, we hereunto set our hands this 27th day of October 1849.

Herman Ridge by
David Walker his Guardian &
Aeneas Ridge by
David Walker his Guardian
Andrew J. Ridge by
J. M. Tebbetts, the attorney of
J. H. Sherman Guardian of said &c
Flora C. Ridge by
J. M. Tebbetts, the attorney of
J. H. Sherman, Guardian of said Flora
Walter Ridge by his Guardian
Stan Watie

(over)

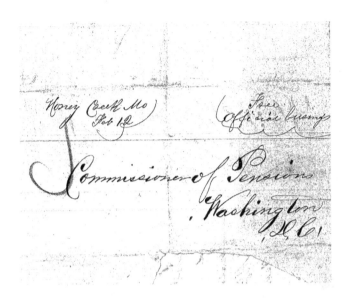

Figure 12. Warrant for the land that Doll received on account of Shoe Boots's military service. Held at and images courtesy of the National Archives and Records Administration, Washington, D.C.

Honey Creek Mo
Feb 11th/58

Commissioner of Pensions

Dear Sir

by last mail I received one Bounty
Land Warant No 93,063 for
120 acres Issued to Dolly Shoeboot
widow of Shoeboot a Cherokee
Indian

very Respectfully
your obt Sevt
R. H. Cleveland
Administrator
of the Estate of B McGhee
deceased

Commissioner of Pension
Washington
DC

Cpd. Dec. 9 - 1872   459

THE UNITED STATES OF AMERICA,

To all to whom these Presents shall come, Greeting:

WHEREAS, In pursuance of the Act of Congress, approved March 3, 1855, entitled "An Act in addition to certain Acts granting Bounty Land to certain Officers and Soldiers who have been engaged in the military service of the United States," there has been deposited in the GENERAL LAND OFFICE, Warrant No. *93063* for *120* acres, in favor of *Dolly Shoeboots widow of "Shoeboots" Captain, Cherokee Volunteers, War 1812*

with evidence that the same has been duly located upon *the South half of the South East quarter and Lot numbered eleven of Section four, in Township twenty two of Range thirty four in the District of Lands subject to sale at Springfield Missouri, containing one hundred and twenty acres.*

according to the Official Plat of the Survey of said Lands returned to the GENERAL LAND OFFICE by the SURVEYOR GENERAL *the said Warrant having been assigned by the said Dolly Shoeboots to David B. Cumming, in whose favor said tract has been located.*

NOW KNOW YE, That there is therefore granted by the UNITED STATES unto the said *David B. Cumming as assignee as aforesaid and to his heirs*

the tract of Land above described: TO HAVE AND TO HOLD the said tract of Land, with the appurtenances thereof, unto the said *David B. Cumming as assignee as aforesaid and to his*

heirs and assigns forever.

In testimony whereof, I, *James Buchanan* PRESIDENT OF THE UNITED STATES OF AMERICA, have caused these Letters to be made Patent, and the SEAL OF THE General Land Office to be hereunto affixed.

GIVEN under my hand, at the City of WASHINGTON, the *first* day of *November* in the year of our Lord one thousand eight hundred and *sixty*, and of the INDEPENDENCE OF THE UNITED STATES the *eighty fifth.*

243

BY THE PRESIDENT: *James Buchanan*

By *J. A. B. Leonard*, Sec'y.

J. N. Granger Recorder of the General Land Office.

Figure 13. Patent for the land sale from Dolly Shoeboots to David B. Cumming, November 1, 1860. Held at and image courtesy of the website (www.glorecords.blm.gov) of the Bureau of Land Management General Land Office Records, United States Department of the Interior, Washington D.C.

Cherokee Emancipation Act, 1863

The Cherokee Emancipation Act passed by the Cherokee National Council on February 21, 1863, freed slaves in the Cherokee Nation prior to the conclusion of the Civil War. The legislation was crucial to the status of blacks in Cherokee country. This particular act, whose text is reproduced here, has often been read as a proactive move on the part of the Cherokee Nation. However, new research indicates that it was produced in negotiation with the U.S. government. Historians Melinda Miller and Rachel Smith Purvis have shown that the Cherokee National Council passed two emancipation acts a few days apart in February 1863, just one month after President Abraham Lincoln's Emancipation Proclamation had taken effect. Purvis and Miller demonstrate that the first act attempted to secure compensation from the U.S. government for owners who freed their slaves but that the second act dropped the compensation request; the scholars argue that this shows Cherokees' keen awareness of the ongoing emancipation debate in Washington, D.C. The Cherokee emancipation acts did not address whether former slaves would be granted Cherokee citizenship. See Melinda Miller and Rachel Smith Purvis, " 'No Right of Citizenship': The 1863 Emancipation Acts of the Loyal Cherokee Council," paper presented at the American Historical Association Annual Meeting, January 3, 2014, Washington D.C.

An Act Providing for the Abolition of Slavery in the Cherokee Nation,
Be it enacted by the Natl Council, That in view of the difficulties and evils which have arisen from the Institution of Slavery and which seem inseperable from its existence in the Cherokee Nation, The Delegation appointed to proceed to Washington are impowered and instructed to assure the President of the U States of the desire of the Authorities and People to remove that Institution from the statures and Soil of the Cherokee Nation and of their wish to provide for that object at once upon the Principle of Compensation to the owners of Slaves not disloyal to the Government of the United States as tendered by Congress to States which shall abolish Slavery to their midst; And in case the Government of the United States accede to this propersition, The Said Delegation are hereby Authorized and instructed to enter into an agreement with the Government for the immediate emancipation of all Slaves in the Cherokee Nation and African Slavery shall therefore be abolished and forever cease to exist in said Nation—and therefore it shall be unlawful for any person to hold a Slave within the limits of the Cherokee Nation. And any person who before any of the Courts of the Nation having jurisdiction in the case shall be found guilty of Holding a Slave or Slaves, Shall be fined in a Sum

not less than One thousand Dollars __ nor more than Five thousand Dollars. And any Slave So held in Bondage shall be forever free.

So it __, Enacted

That it Shall be the duty of all the Solicitors throughout this Nation to see that this law is strictly enforced within the limits of their respective Districts. And in case any Solicitor shall fail in the performance of his duty in any such case it shall be compelent for Any Citizen to prosecute the case before this proper Court and see that the law is enforced.

And the Solicitor So failing to perform his duty Shall be punished as provided by law in other cases of Similar delinquency. And all Acts and parts of Acts which may Conflict with the above acts, are hereby repealed.

Cowskin Prairie Lewis Downing, Prest
Feby 18th 1863 Nat Committee
pro tem

Concurred in Council

With the following Amendment Commencing in the 1st page 26th line after the word (Dollars) And all fines arising from this Act shall be put in the Natil Treasury.

Spring Frog Spkr
N Council
Con by Committee Feb 19th 1863
Lewis Downing, Prest
Comtee pro tem
Enforced

"Cherokee Emancipation Proclamation," February 18–19, 1863, Cherokee Volume 248 (microfilm), Archives and Manuscripts Division, Oklahoma Historical Society, Oklahoma City, transcribed by Dr. Quintard Taylor Jr. as "Primary Documents: Cherokee Emancipation Proclamation (1863)," http://faculty.washington.edu/qtaylor/documents_us/cherokee _emancipation_proclamation.htm

Treaty of 1866 between the United States and the Cherokee Nation

The Reconstruction-era treaty reproduced here reset the relationship between the U.S. government and the Cherokee Nation after the Civil War. It reiterated the end of slavery and articulated a place for former slaves in the Cherokee Nation. Article 9, which states that both slaves freed by Cherokees "and their descendants" would have "all the rights of native Cherokees," is the major basis upon which descendants of these freedmen and freedwomen have argued for their right to citizenship and the franchise in the Cherokee Nation. The meaning and reach of this verbiage are contested. Some interpreters argue that the treaty is clear and ironclad in its promise of rights to freedmen and freedwomen. Others claim that it was developed under pressure and that Cherokee leaders did not exhibit the desire to incorporate blacks as citizens in the post–Civil War period. Still others insist that even if the treaty grants citizenship to slaves freed by Cherokees, later legislation, such as the Five Tribes Act of 1906, which dissolved the Cherokee national government in advance of Oklahoma statehood, nullified this treaty. The heated, ongoing debate over the 1866 treaty and the political intentions of Cherokee leaders at the time of its drafting proves the continued importance of nineteenth-century historical events and legal texts to Cherokee and Afro-Cherokee lives.

Articles of agreement and convention at the city of Washington on the nineteenth day of July, in the year of our Lord one thousand eight hundred and sixty-six, between the United States, represented by Dennis N. Cooley, Commissioner of Indian Affairs, [and] Elijah Sells, superintendent of Indian affairs for the southern superintendency, and the Cherokee Nation of Indians, represented by its delegates, James McDaniel, Smith Christie, White Catcher, S. H. Benge, J. B. Jones, and Daniel H. Ross—John Ross, principal chief of the Cherokees, being too unwell to join in these negotiations.

PREAMBLE.

Whereas existing treaties between the United States and the Cherokee Nation are deemed to be insufficient, the said contracting parties agree as follows, viz:

ARTICLE 1.

The pretended treaty made with the so-called Confederate States by the Cherokee Nation on the seventh day of October, eighteen hundred and sixty-one, and repudiated by the national council of the Cherokee Nation on the eighteenth day of February, eighteen hundred and sixty-three, is hereby declared to be void.

ARTICLE 2.

Amnesty is hereby declared by the United States and the Cherokee Nation for all crimes and misdemeanors committed by one Cherokee on the person or property of another Cherokee, or of a citizen of the United States, prior to the fourth day of July, eighteen hundred and sixty-six; and no right of action arising out of wrongs committed in aid or in the suppression of the rebellion shall be prosecuted or maintained in the courts of the United States or in the courts of the Cherokee Nation.

But the Cherokee Nation stipulate and agree to deliver up to the United States, or their duly authorized agent, any or all public property, particularly ordnance, ordnance stores, arms of all kinds, and quartermaster's stores, in their possession or control, which belonged to the United States or the so-called Confederate States, without any reservation.

ARTICLE 3.

The confiscation laws of the Cherokee Nation shall be repealed, and the same, and all sales of farms, and improvements on real estate, made or pretended to be made in pursuance thereof, are hereby agreed and declared to be null and void, and the former owners of such property so sold, their heirs or assigns, shall have the right peaceably to re-occupy their homes, and the purchaser under the confiscation laws, or his heirs or assigns, shall be repaid by the treasurer of the Cherokee Nation from the national funds, the money paid for said property and the cost of permanent improvements on such real estate, made thereon since the confiscation sale; the cost of such improvements to be fixed by a commission, to be composed of one person designated by the Secretary of the Interior and one by the principal chief of the nation, which two may appoint a third in cases of disagreement, which cost so fixed shall be refunded to the national treasurer by the returning Cherokees within three years from the ratification hereof.

ARTICLE 4.

All the Cherokees and freed persons who were formerly slaves to any Cherokee, and all free negroes not having been such slaves, who resided in the Cherokee Nation prior to June first, eighteen hundred and sixty-one, who may within two years elect not to reside northeast of the Arkansas River and southeast of Grand River, shall have the right to settle in and occupy the Canadian district southwest of the Arkansas River, and also all that tract of country lying northwest of Grand River, and bounded on the southeast by Grand River and west by the Creek reservation to the northeast corner thereof; from thence west on the north line of the Creek reservation to the ninety-sixth degree of west longitude; and thence north on said line of longitude so far that a line due east to Grand River will include a quantity of land equal to one hundred and sixty acres for each person who may so elect to reside in the territory above-described in this article: *Provided*, That that part of said district north of the Arkansas River shall not be set apart until it shall be found that the Canadian district is not sufficiently large to allow one hundred and sixty acres to each person desiring to obtain settlement under the provisions of this article.

ARTICLE 5.

The inhabitants electing to reside in the district described in the preceding article shall have the right to elect all their local officers and judges, and the number of delegates to which by their numbers they may be entitled in any general council to be established in the Indian Territory under the provisions of this treaty, as stated in Article 12, and to control all their local affairs, and to establish all necessary police regulations and rules for the administration of justice in said district, not inconsistent with the constitution of the Cherokee Nation or the laws of the United States; *Provided*, The Cherokees residing in said district shall enjoy all the rights and privileges of other Cherokees who may elect to settle in said district as hereinbefore provided, and shall hold the same rights and privileges and be subject to the same liabilities as those who elect to settle in said district under the provisions of this treaty; *Provided also*, That if any such police regulations or rules be adopted which, in the opinion of the President, bear oppressively on any citizen of the nation, he may suspend the same. And all rules or regulations in said district, or in any other district of the nation, discriminating against the citizens of other districts, are prohibited, and shall be void.

ARTICLE 6.

The inhabitants of the said district hereinbefore described shall be entitled to representation according to numbers in the national council, and all laws of the Cherokee Nation shall be uniform throughout said nation. And should any such law, either in its provisions or in the manner of its enforcement, in the opinion of the President of the United States, operate unjustly or injuriously in said district, he is hereby authorized and empowered to correct such evil, and to adopt the means necessary to secure the impartial administration of justice, as well as a fair and equitable application and expenditure of the national funds as between the people of this and of every other district in said nation.

ARTICLE 7.

The United States court to be created in the Indian Territory; and until such court is created therein, the United States district court, the nearest to the Cherokee Nation, shall have exclusive original jurisdiction of all causes, civil and criminal, wherein an inhabitant of the district hereinbefore described shall be a party, and where an inhabitant outside of said district, in the Cherokee Nation, shall be the other party, as plaintiff or defendant in a civil cause, or shall be defendant or prosecutor in a criminal case, and all process issued in said district by any officer of the Cherokee Nation, to be executed on an inhabitant residing outside of said district, and all process issued by any officer of the Cherokee Nation outside of said district, to be executed on an inhabitant residing in said district, shall be to all intents and purposes null and void, unless indorsed by the district judge for the district where such process is to be served, and said person, so arrested, shall be held in custody by the officer so arresting him, until he shall be delivered over to the United States marshal, or consent to be tried by the Cherokee court: *Provided*, That any or all the provisions of this treaty, which make any distinction in rights and remedies between the citizens of any district and the citizens of the rest of the nation, shall be abrogated whenever the President shall have ascertained, by an election duly ordered by him, that a majority of the voters of such district desire them to be abrogated, and he shall have declared such abrogation: And *provided further*, That no law or regulation, to be hereafter enacted within said Cherokee Nation or any district thereof, prescribing a penalty for its violation, shall take effect or be enforced until after ninety days from the date of its promulgation, either by publication in one or more newspapers of general circulation in said Cherokee Nation, or by posting up copies thereof in the Cherokee and English languages in each district where the same is to take effect, at the usual place of holding district courts.

ARTICLE 8.

No license to trade in goods, wares, or *merchandise* merchandise shall be granted by the United States to trade in the Cherokee Nation, unless approved by the Cherokee national council, except in the Canadian district, and such other district north of Arkansas River and west of Grand River occupied by the so-called southern Cherokees, as provided in Article 4 of this treaty.

ARTICLE 9.

The Cherokee Nation having, voluntarily, in February, eighteen hundred and sixty-three, by an act of the national council, forever abolished slavery, hereby covenant and agree that never hereafter shall either slavery or involuntary servitude exist in their nation otherwise than in the punishment of crime, whereof the party shall have been duly convicted, in accordance with laws applicable to all the members of said tribe alike. They further agree that all freedmen who have been liberated by voluntary act of their former owners or by law, as well as all free colored persons who were in the country at the commencement of the rebellion, and are now residents therein, or who may return within six months, and their descendants, shall have all the rights of native Cherokees: *Provided*, That owners of slaves so emancipated in the Cherokee Nation shall never receive any compensation or pay for the slaves so emancipated.

ARTICLE 10.

Every Cherokee and freed person resident in the Cherokee Nation shall have the right to sell any products of his farm, including his or her live stock, or any merchandise or manufactured products, and to ship and drive the same to market without restraint, paying any tax thereon which is now or may be levied by the United States on the quantity sold outside of the Indian Territory.

ARTICLE 11.

The Cherokee Nation hereby grant a right of way not exceeding two hundred feet wide, except at stations, switches, waterstations, or crossing of rivers, where more may be indispensable to the full enjoyment of the franchise herein granted, and then only two hundred additional feet shall be taken, and only for such length as may be absolutely necessary, through all their lands, to any company or corporation which shall be duly authorized by Congress to construct a railroad from any point north to any point south, and from any point east to any point west of, and which may pass through, the Cherokee Nation. Said company or corporation, and their employés and laborers, while constructing and repairing the same, and in operating said road or roads, including all necessary agents on the line, at stations, switches, water tanks, and all others necessary to the successful operation of a railroad, shall be protected in the discharge of their duties, and at all times subject to the Indian intercourse laws, now or which may hereafter be enacted and be in force in the Cherokee Nation.

ARTICLE 12.

The Cherokees agree that a general council, consisting of delegates elected by each nation or tribe lawfully residing within the Indian Territory, may be annually convened in said Territory, which council shall be organized in such manner and possess such powers as hereinafter prescribed.

First. After the ratification of this treaty, and as soon as may be deemed practicable by the Secretary of the Interior, and prior to the first session of said council, a census or enumeration of each tribe lawfully resident in said Territory shall be taken under the direction of the Commissioner of Indian Affairs, who for that purpose is hereby authorized to designate and appoint competent persons, whose compensation shall be fixed by the Secretary of the Interior, and paid by the United States.

Second. The first general council shall consist of one member from each tribe, and an additional member for each one thousand Indians, or each fraction of a thousand greater than five hundred, being members of any tribe lawfully resident in said Territory, and shall be selected by said tribes respectively, who may assent to the establishment of said general council; and if none should be thus formally selected by any nation or tribe so assenting, the said nation or tribe shall be represented in said general council by the chief or chiefs and headmen of said tribes, to be taken in the order of their rank as recognized in tribal usage, in the same number and proportion as above indicated. After the said census shall have been taken and completed, the superintendent of Indian affairs shall publish and declare to each tribe assenting to the establishment of such council the number of members of such council to which they shall be entitled under the provisions of this article, and the persons entitled to represent said tribes shall meet at such time and place as he shall approve; but thereafter the time and place of the sessions of said council shall be determined by its action: *Provided,* That no session in any one year shall exceed the term of thirty days: *And provided,* That special sessions of said council may be called by the Secretary of the Interior whenever in his judgment the interest of said tribes shall require such special session.

Third. Said general council shall have power to legislate upon matters pertaining to the intercourse and relations of the Indian tribes and nations and colonies of freedmen resident in said Territory; the arrest and extradition of criminals and offenders escaping from one tribe to another, or into any community of freedmen; the administration of justice between members of different tribes of said Territory and persons other than Indians and members of said tribes or nations; and the common defence and safety of the nations of said Territory.

All laws enacted by such council shall take effect at such time as may therein be provided, unless suspended by direction of the President of the United States. No law shall be enacted inconsistent with the Constitution of the United States, or laws of Congress, or existing treaty stipulations with the United States. Nor shall said council legislate upon matters other than those above indicated: *Provided, however,* That the legislative power of such general council may be enlarged by the consent of the national council of each nation or tribe assenting to its establishment, with the approval of the President of the United States.

Fourth. Said council shall be presided over by such person as may be designated by the Secretary of the Interior.

Fifth. The council shall elect a secretary, whose duty it shall be to keep an accurate record of all the proceedings of said council, and who shall transmit a true copy of all such proceedings, duly certified by the presiding officer of such council, to the Secretary of the Interior, and to each tribe or nation represented in said council, immediately after the sessions of said council shall terminate. He shall be paid out of the Treasury of the United States an annual salary of five hundred dollars.

Sixth. The members of said council shall be paid by the United States the sum of four dollars per diem during the term actually in attendance on the sessions of said council, and at the rate of four dollars for every twenty miles necessarily traveled by them in going from and returning to their homes, respectively, from said council, to be certified by the secretary and president of the said council.

ARTICLE 13.

The Cherokees also agree that a court or courts may be established by the United States in said Territory, with such jurisdiction and organized in such manner as may be prescribed by law: *Provided,* That the judicial tribunals of the nation shall be allowed to retain exclusive jurisdiction in all civil and criminal cases arising within their country in which members of the nation, by nativity or adoption, shall be the only parties, or where the cause of action shall arise in the Cherokee Nation, except as otherwise provided in this treaty.

ARTICLE 14.

The right to the use and occupancy of a quantity of land not exceeding one hundred and sixty acres, to be selected according to legal subdivisions in one body, and to include their improvements, and not including the improvements of any member of the Cherokee Nation, is hereby granted to every society or denomination which has erected, or which with the consent of the national council may hereafter erect, buildings within the Cherokee country for missionary or educational purposes. But no land thus granted, nor buildings which have been or may be erected thereon, shall ever be sold or [o]therwise disposed of except with the consent and approval of the Cherokee national council and the Secretary of the Interior. And whenever any such lands or buildings shall be sold or disposed of, the proceeds thereof shall be applied by said society or societies for like purposes within said nation, subject to the approval of the Secretary of the Interior.

ARTICLE 15.

The United States may settle any civilized Indians, friendly with the Cherokees and adjacent tribes, within the Cherokee country, on unoccupied lands east of 96°, on such terms as may be agreed upon by any such tribe and the Cherokees, subject to the approval of the President of the United States, which shall be consistent with the following provisions, viz: Should any such tribe or band of Indians settling in said country abandon their tribal organization, there being first paid into the Cherokee national fund a sum of money which shall sustain the same proportion to the then existing national fund that the number of Indians sustain to the whole number of Cherokees then residing in the Cherokee country, they shall be incorporated into and ever after remain a part of the Cherokee Nation, on equal terms in every respect with native citizens. And should any such tribe, thus settling in said country, decide to preserve their tribal organizations, and to maintain their tribal laws, customs, and usages, not inconsistent with the constitution and laws of the Cherokee Nation, they shall have a district of country set off for their use by metes and bounds equal to one hundred and sixty acres, if they should so decide, for each man, woman, and child of said tribe, and shall pay for the same into the national fund such price as may be agreed on by them and the Cherokee Nation, subject to the approval of the President of the United States, and in cases of disagreement the price to be fixed by the President.

And the said tribe thus settled shall also pay into the national fund a sum of money, to be agreed on by the respective parties, not greater in proportion to the whole existing national fund and the probable proceeds of the lands herein ceded or authorized to be ceded or sold than their numbers bear to the whole number of Cherokees then residing in said country, and thence afterwards they shall enjoy all the rights of native Cherokees. But no Indians who have no tribal organizations, or who shall determine to abandon their tribal organizations, shall be permitted to settle east of the 96° of longitude without the consent of the Cherokee national council, or of a delegation duly appointed by it, being first obtained. And no Indians who have and determine to preserve the tribal organizations shall be permitted to settle, as herein provided, east of the 96° of longitude without such consent being first obtained, unless the President of the United States, after a full hearing of the objections offered by said council or delegation to such settlement, shall determine that the objections are insufficient, in which case he may authorize the settlement of such tribe east of the 96° of longitude.

ARTICLE 16.

The United States may settle friendly Indians in any part of the Cherokee country west of 96°, to be taken in a compact form in quantity not exceeding one hundred and sixty acres for each member of each of said tribes thus to be settled; the boundaries of each of said districts to be distinctly marked, and the land conveyed in fee-simple to each of said tribes to be held in common or by their members in severalty as the United States may decide.

Said lands thus disposed of to be paid for to the Cherokee Nation at such price as may be agreed on between the said parties in interest, subject to the approval of the President; and if they should not agree, then the price to be fixed by the President.

The Cherokee Nation to retain the right of possession of and jurisdiction over all of said country west of 96° of longitude until thus sold and occupied, after which their jurisdiction and right of possession to terminate forever as to each of said districts thus sold and occupied.

ARTICLE 17.

The Cherokee Nation hereby cedes, in trust to the United States, the tract of land in the State of Kansas which was sold to the Cherokees by the United States, under the provisions of the second article of the treaty of 1835; and also that strip of the land ceded to the nation by the fourth article of said treaty which is included in the State of Kansas, and the Cherokees consent that said lands may be included in the limits and jurisdiction of the said State.

The lands herein ceded shall be surveyed as the public lands of the United States are surveyed, under the direction of the Commissioner of the General Land-Office, and shall be appraised by two disinterested persons, one to be designated by the Cherokee national council and one by the Secretary of the Interior, and, in case of disagreement, by a third person, to be mutually selected by the aforesaid appraisers. The appraisement to be not less than an average of one dollar and a quarter per acre, exclusive of improvements.

And the Secretary of the Interior shall, from time to time, as such surveys and appraisements are approved by him, after due advertisements for sealed bids, sell such lands to the highest bidders for cash, in parcels not exceeding one hundred and sixty acres, and at not less than the appraised value: *Provided*, That whenever there are improvements of the value of fifty dollars made on the lands not being mineral, and owned and personally occupied by any person for agricultural purposes at the date of the signing hereof, such person so owning, and in person residing on such improvements, shall, after due proof, made under such regulations as the Secretary of the Interior may prescribe, be entitled to buy, at the appraised value, the smallest quantity of land in legal subdivisions which will include his improvements, not exceeding in the aggregate one hundred and sixty acres; the expenses of survey and appraisement to be paid by the Secretary out of the proceeds of sale of said land: *Provided*, That nothing in this article shall prevent the Secretary of the Interior from selling the whole of said lands not occupied by actual settlers at the date of the ratification of this treaty, not exceeding one hundred and sixty acres to each person entitled to pre-emption under the pre-emption laws of the United States, in a body, to any responsible party, for cash, for a sum not less than one dollar per acre.

ARTICLE 18.

That any lands owned by the Cherokees in the State of Arkansas and in States east of the Mississippi may be sold by the Cherokee Nation in such manner as their national council may prescribe, all such sales being first approved by the Secretary of the Interior.

ARTICLE 19.

All Cherokees being heads of families residing at the date of the ratification of this treaty on any of the lands herein ceded, or authorized to be sold, and desiring to remove to the reserved country, shall be paid by the purchasers of said lands the value of such improvements, to be ascertained and appraised by the commissioners who appraise the lands, subject to the approval of the Secretary of the Interior; and if he shall elect to remain on the land now occupied by him, shall be entitled to receive a patent from the United States in fee-simple for three hundred and twenty acres of land to include his improvements, and thereupon he and his family shall cease to be members of the nation.

And the Secretary of the Interior shall also be authorized to pay the reasonable costs and expenses of the delegates of the southern Cherokees.

The moneys to be paid under this article shall be paid out of the proceeds of the sales of the national lands in Kansas.

ARTICLE 20.

Whenever the Cherokee national council shall request it, the Secretary of the Interior shall cause the country reserved for the Cherokees to be surveyed and allotted among them, at the expense of the United States.

ARTICLE 21.

It being difficult to learn the precise boundary line between the Cherokee country and the States of Arkansas, Missouri, and Kansas, it is agreed that the United States shall, at its own expense, cause the same to be run as far west as the Arkansas, and marked by permanent and conspicuous monuments, by two commissioners, one of whom shall be designated by the Cherokee national council.

ARTICLE 22.

The Cherokee national council, or any duly appointed delegation thereof, shall have the privilege to appoint an agent to examine the accounts of the nation with the Government of the United States at such time as they may see proper, and to continue or discharge such agent, and to appoint another, as may be thought best by such council or delegation; and such agent shall have free access to all accounts and books in the executive departments relating to the business of said Cherokee Nation, and an opportunity to examine the same in the presence of the officer having such books and papers in charge.

ARTICLE 23.

All funds now due the nation, or that may hereafter accrue from the sale of their lands by the United States, as hereinbefore provided for, shall be invested in the United States registered stocks at their current value, and the interest on all said funds shall be paid semi-annually on the order of the Cherokee Nation, and shall be applied to the following purposes, to wit: Thirty-five per cent. shall be applied for the support of the common-schools of the nation and educational purposes; fifteen per cent. for the orphan fund, and fifty per cent. for general purposes, including reasonable salaries of district officers; and the Secretary of the Interior, with the approval of the President of the United States, may pay out of the funds due the nation, on the order of the national council or a delegation duly authorized by it, such amount as he may deem necessary to meet outstanding obligations of the Cherokee Nation, caused by the suspension of the payment of their annuities, not to exceed the sum of one hundred and fifty thousand dollars.

ARTICLE 24.

As a slight testimony for the useful and arduous services of the Rev. Evan Jones, for forty years a missionary in the Cherokee Nation, now a cripple, old and poor, it is agreed that the sum of three thousand dollars be paid to him, under the direction of the Secretary of the Interior, out of any Cherokee fund in or to come into his hands not otherwise appropriated.

ARTICLE 25.

A large number of the Cherokees who served in the Army of the United States having died, leaving no heirs entitled to receive bounties and arrears of pay on account of such service, it is agreed that all bounties and arrears for service in the regiments of Indian United States volunteers which shall remain unclaimed by any person legally entitled to receive the same for two years from the ratification of this treaty, shall be paid as the national council may direct, to be applied to the foundation and support of an asylum for the education of orphan children, which asylum shall be under the control of the national council, or of such benevolent society as said council may designate, subject to the approval of the Secretary of the Interior.

ARTICLE 26.

The United States guarantee to the people of the Cherokee Nation the quiet and peaceable possession of their country and protection against domestic feuds and insurrections, and against hostilities of other tribes. They shall also be protected against inter[r]uptions or intrusion from all unauthorized citizens of the United States who may attempt to settle on their lands or reside in their territory. In case of hostilities among the Indian tribes, the United States agree that the party or parties commencing the same shall, so far as practicable, make reparation for the damages done.

ARTICLE 27.

The United States shall have the right to establish one or more military posts or stations in the Cherokee Nation, as may be deemed necessary for the proper protection of the citizens of the United States lawfully residing therein and the Cherokee and other citizens of the Indian country. But no sutler or other person connected therewith, either in or out of the military organization, shall be permitted to introduce any spiritous, vinous, or malt liquors into the Cherokee Nation, except the medical department proper, and by them only for strictly medical purposes. And all persons not in the military service of the United States, not citizens of the Cherokee Nation, are to be prohibited from coming into the Cherokee Nation, or remaining in the same, except as herein otherwise provided; and it is the duty of the United States Indian agent for the Cherokees to have such persons, not lawfully residing or sojourning therein, removed from the nation, as they now are, or hereafter may be, required by the Indian intercourse laws of the United States.

ARTICLE 28.

The United States hereby agree to pay for provisions and clothing furnished the army under Appotholehala in the winter of 1861 and 1862, not to exceed the sum of ten thousand dollars, the accounts to be ascertained and settled by the Secretary of the Interior.

ARTICLE 29.

The sum of ten thousand dollars or so much thereof as may be necessary to pay the expenses of the delegates and representatives of the Cherokees invited by the Government to visit Washington for the purposes of making this treaty, shall be paid by the United States on the ratification of this treaty.

ARTICLE 30.

The United States agree to pay to the proper claimants all losses of property by missionaries or missionary societies, resulting from their being ordered or driven from the country by United States agents, and from their property being taken and occupied or destroyed by *by* United States troops, not exceeding in the aggregate twenty thousand dollars, to be ascertained by the Secretary of the Interior.

ARTICLE 31.

All provisions of treaties heretofore ratified and in force, and not inconsistent with the provisions of this treaty, are hereby re-affirmed and declared to be in full force; and nothing herein shall be construed as an acknowledgment by the United States, or as a relinquishment by the Cherokee Nation of any claims or demands under the guarantees of former treaties, except as herein expressly provided.

In testimony whereof, the said commissioners on the part of the United States, and the said delegation on the part of the Cherokee Nation, have hereunto set their hands and seals at the city of Washington, this *ninth* [nineteenth] day of July, A.D. one thousand eight hundred and sixty-six.

D. N. Cooley, Commissioner of Indian Affairs.

Elijah Sells, Superintendent of Indian Affairs.

Smith Christie,

White Catcher,

James McDaniel,

S. H. Benge,

Danl. H. Ross,

J. B. Jones.

Delegates of the Cherokee Nation, appointed by Resolution of the National Council.

In presence of—

W. H. Watson,

J. W. Wright.

Signatures witnessed by the following-named persons, the following interlineations being made before signing: On page 1st the word "the" interlined, on page 11 the word "the" struck out, and to said page 11 sheet attached requiring publication of laws; and on page 34th the word "ceded" struck out and the words "neutral lands" inserted. Page 47 1/2 added relating to expenses of treaty.

Thomas Ewing, jr.

Wm. A. Phillips,

J. W. Wright.

Indian Affairs: Laws and Treaties, vol. 2, *Treaties,* edited by Charles J. Kappler (Washington, D.C.: Government Printing Office, 1904), 942–50

NOTES

PREFACE TO THE FIRST EDITION

1. Though Shoe Boots was the first name of the father, his nuclear family adopted Shoeboots as their last name.

2. Sharon Holland, *Raising the Dead: Readings of Death and (Black) Subjectivity* (Durham, N.C.: Duke University Press, 2000), 2.

3. Toni Morrison, *Beloved* (1987; reprint, New York: Plume, 1988), 274–75.

4. Leslie Marmon Silko, "Through the Stories We Hear Who We Are," in *Short Fiction: Classic and Contemporary,* 5th ed., ed. Charles Bohner (New York: Prentice-Hall, 2002).

5. bell hooks, "Revolutionary 'Renegades': Native Americans, African Americans, and Black Indians," in *Black Looks: Race and Representation* (London: Turnaround, 1992), 184.

6. Nell Irvin Painter, "Soul Murder and Slavery: Toward a Fully Loaded Cost Accounting," in *U.S. History as Women's History: New Feminist Essays,* ed. Linda Kerber, Alice Kessler-Harris, and Kathryn Kish Sklar (Chapel Hill: University of North Carolina Press, 1995).

INTRODUCTION

1. Ralph Ellison, *Going to the Territory* (New York: Random House, 1986), 120.

2. Captain Shoe Boots to the Chiefs in Council, October 20, 1824, Cherokee

Nation Papers, roll 46, no. 6508, Western History Collections, University of Oklahoma, Norman, Oklahoma. Many of the quotations in this book come from eighteenth- and nineteenth-century records in which language use is not consistent with contemporary American English writing. To avoid bogging down this quoted material, I often omit the term *sic,* which normally indicates spelling or grammatical errors in the original.

3. For other scholarly accounts of the relationship between Shoe Boots and Doll, see Marion L. Starkey, *The Cherokee Nation* (1946; reprint, North Dighton, Mass.: J. G. Press, 1995), 18–19; Daniel F. Littlefield and Mary Ann Littlefield, "The Beams Family: Free Blacks in Indian Territory," *Journal of Negro History* 61 (January 1976): 21n24; Theda Perdue, *Slavery and the Evolution of Cherokee Society, 1540–1866* (Knoxville: University of Tennessee Press, 1979), 84–85; William G. McLoughlin, *Cherokee Renascence in the New Republic* (Princeton: Princeton University Press, 1986), 343–45; Adriane Strenk, "Tradition and Transformation: Shoe Boots and the Creation of a Cherokee Culture" (master's thesis, University of Kentucky, 1993), 60–74; Circe Sturm, *Blood Politics: Race, Culture, and Identity in the Cherokee Nation of Oklahoma* (Berkeley and Los Angeles: University of California Press, 2002), 59–61; and the forthcoming work of historian Fay Yarbrough.

4. Conversation between anthropologist Circe Sturm and a Cherokee interviewee, quoted in Sturm, *Blood Politics,* 59.

5. Raymond D. Fogelson, "The Ethnohistory of Events and Non-events," *Ethnohistory* 36 (1989): 141.

6. Patricia Hill Collins, "It's All in the Family: Intersections of Gender, Race, and Nation," *Hypatia* 13 (Summer 1998): 62–82. Nancy Cott and Ann Plane have also argued this point effectively. See Nancy F. Cott, *Public Vows: A History of Marriage and the Nation* (Cambridge, Mass.: Harvard University Press, 2000); Ann Marie Plane, *Colonial Intimacies: Indian Marriage in Early New England* (Ithaca, N.Y.: Cornell University Press, 2000); Collins, "It's All in the Family," 63.

7. Challenges to the racial order of the Cherokee Nation demonstrate the notion elaborated by Barbara Fields that race is a social construct grounded in particular historical moments and defined through social relations. See Barbara Fields, "Ideology and Race in American History," in *Region, Race, and Reconstruction,* ed. J. Morgan Kousser and James McPherson (New York: Oxford University Press, 1982): 143–77.

8. My articulation of the tension between emancipation and sovereignty is deeply influenced by Sharon Holland's analysis of Afro-Native literature, in which she argues that works of this genre contest the notion that sovereignty for American Indians and emancipation for African Americans are politically opposed. In an implicit dialogue with cultural theorist Robert Allen Warrior, Holland asserts that this literature expands the definition of sovereignty beyond political

independence for Native nation-states, redefining it to include ideas of personal and social autonomy. The redefinition of sovereignty implied in the literature, Holland argues, connects rather than opposes Indian and black independence struggles. See Sharon Holland, "'If You Know I Have a History, You Will Respect Me': A Perspective on Afro-Native American Literature," *Callaloo* 17 (Winter–Summer 1994): 334–50; Robert Allen Warrior, *Tribal Secrets* (Minneapolis: University of Minnesota Press, 1995).

9. Edmund Morgan, *American Slavery, American Freedom* (New York: Norton, 1975), 4.

10. Fogelson, "Ethnohistory," 141.

11. Fogelson, "Ethnohistory," 135.

12. Toni Morrison, Nobel Lecture, December 7, 1993.

CHAPTER ONE. CAPTIVITY

The epigraph to this chapter is drawn from Thurman Wilkins, *Cherokee Tragedy: The Ridge Family and the Decimation of a People* (Norman: University of Oklahoma Press, 1970), 148.

1. John Howard Payne Papers, 2:53, Ayer Collection, Newberry Library, Chicago, Illinois. John Howard Payne began spending time in the Cherokee Nation in the 1830s. For more on the purpose of his visits, see appendix 1.

2. Citizenship Application of William Stephens, Statement of John McCoy, Cherokee Applications, Applications from the Bureau of Indian Affairs, Muskogee Area Office, Relating to Enrollment in the Five Civilized Tribes Under the Act of 1896, Case 5364 National Archives Microfilm Publication M1650, roll 53, National Archives and Records Administration Southwest Region, Fort Worth, Texas.

3. Citizenship Application of William Stephens, Case Review: Summary Statement of John McCoy. For another description of Shoe Boots's appearance, see Payne Papers, 2:52; parts of this description are quoted in appendix 1.

4. Payne Papers, 2:53.

5. Citizenship Application of William Stephens, Petition of William Stephens.

6. Clarinda Allington's last name is also spelled Ellington in the records. Harry Enoch gives Clarinda's age as eleven, while the Cherokee Agency Records (and historian Adriane Strenk) say she was thirteen when captured. Harry Enoch, *In Search of Morgan's Station and the Last Indian Raid in Kentucky* (Bowie, Md.: Heritage Books, 1997), 104; Records of the Cherokee Indian Agency in Tennessee, 1801–1835, October 19, 1803, Bureau of Indian Affairs, Microfilm Publications RG 75, M208, roll 2, National Archives and Records Administration, Washington, D.C.; Adriane Strenk, "Tradition and Transformation: Shoe Boots and the Creation of a Cherokee Culture" (master's thesis, University of Kentucky, 1993), 1–16.

7. Enoch, *Morgan's Station*, 126.

8. Enoch, *Morgan's Station*, 1, 2.

9. Enoch, *Morgan's Station*, vii, 21, 13, 106–7.

10. Enoch, *Morgan's Station*, 87.

11. Enoch, *Morgan's Station*, 11.

12. Richard Slotkin, *Regeneration Through Violence: The Mythology of the American Frontier, 1600–1860* (Middletown, Conn.: Wesleyan University Press, 1973); Rayna Green, "The Pocahontas Perplex," *Massachusetts Review* 16 (1975): 698–714.

13. William Whitley Papers, 1775–1813, Kentucky Manuscripts, Draper Manuscript Collection 9CC23, State Historical Society of Wisconsin, Madison, Wisconsin.

14. William Whitley Papers, Draper 9CC4–5.

15. I have based Shoe Boots's age on the statement of a contemporary who said that Shoe Boots "must have been sixty years old when he first saw him, about four years after Creek war." Citizenship Application of William Stephens, Case Review: Summary Statement of Nathaniel Fish. Though travel to Kentucky took Shoe Boots far from his home in present-day north Georgia, his involvement in a Shawnee raid would not have been unusual. Ethnohistorian Helen Tanner has demonstrated that Cherokees were frequently involved in Indian affairs in the Ohio Valley in the mid- to late 1700s. A band of Cherokees lived as far north as the Ohio River in 1755, and Cherokees from that settlement and others were engaged in a long-term relationship with the Shawnees; likewise, some Shawnee families lived in Cherokee towns near the Allegheny Mountains. Helen Hornbeck Tanner, "Cherokees in the Ohio Country," *Journal of Cherokee Studies* 3 (Spring 1978): 94–101.

16. William Whitley Papers, Draper 9CC22.

17. William Whitley Papers, Draper 9CC21; Enoch, *Morgan's Station*, 93; Enoch, *Morgan's Station*, 106–7.

18. Enoch, *Morgan's Station*, 104, 126.

19. William Whitley Papers, Draper 9CC25; Enoch, *Morgan's Station*, 125–26. Polly Baker was returned to her family by William Whitley seven to eight years after her capture.

20. The tribes who signed the Treaty of Greenville were the Shawnee, Wyandot, Ottawa, Delaware, Potawatomi, Miami, Chippewa, Kaskaskia, Eelriverwee, and Kickapoo. Enoch, *Morgan's Station*, 114–15, 122.

21. Enoch, *Morgan's Station*, 126.

22. William McLoughlin states that Shoe Boots had a first wife who was Cherokee. This is probable, given the ease of marital separation among Cherokees of the eighteenth century; however, I have found no primary evidence that supports the assertion. William G. McLoughlin, *Cherokee Renascence in the New Republic* (Princeton: Princeton University Press, 1986), 344.

23. William Stephens, a grandson of Shoe Boots and Clarinda, gives the birth order of the couple's children as follows: "William, Sarah (my mother), and John, born in the respective years of 1801, 1796, 1794." Citizenship Application of William Stephens, Petition of William Stephens.

24. William McLoughlin and Adriane Strenk have stated that Clarinda first worked as a servant in Shoe Boots's household. I have yet to find evidence supporting this assertion. However, if the assertion is true it demonstrates a tendency on Shoe Boots's part to make "wives" out of his female captives-servants. McLoughlin, *Cherokee Renascence,* 344; Strenk, "Tradition and Transformation," 20.

25. For an example of the varied experiences of white captives held by Indians, see John Demos, *The Unredeemed Captive* (New York: Vintage, 1994).

26. Records of the Cherokee Agency in Tennessee, June 27, 1803; October 19, 1803.

27. There is some confusion in the records about who actually went to Cherokee country in search of Clarinda. John Howard Payne states that a man named Whitley went after her. Payne gives Whitley's first name as George; however, he says that Whitley was a famous Indian hunter. The only Whitley from Kentucky who fit this description in the late 1700s was William Whitley, whose brother-in-law was named George Clack or Clark. The two explored Kentucky together in 1775. It is probable that Payne confused the brothers' first names. According to Harry Enoch and an article in the *Kentucky Gazette,* it was a relative of Clarinda's named William Rice who went in pursuit of her after hearing from Whitley that she was living with Cherokees. It is likely that William Whitley and William Rice worked together, or successively, to secure Clarinda's release. John Kleber, ed., *The Kentucky Encyclopedia* (Lexington: University Press of Kentucky, 1992), 949; Lewis Collins and Richard Collins, *History of Kentucky* (Covington, Ky.: Collins, 1882), 760; Enoch, *Morgan's Station,* 126–27; *Kentucky Gazette,* November 27, 1804.

28. Kleber, ed., *Kentucky Encyclopedia,* 949.

29. Records of the Cherokee Indian Agency in Tennessee, June 27, 1803.

30. Records of the Cherokee Indian Agency in Tennessee, October 19, 1803.

31. McLoughlin, *Cherokee Renascence,* 344.

32. Payne Papers, 2:57.

33. As Amy Kaplan has elucidated, the nineteenth-century belief that proper white women could positively influence darker, foreign races was tempered by the threat that these same races would penetrate the sanctity of the white home and nation. See Amy Kaplan, "Manifest Domesticity," *American Literature* 70 (September 1998): 589.

34. Cherokee Nation, *Laws of the Cherokee Nation: Adopted by the Council at Various Periods,* 1808–1835 (Tahlequah, C.N.: Cherokee Advocate Office, 1852),

10; A. H. Murchison, "Intermarried Whites in the Cherokee Nation between the Years 1865 and 1887," *Chronicles of Oklahoma* 6, no. 3 (1928): 299, 300.

35. Murchison, "Intermarried Whites," 300.

36. Theda Perdue, "Southern Indians and the Cult of True Womanhood," in *Half Sisters of History*, ed. Catherine Clinton (Durham, N.C.: Duke University Press, 1994): 36–55. As Perdue points out in this article, Cherokee women often incorporated characteristics of "true womanhood" while striving to maintain aspects of Cherokee gender roles and values.

37. Perdue, "Southern Indians," 43. Mary Kelley observes that nineteenth-century American women's writing includes subtle, complex, and dissenting views of the image and ideal of "true womanhood"; Mary Kelley, "Commentary" (on Barbara Welter, "The Cult of True Womanhood: 1820–1860"), in *Locating American Studies: The Evolution of a Discipline*, ed. Lucy Maddox (Baltimore: Johns Hopkins University Press, 1999), 43–70.

38. *Cherokee Phoenix*, July 1, 1829; April 1, 1829; May 27, 1829.

39. Perdue, "Southern Indians," 43–49.

40. "The Wedding," *Cherokee Phoenix*, May 21, 1828.

41. Mary Kelley, Lora Romero, and June Howard all have stressed that the interrelated nineteenth-century ideologies of true womanhood and domesticity were complex, uneven, and contested. Women living in this period adapted some aspects of the notion, abandoned others, and used this set of ideas and social expectations to further their own personal and political causes. Kelley, "Commentary"; Lora Romero, *Home Fronts: Domesticity and Its Critics in the Antebellum United States* (Durham, N.C.: Duke University Press, 1997): 1–11; June Howard, *Publishing the Family* (Durham, N.C.: Duke University Press, 2001): 213–56.

42. The classic article that defines this meaning of the ideology of true womanhood is Barbara Welter, "The Cult of True Womanhood: 1820–1860," *American Quarterly* 18 (1966): 151–74. In this piece Welter notes the relationship between womanly virtues and national uplift, 152, 171, 172; Amy Kaplan extends this argument into a connection between womanly virtues and U.S. empire building in "Manifest Domesticity." Mary Kelley challenges and revises Barbara Welter's paradigm, stating that *deference* is a more accurate word than *submissiveness* for describing white women's relations with white men. Kelley, "Commentary," 67.

43. Welter, "Cult of True Womanhood," 152; Romero, *Home Fronts*, 15. Lora Romero notes that the concept of mothers teaching children to be good citizens has its roots in the revolutionary era and the notion of republican motherhood. For more on this concept, see Mary Beth Norton, *Founding Mothers and Fathers: Gendered Power and the Forming of American Society* (New York: Knopf, 1996).

44. Welter, "Cult of True Womanhood," 171–72; Romero, *Home Fronts*, 15.

45. Payne Papers, 2:54.

46. Starr expresses this sentiment by quoting John McFerrin's comments about intermarriage. Emmet Starr, *Early History of the Cherokees: Embracing Aboriginal Customs, Religion, Laws, Folk Lore, and Civilization* (Claremont, Okla., circa 1917), 96.

47. Butrick Journal, November 21, 1824, Papers of the American Board of Commissioners for Foreign Missions, ABC 18.3.3, vols. 4–5. Houghton Library, Harvard University, Cambridge, Massachusetts. In this statement Butrick is responding to the proposed marriage between John Ridge and Sarah Northrup. In an address to Delaware and Mohican Indians, Thomas Jefferson did in fact advocate white and Indian intermarriage; see Saul K. Padover, ed., *The Complete Jefferson* (New York: Duell, Sloan and Pearce, 1943), 503.

48. Quoted in Enoch, *Morgan's Station,* 127–28, from Commonwealth of Kentucky, *House Journal,* November 20, 1804, 39–41.

49. Enoch, *Morgan's Station,* 127–28.

50. William Whitley Papers, Draper 9CC25.

51. William Whitley Papers, Draper 9CC25. Information about this slave's name comes from: Citizenship Application of William Stephens, Case Review: Summary Statement of William Ellington Shoeboots.

52. Citizenship Application of William Stephens, Petition of William Stephens.

53. Thurman Wilkins, *Cherokee Tragedy: The Ridge Family and the Decimation of a People,* 2nd ed. (Norman: University of Oklahoma Press, 1986), 150.

54. Wilkins, *Cherokee Tragedy,* 131–53; Marion Starkey, *The Cherokee Nation* (1946; reprint, North Dighton, Mass.: J. G. Press, 1995), 71–74; Karen Woods, "One Nation, One Blood: Interracial Marriage in American Fiction, Scandal, and Law, 1820–70" (PhD diss., University of Minnesota, 1999): 11–41.

55. Starkey, *Cherokee Nation,* 72.

56. Harriet Gold, letter to Rev. and Flora Vaill, June 25, 1825, Herman Vaill Collection, Yale University Library, New Haven, Connecticut; also quoted in Woods, "One Nation, One Blood," 20.

57. Starkey, *Cherokee Nation,* 73. Mary Young has argued that the dark skin color of Ridge and Boudinot may have intensified the reaction of white Northerners, as other prominent Cherokee men who were light-skinned had married white women without public protest; Mary Young, "The Cherokee Nation: Mirror of the Republic," *American Quarterly* 33 (Winter 1981): 522. Karen Woods distinguishes between Ridge and Boudinot, noting that Boudinot was the darker of the two, which may have singled him out for worse treatment; Woods, "One Nation, One Blood," 40.

58. Starkey, *Cherokee Nation,* 72.

59. In fact, as Thurman Wilkins points out, John Ridge's wealth was exag-

gerated in this story. At his richest, he had only half the slaves attributed to him; Wilkins, *Cherokee Tragedy,* 153; Starkey, *Cherokee Nation,* 72. Harriet, in contrast to Sarah, had married the poorer of the two cousins, and her story did not receive such a favorable rewrite.

CHAPTER TWO. SLAVERY

The epigraphs to this chapter are drawn from the Cherokee Supreme Court docket, August 10, 1829, Cherokee Collection, microfilm 815, Tennessee State Library and Archives, Nashville, Tennessee, and from Harriet Jacobs, *Incidents in the Life of a Slave Girl Written by Herself* (1861; reprint, Cambridge, Mass.: Harvard University Press, 1987), 1–2.

1. Harriet Jacobs, *Incidents in the Life of a Slave Girl Written by Herself* (1861; reprint, Cambridge, Mass.: Harvard University Press, 1897), 55.

2. Saidiya Hartman, *Scenes of Subjection: Terror, Slavery, and Self-Making in Nineteenth-Century America* (New York: Oxford University Press, 1997), 3.

3. Toni Morrison, *Beloved* (1987; reprint, New York: Plume, 1988), 71, 199; Toni Morrison, "Unspeakable Things Unspoken: The Afro-American Presence in American Literature," *Michigan Quarterly Review* 28 (Winter 1989): 1–34.

4. Marion Starkey, *The Cherokee Nation* (1946; reprint, North Dighton, Mass.: J. G. Press, 1995), 18; John Howard Payne Papers, 2:64, Ayer Collection, Newberry Library, Chicago, Illinois.

5. An online review of South Carolina slave records indicates multiple slave women named Doll in the colony/state from the late eighteenth century through the mid-nineteenth century. South Carolina Department of Archives and History, Combined Index to 30 Records Series, 1675–1929, Columbia, South Carolina, www.state.sc.us/scdah/, topic search "slavery."

6. John Norton, *The Journal of Major John Norton* (1816; reprint, Toronto: Champlain Society, 1970), 147.

7. Peter H. Wood, *Black Majority* (New York: Norton, 1974), 30; Ira Berlin, "Time, Space and the Evolution of Afro-American Society on British Mainland North America," in *Diversity and Unity in Early North America,* ed. Philip Morgan (London: Routledge, 1993), 125.

8. Almon Wheeler Lauber, *Indian Slavery in Colonial Times within the Present Limits of the United States* (Williamstown, Mass.: Corner House Publishers, 1970), 312, 315.

9. Citizenship Application of William Shoeboots, Resubmitted by Rufus Shoeboots, Case 4422, Statement of Thomas Ridge, Cherokee Applications, Applications from the Bureau of Indian Affairs, Muskogee Area Office, Relating to Enrollment in the Five Civilized Tribes Under the Act of 1896, National Archives Microfilm Publication M1650, roll 47, National Archives and Records Admin-

istration Southwest Region, Fort Worth, Texas; Citizenship Application of William Shoeboots, Statement of Nathaniel Fish.

10. Rudi Halliburton, "Origins of Black Slavery among the Cherokees," *Chronicles of Oklahoma* 52 (Winter 1974): 484; Theda Perdue, *Slavery and the Evolution of Cherokee Society, 1540–1866* (Knoxville: University of Tennessee Press, 1979), 36.

11. In 1526 a slave revolt took place in Spanish explorer Lucas Vázquez de Ayllón's short-lived colony on the Peedee River in present-day South Carolina; Perdue, *Slavery*, 36.

12. Wood, *Black Majority*, 119–24; J. Leitch Wright, *The Only Land They Knew* (New York: Free Press, 1981), 262–71; George Lankford, ed., *Native American Legends* (Little Rock, Ark.: August House, 1987). James Mooney discusses similarities between Cherokee and African American rabbit stories in *Myths of the Cherokee* (1900; reprint, New York: Dover, 1995), 233–34.

13. Jack D. Forbes, *Africans and Native Americans: The Language of Race and the Evolution of Red-Black Peoples* (Urbana: University of Illinois Press, 1993), 62; Perdue, *Slavery*, 39; William Loren Katz, *Black Indians: A Hidden Heritage* (New York: Atheneum, 1986), 109, 102.

14. Katz, *Black Indians*, 103; Forbes, *Africans and Native Americans*, 207–9.

15. *South Carolina Gazette*, December 8, 1769.

16. *South Carolina Gazette and Country Journal*, July 5, 1774.

17. *Georgia State Gazette*, January 10, 1793.

18. *Georgetown Gazette*, April 18, 1801.

19. Perdue, *Slavery*, 37.

20. Michael Roethler, "Negro Slavery Among the Cherokee Indians, 1540–1866" (PhD diss., Fordham University, 1964), 38.

21. Perdue, *Slavery*, 36; James Merrell, "The Racial Education of the Catawba Indians," *Journal of Southern History* 50 (1984): 366.

22. Elsa Barkley Brown introduces the notion of the simultaneous occurrence of "seemingly contradictory" behaviors in "African-American Women's Quilting: A Framework for Conceptualizing and Teaching African-American Women's History," in *Black Women in America: Social Science Perspectives*, ed. Micheline R. Malson et al. (Chicago: University of Chicago Press, 1990): 9–18. Patricia J. Williams discusses her perspective of viewing things "simultaneously yet differently" in her essay "The Pain of Word Bondage," in *The Alchemy of Race and Rights* (Cambridge, Mass.: Harvard University Press, 1991), 149–50.

23. Perdue, *Slavery*, 4, 8.

24. Perdue, *Slavery*, 4, 8; Raymond D. Fogelson, "On the 'Petticoat Government' of the Eighteenth-Century Cherokee," in *Personality and the Cultural Construction of Society*, ed. David Jordan and Marc Swartz (Tuscaloosa: University of Alabama Press, 1990): 161–81; Janet Campbell and David Campbell, "The Wolf Clan," *Journal of Cherokee Studies* 7, no. 2 (Fall 1982): 85–91.

25. Perdue, *Slavery*, 19, 22.

26. Perdue, *Slavery*, 37. As the Cherokees sought to increase their supply of goods, such as knives, hatchets, and guns, and to protect their position during a contentious struggle between European powers for control of the Americas, they engaged in strategic trading, at times stealing French slaves to sell to the British, and vice versa.

27. Halliburton, "Origins," 485–86; Rudi Halliburton, *Red over Black: Black Slavery among the Cherokee Indians* (Westport, Conn.: Greenwood, 1977), 8–9.

28. Treaty of Alliance and Commerce between Great Britain and the Nation of Cherokees in America, September 20, 1730, University of Michigan Libraries Electronic Resources: www.sevierlibrary.org/geneaology/indians/dumplin.htm. Quoted in slightly different language in J. B. Davis, "Slavery in the Cherokee Nation," *Chronicles of Oklahoma* 11 (December 1933): 1058; Halliburton, "Origins," 486; Wood, *Black Majority*, 262.

29. Bruce Twyman, *The Black Seminole Legacy and North American Politics, 1693–1845* (Washington, D.C.: Howard University Press, 1999), 78.

30. John Stuart to Thomas Gage, September 26, 1767, Gage Papers, William L. Clements Library, University of Michigan, Ann Arbor, Michigan. Also quoted in William Willis, "Divide and Rule: Red, White and Black in the Southeast," *Journal of Negro History* 48 (July 1963): 163; Perdue, *Slavery*, 39.

31. Halliburton, "Origins," 486.

32. Quoted in Davis, "Slavery in the Cherokee Nation," 1058.

33. Wood, *Black Majority*, 260.

34. Quoted in Willis, "Divide and Rule," 161, and Perdue, *Slavery*, 39.

35. Journals of the South Carolina Commons House of Assembly, quoted in Wood, *Black Majority*, 261–62.

36. Halliburton, "Origins," 486.

37. Perdue, *Slavery*, 40; Merrell, "Racial Education," 367; Roethler, "Negro Slavery," 40; Willis, "Divide and Rule," 163, 167.

38. Willis, "Divide and Rule," 166.

39. James Glen to William H. Lyttelton, January 23, 1758, Lyttelton Papers, William L. Clements Library, University of Michigan, Ann Arbor, Michigan; also quoted in Willis, "Divide and Rule," 165.

40. Halliburton, *Red over Black*, 7.

41. T. Lindsay Baker and Julie Baker, eds., *The WPA Oklahoma Slave Narratives* (Norman: University of Oklahoma Press, 1996), 398.

42. Baker and Baker, eds., *WPA Oklahoma Slave Narratives*, 445.

43. Quoted in McLoughlin, *Cherokee Renascence in the New Republic* (Princeton: Princeton University Press, 1986), 338–39.

44. Rennard Strickland, *Fire and the Spirits: Cherokee Law from Clan to Court* (Norman: University of Oklahoma Press, 1975), 79; Halliburton, *Red over Black*, 4; Davis, "Slavery in the Cherokee Nation," 1065; Adele Logan Alexander, *Am-*

biguous Lives: Free Women of Color in Rural Georgia, 1789–1879 (Fayetteville: University of Arkansas Press), 27.

45. Halliburton, "Origins," 484; Roethler, "Negro Slavery," 63–64.

46. Quoted in Perdue, *Slavery,* 48.

47. Theda Perdue, "Women, Men, and American Indian Policy: The Cherokee Response to 'Civilization,'" in *Negotiators of Change: Historical Perspectives on Native American Women,* ed. Nancy Shoemaker (New York: Routledge, 1995), 110.

48. Treaty with the Cherokee 1791, Article 14, the Avalon Project at Yale Law School: www.yale.edu/lawweb/avalon/ntreaty/chr1791.htm; also quoted in Roethler, "Negro Slavery," 59.

49. Roethler, "Negro Slavery," 59; also quoted in Theda Perdue, *Cherokee Women: Gender and Culture Change, 1700–1835* (Lincoln: University of Nebraska Press, 1998), 111.

50. Perdue, *Cherokee Women,* 111.

51. George Washington to Cherokee Nation of Indians, August 29, 1796, "Talk of the President of the United States to the Beloved Men of the Cherokee Nation," George Washington Papers, 1741–1799, Series 4, General Correspondence, 1697–1799, the Library of Congress. Perdue discusses this letter in *Cherokee Women,* 111.

52. George Washington to Cherokee Nation of Indians.

53. Benjamin Hawkins, "A Sketch of the Creek Country in the Years 1798 and 1799," in *Letters, Journals, and Writings of Benjamin Hawkins,* vol. 1, *1796–1801,* ed. C. L. Grant (Savannah, Ga.: Beehive Press, 1980), 298; also quoted in Joel Martin, *Sacred Revolt: The Muskogees' Struggle for a New World* (Boston: Beacon, 1991), 105.

54. Quoted in Daniel F. Littlefield, *Africans and Creeks: From the Colonial Period to the Civil War* (Westport, Conn.: Greenwood, 1979), 36.

55. Perdue, *Slavery,* 54.

56. Norton, *Journal of Major John Norton,* 66.

57. Norton, *Journal of Major John Norton,* 71.

58. William Harlen Gilbert, *Smithsonian Institution Bureau of Ethnology Bulletin 133: Anthropological Papers Numbers 19–26* (Washington, D.C.: United States Government Printing Office, 1943), 178.

59. Starkey, *Cherokee Nation,* 17; Roethler, "Negro Slavery," 115.

60. Starkey, *Cherokee Nation,* 17.

61. Records Relating to Indian Removal, Records of the Bureau of Indian Affairs Valuations of Property in Cass County, Ga., 1836, by Agents Mays and Hargrove, no. 319, Lizza Shoeboot, Administration Microfilm Publication Record Group 75.6, T 496, Washington, D.C. In this period Cherokees did not own land privately. Instead, they owned any "improvements" they made to the land they had settled on, such as the crops from cultivated fields, cabins, and

other buildings. In a matrilineal kinship system, men lived with their mothers and then their wives. Shoe Boots's nephew maintains that Shoe Boots lived in close proximity to his mother and sister in this period. Because he did not have a Cherokee wife, Shoe Boots would have been unable to relocate to his wife's home. Citizenship Application of William Shoeboots, Statement of John Cochran.

62. Louis Philippe, *Diary of My Travels in America: Louis Philippe, King of France, 1830–1848* (New York, Delacorte Press, 1977), 78.

63. In the early 1800s before the development of a system of roads built by the United States, Cherokee planters conducted most of their commercial trade via the many rivers and smaller waterways that flowed through this central region. Roethler, "Negro Slavery," 114–15; Douglas Wilms, "Cherokee Indian Land Use in Georgia, 1800–1838" (PhD diss., University of Georgia, 1973), 34.

64. Records Relating to Indian Removal, Lizza Shoeboot.

65. Gilbert, *Bulletin 133*, 178; Theda Perdue, *The Cherokee* (New York: Chelsea House Publishers, 1989), 15.

66. Records Relating to Indian Removal, Lizza Shoeboot. Former slaves of Cherokees reported that mid-nineteenth-century Cherokee households with fewer than ten slaves had a variety of living arrangements for those slaves. Some slaves lived in separate, windowless cabins; some lived together in one long cabin; others lived in a designated area of the master's home; Baker and Baker, eds., *WPA Oklahoma Slave Narratives*, 45, 301, 399.

67. Citizenship Application of William Shoeboots, Statement of John Cochran. Given the practice of matrilocality among Cherokees at this time, it is quite possible that the home base described as belonging to Shoe Boots in Indian Agency and Bureau of Indian Affairs records actually belonged to his mother, who seems to have lived on the premises.

68. E. D. Graham, "Slavery as an Issue in Missionary Work," *The American Board and the American Indian (1954)*, 60, Manuscript Histories of Indians, Papers of the American Board of Commissioners for Foreign Missions, ABC 88, Houghton Library, Harvard University, Cambridge, Massachusetts, 28.

69. Graham, "Slavery as an Issue," 28.

70. Norton, *Journal of Major John Norton*, 162; Wilms, "Cherokee Indian Land Use," 29.

71. Ira Berlin, *Many Thousands Gone: The First Two Centuries of Slavery in North America* (Cambridge, Mass.: Harvard University Press, 1998), 370.

72. Berlin, *Many Thousands Gone*, 370.

73. Rowena McClinton, "Possessions of Value: Cherokee Inheritance in the Early Nineteenth Century" (Unpublished paper, Department of History, University of Kentucky, 1992), 25.

74. Shoe Boots's lack of fluency in English is indicated in letters between General John Coffee, former Secretary of War, and Vice President John C. Calhoun,

who write that six of Shoe Boots's associates attested that "he could not speak English intelligibly." John Coffee to Calhoun, December 30, 1829, ed. Larry S. Watson, Senate Document 512, "Letters from the Department to Chiefs and Others; Concerning Quawpaw, Cherokee, Creeks, Ohio Indians, etc.," 23rd Cong., 1st sess., vol. 2, 9. Shoe Boots's lack of English fluency is also suggested by his vulnerability to the financial scheming of white intruders in 1809, discussed in chapter 4. Shoe Boots was fluent in the Creek language, however, and at times served as an interpreter in Cherokee-Creek negotiations. D. B. Mitchell, Account of the Settlement of Cherokees, February 1830, Cherokee Indian Letters, Talks and Treaties Manuscript Collection, 1786–1838, 159, Georgia Department of Archives and History, Atlanta, Georgia.

75. Perdue, *Slavery,* 57, 144.

76. Halliburton, *Red over Black,* 4.

77. In a statistical analysis of WPA interviews with former slaves of Indians, Monroe Billington concludes that Indians were not, in fact, more lenient as masters. To reach this conclusion he determined how many slaves of Indians lived on plantations or farms, finding that more lived on plantations. He tallied the number of times whippings or physical punishment were mentioned, coming up with an undisclosed total for slaves of Indians that was lower than the 61 percent he found for slaves of whites. He also compared the interviewees' assessment of care: 78 percent of slaves owned by whites said their care was good as compared to 81 percent of slaves of Indians, but slaves of Indians reported that they were generally well fed. And finally, he compared slaves' attitudes toward their masters, with 83 percent of slaves of whites reporting good attitudes and 73 percent of Indians reporting the same. Billington's statistics, though informative, take these interviews at face value without considering how dynamics between black former slaves and white interviewers may have skewed responses about white slave owners. In addition, his numerical approach to the question excludes the texture and depth of former slaves' own words about relations with Indians that are apparent in the interviews as well as in slave narratives. Monroe Billington, "Black Slavery in the Indian Territory: The Ex-slave Narrative," *Chronicles of Oklahoma* 61 (1982): 56–65.

78. Celia Naylor-Ojurongbe, "African-American Slave Women's Pathways of Resistance in the Nineteenth-Century Cherokee Nation (Indian Territory)" (paper presented at the sixth meeting of the Southern Conference on Women's History, Athens, Ga., June 2003).

79. Michael F. Doran, "Negro Slaves of the Five Civilized Tribes," *Annals of the Association of American Geographers* 68 (September 1978): 348.

80. Raymond Fogelson, conversation with the author, spring 2002, Chicago; Berlin, *Many Thousands Gone.*

81. Norton, *Journal of Major John Norton,* 60, 67–68.

82. Norton, *Journal of Major John Norton,* 68.

83. Gambold to Reichel, November 9, 1808, Cherokee Mission Papers, Moravian Archives, Winston-Salem, North Carolina.

84. Norton, *Journal of Major John Norton,* 68.

85. Henry Bibb, "Narrative of the Life and Adventures of Henry Bibb, an American Slave," in *I Was Born a Slave,* ed. Yuval Taylor (Chicago: Lawrence Hill Books, 1999), 76.

86. Bibb, "Narrative," 14.

87. Bibb, "Narrative," 76.

88. Polly Colbert in Baker and Baker, eds., *WPA Oklahoma Slave Narratives,* 86.

89. Mary Grayson in Baker and Baker, eds., *WPA Oklahoma Slave Narratives,* 172–73.

90. Katie Rowe in Baker and Baker, eds., *WPA Oklahoma Slave Narratives,* 370.

91. Milton Starr in Baker and Baker, eds., *WPA Oklahoma Slave Narratives,* 409.

CHAPTER THREE. MOTHERHOOD

The epigraphs to this chapter are drawn from Paula Giddings, *When and Where I Enter* (New York: Bantam, 1984), 360, and from Hastings Shade, *Myths, Legends and Old Sayings* ([n.p.], 1994), 43.

1. For more on the dynamic of the jealous mistress, see Catherine Clinton, *The Plantation Mistress: Woman's World in the Old South* (New York: Pantheon, 1982); Elizabeth Fox-Genovese, *Within the Plantation Household: Black and White Women of the Old South* (Chapel Hill: University of North Carolina Press, 1988); Minrose Gwin, "Green-Eyed Monsters of the Slavocracy: Jealous Mistresses in Two Slave Narratives," in *Conjuring: Black Women, Fiction, and the Literary Tradition,* ed. Marjorie Pryse and Hortense Spillers (Bloomington: Indiana University Press, 1985).

2. Details of a Cherokee cabin, circa 1825, are taken from a model cabin, New Echota State Historic Site, Calhoun, Georgia.

3. In testimony before a state court fifty years later, Doll said that her affair with Shoe Boots began in 1802; however, given chronological discrepancies in this court record, I have dated the beginning of the couple's sexual relationship to between 1802 and 1805, approximately one year before the birth of their first child.

4. Captain Shoe Boots to the Chiefs in Council, October 20, 1824, Cherokee Nation Papers, roll 46, no. 6508, Western History Collections, University of Oklahoma, Norman, Oklahoma.

5. Records of the Cherokee Indian Agency in Tennessee, August 7, 1806, Bureau of Indian Affairs, Microfilm Publications RG 75, M208, National Archives and Records Administration, Washington, D.C.

6. Thelma Jennings, "'Us Colored Women Had to Go Through a Plenty':

Sexual Exploitation of African-American Slave Women," *Journal of Women's History* 1 (Winter 1990): 45.

7. Harriet Jacobs, *Incidents in the Life of a Slave Girl Written by Herself* (1861; reprint, Cambridge, Mass.: Harvard University Press, 1987), 51. Though Jacobs says here "resistance is hopeless," she herself and many other slave women resisted sexual exploitation. Her emphasis was probably intended to underscore the rapacity of white men and the vulnerability of slave women in order to propel her northern female readership into abolitionist action.

8. Jacobs, *Slave Girl*, 27.

9. Jennings, "'Us Colored Women,'" 62–64.

10. Jennings, "'Us Colored Women,'" 49.

11. Saidiya Hartman, *Scenes of Subjection: Terror, Slavery, and Self-Making in Nineteenth-Century America* (New York: Oxford University Press, 1997), 81.

12. Henry Bibb, "Narrative of the Life and Adventures of Henry Bibb, an American Slave," in *I Was Born a Slave: An Anthology of Classic Slave Narratives,* vol. 2, *1849–1866,* ed. Yuval Taylor (Chicago: Lawrence Hill Books, 1999), 92.

13. Though it is the case that the system of patriarchy limited and coerced white women's sexual choices as well, the coercion and abuse of slave women and women of color was extreme along a continuum of gender subjugation and arguably unique. Adele Logan Alexander, *Ambiguous Lives: Free Women of Color in Rural Georgia, 1789–1879* (Fayetteville: University of Arkansas Press, 1991), 65. For more on long-term relationships between slave women and masters, see Kent Anderson Leslie, *Woman of Color, Daughter of Privilege: Amanda America Dickson, 1849–1893* (Athens: University of Georgia Press, 1995).

14. Melton McLaurin, *Celia, a Slave* (Athens: University of Georgia Press, 1991).

15. Fred Gearing, *Priests and Warriors: Social Structures for Cherokee Politics in the 18th Century* (Menasha, Wis.: American Anthropological Association, 1962), 31.

16. William Harlen Gilbert, *Smithsonian Institution Bureau of Ethnology Bulletin 133: Anthropological Papers Numbers 19–26* (Washington, D.C.: United States Government Printing Office, 1943), 207.

17. Sarah Hill, *Weaving New Worlds: Southeastern Cherokee Women and Their Baskets* (Chapel Hill: University of North Carolina Press, 1997), 27.

18. Gilbert, *Bulletin 133,* 203–4. Gilbert and other anthropologists note that the English translations for clan names Anisahoni (Blue or Panther), Anigotigewi (Wild Potatoes or Blind Savannah), and Anigilohi (Twisters or Long Hair) are not exact.

19. Hill, *Weaving New Worlds*, 27.

20. Charles Hudson, *The Southeastern Indians* (Nashville: University of Tennessee Press, 1976), 193; Duane Champagne, "Institutional and Cultural Order in Early Cherokee Society," *Journal of Cherokee Studies* 15 (1990): 12.

21. Hudson, *Southeastern Indians,* 185; William Harlen Gilbert, "Eastern Cherokee Social Organization," in *Social Anthropology of North American Tribes,* ed. Fred Eggan (1937; reprint, Chicago: University of Chicago Press, 1955), 296.

22. Orlando Patterson, *Slavery and Social Death* (Cambridge, Mass.: Harvard University Press, 1982), 5.

23. Martha Hodes, *White Women, Black Men: Illicit Sex in the Nineteenth-Century South* (New Haven, Conn.: Yale University Press, 1997), 4, 5.

24. Deborah Gray White, *Ar'n't I a Woman? Female Slaves in the Plantation South* (New York: Norton, 1985), 29, 39–40; Hodes, *White Women, Black Men,* 5, 65, 198.

25. John D'Emilio and Estelle B. Freedman, *Intimate Matters: A History of Sexuality in America* (New York: Harper & Row, 1988), 93–104.

26. Theda Perdue, *Cherokee Women: Gender and Culture Change, 1700–1835* (Lincoln: University of Nebraska Press, 1998), 10.

27. Raymond D. Fogelson, "On the 'Petticoat Government' of the Eighteenth-Century Cherokee," In *Personality and the Cultural Construction of Society,* ed. David Jordan and Marc Swartz (Tuscaloosa: University of Alabama Press, 1990), 170.

28. Gearing, *Priests and Warriors,* 21; Hill, *Weaving New Worlds,* 31–32.

29. James Adair, *Adair's History of the American Indian,* ed. Samuel Cole Williams (1775; reprint, Johnson City, Tenn.: Watauga Press, 1930), 145–46.

30. Louis Philippe, *Diary of My Travels in America: Louis Philippe, King of France, 1830–1848* (New York: Delacorte Press, 1977), 71–72.

31. Cherokee Nation, *Laws of the Cherokee Nation: Adopted by the Council at Various Periods, 1808–1835* (Tahlequah, C.N.: Cherokee Advocate Office, 1852), 53–54; emphasis added.

32. Sharon Block has explained that European and Euro-American men, such as James Adair, who encountered Cherokees in the eighteenth and nineteenth centuries observed that Cherokee men did not have forcible sex with female captives during times of war. In addition to revealing much about white men's notions of sexual identities and behaviors, these accounts may support the notion that rape was uncommon in Cherokee communities at this time. They may also suggest, more concretely, that Cherokee men believed sexual activity was detrimental to their performance in war. Sharon Block, "Rape and Native Americans in Early America" (paper presented at the ninety-sixth annual meeting of the American Historical Association Pacific Coast Branch, Honolulu, Hawaii, August 2003).

33. Hartman, *Scenes of Subjection,* 85.

34. Hill, *Weaving New Worlds,* 28.

35. Cherokee Supreme Court Docket, 1833, Cherokee Collection, microfilm 815, Tennessee State Library and Archives, Nashville, Tennessee. For additional accounts of Molly's case, see William G. McLoughlin, *Cherokee Renascence in*

the New Republic (Princeton: Princeton University Press, 1986), 347, and Rennard Strickland, *Fire and the Spirits: Cherokee Law from Clan to Court* (Norman: University of Oklahoma Press, 1975), 54.

36. Cherokee Supreme Court Docket, microfilm 815.

37. Perdue, *Cherokee Women,* 59.

38. Citizenship Application of William Shoeboots, Statement of Nathaniel Fish.

39. Hill, *Weaving New Worlds,* 11; Gilbert, *Bulletin 133,* 182.

40. Norton, *Journal of Major John Norton,* 51; Louis Philippe, *Diary,* 85.

41. Hill, *Weaving New Worlds,* 14.

42. Perdue, *Cherokee Women,* 31; Gilbert, *Bulletin 133,* 254.

43. Perdue, *Cherokee Women,* 31.

44. Gilbert, *Bulletin 133,* 254.

45. White, *Ar'n't I a Woman?* 110, 111.

46. Citizenship Application of William Shoeboots, Statement of John Cochran.

47. Though it was customary for the father's sister to name the child in the Cherokee kinship system, Shoe Boots seems to have named Kahuga himself, perhaps indicating once again a distance between Doll and his female relatives at this stage in the women's relationship.

48. Loretta Ross, "African-American Women and Abortion: 1800–1970," in *Theorizing Black Feminisms,* ed. Stanlie James and Abena Busia (New York: Routledge, 1993): 141–59.

49. Jacobs, *Slave Girl,* 58.

50. Jacobs, *Slave Girl,* 61–62.

51. Toni Morrison, *Beloved* (New York: Plume, 1987), 31, 30.

52. Morrison, *Beloved,* 61.

53. Morrison, *Beloved,* 62.

54. Morrison, *Beloved,* 140.

55. Morrison, *Beloved,* 6.

56. Morrison, *Beloved,* 16.

57. Morrison, *Beloved,* 202.

58. Morrison, *Beloved,* 163.

59. Morrison, *Beloved,* 23.

60. Sharon Holland, *Raising the Dead: Readings of Death and (Black) Subjectivity* (Durham, N.C.: Duke University Press, 2000), 49.

CHAPTER FOUR. PROPERTY

The epigraphs to this chapter are drawn from Theda Perdue, "Women, Men and American Indian Policy," in Nancy Shoemaker, ed., *Negotiators of Change: His-*

torical Perspectives on Native American Women (New York: Routledge, 1995), 92, and from Cheryl Harris, "Whiteness as Property," *Harvard Law Review* 106 (June 1993): 1716.

1. These details about everyday life are derived from WPA interviews with former slaves of Indians. T. Lindsay Baker and Julie Baker, eds., *The WPA Oklahoma Slave Narratives* (Norman: University of Oklahoma Press, 1996), spinning/weaving 275, 316, 348, 349, 421; dyes 212, 318, 421; baking 275, 233; cooking 315, 317, 318, 348. Also Sarah Hill, *Weaving New Worlds: Cherokee Women and Their Basketry* (Chapel Hill: University of North Carolina Press, 1997), 157.

2. Thurman Wilkins, *Cherokee Tragedy: The Ridge Family and the Decimation of a People* (1970; reprint, Norman: University of Oklahoma Press, 1986), 189.

3. Mission Diary, October 10, 1803, Cherokee Mission Papers, Moravian Archives, Winston-Salem, North Carolina.

4. Gambold to Reichel, April 28, 1808, Cherokee Mission Papers, Moravian Archives; Gambold to Reichel, September 30, 1808, Cherokee Mission Papers, Moravian Archives.

5. Gottlieb and Byhan to Benzien, December 18, 1808, Cherokee Mission Papers, Moravian Archives.

6. Bishop Kenneth Hamilton, "Minutes of the Mission Conference Held in Springplace," *Atlanta Historical Bulletin* 16 (Spring 1971): 50.

7. Mission Diary, July 22, 1802, September 27, 1802, Cherokee Mission Papers, Moravian Archives.

8. Mission Diary, October 18, 1804, August 28, 1805, Cherokee Mission Papers, Moravian Archives; Byhan to Benzien, July 22, 1806, Cherokee Mission Papers, Moravian Archives.

9. John Howard Payne Papers, 8:60–61, Ayer Collection, Newberry Library, Chicago, Illinois.

10. The man with the Wofford surname who gained Shoe Boots's property was a member of the large Wofford family who had settled on Indian land in the eighteenth century. In 1787 Colonel William Wofford moved his family onto Cherokee and Creek territory for which ownership was in dispute. In 1804 Indian Agent Benjamin Hawkins interceded on Wofford's behalf with the Secretary of War, and as a result "the intruders were excused due to their ignorance of the treaties and boundaries that existed at the time of settlement." The Wofford family and twenty-one of their neighbors were awarded ownership of four hundred acres on the Broad River, which became known as the Wofford Settlement. Carl Flowers Jr., "The Wofford Settlement on the Georgia Frontier," *Georgia Historical Quarterly* 61 (Fall 1977): 260.

11. Payne Papers, 8:62.

12. Payne Papers, 8:63. Though Payne does not directly state that Lecroy was removed from Shoe Boots's land along with Wofford, there is no indication that

Lecroy was permitted to remain on Shoe Boots's farm or to retain Shoe Boots's property.

13. Tuscaraga Shoe boots Deed of Gift for Personal property, April 24, 1835, Clerk of Court and Probate Court, Book N, Habersham County, Clarkesville, Georgia. This deed was witnessed by Nathanial Wofford, William Lecroy, and Samuel Bright. The Wofford and Bright families were related by marriage and were co-residents of the Wofford Settlement.

14. Cherokee Supreme Court Docket, October 29, 1823, Cherokee Collection, microfilm no. 815, Tennessee State Library and Archives, Nashville, Tennessee.

15. ABCFM missionary Daniel Butrick wrote about Shoe Boots: "The great warrior Shoe Boots said he was determined to drink no more." Joyce Phillips and Paul Phillips, eds., *The Brainerd Journal: A Mission to the Cherokees, 1817–1823* (Lincoln: University of Nebraska Press, 1998), 475.

16. Rennard Strickland, *Fire and the Spirits: Cherokee Law from Clan to Court* (Norman: University of Oklahoma Press, 1975), 93; quoted by Rowena McClinton, "Possessions of Value: Cherokee Inheritance in the Early Nineteenth Century" (Department of History, University of Kentucky, 1992), 6.

17. Henry Timberlake, *Lieut. Henry Timberlake's Memoirs* (1927; reprint, Marietta, Ga.: Continental Book Company, 1948), 92–93, 90–91.

18. This discussion of the role of animals in eighteenth- and early-nineteenth-century Cherokee society is derived from the Cherokee oral tradition as described in James Mooney, *Myths of the Cherokee* (1900; reprint, New York: Dover, 1995).

19. Theda Perdue, *The Cherokee* (New York: Chelsea House Publishers, 1989), 25. For brief examples of Cherokee practices and beliefs involving animals and hunting, see James Adair, *Adair's History of the American Indian*, ed. Samuel Cole Williams (1775; reprint, Johnson City, Tenn.: Watauga Press, 1930), 251.

20. Perdue, *Cherokee*, 25, 88.

21. Steven Hahn has described a similar free-range method of keeping livestock among white subsistence farmers who occupied land in upper Georgia after Cherokee removal. See Hahn, "The 'Unmaking' of the Southern Yeoman: The Transformation of the Georgia Upcountry, 1860–1890," in *The Countryside in the Age of Capitalist Transformation: Essays in the Social History of Rural America*, ed. Steven Hahn and Jonathan Prude (Chapel Hill: University of North Carolina Press, 1985), 179–203; Hahn, *The Roots of Southern Populism: Yeoman Farmers and the Transformation of the Georgia Upcountry, 1850–1890* (New York: Oxford University Press, 1983).

22. Timberlake, *Memoirs*, 93–94; Louis Philippe, *Diary of My Travels in America: Louis Philippe, King of France, 1830–1848* (New York: Delacorte Press, 1977), 73.

23. Fred Gearing, *Priests and Warriors: Social Structures for Cherokee Politics in*

the 18th Century (Menasha, Wis.: American Anthropological Association, 1962), 4, 5, 6, 31.

24. Gearing, *Priests and Warriors,* 23, 4.

25. Karen Ordahl Kupperman, *Settling with the Indians: The Meeting of English and Indian Cultures in America, 1580–1640* (Totowa, N.J.: Rowman and Littlefield, 1980), 2, 4.

26. Robert K. Miller Jr. and Stephen J. McNamee, "The Inheritance of Wealth in America," in *Inheritance and Wealth in America,* ed. Robert K. Miller Jr. and Stephen J. McNamee (New York: Plenum Press, 1998): 1–2, 11; Peter Dobkin Hall and George E. Marcus, "Why Should Men Leave Great Fortunes to Their Children? Class, Dynasty, and Inheritance in America," in *Inheritance and Wealth in America,* 142; Joan R. Gundersen, "Women and Inheritance in America: Virginia and New York as a Case Study, 1700–1860," in *Inheritance and Wealth in America,* 94, 95, 96, 104.

27. William G. McLoughlin, *Cherokee Renascence in the New Republic* (Princeton: Princeton University Press, 1986), 294.

28. Theda Perdue, "Southern Indians and the Cult of True Womanhood," in *Half Sisters of History,* ed. Catherine Clinton (Durham, N.C.: Duke University Press, 1994), 49–50; McClinton, "Possessions," 1–2.

29. McClinton, "Possessions," 2.

30. McClinton, "Possessions," 9–11.

31. *Cherokee Phoenix,* May 21, 1828. Like the colonial fencing laws that Steven Hahn discusses, this Cherokee fencing law was passed to keep free-ranging livestock out of personal fields rather than to keep the animals penned inside fences. This suggests that as late as 1824, Cherokees were still allowing their livestock to roam. Hahn, *Roots of Southern Populism,* 58–63.

32. *Cherokee Phoenix,* June 25, 1828; October 15, 1828; November 5, 1828.

33. *Cherokee Phoenix,* February 4–March 11, 1829 (Manuel). The tribal status of Joseph Wafford is unclear in the records, though Cherokee public historian and president of the National Trail of Tears Association, Jack Baker, believes him to have been Cherokee. Joseph Wafford's surname is that of a group of white settlers living in Cherokee territory; however, this surname also became a Cherokee name as members from the settler group married Cherokee women. Joseph may have been a white man living among Cherokees or a white man married to a Cherokee woman, but he was most likely the child of a mixed Anglo-Cherokee union. He is *not* named in an 1830 list of white men who were missionaries or traders in the Cherokee Nation or in the accompanying list of white men with Indian families in the Cherokee nation, though a Nathaniel Wafford is. He *is* named in a list of Cherokees who moved West before forced removal; he is said to have emigrated from the Hightower district. This final list supports Jack Baker's assertion that Joseph Wafford was Cherokee but cannot be viewed as conclusive evidence. Cherokee Indian Letters, Talks and Treaties, 1786–1838,

WPA Project no. 4341, Georgia Department of Archives and History, Atlanta, Georgia.

34. *Cherokee Phoenix,* December 11, 1830; November 12, 1831 (Eliza).

35. Don Shadburn, *Cherokee Planters in Georgia 1832–1838: Historical Essays on Eleven Counties in the Cherokee Nation of Georgia,* Pioneer-Cherokee Heritage Series 2 (Roswell, Ga.: Wolfe, 1989), 14.

36. McLoughlin, *Cherokee Renascence,* 286.

37. *Cherokee Phoenix,* June 24, 1829 (Peter), November 4, 1829 (Gabriel), October 8, 1830 (George), December 23, 1830 (Joe, Nelly, and child); *Cherokee Phoenix,* September 24, 1831 ("Two negro boys").

38. Gregory Evans Dowd has suggested that Elias Boudinot may have reprinted these articles condemning the slave trade because he was aware that in the Cherokee fight against removal, northern abolitionist Christians would be important allies. Greg Dowd, comments to the author, June 2003.

39. *Cherokee Phoenix,* June 3, 1829.

40. *Cherokee Phoenix,* May 21, 1828; July 22, 1829; May 7 and 14, 1831. One disparaging story written in dialect and titled "Negro Fun" was reprinted in the *Cherokee Phoenix* as well and shared a page with the poem "Pity for Poor Africans."

41. *Cherokee Phoenix,* July 1, 1829.

42. Both slave advertisements and reprinted articles about slavery and blacks diminished significantly by 1832 as the removal conflict erupted and as a new editor, Elijah Hicks, took over. For another reading of the *Cherokee Phoenix* regarding Cherokee views of slavery, see Theda Perdue, "Cherokee Planters, Black Slaves, and African Colonization," *Chronicles of Oklahoma* 60 (1982): 322–31.

43. McClinton, "Possessions," 26–27.

44. Wilkins, *Cherokee Tragedy,* 61; Rudi Halliburton, "Origins of Black Slavery Among the Cherokees," *Chronicles of Oklahoma* 52 (Winter 1974): 490.

45. Anthropologists classify both Creeks and Cherokees within the Mississippean Mound Culture group. In the 1700s and 1800s both tribes shared a matrilineal kinship system, agricultural methods, and an annual ceremony of renewal celebrating the new corn called the Green Corn Dance. Katja May, *African Americans and Native Americans in the Creek and Cherokee Nations, 1830s to 1920s* (New York: Garland, 1996), 33.

46. Sigmund Sameth, "Creek Negroes" (master's thesis, University of Oklahoma, 1940), 11.

47. Joel Martin, *Sacred Revolt: The Muskogees' Struggle for a New World* (Boston: Beacon, 1991), 79; Sameth, "Creek Negroes," 8.

48. Daniel F. Littlefield, *Africans and Creeks: From the Colonial Period to the Civil War* (Westport, Conn.: Greenwood Press, 1979), 44; Martin, *Sacred Revolt,* 73.

49. Claudio Saunt, *A New Order of Things: Property, Power, and the Trans-*

formation of the Creek Indians, 1733–1816 (New York: Cambridge University Press, 1999), 38–63.

50. Shoe Boots had relational ties with the Creeks, indicated by his fluency in the Creek language and the report that he had relatives who resided among the Creeks. D. B. Mitchell, Account of the Settlement of Cherokees, Feb. 1830, Cherokee Indian Letters, Talks, and Treaties 1786–1838, 159; Wilkins, *Cherokee Tragedy*, 61.

51. Arthur Hall, "The Red Stick War: Creek Indian Affairs During the War of 1812," *Chronicles of Oklahoma* 12 (September 1934): 269, 270.

52. Quoted in Martin, *Sacred Revolt*, 120.

53. Martin, *Sacred Revolt*, 116, 120, 115. For more on Tecumseh and Native spiritualist rebellion, see Gregory Evans Dowd, *A Spirited Resistance: The North American Indian Struggle for Unity, 1745–1815* (Baltimore: Johns Hopkins University Press, 1992).

54. Martin, *Sacred Revolt*, 142. In 1856 the Xhosa nation of South Africa would also turn to killing cattle as part of a prophetic revolution. At the heart of the movement was a young woman's vision that a "new people," who were in fact the ancestors returned, would appear to help dispel British colonists and renew the Xhosa world. To summon the new people and make way for the new world to come, the Xhosa had to dispense with old things: their cattle, supplies of corn, implements of witchcraft, and personal ornaments. This spiritual movement ended in disaster, since the Xhosa, left unaided by British colonial leaders, died of starvation in large numbers. For more on this event, see J. B. Peires, *The Dead Will Arise: Nongqawuse and the Great Xhosa Cattle-Killing Movement of 1856–7* (Bloomington: Indiana University Press, 1989).

55. A. Hall, "Red Stick War," 268.

56. Martin, *Sacred Revolt*, 150, 153; R. S. Cotterill, *The Southern Indians: The Story of the Civilized Tribes Before Removal* (Norman: University of Oklahoma Press, 1954), 177, 181; A. Hall, "Red Stick War," 274; Michael Rogin, *Fathers and Children: Andrew Jackson and the Subjugation of the American Indian* (New Brunswick, N.J.: Transaction, 1995), 145; Saunt, *New Order*, 249.

57. A. Hall, "Red Stick War," 275, 270, 271.

58. Saunt, *New Order*, 259–60.

59. Martin, *Sacred Revolt*, 156.

60. Rogin, *Fathers and Children*, 145, 148.

61. Cotterill, *Southern Indians*, 182, 186. Cotterill's use of the terms *half-bloods* and *full-bloods* should be read as distinguishing between political positions— either "progressive" or "traditionalist"—as well as the racial makeup of a person's ancestry.

62. Martin, *Sacred Revolt*, 137.

63. Wilkins, *Cherokee Tragedy*, 60.

64. Springplace Mission Diary (July 11, 1813), trans. Rowena McClinton as

The Moravian Mission to the Cherokees: Springplace in the Gambold Years, 1805–1821, publication forthcoming.

65. Return Meigs, "An Address to the Cherokees," October 1813, Manuscript Division, no. 1787, Tennessee State Library and Archives, Nashville, Tennessee.

66. Cotterill, *Southern Indians,* 186.

67. Martin, *Sacred Revolt,* 158.

68. Quoted in Rogin, *Fathers and Children,* 151.

69. Rogin, *Fathers and Children,* 151, 156.

70. Marion L. Starkey, *The Cherokee Nation* (1946; reprint, North Dighton, Mass.: J. G. Press, 1995), 24.

71. Payne Papers, 2:55–56.

72. Starkey, *Cherokee Nation,* 25.

73. Quoted in Martin, *Sacred Revolt,* 157.

74. Saunt, *New Order,* 269.

75. Martin, *Sacred Revolt,* 156, 157; Saunt, *New Order,* 269.

76. Martin, *Sacred Revolt,* 163, 73.

77. Cheryl Harris, "Whiteness as Property," *Harvard Law Review* 106 (June 1993): 1716.

CHAPTER FIVE. CHRISTIANITY

The epigraph to this chapter is drawn from Rufus Anderson, *Memoir of Catharine Brown: A Christian Indian of the Cherokee Nation* (Philadelphia: American Sunday School Press, 1832), 24–25.

1. Springplace Mission Diary (November 20, 1812; July 12, 1813), trans. Rowena McClinton as *The Moravian Mission to the Cherokees: Springplace in the Gambold Years, 1805–1821,* publication forthcoming.

2. "Recpt. the Cherokee Officers for Presents to Those Distinguished Themselves," October 1815, Records of the Cherokee Indian Agency in Tennessee, M208, roll 6, National Archives and Records Administration, Washington, D.C.

3. Wm. Crawford to the Secretary of War, May 4, 1816, Letters Sent to the Secretary of War Relating to Indian Affairs, 1800–1824, National Archives Microfilm Publication microfilm 15, roll 3. U.S. War Department Records of the Office of the Secretary of War, National Archives and Records Service, Washington, D.C.

4. James Mooney, *Myths of the Cherokee* (1900; reprint, New York: Dover, 1995), 394.

5. Cherokee Indian Letters, Talks, and Treaties Manuscript Collection, 1786–1838, February 13, 1830, 159, Georgia Department of Archives and History, Atlanta, Georgia.

6. Joyce Phillips and Paul Gary Phillips, eds., *The Brainerd Journal: A Mis-*

sion to the Cherokees, 1817–1823 (Lincoln: University of Nebraska Press, 1998), 475.

7. *Cherokee Phoenix,* June 18, 1828. In this report of the 1828 census, black people are categorized interchangeably either as male or female "negroes" or as male or female "slaves."

8. *Cherokee Phoenix,* June 18, 1828.

9. Ard Hoyt et al. to Jeremiah Evarts, March, 8, 1822, Mission Journal, Papers of the American Board of Commissioners for Foreign Missions, ABC 18.3.1, vol. 2, Houghton Library, Harvard University, Cambridge, Massachusetts.

10. "List of Places in the Cherokee Nation," Cherokee Mission: Joint Communications and Papers, Papers of the American Board of Commissioners for Foreign Missions, microfilm, unit 6, reels 721–858, 168.

11. Hoyt et al. to Evarts.

12. Brainerd Journal, April 14, 1823, April 12, 1823, Cherokee Mission, Papers of the American Board of Commissioners for Foreign Missions, ABC 18.3.1, vol. 2, Houghton Library, Harvard University, Cambridge, Massachusetts.

13. Adriane Strenk, "Tradition and Transformation: Shoe Boots and the Creation of a Cherokee Culture" (master's thesis, University of Kentucky, 1993), 54–56.

14. "Cherokee Chronology," Cherokee Collection, Tennessee State Library and Archives, Nashville, Tennessee.

15. Marion L. Starkey, *The Cherokee Nation* (1946; reprint, North Dighton, Mass.: J. G. Press, 1995), 48.

16. Brainerd Journal, July 25, 1818, Cherokee Mission, Papers of the American Board of Commissioners for Foreign Missions, ABC 18.3.1, vol. 2. Theda Perdue discusses Cherokee women's opposition to land cessions in "Cherokee Women and the Trail of Tears," in *Unequal Sisters: A Multicultural Reader in U.S. Women's History,* ed. Vicki Ruiz and Ellen Carol DuBois (New York: Routledge, 1994), 35.

17. Starkey, *Cherokee Nation,* 49.

18. Strenk, "Tradition and Transformation," 44.

19. Hoyt et al. to Evarts.

20. Brainerd Journal, May 15, 1823, February 13, 1823, Cherokee Mission, Papers of the American Board of Commissioners for Foreign Missions, ABC 18.3.1, vol. 2.

21. Brainerd Journal, May 15, 1823.

22. Brainerd Journal, Hightower School Records, Names of Pupils, July 28, 1824, Cherokee Mission, Papers of the American Board of Commissioners for Foreign Missions, ABC 18.3.1, vol. 2. There is no mention of Shoe Boots's children in this list of pupils, which was recorded three months before Shoe Boots submitted a petition for his children's emancipation.

23. *Cherokee Phoenix,* October 15, 1828.

24. Phillips and Phillips, eds., *Brainerd Journal,* 322–23.

25. Brainerd Journal, July 24, 1822, Cherokee Mission, Papers of the American Board of Commissioners for Foreign Missions, ABC 18.3.1, vol. 2.

26. Vine Deloria Jr., *Custer Died for Your Sins: An Indian Manifesto* (1969; reprint, Norman: University of Oklahoma Press, 1988), 102.

27. Young, "Cherokee Nation," 502, 513.

28. William G. McLoughlin, *Cherokees and Missionaries, 1789–1839* (1984; reprint, Norman: University of Oklahoma Press 1995), 97.

29. Quoted in McLoughlin, *Cherokees and Missionaries,* 105, 114.

30. McLoughlin, *Cherokees and Missionaries,* 102.

31. Daniel Butrick to [illegible], September 27, 1825, Butrick Journal, Papers of the American Board of Commissioners for Foreign Missions, ABC 18.3.1, vols. 4–5. Cherokee Mission: Joint Communications and Papers, American Board of Commissioners for Foreign Missions, Houghton Library, Harvard University, Cambridge, Massachusetts.

32. Peter Hinks, *To Awaken My Afflicted Brethren: David Walker and the Problem of Antebellum Slave Resistance* (University Park: Pennsylvania State University Press, 1997), 127.

33. David Walker, *David Walker's Appeal to the Coloured Citizens of the World,* ed. Peter Hinks (1929; reprint, University Park: Pennsylvania State University Press, 2000), 39.

34. Brainerd Journal, June 7, 1818, Cherokee Mission, Papers of the American Board of Commissioners for Foreign Missions, ABC 18.3.1, vol. 2.

35. E. D. Graham, "Slavery as an Issue in Mission Work," *The American Board and the American Indian* (1954), 60, Papers of the American Board of Commissioners for Foreign Missions, ABC 88, Manuscript Histories of Indians, Houghton Library, Harvard, Massachusetts.

36. Peter Hinks, *To Awaken My Afflicted Brethren: David Walker and the Problem of Antebellum Slave Resistance* (University Park: Pennsylvania State University Press, 1997), 128.

37. Butrick to [illegible], Butrick Journal.

38. Graham, "Slavery as an Issue," 59.

39. Brainerd Journal, April 23, 1822, Cherokee Mission, Papers of the American Board of Commissioners for Foreign Missions, ABC 18.3.1, vol. 2.

40. Michael Roethler, "Negro Slavery Among the Cherokee Indians, 1540–1866" (PhD diss., Fordham University, 1964), 124.

41. Roethler, "Negro Slavery," 125.

42. Brainerd Journal, June 7, 1818, Cherokee Mission, Papers of the American Board of Commissioners for Foreign Missions, ABC 18.3.1, vol. 2.

43. Theda Perdue, *Slavery and the Evolution of Cherokee Society, 1540–1866* (Knoxville: University of Tennessee Press, 1979), 106; Graham, "Slavery as an Issue," 59.

44. Quoted in Perdue, *Slavery,* 106.

45. Perdue, *Slavery,* 106; Joel Martin, *Sacred Revolt: The Muskogees' Struggle for a New World* (Boston: Beacon, 1991), 73.

46. John Howard Payne, "The Green Corn Dance," *Chronicles of Oklahoma* 10 (1932): 175. Previously published as "Green Corn Dance of the Creeks," *Continental Monthly* (Boston), January 1862.

47. Quoted in Katja May, *African Americans and Native Americans in the Creek and Cherokee Nations, 1830s to 1920s* (New York: Garland, 1996), 43.

48. For more on blacks operating as cultural mediators between Native and white people, see William Hart, "Black 'Go-Betweens' and the Mutability of 'Race,' Status, and Identity on New York's Pre-Revolutionary Frontier," in *Contact Points: American Frontiers from the Mohawk Valley to the Mississippi, 1750–1830,* ed. Andrew Clayton and Fredrika Teute (Chapel Hill: University of North Carolina Press, 1998).

49. McLoughlin, *Cherokees and Missionaries,* 139.

50. Charles Hicks to Dr. br. Smith, May 28, 1824, Cherokee Mission Papers, Moravian Archives, Winston-Salem, North Carolina.

51. Graham, "Slavery as an Issue," 60.

52. Hicks to br. Smith, May 26, 1824.

53. Daniel Butrick to Jeremiah Evarts, May 5, 1825, Butrick Journal, Papers of the American Board of Commissioners for Foreign Missions, 18.3.3, vols. 4–5, Houghton Library, Harvard University, Cambridge, Massachusetts.

54. Hicks to Smith, May 28, 1824.

CHAPTER SIX. NATIONHOOD

The epigraphs to this chapter are drawn from Amiri Baraka and crowd, National Black Political Association, 1972; from W. E. B. Du Bois, "The Propaganda of History," in *Black Reconstruction in America, 1860–1880* (1935; reprint, New York: Atheneum, 1992), 714; and from John Ridge, "Letter to Albert Gallatin," 1826, John Howard Payne Papers, 8:212, Ayer Collection, Newberry Library, Chicago, Illinois (reprinted in Theda Perdue and Michael Green, eds., *The Cherokee Removal: A Brief History with Documents* [Boston: Bedford Books, 1995]: 34–43).

1. Citizenship Application of William Shoeboots, Statement of Thomas Ridge, Cherokee Applications, Applications from the Bureau of Indian Affairs, Muskogee Area Office, Relating to Enrollment in the Five Civilized Tribes Under the Act of 1896, National Archives and Records Administration Microfilm Publication M1650, National Archives and Records Administration Southwest Region, Fort Worth, Texas.

2. Thurman Wilkins, *Cherokee Tragedy: The Ridge Family and the Decimation*

of a People (1970; reprint, Norman: University of Oklahoma Press, 1986), 99–100.

3. John Howard Payne Papers, 8:63, Ayer Collection, Newberry Library, Chicago, Illinois.

4. Mark Smith has argued that Christianization often served as an introduction to linear time for slaves, whose West African culture tended toward natural, cyclical time indicators, such as telling time by the sun and counting dates by the moon. These slaves and their descendants later associated their Christian faith with strict time keeping and punctuality. It is possible that Cherokee converts to Christianity also developed a new understanding of time that was linear and precise as an effect of their new faith. Mark Smith, *Mastered by the Clock: Time, Slavery and Freedom in the American South* (Chapel Hill: University of North Carolina Press, 1987), 149.

5. M. Smith, *Mastered by the Clock*, 149.

6. Fred Gearing, *Priests and Warriors: Social Structures for Cherokee Politics in the 18th Century* (Menasha, Wis.: American Anthropological Association, 1962), 3; Circe Sturm, *Blood Politics: Race, Culture, and Identity in the Cherokee Nation of Oklahoma* (Berkeley and Los Angeles: University of California Press, 2002), 36.

7. Duane Champagne, "Institutional and Cultural Order in Early Cherokee Society," *Journal of Cherokee Studies* 15 (1990): 14–15. Men could voice their own opinions at council meetings, but their status—the level of respect they had gained for previous deeds—influenced the reception of their ideas. Richard V. Persico, Jr., "Early Nineteenth-Century Cherokee Political Organization," in *The Cherokee Indian Nation: A Troubled History,* edited by Duane H. King, 92–109 (Knoxville: University of Tennessee Press, 1979), 92; Champagne, "Institutional," 19.

8. Persico, "Cherokee Political Organization," 95–96, 97, 98.

9. Henry Thompson Malone, *Cherokees of the Old South* (Athens: University of Georgia Press, 1956), 76; Persico, "Cherokee Political Organization," 103.

10. Persico, "Cherokee Political Organization," 103; Malone, *Cherokees of the Old South,* 77.

11. Malone, *Cherokees of the Old South,* 83; Wilkins, *Cherokee Tragedy,* 97.

12. Marion L. Starkey, *The Cherokee Nation* (1946; reprint, North Dighton, Mass.: J. G. Press, 1995), 48.

13. Persico, "Cherokee Political Organization," 100.

14. Duane Champagne, "Symbolic Structure and Political Change in Cherokee Society," *Journal of Cherokee Studies* 8 (1983): 87–96, 92.

15. Starkey, *Cherokee Nation,* 220.

16. Theda Perdue, "The Conflict Within: Cherokees and Removal," in *Cherokee Removal: Before and After,* ed. William Anderson (Athens: University of Geor-

gia Press, 1991), 63. Perdue argues in this essay that class divisions among the Cherokee included an aristocracy, an emerging middle class, and "common Indians." She makes a distinction between John Ross and John Ridge, categorizing Ross as aristocratic and Ridge as middle-class.

17. Starkey, *Cherokee Nation*, 220.

18. Mary Young argues that the Cherokee Constitution reflected state constitutions as much as or more than it did the U.S. Constitution; Young, "Cherokee Nation: Mirror of the Republic," *American Quarterly* 33 (Winter 1981): 507.

19. Champagne, "Symbolic Structure," 92. In this essay Champagne argues that local leaders wielded enough influence to maintain behind-the-scenes control of the central government until 1888. Though local leaders do seem to have retained some power, conflicts such as the one over the status of the mission in Hightower, discussed in chapter 4, suggest that the national government sometimes exerted its will against the wishes of local leaders.

20. Persico, "Cherokee Political Organization," 100, 102.

21. Malone, *Cherokees of the Old South*, 124, 122.

22. Malone, *Cherokees of the Old South*, 84; Theda Perdue, *Slavery and the Evolution of Cherokee Society, 1540–1866* (Knoxville: University of Tennessee Press, 1979), 56–57.

23. Malone, *Cherokees of the Old South*, 84, 125; the Vann plantation is a state historic site and tourist attraction in northern Georgia.

24. In her study of a black southern community, Elsa Barkley Brown finds a similar occurrence of the loss of political voice for women and children at a time when black men were consolidating formal political power in response to a new access to state politics during the Reconstruction era. See Brown, "Negotiating and Transforming the Public Sphere: African American Political Life in the Transition from Slavery to Freedom," *Public Culture* 7 (Fall 1994): 107–46.

25. Theda Perdue, *Cherokee Women: Gender and Culture Change, 1700–1835* (Lincoln: University of Nebraska Press, 1998), 104–5.

26. Edmund Morgan, *American Slavery, American Freedom: The Ordeal of Colonial Virginia* (New York: Norton, 1975), 293–362.

27. Morgan, *American Slavery*, 5.

28. Annual Report of Agent Butler, 1859, quoted in Charles C. Royce, "The Cherokee Nation of Indians," in *Fifth Annual Report of the Bureau of Ethnology, 1883–84*, edited by J. W. Powell, 121–373, 322 (Washington, D.C.: Government Printing Office, 1887).

29. Sturm offers an excellent analysis of the development of Cherokee nationalism, racialized citizenship, and racial exclusion in *Blood Politics*, chapter 3, "Race as Nation, Race as Blood Quantum," 52–81.

30. Malone, *Cherokees of the Old South*, 85.

31. Cherokee Nation, *Laws of the Cherokee Nation: Adopted by the Council at Various Periods, 1808–1835* (Tahlequah, C.N.: Cherokee Advocate Office, 1852),

120; Perdue, *Slavery*, 56–57. Note: in the 1839 version of the Constitution, Section 4 quoted here is given as Section 5.

32. Karen Woods, "One Nation, One Blood: Interracial Marriage in American Fiction, Scandal and Law, 1820–70" (PhD diss., University of Minnesota, 1999), 76.

33. Cherokee Nation, *Laws of the Cherokee Nation*, 121. In the 1839 version of the Constitution the parenthetical note referring to "negroes" quoted here is deleted.

34. Cherokee Nation, *Laws of the Cherokee Nation*, 57.

35. Cherokee Nation, *Laws of the Cherokee Nation*, 10; A. H. Murchison, "Intermarried Whites in the Cherokee Nation Between the Years 1865 and 1887," *Chronicles of Oklahoma* 6 (September 1928): 299, 300; Fay A. Yarbrough, "Legislating Women's Sexuality: Cherokee Marriage Laws in the Nineteenth Century" (paper presented at the sixth Southern Conference on Women's History, Athens, Ga., June 2003), 1–2.

36. J. B. Davis, "Slavery in the Cherokee Nation," *Chronicles of Oklahoma* 11 (December 1933): 1064; Cherokee Nation, *Laws of the Cherokee Nation*, 37.

37. Rudi Halliburton, *Red over Black: Black Slavery among the Cherokee Indians* (Westport, Conn.: Greenwood Press, 1977), x.

38. Sturm, *Blood Politics*, 51–52.

39. Sharon Holland, *Raising the Dead: Readings of Death and (Black) Subjectivity* (Durham, N.C.: Duke University Press, 2000), 16.

40. Priscilla Wald, "Terms of Assimilation: Legislating Subjectivity in the Emerging Nation," in *Cultures of United States Imperialism*, ed. Amy Kaplan and Donald Pease (Durham, N.C.: Duke University Press, 1993), 9.

41. William Sturtevant, ed., "John Ridge on Cherokee Civilization in 1826," *Journal of Cherokee Studies* 6 (Fall 1981): 79–91.

42. Sturtevant, "John Ridge," 79–80.

43. Payne Papers, 8:103–15.

44. Historian Robin Kelley borrows the term *hidden transcript* from anthropologist James Scott to describe black working-class resistance in the United States. Kelley quotes Scott's definition of the term as signifying "a dissident political culture that manifests itself in daily conversations, folklore, jokes, songs, and other cultural practices." Robin D. G. Kelley, *Race Rebels: Culture, Politics, and the Black Working Class* (New York: Free Press, 1994), 8.

45. As K. Tsianina Lomawaima has asserted in her study of the Chilocco Indian School that influenced my argument here, the power of an institution, though formidable, is never total. By looking at student letters and diaries as well as official school records, Lomawaima found that a government school meant to transform Indian children into Americans actually served the purpose of shaping a pan-Indian consciousness among the pupils. K. Tsianina Lomawaima, *They Called It Prairie Light* (Lincoln: University of Nebraska Press, 1994).

46. Captain Shoe Boots to the Chiefs in Council, October 20, 1824, Cherokee Nation Papers, roll 46, no. 6508, Western History Collections, University of Oklahoma, Norman, Oklahoma.

47. Payne Papers, 2:57–58.

48. "List of White Men in the Cherokee Nation," September 13, 1830, 227, Cherokee Indian Letters, Talks, and Treaties Manuscript Collection, 1786–1838, Georgia Department of Archives and History, Atlanta, Georgia.

49. Joyce Phillips and Paul Gary Phillips, eds., *The Brainerd Journal: A Mission to the Cherokees, 1817–1823* (Lincoln: University of Nebraska Press, 1998), 521, 246 (November 19, 1821).

50. Ard Hoyt et al. to Jeremiah Evarts, March 8, 1822, Cherokee Mission, Papers of the American Board of Commissioners for Foreign Missions, ABC 18.3.1, vol. 2, Houghton Library, Harvard University, Cambridge, Massachusetts.

51. Brainerd Journal, June 21, 1822, Cherokee Mission, Papers of the American Board of Commissioners for Foreign Missions, ABC 18.3.1, vol. 2, Houghton Library, Harvard University, Cambridge, Massachusetts; Phillips and Phillips, eds., *Brainerd Journal,* 278.

52. Brainerd Journal, July 24, 1822.

53. Brainerd Journal, December 23, 1822; January 3, 1823.

54. Brainerd Journal, May 5, 1825.

55. Isaac Proctor to Jeremiah Evarts, July 17, 1830, Cherokee Mission, Papers of the American Board of Commissioners for Foreign Missions, ABC 18.3.1, vol. 2, Houghton Library, Harvard University, Cambridge, Massachusetts.

56. David Murray, *Forked Tongues: Speech, Writing, and Representation in North American Indian Texts* (Bloomington: Indiana University Press, 1991), 49–53.

57. Genesis 2:23.

58. The story of Selu and Kanati has been told and recorded many times in multiple versions. See James Mooney, *Myths of the Cherokee* (1900; reprint, New York: Dover, 1995), 242–48, for the version told by Cherokee oral traditionalists Swimmer and John Ax. Sarah Hill offers a beautiful retelling and astute interpretation of the myth in *Weaving New Worlds: Cherokee Women and Their Basketry* (Chapel Hill: University of North Carolina Press, 1997), 76–80.

59. Raymond D. Fogelson, "On the 'Petticoat Government' of the Eighteenth-Century Cherokee," in *Personality and the Cultural Construction of Society,* ed. David Jordan and Marc Swartz (Tuscaloosa: University of Alabama Press, 1990), 173–75; Fogelson, "Windigo Goes South: Stoneclad Among the Cherokees," in *Manlike Monsters on Trial: Early Records and Modern Evidence,* ed. Marjorie Ames and Michael Ames (Vancouver: University of British Columbia, 1980), 132–51; Perdue, *Cherokee Women,* 29–30, 35–37; Hill, *Weaving New Worlds,* 79–80; Rowena McClinton, "Reconstructing the Cherokee and Moravian Story through Early Nineteenth Century Missionary Diaries: Transcending Divergent World-

views, Archaic Language, and Time" (paper presented at the University of North Carolina, Chapel Hill, March 5, 2001), 15–18.

60. William Harlen Gilbert, *Smithsonian Institution Bureau of Ethnology Bulletin 133: Anthropological Papers Numbers 19–26* (Washington, D.C.: United States Government Printing Office, 1943), 207; Fogelson, "Petticoat," 173–174; Sturm, *Blood Politics,* 33.

61. Fogelson, "Petticoat," 174.

62. Sturm, *Blood Politics,* 215–16.

63. Henry Bibb, "Narrative of the Life and Adventures of Henry Bibb, an American Slave," in *I Was Born a Slave: An Anthology of Classic Slave Narratives,* vol. 2, *1849–1866,* ed. Yuval Taylor (Chicago: Lawrence Hill Books, 1999), 27.

64. Payne Papers, 7:55–56.

65. Rennard Strickland, *Fire and the Spirits: Cherokee Law from Clan to Court* (Norman: University of Oklahoma Press, 1975), 78.

66. Robert Walker, *Torchlights to the Cherokees* (New York: Macmillan, 1931), 299. This passage is noted by Patrick Minges in "'Go in de Wilderness': Black/Indian Diaspora in the Slave Narratives" (working paper, Union Theological Seminary, New York, N.Y., January 2002), 12.

67. William G. McLoughlin and Walter Conser, "The Cherokee Censuses of 1809, 1825, and 1835," in *The Cherokee Ghost Dance: Essays on the Southeastern Indians, 1789–1861* (Macon, Ga.: Mercer University Press, 1984), 240, 228. Circe Sturm offers a cautionary criticism of the facile association often made between "mixed-bloods" and slaveholding in Cherokee historiography, arguing that although there was a correlation between white ancestry, class status, and slaveholding, there were a number of exceptions to this formula. The biography of Shoe Boots himself, a "full-blood" slaveholder, supports Sturm's argument; Sturm, *Blood Politics,* 55–56.

68. Grievance addressed to the Cherokee Nation North Carolina, Cherokee Supreme Court Docket, 1833, Cherokee Collection, microfilm no. 815, Tennessee State Library and Archives, Nashville, Tennessee.

69. William G. McLoughlin, *Cherokee Renascence in the New Republic* (Princeton: Princeton University Press, 1986), 347.

70. Payne Papers, 7:47–48.

71. Payne Papers, 7:47–48. I found only two petitions requesting emancipation for black slaves in the Cherokee Supreme Court records. The fact that both petitions were submitted by Cherokee men suggests several interpretive possibilities: that more Cherokee men than women were engaging in sexual relations with black slaves, that black-Cherokee families descended from Cherokee men encountered special problems because of their lack of matrilineage and clan membership, that few Cherokees formally freed their slaves, and that acts of slave emancipation were motivated by kinship responsibilities.

72. Captain Shoe Boots to the Chiefs in Council, October 20, 1824.

73. Cherokee Nation, *Laws of the Cherokee Nation*, 38.

CHAPTER SEVEN. GOLD RUSH

The epigraphs to this chapter are drawn from Elijah Hicks, *Cherokee Phoenix,* January 19, 1833, and from a Cherokee song from the 1830s recorded by John Howard Payne, Payne Papers, 2:16–17, Ayer Collection, Newberry Library, Chicago, Illinois.

1. Citizenship Application of William Shoeboots, Statement of William Shoeboots, Cherokee Applications, Applications from the Bureau of Indian Affairs, Muskogee Area Office, Relating to Enrollment in the Five Civilized Tribes Under the Act of 1896, National Archives and Records Administration Microfilm Publication M1650, National Archives and Records Administration Southwest Region, Fort Worth, Texas.

2. Citizenship Application of William Shoeboots, Statement of William Shoeboots; *Cherokee Phoenix,* June 12, 1830.

3. *Cherokee Phoenix,* November 11, 1829.

4. Captain Shoe Boots to the Chiefs in Council, October 20, 1824, Cherokee Nation Papers, roll 46, no. 6508, Western History Collections, University of Oklahoma, Norman, Oklahoma.

5. John Howard Payne Papers, 8:64, Ayer Collection, Newberry Library, Chicago, Illinois. While Payne states that Shoe Boots died before the birth of William and Lewis, William asserts that he knew his father: "I was small when my father died. . . . I can remember him." William gives his age as sixty-seven in 1888, which would have made him eight years old at the time of Shoe Boots's death (Citizenship Application of William Shoeboots, Statement of William Shoeboots). One witness, a Cherokee man named John Cochran who was Shoe Boots's nephew, offered corroborating testimony. He stated that he remembered seeing the twins for the first time "at a big meeting at Red Clay . . . applicant was about 8 or 9 years old when I saw him in Red Clay. . . . I think Shoeboots died about 3 or 4 years before I saw the family at Red Clay" (Citizenship Application of William Shoeboots, Statement of John Cochran). Cochran puts the child's age closer to five at the time of Shoe Boots's death but supports William's claim that he knew his father. The only additional record of William's birth date might have been found in the petition for the emancipation of "Billy and Lewis" submitted by Shoe Boots's sisters after Shoe Boots's death, but the petition does not include the age of the children. William most likely did know his father.

6. In the midst of telling Shoe Boots and Doll's story, Payne breaks narrative form to quote the National Committee's finding on the twins' case. In this find-

ing there is no mention of any involvement on the part of Doll; Payne Papers, 8:64–65.

7. William Harlen Gilbert, *Smithsonian Institution Bureau of Ethnology Bulletin 133: Anthropological Papers Numbers 19–26* (Washington, D.C.: United States Government Printing Office, 1943), 253.

8. Payne Papers, 8:64–65. The only National Committee vote in favor of Peggy and Takesteskee's request to free William and Lewis was made by John Timson, a Cherokee representative from the Aquohee District. I have found no information that would explain the motivation behind Timson's lone vote.

9. Payne Papers, 8:64.

10. Mary Young, "The Cherokee Nation: Mirror of the Republic," *American Quarterly* 33 (Winter 1981): 520.

11. *Cherokee Phoenix,* September 10, 1831; February 12, 1831.

12. *Cherokee Phoenix,* July 16, 1831.

13. *Cherokee Phoenix,* July 27, 1833.

14. Quoted in Katja May, *African Americans and Native Americans in the Creek and Cherokee Nations, 1830s to 1920s* (New York: Garland, 1996), 41.

15. *Cherokee Phoenix,* June 12, 1830.

16. Payne Papers, 8:63–64.

17. William G. McLoughlin, *Cherokee Renascence in the New Republic* (Princeton: Princeton University Press, 1986), 345.

18. Citizenship Application of William Shoeboots, Statement of William Shoeboots.

19. Rennard Strickland, *Fire and the Spirits: Cherokee Law from Clan to Court* (Norman: University of Oklahoma Press), 1975, 99.

20. The regulation of inheritance by mixed-race children is not unique to the Cherokee Nation. For more on familial and state control of property holdings through the disavowal of interracial marriages, see Peggy Pascoe, "Race, Gender, and the Privileges of Property: On the Significance of Miscegenation Law in the U.S. West," in *Over the Edge: Remapping the American West,* ed. Valerie J. Matsumoto and Blake Allmendinger (Berkeley and Los Angeles: University of California Press, 1999), 215–30.

21. Don Shadburn, *Cherokee Planters in Georgia 1832–1838: Historical Essays on Eleven Counties in the Cherokee Nation of Georgia,* Pioneer-Cherokee Heritage Series 2 (Roswell, Ga.: W. H. Wolfe, 1989), 319–20. The Bean family that took up residence on the farm may have been relatives of Shoe Boots.

22. Payne Papers, 2:64.

23. Citizenship Application of William Shoeboots, Statement of William Shoeboots; "Agreement to Free Lizza Shoeboots and Child," Cherokee Nation Papers, 46:6512, Western History Collections, University of Oklahoma, Norman, Oklahoma. Elizabeth Shoeboots changed hands more than once between 1830 and 1837, and it is possible that she ran away from one of her masters during

this period. An advertisement placed in the *Cherokee Phoenix* by a Cherokee slave-owner named Moses Downing offered $20 for the return of a slave called Eliza, who is described as a "mulatto woman," "about 30 years old," who "speaks English and Cherokee well." Eliza was charged with running away with a white man named Michael Doudy (or Dowdy). Though it is not certain, this Eliza may have been Elizabeth Shoeboots. *Cherokee Phoenix*, November 12, 1831.

24. "Agreement to Free Lizza Shoeboots and Child," 46:6512.

25. Citizenship Application of William Shoeboots, Statement of William Shoeboots.

26. Citizenship Application of William Shoeboots, Statement of Thomas Ridge.

27. Citizenship Application of William Shoeboots, Statement of Ed Carey.

28. Citizenship Application of William Shoeboots, Statement of Thomas Ridge.

29. William Stephens, the grandson of Shoe Boots and Clarinda Allington, stated in his application for Cherokee citizenship that his mother, Sarah Ellington Shoeboots, heard of Shoe Boots's passing and returned to the Cherokee Nation to receive a portion of Shoe Boots's estate; however, I have found no corroborating evidence to support this assertion. Citizenship Application of William Stephens, Petition of William Stephens.

30. According to a Cherokee inheritance law passed in 1825, the property of a deceased man would be divided between his wife and "lawful and acknowledged children." Legal citizenship in the Cherokee Nation probably aided Elizabeth in achieving her inheritance, even in a period of such intense political unrest. Rowena McClinton, "Possessions of Value: Cherokee Inheritance in the Early Nineteenth Century" (Department of History, University of Kentucky, 1992), 21.

31. Records Relating to Indian Removal, Records of the Bureau of Indian Affairs Valuations of Property in Cass County, Ga., 1836, by Agents Mays and Hargrove, no. 319, Lizza Shoeboot, Administration Microfilm Publication Record Group 75.6, T 496, Washington, D.C.

32. Records Relating to Indian Removal, 75.6, T 496.

33. Kent Anderson Leslie, *Woman of Color, Daughter of Privilege: Amanda America Dickson, 1849–1893* (Athens: University of Georgia Press, 1995), 37.

34. Leslie, *Woman of Color*, 2.

35. Leslie, *Woman of Color*, 8.

36. Leslie, *Woman of Color*, 4.

37. Quoted in Leslie, *Woman of Color*, 97, 103.

38. Quoted in Leslie, *Woman of Color*, 94.

39. In her study of court cases in the nineteenth-century South involving racially indeterminable plaintiffs or defendants who were suing to prove their whiteness, Ariela Gross demonstrates that in many cases "acting white" and being accepted as white within a community were just as critical to the definition

of a person's racial categorization as physical markers or proof of ancestry. In the trials Gross reviews, plaintiffs were often able to obtain a legal affirmation of their whiteness by pointing to social actions—voting and owning property for men, exhibiting gentility and chastity for women, and socializing with other whites for both sexes—that were generally ascribed to white people. Amanda Dickson's success hinged on her white father's sanity rather than on her own racial categorization. However, there is at least one interesting parallel between the Dickson case and the cases that Gross studies. David Dickson's sanity was demonstrated by evidence that he "acted white" in terms of the social company he kept, despite his having had illicit sex with a black slave woman. Dickson was judged to be sane because he acted within the public bounds of whiteness; acting nonwhite, or publicly associating with black people, would have been evidence of his insanity. Ariela Gross, "Litigating Whiteness: Trials of Racial Determination in the Nineteenth-Century South," *Yale Law Journal* 108 (October 1998): 109–88.

40. Rennard Strickland, *Fire and the Spirits: Cherokee Law from Clan to Court* (Norman: University of Oklahoma Press, 1975), xiv.

41. Young, "Cherokee Nation," 505.

42. Claudio Saunt first made this point in his article "'The English Has Now a Mind to Make Slaves of Them All': Creeks, Seminoles, and the Problem of Slavery," *American Indian Quarterly* 22, no. 2 (Winter/Spring 1998): 161.

43. Citizenship Application of William Shoeboots, Statement of Thomas Ridge. Ridge gives the name of Lewis rather than William in his list of family members living in the Shoeboots household just before removal; however, testimony by William indicates that Lewis was enslaved and separated from the family at this time. It is possible that Thomas confused the two brothers in his memory or inadvertently switched their names in his testimony, since William and Lewis were twins.

44. Homer Walker, *Cherokee Indian Census of 1835* (Washington, D.C., 1835); Jeanne Felldin and Charlotte Tucker, *Index to the 1835 Census of the Cherokee Indians East of the Mississippi* (Tomball, Tex.: Genealogical Publications, 1976); Records Relating to Indian Removal, Records of the Bureau of Indian Affairs Valuations of Property in Cass County, Ga., 1836, no. 94 John, by agents Mays and Hargrove. Another man, named John Boots, appears in the Cherokee census of 1835 and could be Elizabeth's brother. However, his location outside Etowah District suggests he could also have been a different person. In addition to the Shoeboots family, there was a Boots family in the Cherokee Nation in this period.

45. William Shoeboots gives the name and nationality of John's wife, saying that she was a free Cherokee woman; Citizenship Application of William Shoeboots, Statement of William Shoeboots. The quoted description of John's wife comes from the Citizenship Application of William Shoeboots, Statement of Edmond Ross. Ross's spelling of John's wife's name is illegible in the record but begins with the letter *C*.

46. Citizenship Application of William Shoeboots, Statement of William Shoeboots. Nathaniel Fish, a Cherokee man who testified during William Shoeboots's citizenship case, contradicted William's claim that the Cherokee woman named was John's wife. Fish stated that in his recollection the woman in question had been married to a white man and had no children in the East; Citizenship Application of William Shoeboots, Statement of Nathaniel Fish.

47. Citizenship Application of William Shoeboots, Statement of William Shoeboots; Citizenship Application of William Shoeboots, Statement of Thomas Ridge.

48. Mary Young argues in her essay "Racism in Red and Black," *Georgia Historical Quarterly* 73, no. 3 (Fall 1989): 492–518, that Georgia policy in this period discriminated similarly against free people of color and Indians. For instance, under Georgia law, Indians, like free blacks, could not testify in court even on their own behalf. The number of Georgia state officials who supported both Indian removal and black colonization indicates the degree of overlap in the systems of discrimination against blacks and Native people. However, Young extends her argument to include the assertion that in some arenas these similarities did not hold. On the issue of land tenure and removal, for example, Native people in Georgia maintained a privileged position in comparison to that of free blacks. The state of Georgia sought the sanction of the federal government before forcibly removing Cherokees but felt no compunction to seek affirmation of its policy to expel free blacks.

49. Cherokee Nation Papers, 46:6512.

CHAPTER EIGHT. REMOVAL

The epigraphs to this chapter are drawn from Toni Morrison, *Beloved* (New York: Plume, 1987), 104, and from Elijah Hicks, *Cherokee Phoenix,* May 6, 1834.

1. Andrew Jackson, State of the Union Address, December 6, 1830, in *The Cherokee Removal: A Brief History with Documents,* ed. Theda Perdue and Michael Green (Boston: Bedford Books, 1995), 119–20.

2. Jackson, State of the Union Address, 120.

3. William Penn, "A Brief View of the Present Relations between the Government and People of the United States and the Indians within our National Limits," November 1829, in *Cherokee Removal* (see note 1), 97.

4. Cherokee Women, Petition, October 17, 1831, in *Cherokee Removal* (see note 1), 126.

5. Members of the Treaty Party refused to accept the legitimacy of the petition, arguing that a number of the signatures were falsified. Thurman Wilkins asserts that some names appeared more than once on the petition, while others belonged to babies; Thurman Wilkins, *Cherokee Tragedy: The Ridge Family and*

the Decimation of a People, 2nd ed. (Norman: University of Oklahoma Press, 1986), 292.

6. Quoted in Grant Foreman, *Indian Removal* (1932; reprint, Norman: University of Oklahoma Press, 1972), 286.

7. Daniel Butrick, *The Journal of Rev. Daniel S. Butrick, May 19, 1838–April 1, 1839, Monograph One* (1839; reprint, Park Hill, Okla.: Trail of Tears Association Oklahoma Chapter, 1998), 2.

8. James Mooney, *Historical Sketch of the Cherokee* (1897; reprint, Washington, D.C.: Smithsonian Institution, 1975), 124.

9. Foreman, *Indian Removal,* 296.

10. Russell Thornton, "The Demography of the Trail of Tears Period: A New Estimate of Cherokee Population Losses," in *Cherokee Removal,* ed. William Anderson (Athens: University of Georgia Press, 1991), 80.

11. Mooney, *Historical Sketch of the Cherokee,* 126.

12. Quoted in Foreman, *Indian Removal,* 303.

13. Foreman, *Indian Removal,* 302–3.

14. Theda Perdue, *Slavery and the Evolution of Cherokee Society, 1540–1866* (Knoxville: University of Tennessee Press, 1979), 71.

15. Butrick, *Journal,* 32–33, 54, 61, 58.

16. Thornton, "Trail of Tears," 91. The number of blacks who died along the Trail of Tears has not been estimated.

17. Diane Glancy, *Pushing the Bear: A Novel of the Trail of Tears* (New York: Harcourt Brace, 1996), 58, 86.

18. Glancy, *Pushing the Bear,* 128.

19. Glancy, *Pushing the Bear,* 179, 87.

20. Glancy, *Pushing the Bear,* 179, 191.

21. David Lowenthal, "Past Time, Present Place: Landscape and Memory," *Geographical Review* 65 (January 1975): 1–36.

22. Kenneth Foote, *Shadowed Ground: America's Landscapes of Violence and Tragedy* (Austin: University of Texas Press, 1997), 33.

23. Leslie Marmon Silko, *Yellow Woman and a Beauty of the Spirit: Essays on Native American Life Today* (New York: Simon and Schuster, 1996), 25–47. For an in-depth exploration of place and its relationship to Native women's experiences and historical identities as well as black women's lives, see Catherine Griffin, "'Joined Together in History': Politics and Place in African American and American Indian Women's Writing" (PhD diss., University of Minnesota, 2000).

24. N. Scott Momaday, *The Way to Rainy Mountain* (Albuquerque: University of New Mexico Press, 1969), 83.

25. Keith Basso, *Wisdom Sits in Places* (Albuquerque: University of New Mexico Press, 1996); Basso, "Stalking with Stories," in *Western Apache Language and Culture* (Tucson: University of Arizona Press, 1990), 99–137.

26. Basso, "Stalking," 129.

27. Basso, "Stalking," 127, 128, 130.

28. "The Removed Townhouses," in James Mooney, *Myths of the Cherokee* (1900; reprint, New York: Dover, 1995), 335–36. This story might be attributed to one or more of Mooney's major sources, the Cherokee storytellers named Swimmer and John Ax.

29. *Drennen Roll of the Cherokee Indians, 1851* (Tulsa, Okla.: Indian Nations Press, 1851), Delaware District, nos. 1041, 1042.

CHAPTER NINE. CAPTURE

The epigraphs to this chapter are drawn from Daniel F. Littlefield and Mary Ann Littlefield, "The Beams Family: Free Blacks in Indian Territory," *Journal of Negro History* 61 (January 1976): 21, and from Cornelius Neely Nave, Pioneer Papers, Oklahoma Writers Project, Oklahoma Historical Society, Oklahoma City, Oklahoma, 1, 2.

1. William G. McLoughlin, *After the Trail of Tears: The Cherokees' Struggle for Sovereignty, 1839–1880* (Chapel Hill: University of North Carolina Press, 1993), 4; David Keith Hampton, *Cherokee Old Settlers: The 1896 Old Settler Payroll and the 1851 Old Settler Payroll* (Broken Arrow, Okla.: D. K. Hampton, 1993), i–iv.

2. Quoted in McLoughlin, *After the Trail of Tears*, 37, 388n3.

3. Theda Perdue, *Slavery and the Evolution of Cherokee Society, 1540–1866* (Knoxville: University of Tennessee Press, 1979), 75, 84. For more on Cherokee removal, see William Anderson, *Cherokee Removal: Before and After* (Athens: University of Georgia Press, 1991); McLoughlin, *After the Trail of Tears;* Grant Foreman, *Indian Removal* (1932; reprint, Norman: University of Oklahoma Press, 1972).

4. Thurman Wilkins, *Cherokee Tragedy: The Ridge Family and the Decimation of a People,* 2nd ed. (Norman: University of Oklahoma Press, 1986), 307–8.

5. Wilkins, *Cherokee Tragedy,* 307.

6. McLoughlin, *After the Trail of Tears,* 125.

7. McLoughlin, *After the Trail of Tears,* 300–301, 307.

8. McLoughlin, *After the Trail of Tears,* 129, 77.

9. Henry Henderson, Pioneer Papers, Oklahoma Writers Project, Oklahoma Historical Society, Oklahoma City, Oklahoma, 2.

10. McLoughlin, *After the Trail of Tears,* 125–26.

11. Citizenship Application of William Shoeboots, Statement of William Shoeboots, Cherokee Applications, Applications from the Bureau of Indian Affairs, Muskogee Area Office, Relating to Enrollment in the Five Civilized Tribes Under the Act of 1896, National Archives and Records Administration Microfilm Publication M1650, National Archives and Records Administration Southwest Region, Fort Worth, Texas.

12. Citizenship Application of William Shoeboots, Statement of Ed Carey; Citizenship Application of William Shoeboots, Statement of Nathaniel Fish.

13. Wilkins, *Cherokee Tragedy*, 335.

14. Citizenship Application of William Shoeboots, Statement of William Shoeboots. William would have been a teenager at the time of John Ridge's death.

15. Wilkins, *Cherokee Tragedy*, 292.

16. Wilkins, *Cherokee Tragedy*, 49.

17. Katja May, *African Americans and Native Americans in the Creek and Cherokee Nations, 1830s to 1920s* (New York: Garland, 1996), 63.

18. Cherokee Nation, *Laws of the Cherokee Nation: Adopted by the Council at Various Periods, 1808–1835* (Tahlequah, C.N.: Cherokee Advocate Office, 1852), 51, 80.

19. The influx of slave dealers, supported by the Cherokee slave market, also jeopardized Cherokee control over Cherokee borders. Unruly outsiders disrespected the laws of the Nation as they entered Cherokee territory, creating havoc and hunting slaves against the will of many Cherokee people. In their article, Daniel F. Littlefield and Mary Ann Littlefield chronicle the trials of a free black family in the Indian Territory whose distant white and Choctaw relatives sold claims to slave traders for their capture: "The Beams Family: Free Blacks in Indian Territory," *Journal of Negro History* 61 (January 1976): 16–35.

20. *Cherokee Advocate*, March 26, 1846. Celia Naylor-Ojurongbe documents and discusses numerous examples of the kidnapping and theft of slaves during this period of political upheaval. Celia Naylor-Ojurongbe, "'More at Home with the Indians': African-American Slaves and Freedpeople in the Cherokee Nation, Indian Territory, 1838–1907" (PhD diss., Duke University, 2001), 76–138.

21. Daniel F. Littlefield Jr. and Lonnie Underhill, "Slave 'Revolt' in the Cherokee Nation, 1842," *American Indian Quarterly* 3 (Summer 1977): 126–27.

22. Quoted in Theda Perdue, *Slavery and the Evolution of Cherokee Society, 1540–1866* (Knoxville: University of Tennessee Press, 1979), 79, from *Cherokee Advocate*, December 17, 1846. During the Second Seminole War in Florida (1835–1837), General Thomas Jesup promised freedom to black slaves who agreed to leave their Seminole masters. These blacks asserted their freedom in Indian Territory and are referred to disparagingly in this *Cherokee Advocate* quotation; Littlefield and Underhill, "Slave 'Revolt,'" 127.

23. Quoted in Perdue, *Slavery*, 87, from *Cherokee Advocate*, August 3, 1853.

24. Littlefield and Underhill, "Slave 'Revolt,'" 125.

25. Cherokee Nation, *Laws of the Cherokee Nation*, 19.

26. I borrow the phrase "loophole of retreat" from Harriet Jacobs, who uses these words to describe the crawlspace she lived in while hiding from her master in *Incidents in the Life of a Slave Girl* (1861; reprint, Cambridge, Mass.: Harvard University Press, 1987).

27. Watica Watie, "Description of the Falls," November 12, 1868, roll 46, no.

6588, Cherokee Nation Papers, Western History Collections, University of Oklahoma, Norman, Oklahoma.

28. Carolyn Thomas Foreman, "Early History of Webbers Falls," *Chronicles of Oklahoma* 29 (Winter 1951–52): 461.

29. Henderson, Pioneer Papers, 1, 2.

30. Littlefield and Underhill, "Slave 'Revolt,'" 126–27.

31. Naylor-Ojurongbe, "'More at Home,'" 76–82. William McLoughlin argues in an early article that slave rebellions took place in the Cherokee Nation in 1841, 1842, and 1850. William G. McLoughlin, "Red Indians, Black Slavery, and White Racism: America's Slaveholding Indians," *American Quarterly* 26 (October 1974): 367–85.

32. Edward Everett Dale and Gaston Litton, *Cherokee Cavaliers* (Norman: University of Oklahoma Press, 1939), 30; also quoted in Naylor-Ojurongbe, "'More at Home,'" 111.

33. *Fort Smith Elevator* (Fort Smith, Arkansas), February 5, 1897, quoted in C. T. Foreman, "Webbers Falls," 458–59. Though this 1897 newspaper article contends that the slaves were brought from Tennessee, they were in fact brought from Georgia. And though it says the slaves were going to New Mexico, they were actually heading to what would have been the country of Mexico in 1842 when the revolt occurred.

34. Littlefield and Underhill, "Slave 'Revolt,'" 121. Littlefield and Underhill provide a precise and detailed overview of this escape. Celia Naylor-Ojurongbe's treatment of this event in her dissertation is also excellent and provides biographical sketches of many individuals involved; Naylor-Ojurongbe, "'More at Home.'"

35. Ralph Ellison, *Going to the Territory* (New York: Random House, 1986), 131.

36. William Loren Katz, *Black Indians: A Hidden Heritage* (New York: Atheneum, 1986), 71; Kevin Mulroy, *Freedom on the Border* (Lubbock: Texas Tech University Press, 1993); Kenneth Porter, *The Black Seminoles: History of a Freedom-Seeking People,* rev. and ed. Alcione Amos and Thomas Senter (Gainesville: University Press of Florida, 1996).

37. Littlefield and Underhill, "Slave 'Revolt,'" 121–22.

38. Cherokee Nation, *Laws of the Cherokee Nation,* 62–63.

39. Naylor-Ojurongbe, "'More at Home,'" 106.

40. Quoted in Naylor-Ojurongbe, "'More at Home,'" 107, from Statement of Captain John Drew, January 3, 1843, Letters Received by the Office of Indian Affairs, National Archives Microfilm Publications, M234, roll 87, National Archives and Records Administration, Washington, D.C.

41. Littlefield and Underhill, "Slave 'Revolt,'" 125. As Littlefield and Underhill point out (128–29), the Cherokee slave revolt would open up questions about jurisdiction in the case of crimes committed in the Indian Territory by Indian-

owned slaves against Indians of other tribes. The issue of whether such crimes should be tried by the United States or by the tribal nation of the accused slave was decided in favor of Indian jurisdiction under the Indian Intercourse Act of 1834. However, the fact that jurisdiction was debated indicates that slaveholding had opened the Cherokee Nation to further federal intervention and supervision. Where slaves were concerned, the United States broadened its "right" to intervene in Native affairs. The 1850 Fugitive Slave Act, which required the return of escaped slaves to their owners, was applied to the Indian Territory as well as the states.

42. *Fort Smith Elevator,* February 5, 1897, quoted in C. T. Foreman, "Webbers Falls," 459.

43. Betty Robertson, Pioneer Papers, Oklahoma Writers Project, Oklahoma Historical Society, Oklahoma City, Oklahoma, 2–3.

44. Robertson, Pioneer Papers, 1; Naylor-Ojurongbe, "'More at Home,'" 103.

45. Citizenship Application of William Shoeboots, Statement of William Shoeboots. The name of Polly's daughter, Maria, is spelled Mireah on the Drennen Roll. Though her brother William described her as having just three children, Polly may have had additional birth children and probably had additional adopted children under her care, as indicated by the Drennen Roll list of dependents attributed to her.

46. Information about Lewis in William Shoeboots's Citizenship Application is scant and does not include marital status.

47. *Cherokee Advocate,* October 7, 1847.

48. May, *African Americans,* 61.

49. Littlefield and Littlefield, "Beams Family," 21; May, *African Americans,* 63.

50. *Cherokee Advocate,* November 11, 1847.

51. Cherokee Nation, *Laws of the Cherokee Nation,* 156.

CHAPTER TEN. FREEDOM

The epigraphs to this chapter are drawn from Toni Morrison, *Beloved* (New York: Plume, 1987), 141, and from "An Act of Emancipation of the Slaves in the Cherokee Nation," February 21, 1863, Cherokee Nation Papers, 45:6362, Western History Collections, University of Oklahoma, Norman, Oklahoma.

1. "Inventory, Etc. of Estate of Major Ridge & Wife," October 26, 1849, Cherokee Nation Papers, 46:6541, Western History Collections, University of Oklahoma, Norman, Oklahoma.

2. Citizenship Application of William Shoeboots, Statements of Ed Carey and Thomas Ridge, Cherokee Applications, Applications from the Bureau of Indian Affairs, Muskogee Area Office, Relating to Enrollment in the Five Civilized Tribes Under the Act of 1896, National Archives and Records Administra-

tion Microfilm Publication M1650, National Archives and Records Administration Southwest Region, Fort Worth, Texas. These two men, both of whom knew Doll, offer conflicting accounts about the length of her stay with Mrs. Ridge. Ed Carey stated: "It was the common report in the neighborhood that at the death of Mrs. Ridge she gave Dolly her freedom," while Thomas Ridge testified: "She left old Mrs. Ridge and went to live with her daughter Lizzie before the death of Mrs. Ridge."

3. "True List of the Names of Cherokee Indians who have Emigrated," Records of the Cherokee Agency in Tennessee, 1801–1835, transcribed by Marybelle W. Chase, 1990, p. 48, no. 413, Oklahoma Historical Society, Oklahoma City, Oklahoma; Citizenship Application of William Shoeboots, Statement of William Shoeboots.

4. "Anonymous Accounts," 1852, Cherokee Nation Papers, 45:6432.

5. Northern District Citizenship Case Files, Case 32, Mary Swagerty, Statement of Mary Swagerty, National Archives Microfilm Publication M7RA-388, roll 3, Oklahoma Historical Society, Oklahoma City, Oklahoma.

6. Citizenship Files, Mary Swagerty, Statement of Benjamin Hawkins.

7. Arthur Beck, Pioneer Papers, 1, Oklahoma Writers Project, Oklahoma Historical Society, Oklahoma City, Oklahoma; James Duncan, Pioneer Papers, 1.

8. Beck, Pioneer Papers, 1; William Woodall, Pioneer Papers, 2.

9. S. R. Lewis, Pioneer Papers, 1; claim of Charles Landrum, Cherokee Nation Papers, 45:6296.

10. John Rollin Ridge to Stand Watie, Cherokee Nation Papers, 38:3917 and 52:8077.

11. Sarah C. Watie to Stand Watie, November 2, 1864, Cherokee Nation Papers, 38:3904.

12. "Oklahoma Historical Society's Hunter's Home Visitors Guide," George M. Murrell Historic House, Park Hill, Oklahoma.

13. Quoted in Frank Cunningham, *General Stand Watie's Confederate Indians* (1959; reprint, Norman: University of Oklahoma Press, 1998), 47. Cunningham does not cite the source of these quotations from visitors to the Murrells'.

14. "Account of Stand Watie," Cherokee Nation Papers, 41:4661; "Inventory, Etc. of Estate of Major Ridge & Wife," October 26, 1849, Cherokee Nation Papers, 46:6541.

15. "Anonymous Account Books," 1852, Cherokee Nation Papers, 45:6431; "Account Sheets, no date," Cherokee Nation Papers, 46:6470; "Accounts," 1838–1889, Cherokee Nation Papers, 46:6507.

16. "Account of Stand Watie with J. E. Spencer," 1860, Cherokee Nation Papers, 41:4662.

17. Citizenship Application of William Shoeboots, Statement of William Shoeboots.

18. U.S. Census, Eugeni, Kansas, 1860; U.S. Census, Menoken, Shawnee, Kansas, 1880, Oklahoma Historical Society.

19. Bounty Land Files, file 838:39 (Shoeboots), Military Service Records, Veterans Records, National Archives and Records Administration, Washington, D.C.

20. Bounty Land Files, file 838:39 (Shoeboots).

21. Sharon Block, "Rape and Native Americans in Early America" (paper presented at the ninety-sixth annual meeting of the American Historical Association Pacific Coast Branch, Honolulu, Hawaii, August 2003); Ann Marie Plane, *Colonial Intimacies: Indian Marriage in Early New England* (Ithaca, N.Y.: Cornell University Press, 2000), 6.

22. In early Cherokee marriage customs, a woman would often present her intended with ears of corn or a cooked meal, and the man would present her with meat from the hunt, symbolizing the manner in which the couple would care for each other in the marriage. For more on Cherokee marriage ceremonies, laws, and matrimonial customs, see *Cherokee Advocate,* "Marriage Ceremony of the Ancient Cherokees," May 9, 1874, Cherokee Nation Papers 49:7473; Theda Perdue, *Cherokee Women: Gender and Culture Change, 1700–1835* (Lincoln: University of Nebraska Press, 1998), 43–46; Fay A. Yarbrough, "Legislating Women's Sexuality: Cherokee Marriage Laws in the Nineteenth Century" (paper presented at the sixth Southern Conference on Women's History, Athens, Ga., June 2003).

23. Bounty Land Files, file 838:39 (Shoeboots).

24. I borrow this phrasing from Philomena Mariani, ed., *Critical Fictions: The Politics of Imaginative Writing* (Seattle: Bay Press, 1991).

25. This reference to Doll's Cherokee name comes from her associate, Thomas Ridge, a slave of Major Ridge; Citizenship Application of William Shoeboots, Statement of Thomas Ridge.

26. 1860 U.S. Census Indian Lands West of Arkansas, no. 61, Dollay Boots, Cherokee Nation, National Archives Microfilm Publication M653, roll 52, National Archives and Records Administration, Washington, D.C.

27. I am adapting the term *sister-outsider* from the title of Audre Lorde's book *Sister Outsider: Essays and Speeches* (New York: Crossing Press, 1984).

28. Citizenship Application of William Shoeboots, Statement of William Shoeboots. Though William does not explain why his mother died in a distant place, it is possible that Doll had traveled to Choctaw territory to escape the extreme wartime destruction in Cherokee country.

29. Citizenship Application of William Shoeboots, Statement of Ed Carey. This witness gives Doll's Cherokee name as "Cob cob lol." An alternate spelling for Doll's Cherokee name is given as "Con gee loh" by Thomas Ridge; Citizenship Application of William Shoeboots, Statement of Thomas Ridge.

30. William G. McLoughlin, *After the Trail of Tears: The Cherokees' Struggle*

for Sovereignty, 1839–1880 (Chapel Hill: University of North Carolina Press, 1993), 154–56.

31. Quoted in Annie Heloise Abel, *The American Indian in the Civil War, 1862–1865* (1919; reprint, Lincoln: University of Nebraska Press, 1992), 224–25.

32. William McLoughlin argues that the Keetoowahs did not reject these resolutions because their main aim was securing political power for Cherokee traditionalists, not abolishing slavery. By showing support for John Ross during this national crisis, they strengthened their own political influence. McLoughlin, *After the Trail of Tears*, 183–84, 187.

33. Abel, *Civil War*, 25. The treaty stipulated that Cherokee soldiers would be used only as a "homeguard," not in general campaigns of the war. McLoughlin, *After the Trail of Tears*, 187; Abel, *Civil War*, 23.

34. McLoughlin, *After the Trail of Tears*, 220.

35. Daniel F. Littlefield, *The Cherokee Freedmen: From Emancipation to American Citizenship* (Westport, Conn.: Greenwood Press, 1978), 15.

36. By 1866 relations in the Cherokee nation were so contentious that the southern Cherokees who had supported the South in the Civil War wanted to divide into two separate nations. Both the southern Cherokees and the loyal Cherokees met with U.S. officials for the purpose of negotiating treaties. John Ross, who had repositioned himself as chief to the loyal Cherokees, negotiated the treaty that eventually stood as the 1866 treaty between the Cherokee Nation and the United States. For more on the development of this treaty, see William McLoughlin, *After the Trail of Tears*, 222–27; Littlefield, *Cherokee Freedmen*, 15–33; Theda Perdue, *Slavery and the Evolution of Cherokee Society, 1540–1866* (Knoxville: University of Tennessee Press, 1979), epilogue; Circe Sturm, *Blood Politics: Race, Culture, and Identity in the Cherokee Nation of Oklahoma* (Berkeley and Los Angeles: University of California Press, 2002), 52–81.

37. While the incorporation of former slaves into the Cherokee Nation was ethical, it represented an erosion of Cherokee sovereignty, since the Cherokees were forced by the U.S. government to accept a group of people into their citizenry whom they otherwise might have rejected.

38. The Cherokee Nation of Oklahoma entered a period of governmental resurgence in the 1940s and exists today as an independent tribal government. For more on this development see Sturm, *Blood Politics*, 82–107.

39. As a stipulation of the Cherokee Nation's 1866 treaty with the United States government following the Civil War, Cherokees agreed to accept their former slaves as full citizens. Black freedmen and women who wished to claim Cherokee citizenship were required to apply within six months of the treaty's ratification.

40. Morrison Shoeboot, Company Muster Roll, 1 Cherokee Mounted Volunteers, Military Service Records, National Archives and Records Administration, Washington, D.C. Also cited in Grant Foreman, *History of the Five Tribes*

in the Confederate Army, 1:79, Microfilm IAD-5, Oklahoma Historical Society, Oklahoma City, Oklahoma. Morrison's service in the Cherokee Volunteers may have resulted from pressure by powerful Cherokee individuals, such as Stand Watie, who had aided his mother in 1852. A number of Colonel John Drew's regiment defected and joined a band of Unionist Creeks in the Battle of Bird Creek (1861). The Creek forces, led by Opothleyoholo, were composed of radical, traditionalist Creeks and escaped black slaves. However, it seems that Morrison did not participate in the defection, since his Cherokee military service is dated from 1861 to 1863.

Another descendant of Shoe Boots and Doll may also have fought in the Civil War. William Childers, clerk in the Ridge family's general store, married a Cherokee woman named Maria Boots. This woman was probably the daughter of Polly Shoeboots. William Childers and Maria Boots had six children, among them a son named Napoleon Bonaparte Childers. Napoleon Childers's military records are conflicting. National Archives records and additional sources show that he was a scout for the Indian Home Guards of the Union Army and was a "prisoner in the hands of the enemy" from 1864 to 1865. James Manford Carselowey, *Cherokee Old Timers* (Tulsa: Oklahoma Yesterday Publications, 1980), 43; S. R. Lewis, Pioneer Papers, 2; Napoleon Childers, Company Muster Roll, 1st Indian Home Guards Kansas Infantry, Military Service Records, National Archives and Records Administration. However, a Napoleon Childers is also listed as a member of the 1st Cherokee Mounted Rifles, McDaniel's Company; in Janet B. Hewett, ed., *The Roster of Confederate Soldiers 1861–1865* (Wilmington, N.C.: Broadfoot, 1996), 3: 376.

EPILOGUE. CITIZENSHIP

1. The Dawes Rolls do list a woman named Eliza Boots whose history is unclear. In her testimony for inclusion on the roll as a Cherokee by Blood, Eliza Boots, age sixty, stated that she had never had a last name other than Boots, that her father's name was unknown and her mother's name was Ancie, that she did not wish to make a claim for anyone besides herself, and that she came to Indian Territory in the 1838 emigration. She was enrolled as a full-blood in the Cherokee by Blood category, and the recorders noted that she was the same "Lizzie Boot" who was listed in the 1880 Lipe Roll. The 1880 Lipe payment roll lists a Lizzie Boot as the wife of John Boot and mother of William Boot. This Eliza Boot appears in the Guion Miller Roll of 1906, where Eliza gives her deceased husband's name as John Boot, her maiden name as Smith, and her father's and mother's names as Di-ye-ski Smith and Encie (in other records spelled Nancy) Smith. The Dawes enumerators felt that Eliza Boots of the Dawes Rolls was the same person as Lizzie Boot from the Lipe Roll. I have concluded that

Lizzie Boot of the Lipe Roll is the same person as Eliza Boot in the Guion Miller Roll. This Eliza/Lizzie Boot/Boots may indeed have been the same person in all three of these rolls, since the similarities are striking; however, there are enough differences between the descriptions to suggest the possibility that there were two Eliza Boots in the Cherokee Nation at this time. One Eliza (from the Dawes Rolls) seems to have been a woman alone who was unsure of her parentage. The other Eliza/Lizzie (from the Lipe and Guion Miller Rolls) consistently mentions a husband, son, parents, and numerous family members. In addition, this Eliza Boot, married to John Boot, became a Boot through marriage. She married into a family, the Boots, whose name was similar to the Shoeboots and who lived at the same time. The John Boot whom Eliza Boot married was not Doll and Shoe Boots's son and was not descended from the Shoeboots line. It is my tentative conclusion that while Eliza Boots of the Dawes Rolls may be the same woman as Eliza/Lizzie (Smith) Boot of the Lipe and Guion Miller Rolls, she may also be a different person. It is possible that Eliza Boot of the Dawes Rolls is descended from Elizabeth or Polly Shoeboots, whose dependents in 1851 included an Ailse, an Eliza Hammer, and a Lizzy, among others. Dawes Roll Cherokee by Blood, 1898–1914, enrollment no. 7931, National Archives Microfilm Publication M1186, card 3223, National Archives and Records Administration Southwest Region, Fort Worth, Texas; Dawes Roll Applications for Enrollment, 1898–1914, National Archives Microfilm Publication M 1301, cards 3151–3275, National Archives and Records Administration Southwest Region, Fort Worth, Texas; Bureau of Indian Affairs Cherokee Payment Roll "Lipe Roll," 1880, p. 67, no. 205, National Archives Microfilm Publication M7RA-33, roll 1, National Archives and Records Administration Southwest Region, Fort Worth, Texas; Eastern Cherokee Applications of the U.S. Court of Claims ("Guion Miller applications"), 1906–1909, Case nos. 1736–1820, Application no. 1797, National Archives Microfilm Publication M1104, roll 20, National Archives and Records Administration Southwest Region, Fort Worth, Texas; *Drennen Roll of the Cherokee Indians, 1851* (Tulsa, Okla.: Indian Nations Press, 1851), Delaware District nos. 1041, 1042.

2. My attempts to trace the descendants of Elizabeth and Polly came to no conclusive results. Because one dependent of Polly was named Eliza Hammer, because William Shoeboots gave the names of Elizabeth's husbands as simply Ferguson and Morton, and because Mireah, a daughter of Polly, probably married a man named Childers, I searched under the surnames Hammer, Ferguson, Morton, and Childers on multiple online Cherokee rolls. Each of these surnames had long lists of individuals cataloged beneath them (from twenty-five in the case of Ferguson to 144 in the case of Childers). Though in my limited search I did not find exact matches between these surnames and the first names of Elizabeth's and Polly's dependents as recorded in the Drennen Roll of 1851, I am con-

vinced that descendants of Elizabeth and Polly are buried somewhere within these lists or are counted under entirely different surnames in the rolls: userdb.rootsweb .com/nativeamerican/ and arcweb.archives.gov/arc/basic_search.jsp.

3. Citizenship Files, Case 32, Mary Swagerty, Statement of Mary Swagerty, Northern District Citizenship Case Files, National Archives Microfilm Publication M7RA-388, roll 3, Oklahoma Historical Society, Oklahoma City, Oklahoma. It is unclear why Mary Swagerty did not apply for citizenship as a descendant of her mother, who William Shoeboots says was Cherokee in his application for citizenship. However, the men who filed statements in support of William's own claim disagreed about the identity of John's wife, which suggests that perhaps her status was not perfectly clear. In addition, Mary may have felt distant from her mother, since she indicates in her statement cited above: "I don't know if my mother is dead. I left her when I was about thirteen years old in Georgia."

I cannot account for a young man named John Shoeboots who appears in the 1870 U.S. census in Chicot County, Arkansas. This man, described as a black laborer twenty-five years in age, was married to a black woman named Susan. One female child, age two, is listed in their household. There is no clear link between this John and any of Shoe Boots and Doll's children, yet his name and age strongly suggest that he is a grandchild of the couple. It is unlikely that he was the son of Elizabeth, Polly, or William. (The three siblings were in the Cherokee Nation at the time of John's birth in Arkansas.) However, it is quite possible that the original John Shoeboots fathered a son in Arkansas in the mid-1840s, a time when he was in transit between Georgia and Indian Territory. It is also possible that this John Shoeboots was a son of the long-lost twin, Lewis Shoeboots. 1870 Census, Carroll, Chicot Counties, National Archives Microfilm Publication M593, roll 49, National Archives and Records Administration Southwest Region, Fort Worth, Texas.

4. Phrase used by Richard Wilcox, an interviewee in the film *Black Indians: An American Story* (Dallas, Tex.: Rich-Heape Films, 2000).

5. This may also have been the case for John's daughter, Mary Swagerty, who recalled meeting her father only once as a child.

6. William G. McLoughlin, *After the Trail of Tears: The Cherokees' Struggle for Sovereignty, 1839–1880* (Chapel Hill: University of North Carolina Press, 1993), 226–27.

7. Daniel F. Littlefield, *The Cherokee Freedmen: From Emancipation to American Citizenship* (Westport, Conn.: Greenwood Press, 1978), 39, 44.

8. *Indian Affairs: Laws and Treaties,* vol. 2, comp. and ed. Charles J. Kappler (Washington, D.C.: Government Printing Office, 1904). http://www.rootsweb .com/~itcherok/treaties/1866-ending-slavery.htm; Littlefield, *Cherokee Freedmen,* 40. For more on the racial tensions of this period, see Donald A. Grinde Jr. and

Quintard Taylor, "Red vs. Black: Conflict and Accommodation in the Post Civil War Indian Territory, 1865–1907," *American Indian Quarterly* 8, no. 3 (Summer 1984): 211–29.

9. Quoted in Littlefield, *Cherokee Freedmen,* 68, from *Cherokee Advocate,* June 6, 1874; August 26, 1893; October 17, 1894.

10. Littlefield, *Cherokee Freedmen,* 77, 15.

11. For more on the history of the Cherokee freedmen and freedwomen, see Littlefield's extensive study, *Cherokee Freedmen;* Katja May, *African Americans and Native Americans in the Creek and Cherokee Nations, 1830s to 1920s* (New York: Garland, 1996); Grinde and Taylor, "Red vs. Black"; Celia Naylor-Ojurongbe, "'More at Home with the Indians': African-American Slaves and Freedpeople in the Cherokee Nation, Indian Territory, 1838–1907" (PhD diss., Duke University, 2001).

12. Kent Carter, "Deciding Who Can Be Cherokee: Enrollment Records of the Dawes Commission," *Chronicles of Oklahoma* 69, no. 2 (Summer 1991): 175.

13. Carter, "Deciding," 185.

14. Carter, "Deciding," 179.

15. Carter, "Deciding," 184.

16. Citizenship Application of William Shoeboots, Statement of William Shoeboots.

17. Citizenship Application of William Shoeboots, Statement of William Shoeboots.

18. Citizenship Application of William Shoeboots, Statement of Thomas Ridge; Citizenship Application of William Shoeboots, Statement of Ed Carey.

19. Of the four witnesses whose testimony is included in William's application file, it is the two black former slaves who are most willing to posit the notion that the Shoebootses were not enslaved. In a sense, they coconstruct with William the fiction of a free family, downplaying the reality of his family's shifting status. Though Thomas Ridge notes the sale of William's siblings, he leaves open the question of Doll's status. When speaking of the time she spent working for Mrs. Ridge, Thomas Ridge attributes to Doll a great degree of flexibility, implying that the structure and limits of her time in the Ridge household were freely chosen: "The mother of [John] Boots lived with old Mrs. Ridge. . . . She left old Mrs. Ridge and went to live with her daughter Lizzie before the death of Mrs. Ridge"; Citizenship Application of William Shoeboots, Statement of Thomas Ridge. In fact, Doll was probably not free to leave Mrs. Ridge's home at will, even though her position there may have been more elastic than that of other slaves. In another statement made by a former slave named Edmond Ross, the free status of Shoe Boots's wife and children is again asserted: "I knew William Shoeboots back in the old nation, when he lived with Maj Ridge. . . . They were free born." However, on cross-examination by the commissioners, Ross was forced to clarify this claim. He restated, "When I said that these Shoeboots were

freeborn—I meant to say and now say that they were reported. . . . I did not know"; Citizenship Application of William Shoeboots, Statement of Edmond Ross. Ross's qualification of his statement suggests not only the difficulty of knowing the "true" status of a family like the Shoeboots, whose position regularly fluctuated, but also Ross's willingness to overstate the case. It may be that the black men interviewed felt a relational as well as strategic desire to aid William Shoeboots in emphasizing the liberty of the Shoeboots family.

20. William Stephens's case is a primary example of the fact that white-Cherokees could also be excluded by this process. William Stephens was the grandson of Shoe Boots and Clarinda. His mother, Sarah Allington, would have been the half sister of Elizabeth, Polly, John, William, and Lewis, though the two families seemed never to have crossed paths. William Stephens applied to the Cherokee Commission on Citizenship in 1879, claiming Shoe Boots as his grandfather and indicating that his uncle, William Ellington Shoeboots, had appeared on the Cherokee Old Settler Roll of 1851; Citizenship Application of William Stephens, Statement of William Stephens. William Stephens's case included testimony from several witnesses, including his uncle. The majority of the witnesses confirmed that he was descended from Shoe Boots. However, the commission rejected Stephens's application on the grounds that the uncle through whom he traced documentation was not a lineal antecedent; Citizenship Application of William Stephens, Exhibit H. In a letter to Principal Chief Joel B. Mayes, the commissioners unknowingly revealed their confusion over the pending citizenship cases of the black Shoeboots and the white Shoeboots. They indicated that William Stephens (white-Cherokee) was claiming citizenship through William Shoeboots (black-Cherokee) and that William Shoeboots was claiming citizenship through John Shoeboots (black-Cherokee), when in fact William Stephens was claiming citizenship through his uncle William Ellington Shoeboots (white-Cherokee). They stated that neither John nor William Shoeboots was listed on the rolls of the Cherokee Nation but that their sisters Lizzie and Polly Boots were. They decided in November of 1888: "Under the 7th section of the act of December 8, 1886, we cannot re-admit William Shoe-Boots and family and William Stevens to Cherokee citizenship, for they have not proven a 'lineal descent' from a Cherokee ancestor whose name appears on the rolls of Cherokees mentioned in the before cited laws"; Citizenship Application of William Stephens, Exhibit J. Though Stephens hired an attorney and later took his case to the U.S. Dawes Commission in 1896 and to U.S. Special Commissioner Guion Miller in 1909, he was continually rejected. Guion Miller found: "It is plain that he [William Stephens] and his mother were not members of the Eastern Cherokee tribe in 1835, at the time the rights accrued under this government"; Citizenship Application of William Stephens, Special Commissioner to Phillip H. Cass, August 4, 1909.

21. Citizenship Application of William Shoeboots, Statement of Henry Barnes.

22. The outcome of William's case and that of his niece, Mary Swagerty, suggests that the family was trapped in a legal catch-22. William Shoeboots's patrimony was not in question, but Shoe Boots himself did not appear on the 1835 rolls. In contrast, John Shoeboots *was* listed on the 1835 rolls but was not believed to be Mary Swagerty's father.

23. Citizenship Application of William Shoeboots (Rufus Shoeboot Appeal), Statement of Rufus Shoeboot.

24. Citizenship Application of William Shoeboots (Rufus Shoeboot Appeal), Statement of Geo. Hughes, [illegible], and E. P. Porris.

25. Citizenship Application of William Shoeboots (Rufus Shoeboot Appeal), "Demurrer and Answer."

26. Carter, "Deciding," 184.

27. Citizenship Application of William Shoeboots (Rufus Shoeboot Appeal), Hutchings, Hastings and Boudinot, Attorneys for the Cherokee Nation.

28. In fact, the Treaty of 1866 did grant citizenship to free blacks who were residing in the Cherokee Nation at the time that the Civil War broke out and then had returned to the Nation within six months of the treaty; however, the Cherokee attorneys did not reiterate this provision.

29. Citizenship Application of William Shoeboots, Statement of John Cochran.

CODA. THE SHOEBOOTS FAMILY TODAY

1. At least one of William's children continued to live in the Cherokee Nation, despite her lack of political rights. In 1900 this daughter, Lizzie, worked as a "sick nurse" and was designated a "Negro" in the federal census. U.S. Census Indian Territory, 1900, National Archives Microfilm Publication, T623, roll 1845, National Archives and Records Administration Southwest Region, Fort Worth, Texas.

2. Paul W. Stewart and Wallace Yvonne Ponce, *Black Cowboys* (Denver: Black American West Museum and Heritage Center, 1986), 118.

3. Stewart and Ponce, *Black Cowboys*, 117.

APPENDIX ONE. RESEARCH METHODS AND CHALLENGES

1. For more on the private experience of black slaves, see George Rawick, *From Sundown to Sunup: The Making of the Black Community* (Westport, Conn.: Greenwood Press, 1972); and Sterling Stuckey, *Slave Culture* (New York: Oxford University Press, 1987). Theda Perdue has argued that even those white men who married Native women had vague understandings of the realities of Indian

women's lives because of strict gender divisions in Cherokee communities; Perdue, *Cherokee Women: Gender and Culture Change, 1700–1835* (Lincoln: University of Nebraska Press, 1998), 4.

2. Comments by Liza Black at the D'Arcy McNickle Center for American Indian History Lannan Summer Institute, August 1, 2001, Newberry Library, Chicago, Illinois.

3. James Axtell, "The Ethnohistory of Native America," in *Rethinking American Indian History*, ed. Donald Fixico (Albuquerque: University of New Mexico Press, 1997): 11–28.

4. Geographer Michael Doran has charted slave populations among the Five Tribes in the East in 1830 and in Indian Territory in 1830. See Michael F. Doran, "Negro Slaves of the Five Civilized Tribes," *Annals of the Association of American Geographers* 68 (September 1978): 346, table 2; Michael F. Doran, "Population Statistics of Nineteenth-Century Indian Territory," *Chronicles of Oklahoma* 53 (Winter 1975–1976): 501, table 3. Demographer Russell Thornton notes that the 1860 figures given by Doran must be qualified, since whites owning slaves in Cherokee territory were not taken into account in this figure, in *The Cherokees: A Population History* (Lincoln: University of Nebraska Press, 1990), 87.

5. John Howard Payne Papers, 2:52, Ayer Collection, Newberry Library, Chicago, Illinois; Springplace Diary, August 27, 1803, Cherokee Mission Papers, Moravian Archives, Winston-Salem, North Carolina.

6. Payne Papers, 2:52, 2:53, 2:54.

7. My analysis here is inspired by W. E. B. Du Bois, "The Propaganda of History," in *Black Reconstruction in America 1860–1880* (1935; reprint, New York: Atheneum, 1992), 714.

8. See John Howard Payne, *John Howard Payne to His Countrymen*, ed. Clemens de Baillou (Athens: University of Georgia Press, 1961). Also see: "John Howard Payne to His Countrymen" and "The Cherokee Nation to the United States," *Knoxville Register*, December 23, 1835.

9. Gabriel Harrison, *John Howard Payne: His Life and Writings* (London: Lippincott, 1885), 161, 164.

10. Payne, *John Howard Payne*, 15.

11. Payne, *John Howard Payne*, 113; Boston Bibliophile Society, *The Romance of Mary Wollstonecraft Shelley, John Howard Payne, and Washington Irving* (Boston: Boston Bibliophile Society, 1907), with remarks by F. B. Sanborn.

12. Payne, *John Howard Payne*, 176.

13. See Angela Y. Davis, *Women, Race and Class* (New York: Vintage, 1983); bell hooks, *Ain't I a Woman: Black Women and Feminism* (Boston: South End Press, 1981); Paula Giddings, *When and Where I Enter: The Impact of Black Women on Race and Sex in America* (New York: Bantam, 1984); Deborah Gray White, *Ar'n't I a Woman: Female Slaves in the Plantation South* (New York: Norton, 1985).

14. White, *Ar'n't I a Woman,* 23, 24.

15. The WPA interviews, structured by specific questions, reveal details such as diet, housing, work, childbirth and childrearing, methods of punishment, and degree of mobility. While a rich source, these interviews must be read closely and critically, since many of them were conducted by white workers, creating a dynamic that led some interviewees to mask their actual feelings about slavery. Perhaps the most reliable approach to reconstructing a picture of slave women's experience from these interviews is a comparative analysis that teases out common themes and shared experiences across a range of interviews. This type of reading can help us to glean major aspects of slave women's experience without wholly depending on the complete veracity and forthrightness of single interviewees. For more on the use of the WPA materials, see Melvina Johnson Young, "Exploring the WPA Narratives: Finding the Voices of Black Women and Men," in *Theorizing Black Feminisms,* ed. Stanlie James and Abena Busia (New York: Routledge, 1993), 55–74.

In slave narratives by Harriet Jacobs, Old Elizabeth, Mattie Jackson, Lucy Delaney, Kate Drumgoold, and Annie Burton, several key themes emerge. Relationships with family members, especially women, and others of the slave community are paramount in shaping these women's sense of themselves and in providing support and strength for the struggles they face. Sexual coercion and abuse, the struggle to maintain one's autonomy, separation from parents and children, the observation and fear of brutality, power struggles with white mistresses, troubled or brief relationships with black men, incidents of resistance, and attempts at escape all mark these narratives. Most important, these narratives offer a glimpse into the consciousness of slave women, indicating what they thought and how they felt at various moments of their lives. See Harriet Jacobs, *Incidents in the Life of a Slave Girl* (1861; reprint, Cambridge, Mass.: Harvard University Press, 1987); *Six Women's Slave Narratives,* with introduction by William Andrews (New York: Oxford University Press, 1988).

16. John Howard Payne, "The Green Corn Dance," *Chronicles of Oklahoma* 10 (1932): 194, 193, 175; previously published as "Green Corn Dance of the Creeks," *Continental Monthly* (Boston), January 1862.

17. Quoted in Harrison, *John Howard Payne,* 191.

18. Payne Papers, 2:64.

APPENDIX THREE. CHEROKEE NAMES AND MISTAKEN IDENTITIES

1. William G. McLoughlin gives the following description of Shoe Boots in his discussion of Shoe Boots's relationship with Doll: "the famous Cherokee chief and warrior Chulio (Tuskingo, Shoe Boot, or The Boot)"; *Cherokee Renascence in the New Republic* (Princeton: Princeton University Press, 1986), 342.

2. Durbin Feeling, telephone conversation with the author, March 1999.

3. Springplace Letters, May 26, 1824, Moravian Archives, Winston-Salem, North Carolina. McLoughlin quotes this letter in his book *Cherokees and Missionaries, 1789–1839* (1984; reprint, Norman: University of Oklahoma Press, 1995) but does not refer back to it or speculate about whether it complicates his findings on Shoe Boots in *Cherokee Renascence.*

4. Joyce Phillips and Paul Gary Phillips, eds., *The Brainerd Journal: A Mission to the Cherokees, 1817–1823* (Lincoln: University of Nebraska Press, 1998), 475.

5. Colonel Morgan's Regiment of Cherokee Indians, 1812, Shoe Boots no. 1099, Chulio no. 305, Military Service Records, Veterans Records, National Archives and Records Administration, Washington, D.C.

6. Receipt Cherokee Officers, October 1815, Records of the Cherokee Indian Agency in Tennessee, Bureau of Indian Affairs, Microfilm Publications, RG 75, M208, National Archives and Records Administration, Washington, D.C.; letter about pay for officers, August 15, 1819, Records of the Cherokee Indian Agency in Tennessee.

7. John Coffee to Calhoun, December 30, 1829, ed. Larry S. Watson, Senate Document 512, "Letters from the Department to Chiefs and Others; Concerning Quawpaw, Cherokee, Creeks, Ohio Indians, etc.," 23rd Cong., 1st sess., vol. 2, 9.

8. John Howard Payne Papers, 2:52, Ayer Collection, Newberry Library, Chicago, Illinois; Mission Diary, August 27, 1803, Moravian Archives, Winston-Salem, North Carolina.

9. McLoughlin, *Cherokee Renascence;* Theda Perdue, *Slavery and the Evolution of Cherokee Society, 1540–1866* (Knoxville: University of Tennessee Press, 1979); Adriane Strenk, "Tradition and Transformation: Shoe Boots and the Creation of a Cherokee Culture" (master's thesis, University of Kentucky, 1993).

10. Marion Starkey, *The Cherokee Nation* (1946; reprint, North Dighton, Mass.: J. G. Press, 1995), 18.

11. Rudi Halliburton, "Origins of Black Slavery among the Cherokees," *Chronicles of Oklahoma* 52 (Winter 1974): 495; Henry Thompson Malone, *Cherokees of the Old South* (Athens: University of Georgia Press, 1956), 142; Michael Roethler, "Negro Slavery Among the Cherokee Indians, 1540–1866" (PhD diss., Fordham University, 1964), 122–23; Rennard Strickland, *Fire and the Spirits: Cherokee Law from Clan to Court* (Norman: University of Oklahoma Press, 1975), 99.

12. I arrived at the conclusion that Doll was being confused with Shoe Boots's sister in previous histories when I came across a Cherokee roll that listed a woman who I think is Shoe Boots's sister Taskesteskee as "Lucy Takestaske." *Drennen Roll of the Cherokee Indians, 1851* (Tulsa, Okla.: Indian Nations Press, 1851), Delaware District no. 197.

13. Citizenship Application of William Shoeboots, Statement of William Shoeboots, Cherokee Applications, Applications from the Bureau of Indian

Affairs, Muskogee Area Office, Relating to Enrollment in the Five Civilized Tribes Under the Act of 1896, National Archives and Records Administration Microfilm Publication M1650, National Archives and Records Administration Southwest Region, Fort Worth, Texas; Payne Papers, 2:52.

14. Citizenship Application of William Shoeboots, Statement of Ed Carey; Citizenship Application of William Shoeboots, Statement of Thomas Ridge.

15. Citizenship Application of William Shoeboots, Statement of William Shoeboots.

SELECTED BIBLIOGRAPHY

MANUSCRIPT COLLECTIONS AND UNPUBLISHED SOURCES

American Board of Commissioners for Foreign Missions. Cherokee Mission: Joint Communications and Papers Relating to the Mission Generally Received before September 1, 1824. Microfilm Unit 6, reels 721–858. Used by permission of Houghton Library and Wider Church Ministries of the United Church of Christ.

American Board of Commissioners for Foreign Missions. Papers. Archives, Houghton Library, Harvard University, Cambridge, Massachusetts. Used by permission of Houghton Library and Wider Church Ministries of the United Church of Christ.

Biography Files. Kentucky Historical Society, Frankfort, Kentucky.

Cherokee Applications. Applications from the Bureau of Indian Affairs, Muskogee Area Office, Relating to Enrollment in the Five Civilized Tribes Under the Act of 1896. National Archives and Records Administration Microfilm Publication M1650. National Archives and Records Administration Southwest Region, Fort Worth, Texas.

Cherokee Indian Letters, Talks, and Treaties Manuscript Collection, 1786–1838. Georgia Department of Archives and History, Atlanta, Georgia.

Cherokee Nation Papers. Western History Collections. University of Oklahoma, Norman, Oklahoma.

Cherokee Supreme Court Docket. Cherokee Collection, microfilm no. 815. Tennessee State Library and Archives, Nashville, Tennessee.

Gage Papers. William L. Clements Library, University of Michigan, Ann Arbor, Michigan.

Lyttelton Papers. William L. Clements Library, University of Michigan, Ann Arbor, Michigan.

Military Service Records. National Archives and Records Administration, Washington, D.C.

Northern District Citizenship Case Files (National Archives and Records Administration Microfilm Publication 7RA-388). Oklahoma Historical Society, Oklahoma City, Oklahoma.

John Howard Payne Papers. Ayer Collection. Newberry Library, Chicago, Illinois.

Pioneer Papers. Oklahoma Writers' Project. Oklahoma Historical Society, Oklahoma City, Oklahoma.

Records of the Cherokee Indian Agency in Tennessee, 1801–35. Bureau of Indian Affairs. Microfilm Publications, RG 75, M208. National Archives and Records Administration, Washington, D.C.

Records of the Cherokee Indian Agency in Tennessee, 1801–35. Transcribed by Marybeth Chase, 1990. Oklahoma Historical Society, Oklahoma City, Oklahoma.

Records Relating to Indian Removal. Records of the Bureau of Indian Affairs Valuations of Property in Cass County, Georgia, 1836, by Agents Mays and Hargrove. Microfilm Publications RG 75.6, T496. National Archives and Records Administration, Washington, D.C.

Springplace Mission Diary and Letters, 1800–1810. Cherokee Mission Papers, Moravian Archives, Winston-Salem, North Carolina.

U.S. Census Lands West of Arkansas, 1860. Microfilm Publications M653, roll 52. National Archives and Records Administration, Washington, D.C.

U.S. War Department Records of the Office of the Secretary of War, Letters Sent to the Secretary of War Relating to Indian Affairs, 1800–1824. Microfilm 15, roll 3. National Archives and Records Administration, Washington, D.C.

Herman Vaill Collection. Manuscripts and Archives. Yale University Library. New Haven, Connecticut.

William Whitley Papers, 1775–1813, Kentucky Manuscripts. Draper Manuscript Collection. State Historical Society of Wisconsin, Madison, Wisconsin.

NEWSPAPERS

Cherokee Advocate
Cherokee Phoenix and Indian Advocate
Fort Smith Elevator
Georgetown Gazette

Georgia State Gazette
Kentucky Gazette
South Carolina Gazette
South Carolina Gazette and Country Journal

PUBLISHED SOURCES

Abel, Annie Heloise. *The American Indian and the End of the Confederacy, 1863–1866.* 1925. Reprint, Lincoln: University of Nebraska Press, 1993.

———. *The American Indian as Slaveholder and Secessionist.* 1915. Reprint, Lincoln: University of Nebraska Press, 1992.

———. *The American Indian in the Civil War, 1862–1865.* 1919. Reprint, Lincoln: University of Nebraska Press, 1992.

Adair, James. *Adair's History of the American Indian.* Edited by Samuel Cole Williams. 1775. Reprint, Johnson City, Tenn.: Watauga Press, 1930.

Alexander, Adele Logan. *Ambiguous Lives: Free Women of Color in Rural Georgia, 1789–1879.* Fayetteville: University of Arkansas Press, 1991.

Allen, Ivan. *The Cherokee Nation.* Atlanta: Ivan Allen, 1959.

Anderson, William, ed. *Cherokee Removal: Before and After.* Athens: University of Georgia Press, 1991.

Axtell, James. "The Ethnohistory of Native America." In *Rethinking American Indian History,* edited by Donald Fixico, 11–28. Albuquerque: University of New Mexico Press, 1997.

Baker, T. Lindsay, and Julie Baker, eds. *The WPA Oklahoma Slave Narratives.* Norman: University of Oklahoma Press, 1996.

Ball, Edward. *Slaves in the Family.* New York: Ballantine Books, 1998.

Basso, Keith. "Stalking with Stories." In *Western Apache Language and Culture,* 99–137. Tucson: University of Arizona Press, 1990.

———. *Wisdom Sits in Places: Landscape and Language among the Western Apache.* Albuquerque: University of New Mexico Press, 1996.

Beeson, Leola Selman. "Homes of Distinguished Cherokee Indians." *Chronicles of Oklahoma* 11 (September 1933): 927–41.

Bell, Betty Louise. "Pocahontas: 'Little Mischief' and the 'Dirty Men.'" *Studies in American Indian Literatures* 6 (Spring 1994): 63–70.

Berlin, Ira. *Many Thousands Gone: The First Two Centuries of Slavery in North America.* Cambridge, Mass.: Harvard University Press, 1998.

———. "Time, Space and the Evolution of Afro-American Society on British Mainland North America." In *Diversity and Unity in Early North America,* edited by Philip Morgan, 113–46. London: Routledge, 1993.

Bibb, Henry. "Narrative of the Life and Adventures of Henry Bibb, an American Slave." In *I Was Born a Slave: An Anthology of Classic Slave Narratives,* vol. 2, *1849–1866*, edited by Yuval Taylor, 1–102. Chicago: Lawrence Hill Books, 1999.

Billington, Monroe. "Black Slavery in the Indian Territory: The Ex-slave Narrative." *Chronicles of Oklahoma* 61 (1982): 56–65.

Block, Sharon. "Rape and Native Americans in Early America." Paper presented at the ninety-sixth annual meeting of the American Historical Association Pacific Coast Branch, Honolulu, Hawaii, August 2003.

Boston Bibliophile Society. *The Romance of Mary Wollstonecraft Shelley, John Howard Payne, and Washington Irving.* Boston: Bibliophile Society, 1907.

Brooks, James, ed. "Confounding the Color Line: Indian-Black Relations in Historical and Anthropological Perspective." Special Issue, *American Indian Quarterly* 22 (Winter/Spring 1998): 125–258.

Brown, Catharine. *Memoir of Catharine Brown: A Christian Indian of the Cherokee Nation.* Prepared by Rufus Anderson. Philadelphia: American Sunday School Press, 1832.

Brown, Elsa Barkley. "African-American Women's Quilting: A Framework for Conceptualizing and Teaching African-American Women's History." In *Black Women in America: Social Science Perspectives,* edited by Micheline R. Malson et al., 9–18. Chicago: University of Chicago Press, 1990.

———. "Negotiating and Transforming the Public Sphere: African American Political Life in the Transition from Slavery to Freedom." *Public Culture* 7 (Fall 1994): 107–46.

Brown, Kathleen. *Good Wives, Nasty Wenches, and Anxious Patriarchs: Gender, Race, and Power in Colonial Virginia.* Chapel Hill: University of North Carolina Press, 1996.

Burstein, Andrew, Nancy Isenberg, and Annette Gordon-Reed. "Three Perspectives on America's Jefferson Fixation." *Nation,* November 30, 1998.

Burton, Art. *Black, Red, and Deadly: Black and Indian Gunfighters of the Indian Territory, 1870–1907.* Austin, Tex.: Eakin Press, 1991.

Butrick, Daniel. *The Journal of Rev. Daniel S. Butrick, May 19, 1838–April 1, 1839, Monograph One.* 1839. Reprint, Park Hill, Okla.: Trail of Tears Association, Oklahoma Chapter, 1998.

Bynum, Victoria. *Unruly Women: The Politics of Social and Sexual Control in the Old South.* Chapel Hill: University of North Carolina Press, 1992.

Campbell, Janet, and David Campbell. "The Wolf Clan." *Journal of Cherokee Studies* 7, no. 2 (Fall 1982): 85–91.

Carselowey, James Manford. *Cherokee Old Timers.* Tulsa: Oklahoma Yesterday Publications, 1980.

Carter, Kent. "Deciding Who Can Be Cherokee: Enrollment Records of the Dawes Commission." *Chronicles of Oklahoma* 69, no. 2 (Summer 1991): 174–205.

Champagne, Duane. "Institutional and Cultural Order in Early Cherokee Society." *Journal of Cherokee Studies* 15 (1990): 3–26.

———. "Symbolic Structure and Political Change in Cherokee Society." *Journal of Cherokee Studies* 8 (1983): 87–96.

Cherokee Nation. *Laws of the Cherokee Nation: Adopted by the Council at Various Periods, 1808–1835* (Tahlequah, C.N.: Cherokee Advocate Office, 1852).

Clinton, Catherine. *The Plantation Mistress: Woman's World in the Old South.* New York: Pantheon Books, 1982.

Collins, Lewis, and Richard Collins. *History of Kentucky.* Covington, Ky.: Collins, 1882.

Collins, Patricia Hill. "It's All in the Family: Intersections of Gender, Race, and Nation." *Hypatia* 13 (Summer 1998): 62–82.

Cott, Nancy F. *Public Vows: A History of Marriage and the Nation.* Cambridge, Mass.: Harvard University Press, 2000.

Cotterill, R. S. *The Southern Indians: The Story of the Civilized Tribes Before Removal.* Norman: University of Oklahoma Press, 1954.

Cunningham, Frank. *General Stand Watie's Confederate Indians.* 1959. Reprint, Norman: University of Oklahoma Press, 1998.

Dale, Edward Everett, and Gaston Litton. *Cherokee Cavaliers.* Norman: University of Oklahoma Press, 1939.

Dale, Edward Everett, and Morris Wardell. *History of Oklahoma.* New York: Prentice-Hall, 1948.

Davis, Angela Y. *Women, Race, and Class.* 1981. Reprint, New York: Vintage, 1983.

Davis, J. B. "Slavery in the Cherokee Nation." *Chronicles of Oklahoma* 11 (December 1933): 1056–72.

De Baillou, Clemens. "The Chief Vann House at Spring Place, Georgia." *Early Georgia: Society for Georgia Archaeology* 2 (Spring 1957): 3–11.

———. "The Diaries of the Moravian Brotherhood at the Cherokee Mission in Spring Place, Georgia, for the Years 1800–1804." *Georgia Historical Quarterly* 54 (Winter 1970): 571–76.

Debo, Angie. *The Road to Disappearance: A History of the Creek Indians.* Norman: University of Oklahoma Press, 1941.

Deloria, Vine, Jr. *Custer Died for Your Sins: An Indian Manifesto.* 1969. Reprint, Norman: University of Oklahoma Press, 1988.

D'Emilio, John, and Estelle B. Freedman. *Intimate Matters: A History of Sexuality in America.* New York: Harper & Row, 1988.

Demos, John. *The Unredeemed Captive.* New York: Vintage, 1994.

Doran, Michael F. "Negro Slaves of the Five Civilized Tribes." *Annals of the Association of American Geographers* 68 (September 1978): 335–50.

———. "Population Statistics of Nineteenth-Century Indian Territory." *Chronicles of Oklahoma* 53 (Winter 1975–1976): 492–515.

Dowd, Gregory Evans. "North American Indian Slaveholding and the Colonization of Gender: The Southeast Before Removal." *Critical Matrix* 3 (Fall 1987): 1–30.

———. *A Spirited Resistance: The North American Indian Struggle for Unity, 1745–1815.* Baltimore: Johns Hopkins University Press, 1992.

Drennen Roll of the Cherokee Indians, 1851. Tulsa, Okla.: Indian Nations Press, 1851.

Drinnon, Richard. *Facing West: The Metaphysics of Indian-Hating and Empire-Building.* New York: Meridian, 1980.

Du Bois, W. E. B. *Black Reconstruction in America, 1860–1880.* 1935. Reprint, New York: Atheneum, 1992.

Duncan, James. "The Keetoowah Society." *Chronicles of Oklahoma* 4 (1926): 251–55.

Durham, Philip, and Everett Jones. *The Negro Cowboys.* 1965. Reprint, Lincoln: University of Nebraska Press, 1983.

Eggan, Fred, ed. *Social Anthropology of North American Tribes.* 1937. Reprint, Chicago: University of Chicago Press, 1955.

Ellison, Ralph. *Going to the Territory.* New York: Random House, 1986.

Enoch, Harry. *In Search of Morgan's Station and the Last Indian Raid in Kentucky.* Bowie, Md.: Heritage Books, 1997.

Evans, E. Raymond, ed. "Jeddiah Morse's Report to the Secretary of War on Cherokee Indian Affairs in 1822." *Journal of Cherokee Studies* 6 (Fall 1981): 60–78.

Evans, J. P. "Sketches of Cherokee Characteristics." 1835. Reprint, *Journal of Cherokee Studies* 4 (Winter 1979).

Faery, Rebecca Blevins. *Cartographies of Desire: Captivity, Race, and Sex in the Shaping of an American Narrative.* Norman: University of Oklahoma Press, 1999.

Feeling, Durbin. *Cherokee-English Dictionary.* Edited by William Pulte. Tahlequah: Cherokee Nation of Oklahoma, 1975.

Felldin, Jeanne, and Charlotte Tucker. *Index to the 1835 Census of the Cherokee Indians East of the Mississippi.* Tomball, Tex.: Genealogical Publications, 1976.

Fields, Barbara. "Ideology and Race in American History." In *Region, Race, and Reconstruction,* edited by J. Morgan Kousser and James McPherson, 143–77. New York: Oxford University Press, 1982.

Finkelman, Paul. *Slavery in the Courtroom: An Annotated Bibliography of American Cases.* Washington, D.C.: Library of Congress, 1985.

Flowers, Carl, Jr. "The Wofford Settlement on the Georgia Frontier." *Georgia Historical Quarterly* 61 (Fall 1977): 258–67.

Fogelson, Raymond D. "The Ethnohistory of Events and Non-events." *Ethnohistory* 36 (1989): 133–47.

———. "On the 'Petticoat Government' of the Eighteenth-Century Cherokee."

In *Personality and the Cultural Construction of Society,* edited by David Jordan and Marc Swartz, 161–81. Tuscaloosa: University of Alabama Press, 1990.

———. "Who Were the Aní-kutáni? An Excursion into Cherokee Historical Thought." *Ethnohistory* 3 (1984): 255–63.

———. "Windigo Goes South: Stoneclad among the Cherokees." In *Manlike Monsters on Trial: Early Records and Modern Evidence,* edited by Marjorie Ames and Michael Ames, 132–51. Vancouver: University of British Columbia, 1980.

Foote, Kenneth. *Shadowed Ground: America's Landscapes of Violence and Tragedy.* Austin: University of Texas Press, 1997.

Forbes, Jack D. *Africans and Native Americans: The Language of Race and the Evolution of Red-Black Peoples.* Urbana: University of Illinois Press, 1993.

Foreman, Carolyn Thomas. "Early History of Webbers Falls." *Chronicles of Oklahoma* 29 (Winter 1951–52): 444–83.

———. "Miss Sophia Sawyer and Her School." *Chronicles of Oklahoma* 32 (Winter 1954–55): 395–98.

Foreman, Grant. *The Five Civilized Tribes.* Norman: University of Oklahoma Press, 1934.

———. *A History of Oklahoma.* Norman: University of Oklahoma Press, 1942.

———. *Indian Removal.* 1932. Reprint, Norman: University of Oklahoma Press, 1972.

Forts Committee Department of Archives and History. "The Cherokee Removal Forts." *Georgia Magazine* (June–July 1970): 28–29.

Foster, Laurence. "Negro-Indian Relationships in the Southeast." Ph.D. diss., University of Pennsylvania, 1935.

Fox-Genovese, Elizabeth. "Strategies and Forms of Resistance: Focus on Slave Women in the United States." In *In Resistance: Studies in African, Caribbean, and Afro-American History,* edited by Gary Okihiro, 143–65. Amherst: University of Massachusetts Press, 1986.

———. *Within the Plantation Household: Black and White Women of the Old South.* Chapel Hill: University of North Carolina Press, 1988.

Frazier, E. Franklin. *The Free Negro Family.* Nashville, Tenn.: Fisk University Press, 1932.

Gearing, Fred. *Priests and Warriors: Social Structures for Cherokee Politics in the 18th Century* (Menasha, Wis.: American Anthropological Association, 1962).

Giddings, Paula. *When and Where I Enter: The Impact of Black Women on Race and Sex in America.* New York: Bantam, 1984.

Gilbert, William Harlen. "Eastern Cherokee Social Organization." In *Social Anthropology of North American Tribes,* edited by Fred Eggan, 285–338. 1937. Reprint, Chicago: University of Chicago Press, 1955.

———. *Smithsonian Institution Bureau of Ethnology Bulletin 133: Anthropological Papers Numbers 19–26,* "No. 23: The Eastern Cherokees." Washington, D.C.: United States Government Printing Office, 1943.

Glancy, Diane. *Pushing the Bear: A Novel of the Trail of Tears.* New York: Harcourt Brace, 1996.

Gordon-Reed, Annette. *Thomas Jefferson and Sally Hemings: An American Controversy.* Charlottesville: University Press of Virginia, 1997.

Green, Rayna. "The Pocahontas Perplex: The Image of Indian Women in American Culture." *Massachusetts Review* 16 (1975): 698–714.

Griffin, Catherine. "'Joined Together in History': Politics and Place in African American and American Indian Women's Writing." Ph.D. diss, University of Minnesota, 2000.

Grinde, Donald, Jr., and Quintard Taylor. "Red vs. Black: Conflict and Accommodation in the Post Civil War Indian Territory, 1865–1907." *American Indian Quarterly* 8, no. 3 (Summer 1984): 211–29.

Gross, Ariela. "Litigating Whiteness: Trials of Racial Determination in the Nineteenth-Century South." *Yale Law Journal* 108 (October 1998): 109–88.

Gundersen, Joan R. "Women and Inheritance in America: Virginia and New York as a Case Study, 1700–1860." In *Inheritance and Wealth in America,* edited by Robert K. Miller Jr. and Stephen J. McNamee, 91–118. New York: Plenum Press, 1998.

Gwin, Minrose. "Green-Eyed Monsters of the Slavocracy: Jealous Mistresses in Two Slave Narratives." In *Conjuring: Black Women, Fiction, and the Literary Tradition,* edited by Marjorie Pryse and Hortense Spillers. Bloomington: Indiana University Press, 1985.

Hahn, Steven. *The Roots of Southern Populism: Yeoman Farmers and the Transformation of the Georgia Upcountry, 1850–1890.* New York: Oxford University Press, 1983.

———. "The 'Unmaking' of the Southern Yeoman: The Transformation of the Georgia Upcountry, 1860–1890." In *The Countryside in the Age of Capitalist Transformation: Essays in the Social History of Rural America,* edited by Steven Hahn and Jonathan Prude, 179–203. Chapel Hill: University of North Carolina Press, 1985.

Halbert, H. S., and T. H. Ball. *The Creek War of 1813 and 1814.* Edited by Frank L. Owsley Jr. Reprint, Tuscaloosa: University of Alabama Press, 1969.

Hall, Arthur. "The Red Stick War: Creek Indian Affairs During the War of 1812." *Chronicles of Oklahoma* 12 (September 1934): 264–93.

Hall, Peter Dobkin, and George E. Marcus. "Why Should Men Leave Great Fortunes to Their Children? Class, Dynasty, and Inheritance in America." In *Inheritance and Wealth in America,* edited by Robert K. Miller Jr. and Stephen J. McNamee, 139–71. New York: Plenum Press, 1998.

Halliburton, Rudi. "Origins of Black Slavery among the Cherokees." *Chronicles of Oklahoma* 52 (Winter 1974): 483–96.

———. *Red over Black: Black Slavery among the Cherokee Indians.* Westport, Conn.: Greenwood, 1977.

Hamilton, Kenneth. "Minutes of the Mission Conference Held in Springplace." *Atlanta Historical Bulletin* 16 (Spring 1971): 31–59.

Hampton, David Keith. *Cherokee Old Settlers: The 1896 Old Settler Payroll and the 1851 Old Settler Payroll.* Broken Arrow, Okla.: D. K. Hampton, 1993.

Harris, Cheryl. "Whiteness as Property." *Harvard Law Review* 106 (June 1993): 1709–91.

Harris, J. William, ed. *Society and Culture in the Slave South.* London: Routledge, 1992.

Harrison, Gabriel. *John Howard Payne: His Life and Writings.* London: Lippincott, 1885.

Hart, William. "Black 'Go-Betweens' and the Mutability of 'Race,' Status, and Identity on New York's Pre-Revolutionary Frontier." In *Contact Points: American Frontiers from the Mohawk Valley to the Mississippi, 1750–1830,* edited by Andrew Cayton and Fredrika Teute, 88–113. Chapel Hill: University of North Carolina Press, 1998.

Hartman, Saidiya. *Scenes of Subjection: Terror, Slavery, and Self-Making in Nineteenth-Century America.* New York: Oxford University Press, 1997.

Hawkins, Benjamin. "A Sketch of the Creek Country in the Years 1798 and 1799." In *Letters, Journals, and Writings of Benjamin Hawkins,* edited by C. L. Grant. Volume 1, *1796–1801.* Savannah, Ga.: Beehive Press, 1980.

Hazel, Forest. "Black, White, and 'Other': The Struggle for Recognition." *Southern Exposure* 13 (1985): 34–37.

Hewett, Janet B., ed. *The Roster of Confederate Soldiers, 1861–1865.* Wilmington, N.C.: Broadfoot, 1996.

Hicks, Hannah. "The Diary of Hannah Hicks." *American Scene* 13 (1972): 2–24.

Higginbotham, Evelyn Brooks. "African-American Women's History and the Metalanguage of Race." *Signs* 17 (1992): 251–74.

Hill, Sarah. *Weaving New Worlds: Cherokee Women and Their Basketry.* Chapel Hill: University of North Carolina Press, 1997.

Hine, Darlene Clark. "Rape and the Inner Lives of Black Women in the Middle West: Preliminary Thoughts on the Culture of Dissemblance." *Signs* (Summer 1989): 272–80.

Hinks, Peter. *To Awaken My Afflicted Brethren: David Walker and the Problem of Antebellum Slave Resistance.* University Park: Pennsylvania State University Press, 1997.

Hodes, Martha. *White Women, Black Men: Illicit Sex in the Nineteenth-Century South.* New Haven, Conn.: Yale University Press, 1997.

Holland, Sharon. "'If You Know I Have a History, You Will Respect Me': A Perspective on Afro-Native American Literature." *Callaloo* 17 (Winter–Summer 1994): 334–50.

———. *Raising the Dead: Readings of Death and (Black) Subjectivity.* Durham, N.C.: Duke University Press, 2000.

hooks, bell. *Ain't I a Woman: Black Women and Feminism.* Boston: South End Press, 1981.

———. "Revolutionary 'Renegades': Native Americans, African Americans, and Black Indians." In *Black Looks: Race and Representation,* 179–94. London: Turnaround, 1992.

Howard, June. *Publishing the Family.* Durham, N.C.: Duke University Press, 2001.

Hudson, Charles, ed. *Red, White, and Black: Symposium on Indians in the Old South.* Athens, Ga.: Southern Anthropological Society, 1971.

———. *The Southeastern Indians.* Nashville: University of Tennessee Press, 1976.

Hudson, Charles, and Carmen Chaves Tesser, eds. *The Forgotten Centuries: Indians and Europeans in the American South, 1521–1704.* Athens: University of Georgia Press, 1994.

Jacobs, Harriet. *Incidents in the Life of a Slave Girl.* 1861. Reprint, Cambridge, Mass.: Harvard University Press, 1987.

Jennings, Thelma. "'Us Colored Women Had to Go Through A Plenty': Sexual Exploitation of African-American Slave Women." *Journal of Women's History* 1 (Winter 1990): 45–74.

Johnston, Carolyn Ross. *Cherokee Women in Crisis: Trail of Tears, Civil War, and Allotment, 1838–1907.* Tuscaloosa: University of Alabama Press, 2003.

Johnston, James Hugo. "Documentary Evidence of the Relations of Negroes and Indians." *Journal of Negro History* 14 (January 1929).

———. *Race Relations in Virginia and Miscegenation in the South, 1776–1860.* Amherst: University of Massachusetts Press, 1970.

Jordan, Winthrop. *The White Man's Burden: Historical Origins of Racism in the United States.* London: Oxford University Press, 1974.

———. *White over Black: American Attitudes Toward the Negro, 1550–1812.* 1968. Reprint, New York: Norton, 1977.

Kaplan, Amy. "Manifest Domesticity." *American Literature* 70 (September 1998): 581–606.

Kappler, Charles J., comp. and ed. *Indian Affairs: Laws and Treaties.* Vol. 2. Washington, D.C.: Government Printing Office, 1904.

Katz, William Loren. *Black Indians: A Hidden Heritage.* New York: Atheneum, 1986.

———. *The Black West.* Seattle: Open Hand Publishing, 1987.

Kelley, Mary. "Commentary" (on Barbara Welter, "The Cult of True Womanhood: 1820–1860"). In *Locating American Studies: The Evolution of a Discipline,* edited by Lucy Maddox, 43–70. Baltimore: Johns Hopkins University Press, 1999.

Kelley, Robin D. G. *Race Rebels: Culture, Politics, and the Black Working Class.* New York: Free Press, 1994.

King, Duane, ed. *The Cherokee Indian Nation.* Knoxville: University of Tennessee Press, 1979.

Kirkham, E. Kay. *Our Native Americans and Their Records of Genealogical Value.* Vol. 3. Provo, Utah: Stevenson's Genealogy Center, 1984.

Kleber, John, ed. *The Kentucky Encyclopedia.* Lexington: University Press of Kentucky, 1992.

Kupperman, Karen Ordahl. *Settling with the Indians: The Meeting of English and Indian Cultures in America, 1580–1640.* Totowa, N.J.: Rowman and Littlefield, 1980.

Lankford, George, ed. *Native American Legends.* Little Rock, Ark.: August House, 1987.

Lauber, Almon Wheeler. *Indian Slavery in Colonial Times within the Present Limits of the United States.* 1913. Reprint, Williamstown, Mass.: Corner House Publishers, 1970.

Leslie, Kent Anderson. *Woman of Color, Daughter of Privilege: Amanda America Dickson, 1849–1893.* Athens: University of Georgia Press, 1995.

Lewis, Earl. "To Turn as on a Pivot: Writing African Americans into a History of Overlapping Diasporas." In *Crossing Boundaries: Comparative History of Black People in Diaspora,* edited by Darlene Clark Hine and Jacqueline McLeod, 3–32. Bloomington: Indiana University Press, 1999.

Littlefield, Daniel F. *Africans and Creeks: From the Colonial Period to the Civil War.* Westport, Conn.: Greenwood Press, 1979.

———. *The Cherokee Freedmen: From Emancipation to American Citizenship.* Westport, Conn.: Greenwood Press, 1978.

Littlefield, Daniel F., and Mary Ann Littlefield. "The Beams Family: Free Blacks in Indian Territory." *Journal of Negro History* 61 (January 1976): 16–35.

Littlefield, Daniel F., and Lonnie Underhill. "Slave 'Revolt' in the Cherokee Nation, 1842." *American Indian Quarterly* 3 (Summer 1977): 121–31.

Lomawaima, K. Tsianina. *They Called It Prairie Light.* Lincoln: University of Nebraska Press, 1994.

Lorde, Audre. *Sister Outsider: Essays and Speeches.* New York: Crossing Press, 1984.

Louis Philippe. *Diary of My Travels in America: Louis Philippe, King of France, 1830–1848.* New York: Delacorte Press, 1977.

Lowenthal, David. "Past Time, Present Place: Landscape and Memory." *Geographical Review* 65 (January 1975): 1–36.

Malcomson, Scott. *One Drop of Blood: The American Misadventure of Race.* New York: Farrar Straus Giroux, 2000.

Malone, Henry Thompson. "Cherokee Civilization in the Lower Appalachians, Especially in North Georgia, Before 1830." Master's thesis, Emory University, 1949.

———. *Cherokees of the Old South.* Athens: University of Georgia Press, 1956.

Mandell, Daniel. "Shifting Boundaries of Race and Ethnicity: Indian-Black Intermarriage in Southern New England, 1760–1880." *Journal of American History* (September 1988): 466–501.

Mankiller, Wilma. *Mankiller: A Chief and Her People.* New York: St. Martin's Press, 1993.

Mariani, Philomena, ed. *Critical Fictions: The Politics of Imaginative Writing.* Seattle: Bay Press, 1991.

Martin, Joel. *Sacred Revolt: The Muskogees' Struggle for a New World.* Boston: Beacon, 1991.

May, Katja. *African Americans and Native Americans in the Creek and Cherokee Nations, 1830s to 1920s.* New York: Garland, 1996.

McClinton, Rowena. "Notable Persons in Cherokee History: Charles Hicks." *Journal of Cherokee Studies* 17 (1996): 16–27.

———. "Possessions of Value: Cherokee Inheritance in the Early Nineteenth Century." Department of History, University of Kentucky, 1992.

———. "Reconstructing the Cherokee and Moravian Story through Early Nineteenth Century Missionary Diaries: Transcending Divergent Worldviews, Archaic Language, and Time." Paper presented at the University of North Carolina, Chapel Hill, March 5, 2001.

———, ed. and trans. *The Moravian Mission to the Cherokees: Springplace in the Gambold Years, 1805–1821* (forthcoming).

McGoun, William. "Adoption of Whites by Eighteenth-Century Cherokees." *Journal of Cherokee Studies* 9 (1984): 37–41.

McLaurin, Melton. *Celia, a Slave.* Athens: University of Georgia Press, 1991.

McLoughlin, William G. *After the Trail of Tears: The Cherokees' Struggle for Sovereignty, 1839–1880.* Chapel Hill: University of North Carolina Press, 1993.

———. *Cherokee Renascence in the New Republic.* Princeton: Princeton University Press, 1986.

———. *Cherokees and Missionaries, 1789–1839.* 1984. Reprint, Norman: University of Oklahoma Press, 1995.

———. "Experiment in Cherokee Citizenship, 1817–1829." *American Quarterly* 33 (Spring 1981): 3–25.

———. "'The First Man Was Red': Cherokee Responses to the Debate over Indian Origins, 1760–1860." *American Quarterly* 41 (June 1989): 243–64.

———. "Red Indians, Black Slavery, and White Racism: America's Slaveholding Indians." *American Quarterly* 26 (October 1974): 367–85.

McLoughlin, William G., and Walter Conser. "The Cherokee Censuses of 1809, 1825, and 1835." In *The Cherokee Ghost Dance: Essays on the Southeastern Indians, 1789–1861,* 215–47. Macon, Ga.: Mercer University Press, 1984.

Merrell, James. *The Indians' New World: Catawbas and Their Neighbors from European Contact Through the Era of Removal.* New York: Norton, 1991.

———. "The Racial Education of the Catawba Indians." *Journal of Southern History* 50 (1984): 363–84.

Mihesuah, Devon. *Cultivating the Rosebuds: The Education of Women at the Cherokee Female Seminary, 1851–1909.* Urbana: University of Illinois Press, 1993.

———. "Too Dark to Be Angels: The Class System among the Cherokees at the Female Seminary." *American Indian Culture and Research Journal* 15 (1991): 29–52.

Miller, Robert K., Jr., and Stephen J. McNamee, eds. *Inheritance and Wealth in America.* New York: Plenum, 1998.

Minges, Patrick. "'Go in de Wilderness': Black/Indian Diaspora in the Slave Narratives." Working paper, Union Theological Seminary, New York, N.Y., January 2002.

———. "The Keetoowah Society and the Avocation of Religious Nationalism in the Cherokee Nation, 1855–1867." PhD diss., Union Theological Seminary, 1998.

Momaday, N. Scott. *The Way to Rainy Mountain.* Albuquerque: University of New Mexico Press, 1969.

Mooney, James. "Evolution in Cherokee Personal Names." *Journal of Cherokee Studies* 7 (Spring 1982): 40–41.

———. *Historical Sketch of the Cherokee.* 1897. Reprint, Washington, D.C.: Smithsonian Institution Press, 1975.

———. *Myths of the Cherokee.* 1900. Reprint, New York: Dover, 1995.

Moraga, Cherríe. "From Inside the World: Foreword." In *This Bridge Called My Back: Writings by Radical Women of Color,* edited by Cherríe Moraga and Gloria Anzaldúa, xv–xxxiii. 3rd ed. Berkeley: Third Woman Press, 2002.

Morgan, Edmund. *American Slavery, American Freedom: The Ordeal of Colonial Virginia.* New York: Norton, 1975.

Morgan, Philip. *Slave Counterpoint: Black Culture in the Eighteenth-Century Chesapeake and Lowcountry.* Chapel Hill: University of North Carolina Press, 1998.

Morrison, Michael. *Slavery and the American West.* Chapel Hill: University of North Carolina Press, 1997.

Morrison, Toni. *Beloved.* New York: Plume, 1987.

———. Nobel Lecture. December 7, 1993.

———. "Unspeakable Things Unspoken: The Afro-American Presence in American Literature." *Michigan Quarterly Review* 28 (Winter 1989): 1–34.

Mulroy, Kevin. *Freedom on the Border.* Lubbock: Texas Tech University Press, 1993.

Murchison, A. H. "Intermarried Whites in the Cherokee Nation Between the Years 1865 and 1887." *Chronicles of Oklahoma* 6 (September 1928): 299–302.

Murray, David. *Forked Tongues: Speech, Writing, and Representation in North American Indian Texts.* Bloomington: Indiana University Press, 1991.

Nash, Gary. *Red, White, and Black: The Peoples of Early America.* Englewood Cliffs, N.J.: Prentice-Hall, 1974.

Naylor-Ojurongbe, Celia. "African-American Slave Women's Pathways of Resistance in the Nineteenth-Century Cherokee Nation (Indian Territory)." Paper presented at the sixth meeting of the Southern Conference on Women's History, Athens, Ga., June 2003.

———. "'More at Home with the Indians': African-American Slaves and Freedpeople in the Cherokee Nation, Indian Territory, 1838–1907." PhD diss., Duke University, 2001.

Norton, John. *The Journal of Major John Norton.* Edited by Carl F. Klinck and James J. Talman, 1816. Reprint, Toronto: Champlain Society, 1970.

Norton, Mary Beth. *Founding Mothers and Fathers: Gendered Power and the Forming of American Society.* New York: Knopf, 1996.

Oakes, James. *The Ruling Race: A History of American Slaveholders.* New York: Knopf, 1982.

O'Brien, Jean. *Dispossession by Degrees: Indian Land and Identity in Natick, Massachusetts.* New York: Cambridge University Press, 1997.

"Oklahoma Historical Society's Hunter's Home Visitors Guide." Park Hill, Okla.: George M. Murrell Historic House, 2001.

Omi, Michael, and Howard Winant. *Racial Formation in the United States.* New York: Routledge, 1994.

Owens, Louis. *Other Destinies: Understanding the American Indian Novel.* Norman: University of Oklahoma Press, 1992.

Padover, Saul K., ed. *The Complete Jefferson.* New York: Duell, Sloan and Pearce, 1943.

Painter, Nell Irvin. *Exodusters: Black Migration to Kansas after Reconstruction.* 2nd ed. New York: Norton, 1992.

———. "Soul Murder and Slavery: Toward a Fully Loaded Cost Accounting." In *U.S. History as Women's History: New Feminist Essays,* edited by Linda Kerber, Alice Kessler-Harris, and Kathryn Kish Sklar, 125–46. Chapel Hill: University of North Carolina Press, 1995.

Pascoe, Peggy. "Race, Gender, and the Privileges of Property: On the Significance of Miscegenation Law in the U.S. West." In *Over the Edge: Remapping the American West,* edited by Valerie J. Matsumoto and Blake Allmendinger, 215–30. Berkeley and Los Angeles: University of California Press, 1999.

Patterson, Orlando. *Rituals of Blood: Consequences of Slavery in Two American Centuries.* New York: Basic Books, 1998.

———. *Slavery and Social Death: A Comparative Study.* Cambridge, Mass.: Harvard University Press, 1982.

Payne, John Howard. "The Cherokee Nation to the United States." *Knoxville Register,* December 23, 1835.

———. "The Green Corn Dance." *Chronicles of Oklahoma* 10 (1932): 170–95. Previously published as "Green Corn Dance of the Creeks." *Continental Monthly* (Boston), January 1862.

———. *Indian Justice: A Cherokee Murder Trial at Tahlequah in 1840.* Edited by Grant Foreman. Oklahoma City: Harlow Publishing, 1934.

———. *John Howard Payne to His Countrymen.* Edited by Clemens De Baillou. Athens: University of Georgia Press, 1961.

Peires, J. B. *The Dead Will Arise: Nongqawuse and the Great Xhosa Cattle-Killing Movement of 1856–7.* Bloomington: Indiana University Press, 1989.

Perdue, Theda. *The Cherokee.* New York: Chelsea House, 1989.

———. "Cherokee Planters, Black Slaves, and African Colonization." *Chronicles of Oklahoma* 60 (1982): 322–31.

———. "Cherokee Women and the Trail of Tears." In *Unequal Sisters: A Multicultural Reader in U.S. Women's History,* edited by Vicki Ruiz and Ellen Carol DuBois, 32–43. 2nd ed. New York: Routledge, 1994.

———. *Cherokee Women: Gender and Culture Change, 1700–1835.* Lincoln: University of Nebraska Press, 1998.

———. "The Conflict Within: Cherokees and Removal." In *Cherokee Removal: Before and After,* edited by William Anderson, 55–74. Athens: University of Georgia Press, 1991.

———. *Slavery and the Evolution of Cherokee Society, 1540–1866.* Knoxville: University of Tennessee Press, 1979.

———. "Southern Indians and the Cult of True Womanhood." In *Half Sisters of History,* edited by Catherine Clinton, 36–55. Durham, N.C.: Duke University Press, 1994.

———. "Women, Men, and American Indian Policy: The Cherokee Response to 'Civilization.'" In *Negotiators of Change: Historical Perspectives on Native American Women,* edited by Nancy Shoemaker, 90–114. New York: Routledge, 1995.

———, ed. *Nations Remembered: An Oral History of the Cherokees, Chickasaws, Choctaws, Creeks, and Seminoles in Oklahoma, 1865–1907.* 1980. Reprint, Norman: University of Oklahoma Press, 1993.

Perdue, Theda, and Michael Green, eds. *The Cherokee Removal: A Brief History with Documents.* Boston: Bedford Books, 1995.

Persico, Richard V., Jr. "Early Nineteenth-Century Cherokee Political Organization." In *The Cherokee Indian Nation: A Troubled History,* edited by Duane H. King, 92–109. Knoxville: University of Tennessee Press, 1979.

Phillips, Joyce, and Paul Gary Phillips, eds. *The Brainerd Journal: A Mission to the Cherokees, 1817–1823.* Lincoln: University of Nebraska Press, 1998.

Plane, Ann Marie. *Colonial Intimacies: Indian Marriage in Early New England.* Ithaca, N.Y.: Cornell University Press, 2000.

Porter, Kenneth W. *The Black Seminoles: History of a Freedom-Seeking People.* Revised and edited by Alcione Amos and Thomas Senter. Gainesville: University Press of Florida, 1996.

———. "Negroes and Indians on the Texas Frontier." *Journal of Negro History* 41 (October 1956): 285–310.

————. "Notes Supplementary to 'Relations Between Negroes and Indians.'" *Journal of Negro History* 18 (July 1933): 282–88.

————. "Relations Between Negroes and Indians Within the Present Limits of the United States." *Journal of Negro History* 17 (July 1932): 287–367.

Rawick, George. *From Sundown to Sunup: The Making of the Black Community.* Westport, Conn.: Greenwood Press, 1972.

Reid, John Phillip. *A Law of Blood: The Primitive Law of the Cherokee Nation.* New York: New York University Press, 1970.

Roethler, Michael. "Negro Slavery Among the Cherokee Indians, 1540–1866." PhD diss., Fordham University, 1964.

Rogin, Michael Paul. *Fathers and Children: Andrew Jackson and the Subjugation of the American Indian.* 1975. Reprint, New Brunswick, N.J.: Transaction, 1991.

Romero, Lora. *Home Fronts: Domesticity and Its Critics in the Antebellum United States.* Durham, N.C.: Duke University Press, 1997.

Ross, Loretta. "African-American Women and Abortion: 1800–1970." In *Theorizing Black Feminisms,* edited by Stanlie James and Abena Busia, 141–59. New York: Routledge, 1993.

Royce, Charles C. *The Cherokee Nation of Indians.* Chicago: Aldine Publishing, 1975.

————. "The Cherokee Nation of Indians." In *Fifth Annual Report of the Bureau of Ethnology, 1883–84,* edited by J. W. Powell, 121–373, 322. Washington, D.C.: Government Printing Office, 1887.

Sameth, Sigmund. "Creek Negroes." Master's thesis, University of Oklahoma, 1940.

Saunt, Claudio. "'The English Has Now a Mind to Make Slaves of Them All': Creeks, Seminoles, and the Problem of Slavery." *American Indian Quarterly* 22, no. 2 (Winter/Spring 1998): 157–80.

————. *A New Order of Things: Property, Power, and the Transformation of the Creek Indians, 1733–1816.* New York: Cambridge University Press, 1999.

Shadburn, Don. *Cherokee Planters in Georgia 1832–1838: Historical Essays on Eleven Counties in the Cherokee Nation of Georgia.* Pioneer-Cherokee Heritage Series 2. Roswell, Ga.: W. H. Wolfe, 1989.

Shoemaker, Nancy. "How Indians Got to Be Red." *American Historical Review* 102 (June 1997): 625–44.

Silko, Leslie Marmon. "Through the Stories We Hear Who We Are." In *Short Fiction: Classic and Contemporary,* edited by Charles Bohner. 5th ed. New York: Prentice-Hall, 2002.

————. *Yellow Woman and a Beauty of the Spirit: Essays on Native American Life Today.* New York: Simon and Schuster, 1997.

Six Women's Slave Narratives, with an introduction by William L. Andrews. Schomburg Library of Nineteenth-Century Black Women Writers. New York: Oxford University Press, 1988.

Slotkin, Richard. *Regeneration Through Violence: The Mythology of the American Frontier, 1600–1860.* Middletown, Conn.: Wesleyan University Press, 1973.

Smith, James. *The Cherokee Land Lottery.* Baltimore: Genealogical Publishing Company, 1969.

Smith, Mark. *Mastered by the Clock: Time, Slavery, and Freedom in the American South.* Chapel Hill: University of North Carolina Press, 1987.

Smyers, Robyn Minter. "Remaking the Past: The Black Oral Tradition in Contemporary Art." *The Black Indian Connection in American Art: The International Review of African American Art* 17 (2000): 47–53.

Sparks, Carol Douglas. "The Land Incarnate: Navajo Women and the Dialogue of Colonialism, 1821–1870." In *Negotiators of Change: Historical Perspectives on Native American Women,* edited by Nancy Shoemaker, 135–56. New York: Routledge, 1995.

Starkey, Marion L. *The Cherokee Nation.* 1946. Reprint, North Dighton, Mass.: J. G. Press, 1995.

Starr, Emmet. *Early History of the Cherokees.* Claremore, Okla., 1917.

———. *History of the Cherokee Indians and Their Legends and Folklore.* Oklahoma City: Warden Company, 1921.

Stewart, Paul, and Wallace Yvonne Ponce. *Black Cowboys.* Denver: Black American West Museum and Heritage Center, 1986.

Strenk, Adriane. "Tradition and Transformation: Shoe Boots and the Creation of a Cherokee Culture." Master's thesis, University of Kentucky, 1993.

Strickland, Rennard. *Fire and the Spirits: Cherokee Law from Clan to Court.* Norman: University of Oklahoma Press, 1975.

———. "In Search of Cherokee History: A Review Essay." In *A Political History of the Cherokee Nation, 1838–1907,* edited by Morris Wardell, xi–xxxv. 1938. Reprint, Norman: University of Oklahoma Press, 1977.

Stuckey, Sterling. *Slave Culture.* New York: Oxford University Press, 1987.

Sturm, Circe. *Blood Politics: Race, Culture, and Identity in the Cherokee Nation of Oklahoma.* Berkeley and Los Angeles: University of California Press, 2002.

Sturtevant, William. "Louis-Philippe on Cherokee Architecture and Clothing in 1797." *Journal of Cherokee Studies* 3 (Fall 1978): 198–205.

———, ed. "John Ridge on Cherokee Civilization in 1826." *Journal of Cherokee Studies* 6 (Fall 1981): 79–91.

Takaki, Ronald. *A Different Mirror: A History of Multicultural America.* Boston: Little, Brown, 1993.

———. *Iron Cages: Race and Culture in Nineteenth-Century America.* New York: Oxford University Press, 1990.

Tanner, Helen Hornbeck. "Cherokees in the Ohio Country." *Journal of Cherokee Studies* 3 (Spring 1978): 94–101.

Taylor, Quintard. *In Search of the Racial Frontier: African Americans in the American West, 1528–1990.* New York: Norton, 1998.

Thornton, Russell. *The Cherokees: A Population History.* Lincoln: University of Nebraska Press, 1990.

———. "The Demography of the Trail of Tears Period: A New Estimate of Cherokee Population Losses." In *Cherokee Removal: Before and After,* edited by William Anderson, 75–95. Athens: University of Georgia Press, 1991.

Tilton, Robert. *Pocahontas: The Evolution of an American Narrative.* New York: Cambridge University Press, 1994.

Timberlake, Henry. *Lieut. Henry Timberlake's Memoirs, 1756–1765.* 1927. Reprint, Marietta, Ga.: Continental Book Company, 1948.

Turner, C. W. "Events Among the Muskogees During Sixty Years." *Chronicles of Oklahoma* 10 (1932): 21–34.

Twyman, Bruce. *The Black Seminole Legacy and North American Politics, 1693–1845.* Washington, D.C: Howard University Press, 1999.

Vipperman, Carl. "'Forcibly If We Must': The Georgia Case for Cherokee Removal, 1802–1832." *Journal of Cherokee Studies* 3 (Spring 1978): 103–9.

Wald, Priscilla. "Terms of Assimilation: Legislating Subjectivity in the Emerging Nation." In *Cultures of United States Imperialism,* edited by Amy Kaplan and Donald Pease, 59–84. Durham, N.C.: Duke University Press, 1993.

Walker, Alice. *In Search of Our Mother's Gardens.* New York: Harcourt, Brace, Javonovich, 1983.

Walker, David. *David Walker's Appeal to the Coloured Citizens of the World.* Edited by Peter Hinks. 1829. Reprint, University Park: Pennsylvania State University Press, 2000.

Walker, Homer. *Cherokee Indian Census of 1835.* Washington, D.C., 1835.

Walker, Juliet. *Free Frank: A Black Pioneer on the Antebellum Frontier.* Lexington: University of Kentucky Press, 1983.

Walker, Robert. *Torchlights to the Cherokees.* New York: Macmillan, 1931.

Walton-Raji, Angela. *Black Indian Genealogy Research.* Bowie, Md.: Heritage Books, 1993.

Walvin, James. *Questioning Slavery.* London: Routledge, 1996.

Warrior, Robert Allen. *Tribal Secrets: Recovering American Indian Intellectual Traditions.* Minneapolis: University of Minnesota Press, 1995.

Welter, Barbara. "The Cult of True Womanhood: 1820–1860." *American Quarterly* 18 (1966): 151–74.

White, Deborah Gray. *Ar'n't I a Woman: Female Slaves in the Plantation South.* New York: Norton, 1985.

Wilkins, Thurman. *Cherokee Tragedy: The Ridge Family and the Decimation of a People.* 2nd ed. Norman: University of Oklahoma Press, 1986.

Williams, David. "The Cherokee Gold Lottery and Georgia's Gubernatorial Campaign of 1831." *Journal of Cherokee Studies* 15 (1990): 40–58.

Williams, Patricia. *The Alchemy of Race and Rights.* Cambridge, Mass.: Harvard University Press, 1991.

————. "What's Love Got to Do With It?" *Nation,* November 23, 1998.

Williamson, Joel. *New People: Miscegenation and Mulattoes in the United States.* Baton Rouge: Louisiana State University Press, 1995.

Willis, William. "Divide and Rule: Red, White and Black in the Southeast." *Journal of Negro History* 48 (July 1963): 157–76.

Wilms, Douglas. "Cherokee Land Use in Georgia, 1800–1838." PhD diss., University of Georgia, 1973.

Wilson, Raleigh Archie. "Negro and Indian Relations in the Five Civilized Tribes from 1865 to 1907." PhD diss., State University of Iowa, 1949.

Wood, Betty. *The Origins of American Slavery: Freedom and Bondage in the English Colonies.* New York: Hill and Wang, 1997.

Wood, Peter H. *Black Majority: Negroes in Colonial South Carolina from 1670 through the Stono Rebellion.* New York: Norton, 1974.

Woods, Karen. "One Nation, One Blood: Interracial Marriage in American Fiction, Scandal and Law, 1820–70." PhD diss., University of Minnesota, 1999.

Woodson, Carter G. "The Relations of Negroes and Indians in Massachusetts." *Journal of Negro History* 5 (January 1920): 45–62.

Wright, J. Leitch. *Creeks and Seminoles: The Destruction and Regeneration of the Muscogulge People.* Lincoln: University of Nebraska Press, 1986.

————. *The Only Land They Knew: The Tragic Story of the American Indians in the Old South.* New York: Free Press, 1981.

Wright, Muriel. "American Indian Corn Dishes." *Chronicles of Oklahoma* 36 (Summer 1958): 155–62.

————. *Our Oklahoma.* Guthrie, Okla.: Co-operative Publishing, 1939.

Yarbrough, Fay A. "Legislating Women's Sexuality: Cherokee Marriage Laws in the Nineteenth Century." Paper presented at the sixth Southern Conference on Women's History, Athens, Georgia, June 2003.

Young, Mary. "The Cherokee Nation: Mirror of the Republic." *American Quarterly* 33 (Winter 1981): 503–24.

————. "Racism in Red and Black: Indians and Other Free People of Color in Georgia Law, Politics, and Removal Policy." *Georgia Historical Quarterly* 73, no. 3 (Fall 1989): 492–518.

Young, Melvina Johnson. "Exploring the WPA Narratives: Finding the Voices of Black Women and Men." In *Theorizing Black Feminisms,* edited by Stanlie James and Abena Busia, 55–74. New York: Routledge, 1993.

INDEX

Page numbers in *italics* indicate maps.

Georgia militia's takeover, 132–33; on Indian Removal Act, 151–52; political role of, 102, 307n7; pregnancy practices of, 58; sexual/social autonomy of, 52–54, 296n32; as War Women, 31; white intermarriage with, 18–19; white womanhood ideal of, 19–20, 286nn36,37,41–43

Chickamauga Valley, 37

Chickaua/Molly (black slave), 56–57, 87, 125

Childers, Napoleon Bonaparte, 324–25n40

Childers, William, 324–25n40

Choctaws, 42, 80, 171

Christian missions: Cherokees' education at, 22, 101; colonization linked to, 91; as culturally disruptive, 98–99; Hightower location for, 88–90; intermarried white women of, 86–87; kinship discourse of, 120, 122; slaves' education at, 93–95; time management at, 101–2, 307n4. *See also* Hightower mission

Chulio, 216–18, 332n1

citizenship: Cherokee Commission's regulation of, 193–94, 195–96, 201–2; Constitutional definition of, 108–12, 114; Dawes applications for, 194–95, 200–201; of intermarried white women's children, 19; kinship code of, 125–27, 141–42, 177–78, 311n71; lineage issue of, 198–200, 329n20, 330n22; patrilineal recognition of, 128; property rights linked to, 140; under Treaty of 1866, 188, 193, 202, 324n37,39, 330n28

citizenship/emancipation petition of Shoe Boots: abolitionist ties to, 97–98; children excluded from, 130, 312n5; confessional form of, 118–19; Doll's status in, 123, 126; drafter of, 97, 116; kinship discourse of, 119–23; General Council's reply to, 126–27; text of, 1, 115, 281n2

citizenship petitions: by Doll Shoeboots, for children, 130–32, 312nn5,6, 313n8; by William Shoeboots, 196–201, 328–

29n19, 330n22; by William Stephens, 329n20. *See also* citizenship/ emancipation petition of Shoe Boots

Civills, Jack, 33–34

Civil War, 4–5; blacks' dislocation during, 193–94, 330n28; factional debate on, 186–87, 324n32; impact of, on Cherokee Nation, 187–89, 324nn36,37,39

Clack (or Clark), George, 285n27

clan membership: adoption form of, 56–57, 125; in intermarriage, 86; kinship relations of, 55–56; and names of clans, 50, 295n18; rules of, 50–52. *See also* matrilineal kinship

Cochran, John (Shoe Boots's great-nephew), 202–3, 312n5

Coffee, John, 217–18, 292–93n74

Collins, Patricia Hill, 3

colonists. *See* British colonists

concubinage: of Doll Shoeboots, 45–46, 54–55, 294n3; power relations of, 48–50, 295n13

Confederacy, 4–5, 186–87

Constitutional Convention (1827). *See* Cherokee Constitution

Cotterill, R. S., 80, 302n61

creation stories: of Cherokees, 120–22; of Christians, 120

Creeks, 29; anthropological classification of, 301n45; in Civil War, 324–25n40; in Creek War, 79–82; elite slaveholder class of, 42–43, 76–77; in Redstick rebellion, 78–79; slaves of, in Cherokee revolt, 171; in U.S. road dispute, 77–78

Creek War (1813–1814): background of, 77–79; Chulio's service in, 217; class component of, 80, 302n61; Shoe Boots's role in, 81–83, 85

Cunestuta (Isaac Tucker), 56–57

Curtis Act (1898), 194

Davis, Angela, 211

Dawes, Henry L., 194, 201

Dawes Allotment Act (1887), 194

Dawes Commission, 194–95, 200–201

Jacobs, Harriet, 25–26, 319n26, 332n15; on sexual abuse of slaves, 47–48, 295n7; on slave motherhood, 59–60
Jefferson, Thomas, 21, 287n47
Jennings, Thelma, 47, 48
Jesup, Thomas, 319n22
Jolly, John, 89
Jones, Calvin, 117
Jones, John, 163
Junaluska, 80

Kaplan, Amy, 285n33, 286n42
Katz, William Loren, 29
Keetoowah secret society, 186, 187, 324n32
Kelley, Mary, 286nn37,41,42
Kelley, Robin, 309n44
Kentucky settlers, 14–15
Kidd, Meredith, 194
Kingsbury, Cyrus, 91
kinship: as citizenship protection, 125–27, 141–41, 177–78, 311n71; John Cochran's affirmation of, 202–3; in creation myths, 120–22; exclusion of, in citizenship cases, 140–41, 198–200, 201–2, 329n20, 330n22; paternal aunt's ties of, 131; meanings of, as freedom, 4, 51–52, 56, 122–23, 128, 141–42; patrilineal recognition of, 71–72, 128; in Shoe Boots's petition, 119–23. See also matrilineal kinship
Knights of the Golden Circle, 186
Knox, Henry, 35, 64, 91

land: Cherokee identification with, 156–61; communal use of, 36, 69, 75, 291–92n61; as Creek War issue, 77–78; Dawes Commission's allotment of, 194–95; Doll's application for, 183–85, 323n22; of emigrants, in West, 162–63; fencing's protection of, 72–73, 300n1; Georgia's proposed exchange of, 89; Indian Removal from, 149–54. See also Cherokee territory
Landrum, Charles, 176–77, 180
language skills: of Cherokee slaves, 94–95, 96–97; of Shoe Boots, 292–93n74
Lecroy, John, 66–67, 68, 298–99n12, 299n13

Leslie, Kent, 138, 139
The Liberator (abolitionist newspaper), 75
Light Horse (Cherokee police force), 103
Lipe Roll (1880), 325–26n1
Littlefield, Daniel F., 162, 170, 188, 193, 319n19, 258–59n41
Littlefield, Mary Ann, 162, 170, 319n19, 258–59n41
Little Turkey, 34
Lomawaima, Tsianina K., 309n45
Loowaga, Wilson, 185
Louisiana Purchase (1803), 89
Louis Philippe (king of France), 53–54
Lovely, William, 34
Lowenthal, David, 158
Lucy Walker (steamboat ferry), 169
Lynch, Joseph, 74

Madison, James, 79–80
Martin, Joel, 78, 95–96, 302n54
matrilineal kinship: adoption alternative to, 56–57, 125; blood/bone symbolism of, 120–22; child naming custom of, 297n47; clan rules of, 50–52; Constitutional revision of, 128; inheritance laws' impact on, 71–72; matrilocality of, 55–56, 291–92n61, 292n67; property ownership in, 19, 36; in white-Cherokee marriage, 86
May, Katja, 175
Mayes, Joel B., 329n20
McClinton, Rowena, 39, 72
McKennon, Archibald, 194
McLaurin, Melton, 49
McLoughlin, William: on Clarinda Allington, 285n24; on Cherokee elite, 164–65; on Cherokee slave rebellions, 320n31; on Civil War's impact, 187–88; final Shoe Boots account by, 134; on Keetoowahs' mission, 324n32; on Molly/Chickaua's citizenship, 125; on Shoe Boots as Chulio, 216–17, 332n1, 333n3; on Shoe Boots's first wife, 284n22
Meigs, Return Jonathan, 17–18, 46, 67, 80, 89
Mexico, 171

Miko, Hopoithle, 77–78
Miller, Guion, 329n20
Mims, Samuel, 79
Molly/Chickaua (black slave), 56–57, 87, 125
Momaday, N. Scott, 158
Mooney, James, 85–86, 160
Moravian Mission school (Spring Place), 22, 65, 101, 217
Morgan, Edmund, 5, 107
Morgan, Ralph, 14–15
Morgan's Station raid (Kentucky), 14–16, 284n15
Morrison, Toni, 6, 26, 149, 179; disremember theme of, xxvi–xxvii; slave motherhood story by, 60–63
Murray, David, 118–19
Murrell, George, 181

National Committee, 104–5, 131–32, 308n19, 312n6, 313n8. *See also* General Council
National Council: centralization initiatives of, 103–5, 308nn18,19; citizenship legislation of, 193–94; Civil War resolutions of, 187, 324n32; Doll's petition to, 130–32, 312n5; formation of, 103; in Indian Removal controversy, 151–52; intermarriage provisions of, 19; land sale legislation of, 89; population census by, in 1824, 87; on Shoe Boots's rescued granddaughters, 177; on slave revolt of 1842, 171–72; on Vann inheritance dispute, 72. *See also* General Council
Native Americans: disremember imperative of, xxvi–xxviii; Indian Removal of, 150–54; land's meaning to, 157–59; in Morgan Station's raid, 14–16, 284n15; Payne's accounts of, 208–10; racialized property's exclusion of, 83–84; slaves' treatment by, 40–43, 293n77; terms used to identify, 215; as war captive slaves, 31, 290n26; written confessions by, 118–19. *See also* Cherokees; Creeks
Nave, Cornelius Neely, 162

Naylor-Ojurongbe, Celia, 40, 170, 319n20
Neugin, Rebecca, 155
New Echota (New Town), 105
New Echota, Treaty of (1835), 152, 163, 316n5
newspaper notices on slaves, 29–30, 73–74
Newton, Ebenezer, 95
Northrup, Sarah, 22–24, 86, 287nn47,59
Norton, John, 37, 41

Ohkilunakah/Ferguson (Elizabeth Shoeboots's husband), 142
Oklahoma: Cherokee Nation of, 162–63, 324n38; statehood of, 188
Old Settlers (Western Cherokee Nation), 162–63, 166, 170

Painter, Nell Irvin, xxviii
Pardo, Juan, 28
Path Killer, 85, 89, 103, 123
Patterson, Orlando, 51–52
Payne, John Howard: on Clarinda Allington, 20, 24, 285n27; as biographer/historian, 209–10; on blacks, 212–13; on Indian Removal, 151; on Shoe Boots's citizenship petition, 116; on Shoe Boots's deed of gift, 66–68, 134, 298–99n12; on Shoe Boots's traits, 13, 18, 81–82, 208–9, 218; on Shoeboots twins' petition, 130, 131–32, 312nn5,6; on slaves as mediators, 96; on Wofford kidnap case, 135
Peedee River colony, 28, 289n11
Peggy (Shoe Boots's sister), 130–31, 134, 135
Perdue, Theda, 35, 40, 218, 268–69n1; on Cherokee emigrants, 163–64; on Cherokees' prejudice, 34; on Cherokee women, 52, 286n36; on property law, 72; on John Ross, 104; on slaves' linguistic skills, 95
Pettit, Thomas, 106
Phillips, Joyce, 217
Phillips, Paul Gary, 217
Plane, Ann, 184
political community. *See* social/political community
poverty relief, 69
pregnancy practices, 58–59

Proctor, Isaac, 89–90

property: black slaves defined as, 73–75, 301nn38,40,42; Cherokee women's rights to, 19, 36; citizenship's linkage to, 140; as Creek/Cherokee class issue, 76–77; fencing's protection of, 72–73, 300n1; of Hightower residents, 87; patrilineal inheritance of, 71–72; racialized ownership of, 83–84, 114; Shoeboots's family deeded as, 66–68, 133–34, 299n13; traditional value of, 69–70; U.S. civilization program on, 35–36, 113–14. *See also* inheritance; land

Pushing the Bear (Glancy), 156–57

race: American ideology of, 49, 83–84, 107, 113–14, 295n13; citizenship defined by, 108–12, 168, 201–2; Doll's omission of, in land application, 185; first Cherokee bias against, 34; Georgia's policies on, 142–43, 316n48; "hidden transcript" on, 114, 309nn44,45; property's conflation with, 73–75, 83–84, 301nn38,40,42; reconfigured fixed categories of, 87, 106–8, 110; Shoeboots family drama of, 2–4; socialization's definition of, 138–39, 314–15n39

rape laws, 54, 167, 296n32

Red Paint Clan *(Aniwodi)*, 50

Redstick rebellion, 78–83

"The Removed Townhouses" (Cherokee story), 160

research: on black slave women, 211–12, 332n15; key sources for, 213; problematic context of, 207–11, 268–69n1; reconstruction methodology of, 5–6, 212–13

Rice, William, 285n27

Ridge, John, 100, 105, 115, 129; as Doll's pseudoguardian, 136–37, 165, 179–80, 197, 328–29n19; execution of, 166; Honey Creek home of, 164; on Indian Removal, 152; intermarriage of, 22–24, 86, 287nn47,57,59; mission education of, 22, 101–2, 307n4; as

slaveowner, 180–81; on U.S. civilization program, 113–14

Ridge, John Rollin, 181, 183

Ridge, Major (The Ridge), 80, 85, 115; centralization initiatives of, 104; execution of, 166; on Indian Removal, 152; Shoe Boots's ties to, 100–101; as slaveowner, 164

Ridge, Susannah, 101, 179–80, 181, 321–22n2

Ridge, Thomas, 100–101, 197, 321–22n2, 323n25, 328–29n19

Robertson, Betty, 172–73

Rocky Mountain News, 204

Rogin, Michael, 79, 81

Romero, Lora, 286nn41,43

Ross, Edmond, 328–29n19

Ross, John, 80, 103, 165, 181; Civil War position of, 186, 187, 324n36; at Constitutional Convention, 105–6; on Indian Removal, 152, 154; Payne's friendship with, 209; slaveholder status of, 104

Ross, Lewis, 170

Ross, Minerva, 181

Ross, Quatie, 155

Ross, William, 175–76

Rowe, Mary, 90

Rowe, Richard, 90, 97

runaway slaves: British treaty provisions on, 31–32; *Cherokee Advocate* on, 167–68, 319n22; of 1842 slave revolt, 169–73, 320nn31,33,41; newspaper notices on, 29–30; of James Vann, 65–66

Sawyer, Sophia, 124

Scott, James, 309n44

Scott, Winfield, 153, 154

Seminole slaves, 29, 167–68, 169, 319n22

Sequoyah, 80

sexual relations: brutality of, with slave women, 46–47, 295n7; of Cherokee women, 53–54, 296n32; in polygynous cultures, 45; of slave concubines, 47–50, 295n13; white womanhood issue of, 21–22, 52

Shade, Hastings, 44

Shane, Rev. John, 15

Shawnees, 14–16, 284nn15,20

Shelby, Isaac, 17, 209

Shoeboot, Haskell James (Shoe Boots and Doll's descendant), 204–5

Shoeboot, Morrison (Shoe Boots and Doll's grandson), 189, 324–25n40

Shoe Boots: in Creek War, 77, 80, 81–83, 85, 302n50; death/estate of, 129–30, 137, 312n5, 314nn29,30; in deed of gift incident, 66–68, 133–34, 298nn10,12, 299nn13,15; description of, 13–14, 208–9; Doll's sexual relationship with, 45–46, 54–55, 294n3; kidnapped granddaughters of, 174–77; language skills of, 292–93n74; marriage of, to Clarinda, 16–18, 20, 46, 284n22, 285nn23,24; marriage of, to Doll, 2, 183–85, 323n22; missionary education sentiments of, 88–89, 90, 98–99, 304n22; in Morgan's Station raid, 14–16, 284n15; names used for, 216–18, 332n1, 333n3; naming of child by, 59, 297n47; Payne's biography of, 208–10; property holdings of, 37–38, 291–92n61, 292n67; Ridge family's ties to, 100–101; as slave-owner, 75–76; warrior celebrity of, 81–82, 85–86. *See also* citizenship petition of Shoe Boots

Shoeboots, Clarinda Allington. *See* Allington, Clarinda

Shoeboots, Conmenoula (John Shoe-boots's wife), 142, 315n45, 316n46

Shoeboots, Doll (Shoe Boots's wife): citizenship petition of, for children, 130–32, 312nn5,6, 313n8; clan's exclusion of, 55–56, 57; Clarinda's relations with, 44–45; complex identities of, 86–87; as concubine of Shoe Boots, 45–46, 54–55, 294n3; death of, 185–86, 323n28; in deed of gift incident, 66–68, 298nn10,12, 299n13; emancipation of, 180, 321–22n2; in Indian Removal, 161; kidnap/

enslavement of, 133–36; land application of, 183–85, 323n22; marriage/children of, 2; names of, 26–27, 185, 216, 218, 288n5, 323nn25,29, 333n12; pregnancy of, 58–59, 297n47; research approach to, 212–13; in Ridge household, 136, 165, 179–80, 328–29n19; slave status of, 39–40, 64–65, 100, 123, 126; as undocumented life, 27–28, 211

Shoeboots, Elizabeth/Kahuga (Shoe Boots and Doll's daughter), 2, 67, 86, 197; birth/naming of, 59, 297n47; Cherokee acceptance of, 173–74; complex identities of, 142–43, 316n48; Delaware District community of, 180, 182; descendants of, 191, 326–27n2; emigration of, to West, 161, 165; inheritance of, 137–38, 139, 141–42, 314n30; kidnap/enslavement of, 133–36, 313–14n23; kidnapped daughters of, 174–77; marriage/children of, 173

Shoeboots, John (black laborer), 327n3

Shoeboots, John (Shoe Boots and Doll's son), 2; birth of, 86; Cherokee acceptance of, 173–74; daughter Mary of, 142, 191, 327n3, 330n22; Delaware District community of, 180, 182; kidnap/enslavement of, 133–34; marriage of, 142, 315n45, 316n46

Shoeboots, John Ellington (Shoe Boots and Clarinda's son), 16, 285n23

Shoeboots, Lewis (Shoe Boots and Doll's son), 2, 134, 135, 173, 192, 197, 315n43; Doll's citizenship petition for, 130–32

Shoeboots, Lizzie (William and Dicey Shoeboots's daughter), 200–201, 332n1

Shoeboots, Polly (Shoe Boots and Doll's daughter), 2, 142; birth of, 86; Cherokee acceptance of, 173–74; children of, 173, 321n45; Delaware District community of, 180, 182; descendants of, 191, 326–27n2; emigration of, to West, 161, 165; kidnap/enslavement of, 133–36; kidnapped daughter of, 174–77

Timberlake, Henry, 69–70

Timson, John, 131, 313n8

tobacco trade, 107

towns: centralized supervision of, 103–4, 105, 308n19; traditional system of, 36–37, 102, 307n7

Trail of Tears, 154–57. *See also* Indian Removal

Treaty of Dover (1730), 31–32

Treaty of 1866, 188, 192–93, 202, 324nn36,39, 330n28

Treaty of Holston (1791), 35

Treaty of New Echota (1835), 152, 163, 316n5

Treaty Party members: Civil War loyalties of, 186–87; execution of, 165–66; New Echota Treaty with, 152, 316n5; slave labor economy of, 164–65; Western settlement sites of, 163, 180–81

Tucker, Isaac (Cunestuta), 56–57

Twisters or Long Hair Clan *(Anigilohi)*, 50, 295n18

United States: Christianization role of, 91; in Creek War, 77–78, 79–81; criminal jurisdiction issues of, 320–21n41; Dawes subdivision initiative of, 194–95; Georgia's land compact with, 149–50; gifts to Shoe Boots from, 85; Indian civilizing program of, 35–36, 39, 71, 77, 113–14; Indian Removal initiatives of, 150–51, 153–54; racial ideology of, 49, 83–84, 107, 113–14, 295n13; Treaty of 1866 with, 188, 192–93, 202, 324nn36,39, 330n28; Treaty of Holston with, 35; Treaty of New Echota with, 152, 163, 316n5; unauthorized land sales to, 89. *See also* Euro-American culture; U.S. Congress

"Upon a Watch" (John Ridge), 101

U.S. Congress: Creek War veterans act of, 183; Curtis Act of, 194; General Allotment Act of, 194; Indian Removal Act of, 151

U.S. Constitution (1787), 112

Vann, James, 28, 41, 65–66, 72

Vann, Joseph, 72, 106, 115, 187; death of, 173; slaves' revolt against, 169–72, 320n33

Vann, Martin, 169

Virginia (state), 28–29, 107

Wade, James, 22

Wafford, Joseph, 73, 300n33

Wafford, Nathaniel, 300n33

Wald, Priscilla, 113

Walker, David, 92

war captive slaves, 31, 290n26

War of 1812, 79

Warrior, Robert Allen, 282–83n8

War Women (Cherokee elders), 31

Washington, George, 16, 35

Watie, Buck. *See* Boudinot, Elias

Watie, Sarah, 181

Watie, Stand, 152, 166, 180–81, 182, 185, 187

Watie, Watica, 169

Wayne, "Mad Anthony," 16

The Way to Rainy Mountain (Momaday), 158

Webbers Falls (Canadian District), 169

Welter, Barbara, 286n42

Western Apache stories, 158–59

Western Cherokee Nation (Old Settlers), 162–63, 166, 170

Wheatley, Phillis, 27

Wheelock, Elizur, 118–19

White, Deborah Gray, 211–12

white-Cherokee marriage: citizen children of, 19, 111; elite emigrant families of, 164–65; matrilineal kinship issue of, 86; negative views of white women in, 18, 21–22, 285n33; proving lineage from, 329n20; of Ridge family, 22–23, 86–87, 287nn57,59; slavery component of, 23–24, 124, 311n67; white womanhood ideal of, 19–21, 286nn36,37,41–43, 287n47

White Path, 123–24, 125, 154–55

whites: as captives of Indians, 17, 285n25; citizenship status of, 19, 111; as historical sources, 207–8, 330–31n1; ideal family as, 3–4; property ownership status of, 83–84; sexual ideology